Australian Courts

"This book brings together the theoretical perspectives of leading criminologists in Australia balanced with the viewpoints of practitioners to provide a comprehensive criminological appraisal of courts in Australia. The authors discuss the controversies and challenges involved in the administration of various types of courts across disparate geographical jurisdictions in Australia and discuss potential reforms to improve equity in access to justice. This book is an excellent resource for students in law, criminology, policing and social work as well as practitioners and policymakers; indeed, anyone seeking to understand the complexities of Australian Courts."

—Elaine Barclay, *former Associate Professor in Criminology, University of New England (retired)*

"A book which explores the contexts, complexities and challenges of courts is therefore extremely timely and, given the dearth of systematic reviews in this area, presents a wonderful contribution to better understanding what Australian courts do and how they work. It provides an excellent informed introduction to one of our most important social institutions. I commend the editors and contributors for putting together an informative and critical text that interrogates the relationship between courts and justice—past, present, and future."

—Rob White, *Emeritus Distinguished Professor of Criminology, University of Tasmania, Australia*

Adjunct Professor of Criminology, University of New England, Australia

Marg Camilleri · Alistair Harkness
Editors

Australian Courts

Controversies, Challenges and Change

palgrave
macmillan

Editors
Marg Camilleri
Federation University Australia
Ballarat, VIC, Australia

Alistair Harkness
University of New England
Armidale, NSW, Australia

ISBN 978-3-031-19062-9 ISBN 978-3-031-19063-6 (eBook)
https://doi.org/10.1007/978-3-031-19063-6

Cover illustration: @ Gettyimages/Gema Ibarra/EyeEm

This Palgrave Macmillan imprint is published by the registered company Springer Nature Switzerland AG
The registered company address is: Gewerbestrasse 11, 6330 Cham, Switzerland

This book is dedicated to my son, Bren, who took his life in late 2019.

Heartbroken that you passed alone, that I will never see you again and that you couldn't see another way.

Readers are encouraged to consider donating to any suicide support services. Two, in particular, would be worthy recipients:

Lifeline, for suicide prevention – https://www.lifeline.org.au/
Jesuit Social Services, for support after suicide – https://jss.org.au/what-we-do/mental-health-and-wellbeing/support-after-suicide/

—*Marg Camilleri*

Foreword

The principles and practices of justice are contested in courts, and courts themselves are part of the contest over justice. Different kinds of courts deal with diverse aspects of the human condition, from family relationships through to harmful conduct. Courts are, therefore, a central part of the everyday architecture of Australian society, with significant impacts and influences at the individual and communal levels across a wide spectrum of social, political and economic activities.

Courts are of course vital to conflict resolution; but they also reproduce and reinforce significant institutional inequalities and social disparities. Courts are not merely the arbiter of 'right' and 'wrong'. They reflect particular social interests and power dynamics, both contemporary and as evolved and entrenched over time.

In part, the political nature of courts is associated with the 'letter of the law' and how this circumscribes what a court may do or not do. Courts are bound by the legislation that gives them the mandate for their specific operation. Their powers and philosophical orientation in relation to specific justice matters are embedded in law, as determined by parliament, and it is up to judicial officers to interpret their duties and the law in the light of this legislative framing.

Yet, there is also judicial discretion, so decisions made in court also reflect the human element. In criminal law, this is sometimes referred to as the 'intuitive synthesis', whereby judges and magistrates weigh up objective and subjective factors when determining the extent of harm and the most suitable sanction.

Specific courts in particular jurisdictions also tend to develop their own ways of doing things, partly due to precedent in specific areas of substantive law but also because expertise and general operational approach become part of the culture of a court as influenced by its leading judicial administrators over time. Thus, specific court cultures also shape decision-making in particular court settings.

Generalist courts, such as magistrates' courts, have in recent years been complemented by specialisms of various kinds. This takes the form of specific judicial appointments (such as selection of specific magistrates within Magistrates Courts to exclusively hear Children's Court cases); specific Divisions of the Court (such as therapeutic courts such as 'drug courts'); and specialist stand-alone courts (such as the New South Wales Land and Environment Court). A drug court, an environment court, a family court—each represents areas of law where specific expertise and remedies are required. Indeed, the trend towards problem-solving and specialist courts of many kinds is symptomatic of a shift in thinking that recognises the complexity of social life, including longstanding barriers to justice.

For criminology, and critical criminology especially, the question of harm is central. Accordingly, it is important to acknowledge how harm is reflected in, prevented and/or reproduced by non-criminal as well as criminal courts. The separation of children from parents and communities (such as via child protection), for example, is intertwined with prosecution of children in Children's Courts (e.g. juvenile justice). The law is never partial. Nor is it socially neutral in regards composition of judicial officers, how interests and rights are weighed up, and who most benefits or suffers from civil and criminal proceedings.

Courts are integral to Australian social life. For good or for bad, courts deliver verdicts that impact us all. Justice is defined in practice by who makes decisions, how they do so, the principles which guide consideration and the consequences they engender.

A book which explores the contexts, complexities and challenges of courts is, therefore, extremely timely and, given the dearth of systematic reviews in this area, presents a wonderful contribution to better understanding what Australian courts do and how they work. It provides an excellent informed introduction to one of our most important social institutions. I commend the editors and contributors for putting together an informative and critical text that interrogates the relationship between courts and justice—past, present and future.

Rob White
Emeritus Distinguished Professor
of Criminology
University of Tasmania
Hobart, Australia

Adjunct Professor of Criminology
University of New England
Armidale, Australia

Preface

The impetus for this edited collection stemmed from a realisation that there was no single contemporary consolidated volume which assesses the courts in Australia from a criminological rather than a legal perspective.

And, so, this book serves as the first comprehensive collection of its kind to canvas the diversity of courts in Australia, providing critical analysis of contemporary issues, debates and reforms. Contributors consider the array of courts across state, territory and national jurisdictions in Australia, including coroners' courts, family courts, criminal, Indigenous Sentencing courts, civil courts and problem-solving courts.

Australian Courts brings together scholars and practitioners with a unique exploration of courts in Australia. The primary focus of this volume is to identify controversies and challenges—and opportunities for change, in the form of potential reforms within the courts across Australian jurisdictions. The intention has been to bring to the forefront original research and scholarship on a wide array of courts in Australia, combined with insightful practitioner perspectives, to integrate research with practice.

Each chapter has been structured similarly:

- providing the *context* for the topic and importantly identifying areas for reform, including the historical and contemporary context of the topic at hand
- identifying and exploring key *controversies* within the current context
- outlining and assessing key relevant and contemporary *challenges*
- advocating for *change* and areas for reform.

Chapters will not address each and every aspect of courts and processes. Rather, contributors provide insights into relevant controversies, challenges and opportunities for reform, considering the perspectives of various participants in the court system in Australia, including court users such as people with disability, ethnic minorities, Indigenous Australians and victims of crime. Each chapter seeks to provide opportunities for further debate among scholars, practitioners and students alike regarding potential future directions for reform to improve the efficacy, equity and accessibility of Australian courts.

Ballarat, Victoria, Australia — Marg Camilleri
Armidale, New South Wales, Australia — Alistair Harkness

Acknowledgements

We would like to thank, most profusely, Dr. Rachel Hale for her input into the proposal from which this volume has emerged. Her conceptualisation of an array of issues associated with elements of the court system in Australia is really very much appreciated.

We wish to thank each of the contributors, whether involved in academia or as practitioners, for their research and insights and their ongoing commitment to just outcomes.

Finally, much gratitude is offered to Josie Taylor and her team at Palgrave for taking on this project and for all the support which has been provided.

September 2022

Marg Camilleri
Alistair Harkness

Contents

1 **Context and Controversies of Australian Courts** 1
Marg Camilleri and Alistair Harkness

2 **Politics, Parliament and the Courts** 19
Alistair Harkness

Practitioner Perspective: The Role of Parliamentarians in Making Laws 38
Simon Finn

3 **Juries in the Digital Age: Managing Juror Online and Social Media Use During Trial** 45
Jane Goodman-Delahunty and David Tait

Practitioner Perspective: A View from the Bench—Juries in the Digital Age 65
Judge W. Graham Turnbull SC

4 **Courts and the Media** 73
Lisa Waller and Katrina Clifford

Practitioner Perspective: Pell, the Press and a Pandemic 90
Danny Tran

5 **Prosecutions in the Summary Jurisdictions** 95
Sophie Ellis and Marg Camilleri

Practitioner Perspective: Police-Led Prosecutions in the Magistrates' Court 115
Sophie Ellis

6 **Bail Decisions: Key Challenges Driving Bail Refusal** 121
Emma Colvin

Practitioner Perspective: Key Challenges Driving Bail Refusal 137
Lydia Hamilton

7 **Delaying Justice** 143
Liz Curran

Practitioner Perspective: Justice Delayed 164
Sharon E. Lacy

8 **Injustices and Inequitable Outcomes: Miscarriages of Justice and Wrongful Convictions** 169
Rachel Dioso-Villa and Caitlin Nash

Practitioner Perspective: Wrongful Conviction—*The Case of Terry Irving* 190
Michael O'Keeffe

9 **Problem-Solving Courts** 197
Lacey Schaefer and Caitlyn Egan

Practitioner Perspective: A Reflection on Problem-Solving Courts in Australia 215
Elizabeth Daniels

10 **Indigenous Sentencing Courts** 221
Elena Marchetti and Linda M. Ryle

Practitioner Perspective: Murri Court 238
Jacqueline Payne

11 **Coroners Courts and Death Investigations** 247
Fiona Allison and Chris Cunneen

Practitioner Perspective: Chasing Professionalism—The Practitioner Role in Responding to First Nations Deaths in Custody 264
Craig Longman and Alison Whittaker

12 **Victims' Participatory Rights** 269
Marg Camilleri

Practitioner Perspective: Victims/Survivors and the Courts—From Alienation and Secondary Victimisation to Participatory Rights 292
Dagmar Jenkins

13 **Children and Young People in Court** 297
Rosemary Sheehan and Susan Baidawi

Practitioner Perspective a Participatory Approach to Young Offenders in the Children's Court 314
Laura Chipp

14 **Family Courts and Family Violence** 321
Thea Brown and Renata Alexander

Practitioner Perspective: Family Law Professionals and the Court 341
Renata Alexander

15 **The Ur-controversy of Civil Justice** 345
Joe McIntyre

Practitioner Perspective: A Reflection on Civil Litigation 363
Ben Doyle KC and Stephen McDonald SC

16 **Challenging Court Landscapes and Opportunities for Change** 367
Marg Camilleri and Alistair Harkness

Correction to: Australian Courts C1
Marg Camilleri and Alistair Harkness

Index 391

Notes on Contributors

Renata Alexander is a family law barrister in Victoria, Australia, specialising in parenting cases and the separate representation of children. She completed her Ph.D. on gender issues in family law decision-making. She occasionally teaches family law in the Faculty of Law at Monash University. She is the author/co-author of various publications including five books on family law and family violence.

Fiona Allison is a research fellow at the Jumbunna Institute for Indigenous Education and Research, University of Technology Sydney, and data/policy lead at Just Reinvest NSW. Her work is focused on improving civil/family law access to justice and reduced contact with and better outcomes in the criminal justice system for First Nations peoples.

Susan Baidawi is a senior lecturer in the Department of Social Work at Monash University in Victoria, Australia. She received a DECRA Fellowship (2019–2021) from the Australian Research Council, and her primary research interests are child protection, youth offending and crossover children at the child protection–youth justice system nexus.

Thea Brown is a Monash University researcher and policy consultant in family violence. She is one of the founders and directors of the Monash Deakin Filicide Research Hub. She has published three books, as well as many articles and government reports. She focuses on intervention and prevention in family violence and has been a contributor to new Family Court programmes funded by the Australian Commonwealth government.

Marg Camilleri is a senior lecturer in criminology and criminal justice at Federation University Australia. She worked in the community, legal and government sectors for over 20 years, returning to academia in 2014. Her main areas of research include the systemic, legislative and policy responses to victims of crime, in particular police response to victims/survivors with disabilities.

Laura Chipp has worked as a lawyer in the justice system for 15 years, leading Victoria Legal Aid's Statewide Youth Crime Program and creating Victoria Police's Statewide Specialist Children's Court Prosecution Unit. She has been awarded a Churchill Fellowship to find the best practice pre-Court diversion system to stop children re-offending.

Katrina Clifford is a senior lecturer in communication at Deakin University, Australia, and a specialist in media criminology and media framing analysis. She is the co-author of *Media and Crime: Content, Context and Consequence* (with Rob White, Oxford University Press, 2017) and author of *Policing, Mental Illness and Media: The Framing of Mental Health Crisis Encounters and Police Use of Force* (Palgrave, 2021).

Emma Colvin is a senior lecturer in law and criminology at Charles Sturt University in Australia. Her research focus is on issues that affect access to justice, particularly for vulnerable groups in the community. Her most recent research, which has received federal funding, includes an examination of bail practices in several Australian states and exploring the criminalisation of children in out-of-home care in the Children's Court.

Chris Cunneen is professor of criminology at the Jumbunna Institute for Indigenous Education and Research, University of Technology Sydney. He has published widely on Indigenous legal issues, juvenile justice, policing, penality and restorative justice. His most recent book is *Youth Penality in Comparative Context* (with Goldson et al., Routledge, 2021).

Liz Curran is associate professor Clinical Legal Education and the School Research Impact Lead at Nottingham Law School, Nottingham Trent University in the United Kingdom, and is an honorary associate professor at the Australian National University College of Law. Her areas of research endeavour include access to justice, multidisciplinary practice and impact evaluation.

Elizabeth Daniels commenced work in general practice law upon being admitted as a solicitor in 2011 in Queensland, Australia. In 2014, she was employed as a legal officer with the Queensland Police Service prosecuting in several locations across Queensland. She commenced as the Southport Domestic and Family Violence Court Coordinator in 2018 and continues to be employed by the Queensland Department of Justice and Attorney General as a Principal Legal Officer.

Rachel Dioso-Villa is a senior lecturer in the School of Criminology and Criminal Justice at Griffith University and a member of the Griffith Criminology Institute in Queensland, Australia. Her research investigates wrongful convictions and miscarriages of justice in Australia and the admissibility and evaluation of forensic sciences as expert testimony.

Ben Doyle KC is a barrister at Hanson Chambers in Adelaide, South Australia, practising predominantly in civil and commercial matters and appeals across a broader range of practice areas. He was formerly a solicitor with Kelly & Co Lawyers and an associate to the Honourable Chief Justice A.M. Gleeson AC.

Caitlyn Egan is an honours student and research assistant with the School of Criminology and Criminal Justice at Griffith University in Queensland, Australia. Her honours thesis includes a mixed-methods examination of the opinions of university students on crime and punishment. Her research interests include public opinion, correctional ideology and practice, rehabilitation and reintegration.

Sophie Ellis has over a decade of experience practising in law, across human rights, civil and criminal law spheres. She has also worked as a tutor and researcher in criminology, and as an independent researcher.

Simon Finn is a former member of the Queensland Parliament and served as Minister for Government Services, Building Industry and Information and Communication Technology from 2011–2012. He has worked in various executive roles in higher education and as an education consultant.

Jane Goodman-Delahunty is a professor at Newcastle Law School and a Member of the New South Wales Civil and Administrative Tribunal in Australia. Trained in law and experimental psychology, her empirical legal studies promote evidence-based practices to enhance justice. Her expertise on jury behaviour has been admitted internationally in civil and criminal cases.

Lydia Hamilton has been working in community and custodial settings in regional, rural and metropolitan settings throughout Australia with both adults and youth for nearly 30 years. She has substantial operational, management and policy/project experience combined with post-graduate qualifications in public administration, criminology and correctional management, and undergraduate degrees in philosophy, psychology and social work.

Alistair Harkness is a senior lecturer in criminology and co-director of the Centre for Rural Criminology at the University of New England in Australia. His primary research interests are in rural acquisitive crime (with a particular emphasis on crime prevention, policing responses and community partnerships) and the politics of criminal justice.

Dagmar Jenkins is a social worker, working for a Victorian sexual assault support service as a counsellor/advocate and in leadership roles until 2021. In her current position, she continues to assist victims/survivors of sexual violence as they navigate the criminal justice system.

Sharon E. Lacy commenced in general practice as a solicitor advocate in the Northern Territory and has practised as a barrister in Victoria,

Australia, for over 20 years, principally in criminal law and coronial inquests. She often appears in coronial inquests and other public inquiries.

Craig Longman is Head of Legal Strategies at Jumbunna Research Unit at the University of Technology Sydney, Australia, and is a Barrister at Black Chambers in Sydney. He has collaborated with families in multiple inquests into Indigenous deaths in custody including the complaint by Leetona Dungay to the United Nations in relation to the death in custody of her son David Dungay Jnr.

Elena Marchetti is a professor and Deputy Head of School (Research) in the Griffith Law School at Griffith University in Queensland, Australia. She also serves as the Deputy Chair of the Queensland Sentencing Advisory Council. She is an acclaimed researcher with significant experience in researching how Aboriginal and Torres Strait Islander people experience the criminal justice system.

Stephen McDonald SC is a barrister who practises mainly in public law and appellate matters, in state and federal courts. He is also an Adjunct Associate Professor at the University of Adelaide Law School in South Australia, and is co-author of a student text on Administrative Law. He was appointed senior counsel in 2020.

Joe McIntyre is an associate professor in public law and legal theory at the University of South Australia. His research specialises in judicial theory—the study of courts and how they function in society. He has held teaching posts in Canada, the United Kingdom and Australia.

Caitlin Nash is a Ph.D. candidate at the School of Criminology and Criminal Justice at Griffith University in Queensland, Australia. Her research focuses on guilty plea wrongful convictions in Australia, particularly on the underlying structural and organisational features of the criminal justice system that may contribute to this issue.

Michael O'Keeffe is a retired Queensland lawyer. He graduated from the Australian National University Law Faculty in 1987, and previously worked in the areas of criminal law, environmental law and human rights law. He continues to work as a volunteer solicitor in criminal appeal and restitution cases, particularly those involving the wrongful conviction of innocent Indigenous Queensland exonerees.

Jacqueline Payne was admitted as a solicitor in Queensland, Australia in 1985, and her first role as a solicitor was with the Aboriginal and Torres Strait Islander Legal Service. She was appointed as a magistrate in 1999, the first aborigine to be appointed to judicial office in Queensland. Jacqui is Butchulla from K'Gari (Fraser Island) and her clan group is Wonamutta.

Linda M. Ryle is a Birrigubba and Kamilaroi Woman, a lawyer, equity advocate and a Culturally Principled Practitioner. Her contribution to First Nations community, legal and affairs of equity and justice has spanned more than three decades, including more than a dozen years attempting to influence and reform the legal profession and courts/legal policy in Queensland and across Australia.

Lacey Schaefer is a senior lecturer in the School of Criminology and Criminal Justice at Griffith University and a Research Associate with the Griffith Criminology Institute in Queensland, Australia. She holds research expertise in criminological theory and correctional ideologies. As an applied researcher, she trains community corrections agencies in supervision frameworks and interventions.

Rosemary Sheehan has published extensively on child welfare and the law, and was awarded the Order of Australia for her significant work in this field. She has 17 years of experience as a Dispute Resolution Convenor in the Children's Court of Victoria; and as a member of Victoria's Child Death Review Committee.

David Tait is a scholar in criminology and sociology, and professor of justice research at Western Sydney University, Australia. He researches justice policy issues including physical and psychological setting of courts, uses of justice technologies, processes and rituals of justice, and court safety and security. He co-ordinates the Court of the Future Network and is currently investigating distributed and virtual courts.

Danny Tran is the court reporter for ABC News in Melbourne, Australia. He was the ABC's Andrew Olle Scholar in 2019 and is a former finalist in the Walkley Young Australian Journalist of the Year Awards and the Melbourne Press Club Quill awards.

Judge W. Graham Turnbull SC has worked as a solicitor in private practice, for the Australian Legal Aid Office and Legal Aid Commission, and with the Criminal Law Review Division and the Crown Prosecution Service Special Case Work division in London. Prior to his appointment in 2018 as a Judge of the District Court of New South Wales, Australia—sitting as a full-time judge in Orange, Bathurst and Parkes—he was a barrister in private practice.

Lisa Waller is professor and Associate Dean of Communication in the School of Media and Communication at RMIT University in Victoria, Australia, and is a Research Associate at the Centre for Rural Criminology at the University of New England in New South Wales, Australia. Her research investigates how the news media shapes a range of social domains, including the justice system.

Alison Whittaker is a Gomeroi legal researcher and author. She is senior researcher at the University of Technology Sydney's Jumbunna Institute in New South Wales, Australia. Between 2017–2018, she was a Fulbright scholar at Harvard Law School, where she was named the Dean's Scholar in Race, Gender and Criminal Law.

1

Context and Controversies of Australian Courts

Marg Camilleri and Alistair Harkness

Introduction

As with most criminal justice systems the world over, the Australian system is not immune from an array of controversies—both historically and contemporaneously. The arrival of the First Fleet in 1788 imposed monumental and ongoing systemic change for First Nations peoples, the impacts of which remain over two centuries later.

This chapter is divided into two parts. The first charts the development of courts within the Australian criminal justice system, both historically and theoretically, from pre-colonisation forms of justice

M. Camilleri (✉)
Federation University Australia, Ballarat, VIC, Australia
e-mail: m.camilleri@federation.edu.au

A. Harkness
University of New England, Armidale, NSW, Australia
e-mail: alistair.harkness@une.edu.au

M. Camilleri and A. Harkness (eds.), *Australian Courts*,
https://doi.org/10.1007/978-3-031-19063-6_1

delivery to the contemporary era. The second identifies controversies which exist across various Australian court jurisdictions.

A critical role of a justice system is to ensure fair and equitable access to all its systems and processes. To this end, five critical matters can be considered when contemplating access to the courts: (i) access to and costs of legal representation; (ii) physical infrastructure of courts; (iii) access to rehabilition options; (iv)justice delays; and (v) participatory justice.

A key element of *Australian Courts* is the inclusion of a collection of diverse perspectives contributed by practitioners, many with years of experience and expertise within the specific jurisdiction. These contributions offer valuable and nuanced tangible insights: much benefit is derived, indeed, from considering lived experiences in deciphering and making sense of the functioning of courts in Australia in the decade of the twenty-first century and beyond and in responding to identified need for reform.

Contextualising the Australian Courts

Historically, the Australian court system and courts have developed over time, adapting from British foundations to an Australian context, although by international standards the gestation and growth period has been relatively short. Theoretically, there exist two diametrically opposed considerations of the purpose of courts, adopting notions of consensus on the one hand and conflict on the other.

Informed by English common law traditions, a jury trial in an Australian court is an adversarial contest with winners and losers, contrasting with the inquisitorial systems in places such as France, Germany and Japan. This can, therefore, lead to a sense of battle as opposed to the finding of truth and the delivery of justice. As the American poet Robert Frost wrote: "A jury consists of twelve people chosen to decide who has the better lawyer". Criminal trials are highly formalised and with a ritualised sets of procedures. The trial is the showcase of the criminal justice system and, whilst it is tempting to focus on jury trials, it is important to remember that only a minority of matters are attended to with a trial by jury (White & Perrone, 2005). Thus, it is crucial to cast a critical eye over all aspects of the court system, even those which might not receive any prominence.

Courts are, generally though, rightly held to an elevated level of scrutiny from the media, community and those who interact with the courts seeking justice. Whilst to be heard and treated fairly are expectations common to anyone who interacts with the courts—and the justice system more broadly—the meaning of 'justice' and a 'just' outcome is more nebulous, as they relate to individual expectations of the outcomes and, importantly, how individuals are treated by the court. There are also times when procedural and legislative mechanisms cease or struggle to function effectively and require review and reform (see Camilleri and Harkness, Chapter 16).

Historical Context

First Nations peoples in Australia belong to the longest ongoing civilisation, spanning at least 65,000 years (Mawson, 2021; Rasmussen et al., 2011). Indigenous peoples had their own systems of law, but European settlement saw the displacement of existing practices and their replacement "immediately and unilaterally" with "a foreign system of law, including the criminal law" (ALRC, 2018, p. 56). A report prepared by the Australian Law Reform Commission (ALRC, 2018, p. 57) notes that:

> While the general body of British law was considered to apply in the new colony, the application of criminal laws to Aboriginal people was less clear, especially where offences were committed by one Aboriginal person against another Aboriginal person.

The notion of *terra nullius*—nobody's land—remained firmly entrenched for two centuries until the *Mabo* judgement of the High Court in 1992 (*Mabo v Queensland (No 2)*) rejected this, solidified native title and changed the foundation of land law and common law in Australia (see, e.g., Hughes et al., 2003; Sharp, 1996).

Transplanting the English common law tradition, system and processes was no mean feat. Notwithstanding every intention of the

Charter of Justice (GB) of 2 April 1787 in providing for the establishment of courts in the new colony, the sheer size of the Australian landmass and absence of any pre-existing formalised infrastructure, coupled with the demographics of the newly arrived population—initially being dominated by convicts transported from England for various indiscretions—meant that deviations to legal processes occurred in practice (see Neal, 1991; Wise & Roberts, 2016). Significant was the passing of the *Australian Courts Act 1828*, establishing a departure from autocratic rule to applying the rules of England, strengthening civil rather than militaristic processes, and allowing for trials by jury (York, 2018).

Since Federation in 1901, the hierarchy of the courts in Australia has evolved (depicted in Fig. 1.1). In essence, although some differences do exist between states and territories, the criminal courts deal with offences seen as violations of state's sovereignty. Summary (less serious) offences are heard in the lower courts, and cases are often prosecuted by a police prosecutor; indictable offences, typically of a more serious nature, are tried in the higher courts (and on pleas of innocence in the presence of a jury); and some offences (hybrid offences) can be tried either way (see White & Perrone, 2005, p. 85).

Generally, decisions made by a single judge in one court can be appealed and heard by a Court of Appeal, if leave for appeal is granted. Up until the passing of the *Australia Acts*, 1986 (Cth), appeals could be heard at the Privy Council in London. Whilst this reform finally centred the ultimate judicial decision-making in the High Court in Canberra, throwing off the shackles of imperialism, the process to get there was a "gradual, and messy, legislative process" (Gleeson, 2008, p. 2).

Foreseeing a need for a civil jurisdiction, in 1787 by letters patent, a court of Civil Jurisdiction was established (*Charter of Justice (GB)* of 2 April 1787). Following this was the appointment of justices of the peace to resolve smaller claims generally regarding debts owed (Windeyer, 1962). By the turn of the twenty-first century, an array of other courts and tribunals have been established including, for instance, the Administrative Appeals Tribunal, Australian Human Rights Commission, Industrial Relations Court of Australia, the National Native Title Tribunal and the Federal Circuit and Family Law Court at the Federal level. At the State level, specialist courts exist, such as the Children's Court, Coroner's

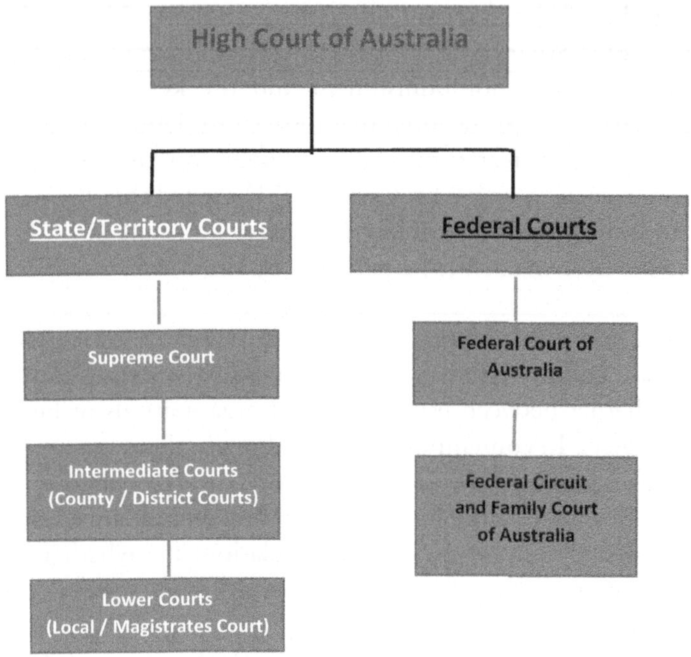

Fig. 1.1 Hierarchy of the courts in Australia

Court, Family Violence Court, Koori Court, Drugs and Alcohol Treatment Court, Victorian Civil and Administrate Tribunal in Victoria. The Court of Disputed Returns (at the High Court federally and the Supreme Court in the states) will meet as required to resolve matters pertaining to election outcomes.

Theoretical Context

'Justice' (as opposed to punishment) is a social and political concept, and laws and precedents are determined. Whereas in times of ecclesiastical justice inspired by the Old Testament, where "an eye for an eye, a tooth for a tooth" was a key consideration in the delivery of justice, times have changed, and courts have evolved.

Key thinkers have for eons, though, grappled with considerations of justice. John Stuart Mill (1998 [1861]) considered social utility as the only justification for punishment and the key to justice; Jeremy Bentham (2017 [1780]) believed that justice was defined in terms of "the greatest good of the greatest number", although this denied justice for the minorities in society; and John Rawls (1971) argued that the concepts of justice and fairness are essentially the same. Foucault (1977), though, questioned whose interest is perpetuated by the concept and imposition of justice.

Essential for a functioning and ordered society are guiding rules that regulate conduct, and of course the places where disputes can be settled—whether between individuals and organisations or between the State and others. In contemporary times, though, there is a need to regularly pause and reflect on whether the courts are fair; whether justice in the courts means the same for all; whether the courts are accessible and meet the cultural needs of the diverse population; and whether the courts offer a utilitarian purpose for society. Chapters in *Australian Courts* seek to do just this.

There are two main theories in relation to the functions of the criminal courts. The consensus theory argues that the principles of criminal justice evolve from laws, values and norms that are shared in common by the people. The objective of social order benefits all members of society, and the courts should exist to settle disputes, respond to violations of the law, form part of the social control apparatus of society, uphold the moral correctness of the law and legitimacy of government, and be progressive in the process of social change. Conflict theory, though, views the law as an expression of the capitalist economic structure and a mechanism for controlling the population. That is, the law is a tool of the white ruling class, and the criminal courts exist to protect interests of powerful groups (see Light, 1999; White & Perrone, 2005).

Purposes and Functions of the Courts in Contemporary Practice

The purpose of the courts is to adjudicate, to apply the law and to deliver just outcomes. Decisions can, and must, be made based on notions of fairness and equity before the law, on legislative requirements and common law precedent—and not on 'the vibe of it' as comically proffered in a High Court scene in the iconic Australian movie *The Castle* (IMDb, 2015).

The courts have two key functions: crime control and rehabilitation. For the former, central goals are deterrence and community protection (see Harkness on sentencing in Chapter 2). The latter is not so much focused on punitive action but rather on providing a therapeutic and rehabilitative response through individualised treatment. Regardless of which function may take primacy in a particular case, it is vital to appreciate that 'due process' is a concept enshrined in the Australian Constitution (Basteman, 2009). In essence, due process is aimed at ensuring that the criminal courts act as impartial arbiters and that the rights of an individual are protected against the heavily resourced might of the State.

Many aspects of contemporary court processes, which we often simply take as given, emanate from Cesare Beccaria's principle of justice: that laws should be clear and simple; judges should act only in the determination of guilt; punishment should be proportionate to the crime committed, certain and swift (White et al., 2017). For defendants, there ought to exist the presumption of innocence; restraints on arbitrary power, a right to counsel, judgement by peers, no secret accusation by government, and determinate sentencing. Such due processes attempt to ensure a smooth-running, fair and impartial system (Fagin, 2006; see also Findlay et al., 2015 who offer a comprehensive articulation of the criminal justice in a contemporary Australian context).

Courting Controversy

Whilst the criminal justice system generally works for most (Wimshurst & Harrison, 2000), there are no shortage of controversies which exist and opportunities for reform. White and Perrone (2005) argue that a transformation in power relations in the courts is necessary, pointing to the hitherto close-knit nature of the legal profession itself, the male-centeredness of laws and legal institutions; the affordability of legal services; the lack of representativeness amongst the judiciary; the overly adversarial nature of trials that disempower minorities and those of low socio-economic status; and delays in proceedings.

Courts are a vital pillar in a functioning society, but in an Australian context matters such as access to justice, treatment of First Nations peoples and blurred boundaries between various arms of the justice system or with government all provoke debate.

Access to Justice

Anyone who appears before a court or needs to access the courts ought to be supported to do so processes must be clear and transparent, and courts must be accessible, responsive and appropriately resourced (see, e.g., Law Council of Australia, 2018). 'Access to justice', therefore, is critically important. The term, although ubiquitous (Sackville, 2004) is imprecise (Coverdale, 2016), and the notion are under-developed both empirically and theoretically (Donnermeyer, 2022). It is, though, "an essential element of the rule of law" (ALRC, 2018, p. 319).

The concept can be considered in terms of both physical access (i.e. the actual infrastructure) as well as the less tangible aspects of access for certain individuals or demographics—such as for persons with physical or cognitive impairment; survivors of family violence; witnesses; the socio-economically disadvantaged; single parents in outer suburbs and people residing in certain rural, regional and remote areas; Indigenous persons; and people for whom English is a second language. Five critical matters can be considered when contemplating access to the courts: (i) access to and costs of legal representation; (ii) physical infrastructure; (iii) access to rehabilitation options; (iv) justice delays; and (v) participatory justice.

i. **Access to and costs of legal representation**

Access to legal representation is a cornerstone principle of the court system, for all who appear before the courts. Nevertheless, we live in an era in which self-representation has become common. This is perhaps most acutely relevant for First Nations peoples in order to address a chronic level of over-representation in the corrections system brought about by any or adequate legal advice, or a lack of awareness of possible defences or pleas of mitigation (ALRC, 2018).

Accessing justice can take a significant toll both emotionally and financially, and requires a significant investment of time. The cost of legal advice and representation, as well as other court costs, can be debilitating for many people (see, for practical examples, Wells, 2018). The financial costs of appearing in court can thus limit those who might wish to access judicial redress. That is, some might consider the costs to outweigh the desire for seeking an adjudicated outcome, and this will have the effect of limiting court processes to those with deeper pockets. McIntyre (Chapter 15) focuses on access to justice in the civil courts, noting that access in this sphere (and here we can think of actions around defamation for instance) is primarily the domain of the wealthy, and that there exists an 'unacknowledged crisis'.

Dioso-Villa and Nash (Chapter 8) identify the access to justice consequences for defendants amidst insufficient funding for legal aid representation and the cost of private legal representation being out of reach for many individuals. Limited or no access to government-funded representation is particularly an issue for people from vulnerable populations who are then faced with the scenario of self-representation. Added to this is the pressure from a backlog of cases in the courts, leading to significant time delays which result in people foregoing legal redress or settling for outcomes not in their interest such as pleading guilty. Lack of access to appropriate legal representation may well result in wrongful convictions, which often only gain prominence following public campaigning.

The consequence of a lack of private legal representation is felt acutely in rural, regional and remote places (Davies & Peck, 2023), and when lawyers are not available access to justice will be undermined and costs both to participants and the courts themselves will increase (Pruitt & Davies, 2022). Initiatives to overcome this matter in an Australian context include the Digital Treechange project of the Law Council of Australia (2021), which encourages lawyers to work remotely for a rural community for a trial period.

ii. **Physical infrastructure of courts**

Many courts throughout Australia were built either in the latter part of the nineteenth century or in the post-Second World War building boom at times when the population was much smaller and due regard for people with disabilities was limited or non-existent. Physical infrastructure for such older physical infrastructure can inhibit accessibility. For instance, steps leading up to a court will inhibit people with disabilities from easily accessing the facility; in rural and outer-suburban areas, lack of transport options will also limit accessibility (Camilleri, 2019; George & Harris, 2014).

The physical infrastructure and geographies of courts will also impact on a person's need for privacy of access to justice. In rural areas, there may well be a lack of private meeting spaces and 'safe spaces' meaning that victims and witnesses may well be sharing the same spaces with an accused. In small communities, when anonymity is already unlikely, a person's personal matters might be on full public display, leading to a fear of giving evidence, shame and public exposure. As one interviewee reported in a study of women surviving family violence in regional and rural Victoria: "You can hear the names from the court loudspeaker in the supermarket across the road" (George & Harris, 2014, p. 83).

iii. **Access to rehabilitation options**

There was a marked shift in criminological thinking in the 1980s, with the emergence of Left Realism not only as a theoretical construct but also a roadmap of sorts for pragmatic crime control. Key to this approach is a focus on active cooperation between criminal justice agencies and the adoption of problem-solving strategies. Simultaneously, Right Realism emerged as a political philosophy, of which populist tough-on-crime rhetoric manifests into a greater focus on retribution, deterrence and incarceration rather than using the criminal justice system to engage in rehabilitative approaches (White et al., 2017). Here, then, a significant divergence exists not only theoretically but also in legislative decision-making and court processes.

Problem-solving courts—such as specialist drug, family violence and Indigenous sentencing courts—have emerged as a non-adversarial mechanism for dealing with criminal cases in a rehabilitative manner. Therapeutic jurisprudence, in the form of problem-solving courts, recognises that traditional court processes inadequately address causes of offending. Issues such as homelessness and drug and alcohol addiction, if not addressed, will fuel the cycle of offending, which can then be extremely difficult to break. Schaefer and Egan (Chapter 9) identify some of the traditional elements of the criminal courts which have been maintained or worsened in with the introduction of problem-solving courts; which include the notion of pressured participation, unforeseen sentencing outcomes, 'net-widening', potential for stigmatisation, and less transparency (see also Castellano, 2011).

iv. **'Justice delayed is justice denied'**

For Sourdin and Burstyner (2014, p. 49), borrowing the phrase credited to the former British Prime Minister William Gladstone that 'justice delayed is justice denied', "the time taken to deal with a dispute is a, and in many cases the, critical factor in determining whether or not people consider that the justice system is just and fair". Empirical studies suggest that higher levels of quality of justice will be derived from speedier judicial processes (Melcarne et al., 2021).

In an Australian context, delay in access to timely justice remains a critical issue for an accused, victims and witnesses alike. The impact of the COVID-19 pandemic has added further strain on a system already struggling to hear matters in a timely manner (Curran, Chapter 7). Other issues contributing to delays are legislative changes to the bail laws

(Colvin, Chapter 6) where, for example in Victoria, the onus provision and presumptions against bail has been shifted. This change has resulted in those accused of crimes being remanded in custody until the matter could be heard by the court. In some instances, those remanded have been found subsequently innocent of the charges.

v. **Participatory Justice**

Another aspect of access to the courts, or indeed lack thereof, revolves around the concept of 'participatory justice'. Sheehan and Baidawi (Chapter 13) consider the perspective of children and young people in what is effectively an adult system, arguing that the lack of cognitive understanding, maturity and ability to engage in processes inhibits children and young people appearing before the courts. They also argue that the minimum age of criminal responsibility of ten years sits outside of Australia's signatory responsibilities to the United Nations Convention on the Rights of the Child.

Camilleri (Chapter 12) adds voice to calls for greater participatory rights for victim/survivors of sexual assault. Noting that despite their role of holding perpetrators to account, victim/survivors will often feel alienated from an adversarial system which at times can be a source of secondary victimisation. Camilleri argues that whilst there have been numerous reforms to increase the status of victim/survivors in the criminal justice system, these are not implemented consistently.

Participation in court processes is not limited only to those actively involved, but ought to also include the community at large. Clearly not all citizens have the time or desire to attend court hearings, and so media outlets serve an important role in distilling and reporting on outcomes. The media, as Waller and Clifford (Chapter 4) argue, "have a special role in our democracy - they are uniquely and inseparably linked to open and accountable government".

Open and accessible justice is a fundamental principle in systems of justice, allowing accessibility of the courts to the public directly, or to the public via media reporting (see, e.g., chapters in Hess & Harvey, 2019). However, restrictions on in-person gatherings because of COVID-19 and technological issues with online meeting platforms meant reporters were unable to access hearings. The use by courts of suppression and non-publication orders also limits public accessibility to open justice, and rankles with reporters (Waller and Clifford, Chapter 4).

Court Impacts on First Nations Peoples

Central to several chapters of *Australian Courts* is a recognition that a key measure of a justice system is how the justice system responds to those deemed most vulnerable and who have the most to lose. In particular, the impact of embedded long-established practices and processes continues to have an enduring impact on First Nations peoples.

Despite the recommendations and significant learnings and opportunities for change offered by the Royal Commission into Aboriginal deaths in Custody (RCIADIC, 1991), Marchetti and Ryle (Chapter 10) highlight that the incarceration rate of First Nations peoples continues to rise and that court practices in the form of pre-sentence reports have significant bearing on 'hyper-incarceration'. These reports, they note, are an inadequate tool through which to "represent the experiences and perspectives of First Nations peoples and facilitate erroneous risk evaluations".

Considering the responses to First Nations peoples from the perspective of the families of people who have died in custody, and who seek justice for and explanations of how their loved one has died while in the 'protection' of the state, Allison and Cunneen (Chapter 11) note that: "A fundamental controversy arises with respect to First Nations deaths investigations by coroners courts; that institutional racism within these courts prevents First Nations peoples from attaining the justice to which they are entitled".

There is a real danger that existing practices, which may lack due regard for cultural safety, can be triggering and retraumatising for families. Such practices can nullify opportunities for families to experience any measure of 'peace' which might emerge from knowing that the processes utilised to understand the circumstances leading to a person's death are clear and have been investigated thoroughly. Just outcomes, identified by families who have shared their experiences, include the need to 'find fact', prevent future deaths, ensure accountability and deliver therapeutic outcomes (Allison and Cunneen, Chapter 11).

Another dimension of institutionalised practices are wrongful convictions, which impact most heavily on marginalised and disadvantaged people. Indigenous peoples, certainly, are over-represented in the criminal justice system and are therefore at disproportionally higher risk of suffering from miscarriages of justice and wrongful convictions. The vulnerability of Indigenous peoples to wrongful conviction in the first instance lays the foundations for pressure for guilty pleas, and thus "creating a particular barrier for Indigenous defendants to have their wrongful convictions recognised and remedied" (Dioso-Villa and Nash, Chapter 8).

Blurred Boundaries

Controversies, Schaefer and Egan (Chapter 9) argue, include the 'blurred boundaries' of problem-solving courts, some of which do not address underlying problems leading to offending. In what they call 'slippery sentencing', the requirement to plead guilty and the potential of further harm which stems from constant surveillance and the threat of returning to the original sentence are significant issues.

Blurred boundaries exist between various arms of the justice system or with government. Brown and Alexander (Chapter 15) refer to women and children who are not protected from the harm of family violence within the family law system. They detail the controversies which arise in the Family Court when family violence is present in relationships between separating and divorcing couples. The family law system, they argue, has been beset by crisis, notwithstanding reviews and reform attempts "without ever successfully addressing family violence".

Ellis and Camilleri (Chapter 5) expand upon the blurring of boundaries in police-led prosecutions, noting the lack of separation and the "opaque nature [of] police prosecutor decision making in the summary jurisdiction". This is particularly concerning in instances when the police informant is also the victim, and the prosecutor is also a police member. Blurred boundaries also exist between the public, media, parliament and the courts, a consequence of which might be knee-jerk reactions made by government in the form of legislative reform following public pressure (see Harkness, Chapter 2). In a technologically-advanced social-media age, there are blurred boundaries for jurors, too—Facebook and internet searches can have a prejudicial impact on an accused presumption of innocence (Goodman-Delahunty and Tait, Chapter 3).

Conclusion

Chapters included in *Australian Courts* outline critical issues which impact directly on court processes and functions, and importantly on those who interact with the courts. In the third decade of the twenty-first century, there is a growing demand that courts reflect both the expectations of society and the access needs of a diverse community. This means universal access to justice—regardless of geography, demography or socio-economic factors. As courts change to meet new demands, it is of course inevitable that further reforms will be needed at some point in the future, as controversies persist, and with them opportunities for meaningful change.

References

ALRC (Australian Law Reform Commission). (2018). *Pathways to justice: Inquiry into the incarceration rate of aboriginal and torres strait islander peoples* (ALRC Report 133). Australian Government.https://www.alrc.gov.au/publication/pathways-to-justice-inquiry-into-the-incarceration-rate-of-aboriginal-and-torres-strait-islander-peoples-alrc-report-133/

Basteman, W. (2009). Procedural due process under the Australian Constitution. *Sydney Law Review, 31*(3), 411–442.

Bentham, J. (2017 [1780]). Of the principle of utility. In J. Bennett (Ed.), *An introduction to the principles of morals and legislation.* T. Payne and Sons.

Camilleri, M. (2019). Disabled in rural Victoria: Exploring the intersection of victimisation, disability and rurality on access to justice. *International Journal of Rural Criminology, 5*(1), 88–112.

Castellano, U. (2011). Problem-solving courts: Theory and practice. *Sociology Compass, 5*(11), 957–967.

Coverdale, R. (2016). Accessing justice in regional Australia: Evolving perspectives and contexts. In A. Harkness, B. Harris, & D. Baker (Eds.), *Locating crime in context and place: Perspectives on regional, rural and remote Australia* (pp. 108–119). The Federation Press.

Davies, A. L. B., & Peck, S. (2023). Access to legal representation. In A. Harkness, J. R. Peterson, M. Bowden, C. Pedersen, & J. F. Donnermeyer (Eds.), *Encyclopedia of rural criminology.* Bristol University Press.

Donnermeyer, J. F. (2022). Theoretical and empirical gaps in rural criminology. In M. Bowden & A. Harkness (Eds.), *Rural transformations and rural crime: International critical perspectives in rural criminology* (pp. 31–48). Bristol University Press.

Fagin, J. A. (2006). *Criminal justice*. Pearson/Allyn and Bacon.

Findlay, M., Odgers, S., & Yeo, S. (2015). *Australian criminal justice* (5th ed.). Oxford University Press.

Foucault, M. (1977). *Discipline and punish: The birth of the prison.* Random House.

George, A., & Harris, B. (2014). *Landscapes of violence: Women surviving family violence in rural and regional Victoria.* Centre for Rural and Regional Law and Justice. Deakin University.https://www.deakin.edu.au/__data/assets/pdf_file/0003/287040/Landscapes-of-Violence-online-pdf-version.pdf

Gleeson, M. (2008, June 18). *The privy council: An Australian perspective.* Address to The Anglo-Australian Lawyers Society, the Commercial Bar Association and the Chancery Bar Association. London.https://www.hcourt.gov.au/assets/publications/speeches/former-justices/gleesoncj/cj_18jun08.pdf

Hess, B., & Harvey, A. K. (Eds.). (2019). *Open justice: The role of courts in democratic society.* Max Planck Institute Luxembourg for International European and Regulatory Procedural Law.

Hughes, R. A., Leane, G. W. G., & Clarke, A. D. (2003). *Australian legal institutions: Principles, structure and organisation* (2nd ed.). Lawbook Co.

IMDb. (2015). *The Castle (1997)* [online]. http://www.imdb.com/title/tt0118826/quotes

Law Council of Australia. (2018, August). *The justice project: Introduction and overview.* Law Council of Australia.https://www.lawcouncil.asn.au/files/web-pdf/Justice%20Project/Final%20Report/Justice%20Project%20_%20Final%20Report%20in%20full.pdf

Law Council of Australia. (2021, September 22). *New program to bring more lawyers to the bush* [Media Release].https://www.lawcouncil.asn.au/media/media-releases/new-program-to-bring-more-lawyers-to-the-bush

Light, S. C. (1999). *Understanding criminal justice*. Wadsworth.

Mawson, S. (2021). The deep past of pre-colonial Australia. *The Historical Journal, 64*(5), 1477–1499.

Melcarne, A., Ramello, G. B., & Spruk, R. (2021). Is justice delayed justice denied? An empirical approach. *International Review of Law and Economics, 65*, 1–9.

Mill, J. S. (1998 [1861]). *Utilitarianism* (R. Crisp, Ed.). Oxford University Press.

Neal, D. (1991). *The rule of law in a penal colony*. Cambridge University Press.

Pruitt, L. R., & Davies, A. (2022). Investigating access to justice, the rural lawyer shortage, and implications for civil and criminal legal systems. In R. A. Weisheit, J. R. Peterson, & A. Pytlarz (Eds.), *Research methods for rural criminologists* (pp. 67–78). Routledge.

Rasmussen, M., Gou, X., Wang, Y., Lohmueller, K. E., Albrechtsen, A., Skotte, L., Lindgreen, S., Metspalu, M., Jombart, T., Kivisild, T., Zhai, W., Eriksson, A., Manica, A., Orlando, L., De La Vega, F. M., Tridico, S., Metspalu, E., Nielsen, K., Avila-Arcos, M. C., Moreno-Mayar, J. V. … Willerslev, E. (2011). An Aboriginal Australian Genome reveals separate human dispersals into Asia. *Science, 334*(6052), 94–98.

Rawls, J. (1971). *A theory of justice*. The Belknap Press.

Royal Commission into Aboriginal Deaths in Custody (RCIADIC). (1991). *Royal Commission into aboriginal deaths in custody: National Report* (Vols. 1–5). Australian Government Publishing Service.

Sackville, R. (2004). Some thoughts on access to justice. *New Zealand Journal of Public and International Law, 2*(85), 85–111.

Sharp, N. (1996). *No ordinary judgement: Mabo, the Murray Islanders' land case*. Aboriginal Studies Press.

Sourdin, T., & Burstyner, N. (2014). Justice delayed is justice denied. *Victoria University Law and Justice Journal, 4*(1), 49–62.

Wells, J. (2018, December 20). The cost of a day in court is more emotionally, and financially draining than you might think. *ABC News*. https://www.abc.net.au/news/2018-12-20/the-true-cost-of-a-day-in-court/10610408

White, R., Haines, F., & Asquith, N. (2017). *Crime & criminology* (6th ed.). Oxford University Press.

White, R., & Perrone, S. (2005). *Crime and social control*. Oxford University Press.

Wimshurst, K., & Harrison, A. (2000). The Australian criminal justice system: Issues and prospects. In D. Chappell & P. Wilson (Eds.), *Crime and the criminal justice system in Australia: 2000 and beyond* (pp. 3–21). Butterworths.

Windeyer, V. (1962). A birthright and inheritance: The establishment of the rule of law in Australia. *Tasmanian University Law Review, 1*(5), 635–669. http://www.austlii.edu.au/au/journals/UTasLawRw/1962/1.pdf

Wise, J., & Roberts, D. A. (2016). Development of crime and the criminal justice system in Australia. In A. Harkness, B. Harris, & D. Baker (Eds.), *Locating crime in context and place: Perspectives on regional, rural and remote Australia* (pp. 35–48). The Federation Press.

York, B. (2018, July 24). *Australian Courts Act 1828*. Blog post. The Museum of Australian Democracy at Old Parliament House. https://www.moadoph.gov.au/blog/australian-courts-act-1828/#

Legislation and Cases

Australia Act 1986 (Cth).

Mabo and others v Queensland (No 2) [1992] HCA 23, (1992) 175 CLR 1 1 F.C. 92/014 (3 June 1992).

New South Wales Charter of Justice, Letters Patent 2 April 1787.

2

Politics, Parliament and the Courts

Alistair Harkness

Introduction

Recognising the oftentimes polarising nature of court decision-making—and the overt public interest and political sensitivities which exist—this chapter focuses on the public influence on legislative decision-making with regard to the courts and court processes. It considers the blurring of boundaries in regard to mandatory sentencing; the parliamentary appetite for sentencing reform; and the questioning of sentencing outcomes and other court practices.

How to reconcile public attitudes (and thus parliamentary action) with magisterial, judicial, parole board and bail justice decision-making is

The original version of this chapter was revised: The author's "Simon Finn" affiliation has been corrected. The correction to this chapter is available at https://doi.org/10.1007/978-3-031-19063-6_17

A. Harkness (✉)
University of New England, Armidale, NSW, Australia
e-mail: alistair.harkness@une.edu.au

M. Camilleri and A. Harkness (eds.), *Australian Courts*,
https://doi.org/10.1007/978-3-031-19063-6_2

a significant challenge. The role of various actors is considered, including sentencing advisory councils, parliamentary law reform committees, legal services boards, community legal centres and other bodies in advocating for positive change, fairness and equity based on sound evidence rather than potentially knee-jerk reactions to public conjecture.

Parliament and the Courts in Australian Context

Following British colonisation of Australia in 1788 and the commencement of transportation of convicts, an English model of criminal justice was, in effect, transplanted upon the new colony. Given the size and ruggedness of the Australian landscape, this was by no means a smooth process, and adaptation to starkly different conditions by appointed magistrates was necessary. This was an era, too, where no notion of sovereignty or existing justice systems of First Nations People was provided any countenance (Wise & Roberts, 2016).

The early incarnation of a colonial judicial system was very militaristic in nature. Until 1823, a Judge Advocate of New South Wales was the highest judicial officer in the colony: the first incumbent was a British naval officer (Nagle, 1996). It was not until 1855 that the Colony of New South Wales became self-governing with its own constitution and elections. Prior to this, a governor appointed by Britain administered the colony. By 1901, what had become six colonies federated to form the Commonwealth of Australia.

The making of laws in contemporary Australia essentially occurs in two places: parliament and the courts. The parliamentary process involves drafted legislation (Bills) proceeding to become Acts of Parliament; and in the courts, decisions are made by judges that subsequently become binding in the determination of future cases—the establishment of precedents. At the State level, the courts achieve their raison d'être from Acts of Parliament. In Victoria, for instance, the *Magistrates' Court Act 1989* (Vic), the *County Court Act*, 1958 (Vic) and the Supreme Court Act *1986* (Vic) provide the basis for the existence and powers of each court.

There is, then, a symbiotic relationship between parliament and the courts. The courts rely on the parliament to provide their powers and for legislation upon which to adjudicate; and parliaments require courts to adjudicate and administer the law. Parliamentary supremacy holds that the law-making powers of parliament take precedence over that of the courts; and by way of the principle of separation of powers, the courts cannot challenge parliamentary law-making (Parliamentary Education Office, 2022b). Nevertheless, the High Court in interpreting the Australian Constitution can confirm or change the Federal Parliament's ability to make certain laws (Parliamentary Education Office, 2022a).

A court is a place where arguments are settled through the application of the law, and a court's legitimacy is based on impartiality and independence. Theoretically, each party must have an equal chance to present their case and no outside factors—whether political, financial, fame or notoriety—should influence the court's decision. That is, everyone is entitled to a fair trial.

A sentence follows the finding of guilt, the punishment for a crime as determined by a magistrate or a judge. Sentencing is considered the 'punch-line' of the criminal justice system because it is where the law is seen to have the most impact (Sallman & Willis, 1984). Of course, any sentence must be consistent with the verdict of a jury—if the particular case has been presented to a jury as opposed to just the judge as in cases where a plea of guilt has been entered. Sentencing occurs after conviction; if it is a trial by jury, the jury has no say in the sentencing process and the judge has considerable discretion within parameters that are set by parliament.

Sentencing options vary from state to state, but there is often commonality about what is considered either a minor or a serious crime and the nature of the sanctions to be imposed by the court on findings of guilt, ranging from good behaviour bonds through to custodial sentences. Sentencing will involve consideration of parsimony (the least severe sentence to meet the purposes of sentencing), proportionality of the sentence to the offence, parity between a sentence for one offence with a similar offence, and of both aggravating and mitigating circumstances. The main purposes of sentencing and punishment are retribution, deterrence, denunciation, incapacitation, rehabilitation and restitution (Livings, 2020; for more on the principles and purposes of sentencing in the context of Victoria, Australia, refer to the Victorian Sentencing Advisory Council, 2022a).

Controversies of Politics and Sentencing

In sentencing, judges must be guided not just by relevant legislation pertaining to the matters before them, such as for instance in Victoria the *Crimes Act*, 1958 (Vic), but also by specific sentencing legislation: such as the *Sentencing Act*, 1991 (Vic) for adults and the *Children, Youth and Families Act 2005* (Vic) for a child. These latter two Acts seek to ensure 'fair', 'just' and consistent sentencing outcomes. Regardless of the legislative and common law framework which exists, nuances of particular cases and a fine focus on the evidence provided can be lost when sentencing outcomes are distilled into media reports of a case and second-hand considerations—and thus the creation, potentially, of public consternation with outcomes.

Notwithstanding ongoing reforms, controversy around aspects of sentencing and the administration of justice persist (for a useful timeline of sentencing reforms in Victorian refer to Sentencing Advisory Council, 2021). Following is an outline of six controversies with regard to sentencing, with a focus on circumstances in Victoria: (i) bail law reform; (ii) mandatory sentencing; (iii) abolition of suspended sentencing; (iv) access to parole; (v) retrospective sentencing; and (vi) guilty plea sentencing discounts.

Bail Law Reform

Victoria's *Bail Act*, 1977 (Vic) was changed in 2018, a key consequence being a requirement for an accused to provide 'compelling reasons' or 'exceptional circumstances' to be released on bail (Kolovos, 2022). Two statutory amendments—the *Bail (Stage One) Amendment*

Act 2017 (Vic) and the *Bail (Stage Two) Amendment Act 2018* (Vic)—increased the number of offences for which a reverse onus test would apply (McMahon, 2019). A key impetus for bail law reform was the circumstance of James Gargasoulas who, whilst on bail, drove a stolen vehicle along a crowded footpath in Melbourne's central business district, killing six and injuring a further 27 people (McMahon, 2019; *DPP v Gargasoulas [2019] VSC 87*).

The political driver for bail law reforms centred on concerns around community protection and a perceived need to remand an accused person in custody rather than await trial in the community. A significant issue here, though, is that some 38% of adult prisoners in Victoria are being held on remand (see McMahon 2019 research paper prepared for the Parliament of Victoria which provides a detailed contextualisation and assessment of issues around public safety, bail and political/community interests).

A number of stakeholder and advocacy groups demand greater access to bail, including the Victorian Aboriginal Legal Services (2021)—although there was not much political appetite for reform in advance of the 2022 state election (Millar & Vedelgos, 2021). This organisation's Chief Executive, Nerita Waight, argued that:

> When politicians make cynical political calculations and sacrifice Aboriginal and Torres Strait Islander people for votes, the message they send is that our lives, our families, our communities and our dignity do not matter. Every day that we wait for Government action on bail reform in Victoria, more Aboriginal people are thrown into Victoria's prisons for minor offending that would be more effectively addressed within community. This is a crisis.

A direct correlation exists between 'tough on crime' legislative reform and the budget bottom line, and governments must weigh up the political opportunity costs of spending more on courts and prisons and other public-sector expenditure in tightened financial times following the COVID-19 pandemic.

Mandatory Sentencing

Blurring the boundaries of judicial and magisterial discretion is mandatory sentencing imposed on the courts by legislatures. Drawing theoretically upon contemporary 'new right' criminology, mandatory sentencing stems from a political shift in the 1970s and 1980s and a reversion to aspects of neo-classical criminology with a focus on the offender rather than on the offence or on the social constructs leading to criminal behaviour. A 'tough on crime' narrative established itself in many Western liberal democracies from the 1990s (White et al., 2017). Absent here is recognition of structural determinism (such as poverty and inequality) and on rehabilitation as a criminal justice response, but rather a focus is placed on individual responsibility, 'just deserts', incapacitation and punitive populism (see, e.g., Newburn, 2007; Walton & Young, 1998; Wood, 2014).

Ordinarily, parliaments will set maximum rather than minimum penalties for specific offences, and also on occasions for specific defendants (such as repeat offenders). Mandatory sentencing guidelines, though, are determined punishments that must be applied to those who are convicted of specific crimes. That is, they mandate a minimum or fixed sentence such as a specific term of imprisonment (see ALRC, 2022). Set by parliament, firm standards for certain crimes are stipulated and no discretion is left to the courts. Mandatory sentencing guidelines stem from public dissatisfaction with determinate sentencing regarded as being 'too soft on crime'.

Proponents of mandatory sentencing point to advantages including equality (same sentences for same offences); certainty (truth in sentencing); just deserts (violent and/or repeat offenders receive harsh treatment); deterrence (a strong message is sent that offenders will be incarcerated); incapacitation (thus protecting public safety). Negative aspects, though, include inflexibility and removal of judicial discretion for mitigating circumstances; the potential for prison overcrowding, increased court workloads and increased prison costs; disparity in sentencing and discrimination (including of Indigenous persons and people with mental or intellectual impairment); the punishment being disproportionate to the actual offence; and the compromising of the tenet of the separation of powers. It is also debatable about whether such sentencing serves as a deterrence and actually reduces crime (ALRC, 2022; Brown, 2001; Law Council of Australia, 2014; Roche, 1999).

Under previous Northern Territory law (repealed in 2001), a first property offence mandated 14 days imprisonment, the second 90 days and the third a one-year minimum sentence. Juveniles aged 15–17 years received a mandatory 28 days in custody for a second property offence (Law Council of Australia, 2014). Such sentences were imposed regardless of an individual's characteristics or any variables which surround the crime.

Victoria maintains a form of mandatory sentencing. Changes to the *Sentencing Act*, 1991 (Vic) in 2016 requires judges in certain instances to provide a custodial sentence only unless it can be demonstrated that compelling and substantial reasons could be offered to sentence otherwise. An amendment in 2018 legislated that previous good character and prospects for rehabilitation were insufficient reasons to avoid jail time. Limiting of judicial discretion, though, is controversial. A particular case of dangerous driving causing death prompted a prominent Melbourne talk-back radio host to declare that "jail is not always constructive... Some people deserve jail, and lots of it. Some do the wrong thing and don't deserve any. Judges should decide that, not vote-hungry politicians" (Mitchell, 2022).

Another prominent critic of limiting judicial discretion is a former Director of Public Prosecutions in New South Wales, Nicholas Cowdery QC, who argues that: "Anybody arguing that mandatory sentencing is not a bad thing, and even worse for juveniles, has not been paying attention... Why, then, do we see politicians returning like dogs to lick at it and why should we need to be discussing it at all?" (Wilkinson, 2011).

Abolition of Suspended Sentencing

A degree of controversy exists around the use of—and abolition of—suspended sentences. These have been traditionally deployed as a sentencing option whereby a court can suspend all or part of a custodial sentence for a period of time, subject to the offender not reoffending during that period: if they were to reoffend, the sentence would need to be actually served (see Baker et al., 2005). In Victoria, these were phased out during 2011 and 2014, replaced by community corrections orders which could set curfews, restrict an offenders' movements and require community service. Other abolished sentencing options are intensive correction orders, combined custody and treatment orders, community-based orders and home detention (Victorian Sentencing Advisory Council, 2022c). Suspended sentences have also be abolished in New South Wales (in 2018) and Tasmania is, as at 2022, in the process of also doing so.

The Victorian Attorney General in 2014 argued that: "If a magistrate does not believe an offender should go to prison, the law will in future require that to be done openly instead of the law pretending an offender is going to prison". Opponents of this move suggest that there would be detrimental impacts in terms of prison overcrowding and higher rates of recidivism (Australian Associated Press, 2014). A research report prepared for Catholic Social Services Victoria (Gelb, 2013) argued that the removal of such a "valuable sentencing option" would significantly increase the prison population, workloads of various participants in the criminal justice process and would not improve community safety (Gelb, 2013, p. iii).

Access to Parole

The horrendous murder of Jill Meagher in inner-city Melbourne in 2012 by Adrian Bayley sparked very significant public and political attention and consternation. Bayley was a recidivist offender who had previously served three years of a five-year sentence for rape (1990–1993), and who had been sentenced in 2002 to 11 years with a minimum of eight for 16 counts of rape and was released on parole in 2010. He had not been added to the sexual offenders register which would have lengthened his sentence. He attacked a man in public in 2011 but his parole was not cancelled. He went on to violently rape and murder Meagher whilst still on parole (Bucci & Spooner, 2015). He was sentenced to life imprisonment with a non-parole period of 43 years, reduced to a single non-parole period of 40 years on appeal (Supreme Court of Victoria, 2016; *The Queen v Bayley [2013] VSC 313).*

Typical of media opinion on this case was the view expressed by newspaper crime columnist John Silvester (2015):

> The simple fact is that on September 22, 2012 Adrian Earnest Bayley should have been in jail. He should never have been in a position to attack, rape and kill Jill Meagher as she walked home in Brunswick after a night out with friends.

Focus on parole laws in Victoria had been accentuating for some time, but the Meagher case projected attention to the forefront of public attention through front-page media coverage and speeches in Parliament. In 2013, the *Corrections Amendment (Parole Reform) Bill 2013* was introduced, following review recommendations made by former High Court Justice Ian Callinan (2013). The Bill amended the *Corrections Act 1986* (Vic) "to provide that safety and protection of the community is paramount in parole decisions; to reform membership of the Adult Parole Board; and to provide for the notification of registered victims before the release of a prisoner on parole" (Parliamentary Library Research Service, 2013).

Retrospective Sentencing

In accord with s.27 of the *Victorian Charter of Human Rights and Responsibilities 2006 (Vic)*, people have the right to protection from retrospective criminal laws. That is, the penalty for someone sentenced ought not to be greater than it would have been possible at the time of the offending (VEOHRC, 2022). In 2018, the Victorian Parliament passed amendments to the *Sentencing Act*, 1991 (Vic) which introduced 'standard sentences' for 12 serious offence types, set at 40% of the maximum penalty. Treatment and monitoring orders were also mandated for some serious offences against emergency workers (Victorian Sentencing Advisory Council, 2022d). These changes meant that (Victorian Sentencing Advisory Council, 2022d, p. 3):

> … courts [must] take 'current sentencing practices' into account; that is, courts must consider any trends in how an offence is usually sentenced, particularly in comparable cases. When sentencing a standard sentence offence, however, courts are now prohibited from having regard to any sentences imposed on offences prior to the standard sentence legislation coming into operation. This effectively means that sentencing practices for the 12 standard sentence offences have been wiped clean, and courts must start afresh.

Laws passed by the Commonwealth Parliament which are retrospective in nature are not uncommon, and in terms of criminality have attended to war crimes, hoaxes using the postal services, offences against Australians overseas and people smuggling (ALRC, 2016). Sparking controversy at the State level, though, is the passing of retrospective legislation which extends the time in custody beyond that which was set by the sentencing judge at the time of trial.

An example of such an occurrence involves the mass murderer, Julian Knight, who in 1987 killed seven people and injured a further 19 by opening fire as they passed on Hoddle Street in an inner-suburb of Melbourne. Knight was sentenced to a minimum non-parole period of 27 years. The sentencing judge noted (*R v Knight*), and the Crown prosecutor "did not contend that a minimum term should not be fixed", that:

> In my view, the fixing of a minimum term in this case is appropriate because of your age and your prospects of rehabilitation, as well as the other mitigatory factors I have already mentioned which justify some amelioration of your sentence, not only in your interest, but in the interest of the community.

Prior to Knight's non-parole period expiry in 2015, the Victorian Parliament introduced specific legislation—the *Corrections Amendment (Parole) Act 2014* (Vic)—to ensure that the Adult Parole Board could not order Knight's release "unless satisfied, amongst other things, that Mr Knight is in imminent danger of dying or is seriously incapacitated and that, as a result, he no longer has the physical ability to do harm to any person"

(*Corrections Act 1986* (Vic), s.74AA 'Conditions for making a parole order for Julian Knight').

In addition to the horrific nature of his crimes, Knight elicited little sympathy from the public owing to his ongoing legal action which led him to being declared a vexatious litigant (Younger, 2016). In introducing the legislation, the then Premier Denis Napthine declared that (ABC News, 2014):

> This is a special situation for Julian Knight… Julian Knight is our worst mass murderer. (He was) convicted of seven murders and has a history of further inappropriate behaviour and disrespect for our fellow man whilst in jail. He deserves to rot in jail.

Opposition to this legislation was expressed by Greg Barnes from the Australian Lawyers Alliance who argued that (ABC News, 2014):

> Julian Knight, whatever you think of him, has certain rights… When he was sentenced to life with 27 years, to then retrospectively say no, that's not your right, that is grossly unfair. It also means that it sets a very dangerous precedent for governments to think they can make policy on the run to undermine peoples' rights.

Guilty Plea Sentencing Discounts

A plea of guilty has long been considered a mitigating factor in sentencing decision-making—it does, after all, save considerable resources—and a lesser sentence will be imposed (*Sentencing Act*, 1991 (Vic), s.6AAA). However, there exists ongoing debate about the merits and application of sentencing discounts (Warner et al., 2022): questions are raised as to issues of consistency and fairness; and it is acknowledged that someone ought not be penalised for their right to a trial. MacKenzie (2007, p. 206) for instance argues that:

> …there is little appropriate justification for the discount, and that it creates, in effect, a penalty for those defendants who exercise their right to trial (for whatever reason) [and that] in some cases the existence of the

discount can provide an inappropriate incentive to plead guilty, when in some cases, defendants ought not to have done so.

Warner et al. (2022) note other opposition for discounts include that a sentence reduction based on something other than related directly to the offence; discounts do not necessarily attend to the problem of court delays; and there is a scarcity of evidence as to its effectiveness in producing pleas of guilt. However, proponents point to reductions in court delays; possible reduced costs; and the saving of victims needing to provide evidence (Warner et al., 2022). Their national study of public sentiments of sentencing discounts found that a third of respondents would have supported a discount on a plea of guilt, and over half supported an increase in sentence had the matter gone to trial.

The Challenge of Balancing Sentencing Policy and Public Opinion

Public attitudes towards punishment can influence individual parliamentarians and political parties alike. This influence, as well as geographic and social differences, can affect legislative decision-making, presenting a challenge for the fair, impartial conduct of the courts. How to reconcile public attitudes (and thus parliamentary action) with magisterial, judicial, parole board and bail justice decision-making is a significant challenge. A key question inevitably arises: How much influence should the public—whether interest groups, the public in general or via their elected representatives—have on sentencing?

For Justice Lex Lasry QC (2016, p. 4), there exists a significant overlap between sentencing outcomes, political action and media influence. A key concern for him is the "politics of sentencing to the extent that it becomes a political point scoring issue and is used as a weapon in the contest between political parties", and the oft-made accusations promulgated in sections of the media that the judiciary is out of touch with community expectations.

An example of when political decision-making was widely viewed as out of step with public opinion is that of Ronald Ryan who was convicted and sentenced to death by hanging—the mandatory sentence at the time (and the last person executed in Victoria)—for the killing of a prison officer during an escape attempt from Pentridge Prison in Melbourne in 1965 (*The Queen v. Ryan and Walker*). Appeal attempts were dismissed and the State Cabinet declined to commute the sentence (Richards, 2002). Significant public opposition to this determination ensued: public opinion was most certainly divided (Richards, 1976).

Much public discourse on sentencing verges on dissatisfaction with outcomes. For example, in 2022 a mentally impaired man convicted of viciously assaulting two police officers was sentenced to three years and two months of imprisonment. Reaction was swift, with the Victorian Police Commissioner and the Secretary of the Victoria Police Association denouncing the sentence as inadequate—the latter attributed blame not to the presiding judge but to the system itself (Jeuniewic & Neal, 2022).

Following a change of government in Victoria in 2010 and having campaigned heavily on law-and-order issues, the new Government launched a survey of Victorian attitudes to sentencing (the survey instrument used can be accessed from https://www.abc.net.au/mediawatch/transcripts/1128_survey.pdf [ABC, n.d.]). The survey was published in the state's major tabloid newspaper, the *Herald Sun*, with readers invited to nominate sentencing outcomes for cases such as murder, rape, armed robbery and so on based on very short blurbs of a given case. 18,000 responses were received, and the Attorney General noted that the results strengthened the government's resolve to adopt a hardline stance on tougher sentencing (Nine News, 2011). Nicholas Cowdery QC, a former New South Wales Director of Public Prosecutions, though, described the survey as "totally useless… to formulate policy on the basis of some sort of public opinion poll I think is deeply flawed" (Wilkinson, 2011). Questions can also be raised about the veracity of the methodology adopted (Cunliffe, 2011).

But how true is it that a significant gulf exists between sentencing outcomes and pubic expectations? To determine the similarities or differences between public opinion and jury sentencing outcomes, a landmark study was undertaken in Tasmania considering 138 trial outcomes form between 2007 and 2009. The Tasmania Jury Sentencing Survey (Warner et al., 2011) found that 90% of jurors believed the judicial outcome to be very or fairly appropriate, with over half proposing a more lenient sentence than was handed down by the judge. A similar study of 987 jurors conducted in Victoria between 2013 and 2015 (Warner et al., 2017a, p. 180; see also Warner et al., 2017b) found that "the views of judges and jurors are much more closely aligned than mass public opinion surveys would suggest".

Mechanisms for Accountability and Change

One significant step forward has been the creation of the Victorian Sentencing Advisory Council, established to assist in the development of guideline sentencing judgements. These guidelines are advisory, they are not binding on the courts and judicial independence is maintained. A *Sentencing Review: Discussion Paper* (Freiberg, 2001) announced a Victorian policy of gauging public opinion in relation to offenders, offences, maximum penalties and sentencing.

Educating the public as to the complexities of sentencing decision-making is critical. Although perhaps easier said than done, a number of mechanisms exist. For example, all sentencing outcomes are provided publicly via the AusLII (the Australasian Legal Information Institute) website. One innovative mechanism which enables members of the public to assess their own determinations on real cases with actual outcomes is the *You be the judge* scenarios provided by the Victorian Sentencing Advisory Council (2022b).

Other various actors, including parliamentary law reform committees, legal services boards, community legal centres and other bodies, are critical in advocating for positive change, fairness and equity based on sound evidence rather than potentially knee-jerk reactions to public conjecture.

Conclusion

Sentencing decision-making will always evoke emotive sentiment. For parliaments, though, a primary objective is to legislate for the betterment of society, drawing upon advice and input from the community as well as from government departments, police, the not-for-profit sector; and considering case law, human rights and equal opportunities. Everyone has a vested interest in ensuring that the courts work—even members of parliament—and the courts must be allowed to perform their vital role in civil society without being micro-managed and at the mercy of daily public opinion.

References

ABC News. (2014, February 18). Government to legislate to keep Hoddle Street Killer Julian Knight in jail indefinitely. *ABC News*. https://www.abc.net.au/news/2014-02-18/government-to-legislate-to-keep-julian-knight-in-jail-indefinit/5266120

ABC. (n.d.). *Sentencing survey*. https://www.abc.net.au/mediawatch/transcripts/1128_survey.pdf

ALRC (Australian Law Reform Commission). (2016). *Laws with retrospective operation*. Canberra: Australian Law Reform Commission. Retrieved from https://www.alrc.gov.au/publication/traditional-rights-and-freedoms-encroachments-bycommonwealth-laws-alrc-report-129/13-retrospective-laws/laws-with-retrospective-operation-2/

ALRC (Australian Law Reform Commission). (2022). *Mandatory sentencing*. Australian Law Reform Commission. https://www.alrc.gov.au/publication/incarceration-rates-of-aboriginal-and-torres-strait-islander-peoples-dp-84/4-sentencing-options/mandatory-sentencing/

Australian Associated Press. (2014, September 1). Suspended prison sentences now banned in all Victorian Courts. *The Guardian*. https://www.theguardian.com/world/2014/sep/01/suspended-prison-sentences-now-banned-in-all-victorian-courts

Baker, J., Burns, K., & Moore, V. (2005, April). *Suspended sentences: Discussion paper*. Sentencing Advisory Council. https://www.vgls.vic.gov.au/client/en_AU/search/asset/1289074/0

Brown, D. (2001). Mandatory sentencing: A criminological perspective. *Australian Journal of Human Rights, 7*(2), 31–49.

Bucci, N., & Spooner, R. (2015, March 26). Adrian Bayley: How the justice system left him free to stalk Melbourne's streets. *The Age*. https://www.theage.com.au/national/victoria/adrian-bayley-how-the-justice-system-left-him-free-to-stalk-melbournes-streets-20150325-1m70ps.html

Callinan, I. (2013, July). *Review of the parole system in Victoria*. https://files.corrections.vic.gov.au/2021-06/ReviewAdultParoleBoard%20v1.pdf
Cunliffe, I. (2011). Sentencing made simple. *Dissent, 37*, 38–41.
Freiberg, A. (2001, August). *Sentencing review: Discussion paper*. Department of Justice.
Gelb, K. (2013, December). *The perfect storm? The impacts of abolishing suspended sentences in Victoria*. Catholic Social Services Victoria. https://researchdirect.westernsydney.edu.au/islandora/object/uws:32115/datastream/PDF/download/citation.pdf
Jeuniewic, L., & Neal, M. (2022, July 22). Steven John Cleary jailed for brutal assault captured on police body cam. *ABC Ballarat*. https://www.abc.net.au/news/2022-07-22/steven-john-cleary-sentenced-for-attack-on-warrnambool-police/101260268
Kolovos, B. (2022, March 25). 'Long overdue': MPs call for reviews of Victoria's bail laws that disproportionately affect women. *The Guardian*. https://www.theguardian.com/australia-news/2022/mar/25/long-overdue-mps-call-for-review-of-victorias-bail-laws-that-disproportionately-affect-women
Lasry, L. (2016, October 14). *Sentencing, politics and the media*. Address to the Criminal Law Congress, South Australia. https://www.supremecourt.vic.gov.au/about-the-court/speeches/sentencing-politics-and-the-media
Law Council of Australia. (2014). *Policy discussion paper on mandatory sentencing*. Law Council of Australia. https://www.lawcouncil.asn.au/publicassets/f370dcfc-bdd6-e611-80d2-005056be66b1/1405-Discussion-Paper-Mandatory-Sentencing-Discussion-Paper.pdf
Livings, B. (2020). Sentencing to protect the safety of the community. *Adelaide Law Review, 41*(2), 395–420.
MacKenzie, G. (2007). The guilty plea discount: Does pragmatism win over proportionality and principle? *Southern Cross University Law Review, 11*, 205–223.
McMahon, M. (2019, August). *No bail, more jail? Breaking the nexus between community protection and escalating pre-trial detention* (Research Paper No. 3). Parliamentary Library and Information Service, Parliament of Victoria. https://apo.org.au/sites/default/files/resource-files/2019-08/apo-nid253906.pdf
Millar, R., & Vedelgos, C. (2021, November 15). Labor shelves plans to revamp justice laws until after state election. *The Age*. https://www.theage.com.au/national/victoria/labor-shelves-plans-to-revamp-justice-laws-until-after-state-election-20211115-p598xn.html

Mitchell, N. (2022, July 20). Judges should decide sentences, not vote-hungry politicians. *9News*. https://www.9news.com.au/national/neil-mitchell-judges-should-decide-sentences-not-votehungry-politicians/f9768087-4735-4ff5-952e-1b585719229c

Nagle, J. F. (1996). *Collins, the courts and the colony: Law and society in colonial New South Wales, 1788–1796*. University of New South Wales Press.

Newburn, T. (2007). "Tough on crime": Penal policy in England and Wales. *Crime and Justice, 36*(1), 425–470.

Nine News. (2011, December 5). *Make serious offenders pay, says survey*. https://www.9news.com.au/national/make-serious-offenders-pay-says-survey/93c40c8b-a8dc-45dd-bb9c-717e735ad7d4

Parliamentary Education Office. (2022a). *Parliament and the courts*. https://peo.gov.au/understand-our-parliament/how-parliament-works/system-of-government/parliament-and-the-courts/

Parliamentary Education Office. (2022b). *Separation of powers: Parliament, executive and judiciary*. https://peo.gov.au/understand-our-parliament/how-parliament-works/system-of-government/separation-of-powers/

Parliamentary Research Office. (2013, October). *Corrections Amendment (Parole Reform) Bill 2013* (Research Brief No. 6). Parliament of Victoria. https://www.parliament.vic.gov.au/publications/research-papers/download/36-research-papers/13613-corrections-amendment-parole-reform-bill-2013-final

Richards, M. J. (1976). *The Ryan case: An analysis of the decision of the Victorian Cabinet to impose the death sentence on Ronald Joseph Ryan, and of the public and mass media protest campaign* (Masters Research thesis), School of Political Science, The University of Melbourne. https://minerva-access.unimelb.edu.au/items/cbc6b33e-9232-5348-b330-4a74a99cbef8

Richards, M. J. (2002). Ryan, Ronald Joseph (1925–1967). *Australian Dictionary of Biography*. National Centre of Biography, Australian National University (published first in hardcopy 2002). https://adb.anu.edu.au/biography/ryan-ronald-joseph-11592

Roche, D. (1999). Mandatory sentencing. *Trends and Issues in Criminal Justice, 138*. Australian Institute of Criminology. https://www.aic.gov.au/sites/default/files/2020-05/tandi138.pdf

Sallman, P. A., & Willis, J. (1984). *Criminal justice in Australia*. Oxford University Press.

Silvester, J. (2015, March 26). Adrian Bayley's reign of terror: How the system failed us. *The Age*. https://www.theage.com.au/national/victoria/adrian-bayleys-reign-of-terror-how-the-system-failed-us-20150324-1m6aj3.html

Supreme Court of Victoria. (2016, July 13). *Summary of Judgement: Bayley v The Queen [2016] VSCA 160*. https://www.supremecourt.vic.gov.au/sites/default/files/assets/2017/09/ab/da9fc5f29/summaryofjudgmentbayleyvthe%2Bqueen2016vsca160.pdf

VEOHRC (Victorian Equal Opportunity and Human Rights Commission). (2022). *Right to protection from retrospective criminal laws*. https://www.humanrights.vic.gov.au/for-individuals/right-to-protection-from-retrospective-criminal-laws/

Victorian Aboriginal Legal Service. (2021, December 14). *Victorian must not wait to act on bail reform*. https://www.vals.org.au/victoria-must-not-wait-to-act-on-bail-reform/

Victorian Sentencing Advisory Council. (2021). *Key evets for sentencing in Victoria*. https://www.sentencingcouncil.vic.gov.au/about-sentencing/key-events-for-sentencing-in-victoria

Victorian Sentencing Advisory Council. (2022a). *Sentencing principles, purpose, factors*. https://www.sentencingcouncil.vic.gov.au/about-sentencing/sentencing-principles-purposes-factors

Victorian Sentencing Advisory Council. (2022b). *You be the judge*. https://virtualjudge.sentencingcouncil.vic.gov.au/

Victorian Sentencing Advisory Council. (2022c). *Suspended sentences and other abolished sentencing orders*. https://www.sentencingcouncil.vic.gov.au/about-sentencing/suspended-sentences-and-other-abolished-orders

Victorian Sentencing Advisory Council. (2022d). *Changes to sentencing law in Victoria: An overview of 2018*. https://www.sentencingcouncil.vic.gov.au/sites/default/files/2019-08/Changes_to_Sentencing_Law_in_Victoria_2018.pdf

Walton, P., & Young, J. (Eds.). (1998). *The new criminology revisited*. Palgrave Macmillan.

Warner, K., Davis, J., Spiranovic, C., Cockburn, H., & Freiberg, A. (2017a). Measuring jurors' views on sentencing: Results from the second Australian Jury Sentencing Study. *Punishment and Society, 19*(2), 180–202.

Warner, K., Davis, J., Spiranovic, C., Cockburn, H., & Freiberg, A. (2017b). Why sentence? Comparing the views of jurors, judges and the legislature on the purposes of sentencing in Victoria, Australia. *Criminology & Criminal Justice, 19*(1), 26–44.

Warner, K., Davis, J., Walter, M., Bradfield, R., & Vermey, R. (2011). *Public judgement on sentencing: Final results from the Tasmania Jury Sentencing Study* (Trends & Issues in Crime and Criminal Justice no. 407). Australian Institute of Criminology. https://www.aic.gov.au/publications/tandi/tandi407

Warner, K., Spiranovic, C., Bartels, L., Roberts, L., & Gelb, K. (2022). Juror and community views of the guilty plea sentencing discount: Findings from a national Australian study. *Criminology & Criminal Justice, 22*(1), 78–96.

White, R., Haines, F., & Asquith, N. L. (2017). *Crime & criminology* (6th ed.). Oxford University Press.

Wilkinson, G. (2011, July 29). Former DPP raps government over public survey on issue. *Herald Sun*. https://www.heraldsun.com.au/news/former-dpp-fixed-penalties-a-sham/news-story/be6aa1fca18903e1a48a165ff31c3d5a

Wise, J., & Roberts, D. A. (2016). Development of crime and the criminal justice system in Australia. In A. Harkness, B. Harris, & D. Baker (Eds.), *Locating crime in context and place: Perspectives on regional, rural and remote Australia* (pp. 35–48). The Federation Press.

Wood, W. R. (2014). Punitive populism. In J. M. Miller (Ed.), *The encyclopedia of theoretical criminology* (pp. 678–682). Wiley Online Library.

Younger, E. (2016, August 30). Hoddle Street killer Julian Knight declared vexatious litigant for life. *ABC News*. https://www.abc.net.au/news/2016-08-30/julian-knight-declared-vexatious-litigant-for-life/7798920

Legislation and Cases

Bail Act 1977 (Vic).

Children, Youth and Families Act 2005 (Vic).

Corrections Act 1986a (Vic).

Corrections Amendment (Parole Reform) Bill 2013 (Vic).

Corrections Amendment (Parole) Act 2014 (Vic).

County Court Act 1958 (Vic).

Crimes Act 1958 (Vic).

DPP v Gargasoulas [2019] VSC 87.

Magistrates' Court Act 1989 (Vic).

R v Knight [1989] Vic Rp 62; [1989] VR 705 (10 November 1988).

Sentencing Act 1991 (Vic).

Supreme Court Act 1986b (Vic).

The Queen v Bayley [2013]. VSC 313 (19 June 2013).

The Queen v. Ryan and Walker [1966] VR 553.

Victorian Charter of Human Rights and Responsibilities 2006 (Vic).

Practitioner Perspective: The Role of Parliamentarians in Making Laws

Simon Finn

Australian criminal justice can be characterised fairly simply in terms of its key components. Laws are determined by parliaments, enforced by police services and interpreted by courts. Practitioners in these segments of the system, however, operate within a vast range of complexities that influence the capabilities and success of their work.

Ultimately the Australian legal system is designed to construct and define an orderly society. But the end game of an orderly society is not the sole goal of the criminal justice practitioner. An orderly society relies on ensuring that the constructs, practices and outcomes of the system are 'just' and 'fair', and that the interpretation of these principles contributes to the complexities across the system.

The core components of the system are also not silos, and practitioners across the system share common goals—both operational and aspirational. Elected representatives, police officers and judges are acutely aware that loopholes in laws will be exploited, and this will influence their design, enforcement and interpretation. Operational tensions between the segments are common, with the success of the system relying on diligent application at every stage within an environment where the interpretation of 'just' and 'fair' can vary widely. Despite these tensions and challenges, the common goal for all practitioners is the application of justice through the successful operation of the courts.

My experience within this system has been at the stage of determining the laws, having had the honour of serving as an elected representative in an Australian state parliament. Whilst it is common in the United States for elected representatives to be referred to as 'lawmakers', in Australia the common terms reflect the Westminster terminology of 'parliamentarian' or more commonly 'elected representative', 'politician' or the abbreviated 'MP'. Without seeking to debate the relative differences in terminology,

S. Finn
Former member of the Queensland Parliament, Melbourne, VIC, Australia

few Australian parliamentarians would describe themselves as 'criminal justice practitioners', yet the diligent application of their representative and parliamentary functions is critical to the success of the system.

In simple terms, the Australian parliamentarian undertakes two key stakeholder engagement functions as a practitioner in the criminal justice system: (i) community consultation to inform the principles of 'just' and 'fair'; and (ii) applying the product of that consultation in the development of laws.

First, the work of an elected community representative contributes an essential building block of the principles of 'just' and 'fair' in the legal environment. Their day-to-day work often sees them connecting with the broad Australian community through active engagement with organisations, opinion leaders and the general community. In addition to being approached by community members seeking representation on issues impacting their livelihoods, elected representatives engage in direct local consultation with activities targeted at seeking the views of constituents on a range of government issues, including proposed laws.

As an elected representative I met with victims of crime, offenders, prisoners and police officers. I met with health services, domestic violence shelters, community service organisations, churches, schools and parent organisations, and business groups. These experiences invariably present a range of views and, whilst challenging to distil, enable the representative to be informed on community impacts beyond their own personal life experience.

This community representative function serves as direct consultation on community expectations of the criminal justice system, informs the representative's understanding of how the community interprets the principles of 'just' and 'fair', and shapes an understanding of how changes to the existing legal framework—including their design, enforcement and application—might benefit the community. The critical point here is consultation. By engaging with their community, the representative undertakes essential 'stakeholder engagement' that informs their work as a parliamentarian.

The second stage of the criminal justice function of an elected representative is their work as a parliamentarian. Whilst the capability to influence the early drafting of laws varies based on a parliamentarian's status as a government or non-government member, their parliamentary committee membership or whether they are a member of the executive (i.e. a cabinet minister), ultimately all parliamentarians have an equal capacity to influence the development of laws as they pass through the parliament.

In the usual circumstances, the government 'introduces' proposed laws to the parliament through the relevant minister tabling a draft of the legislation along with explanatory notes and delivering the 'Second Reading Speech' that outlines the purpose and intent of the proposed law. The text of this speech serves as a critical document in the criminal justice system, providing guidance to the courts on the intent of laws where questions of interpretation might later arise.

Introduction of a Bill to parliament is the first opportunity for the community to view draft laws the government intends to implement. This stimulates a consultative opportunity for elected representatives to engage with constituents with exposure to the detail of draft laws and explanatory notes that detail the purpose of the laws and provide fiscal, legal and human rights impact assessments. The introduction of draft legislation will also stimulate the lobbying of elected representatives by interested parties seeking to further inform or influence their deliberations.

The processes that attach to the passage of legislation enable the elected representative to implement their parliamentary functions through informed consideration of the detail of proposed laws and their likely societal and community impacts. This can include questioning the relevant minister on the intention and purpose of specific clauses or moving amendments to the proposed legislation.

Whilst the passage of legislation through the parliament is frequently identified as a measure of a government's success, its passage alone is not an indicator of whether laws will be successfully enforced or applied. Again, a key indicator of likely success will be the extent of consultation informing parliamentary processes. Draft legislation is usually introduced by the government, following detailed consideration by the executive, diligent consultation with impacted parties and extensive legal advice. Legislation that has arisen following comprehensive consultation including existing legislative reviews, release of discussion papers, consideration by parliamentary committees or community engagement events has a greater likelihood of reflecting community principles of 'just' and 'fair'. In turn, this drives a greater understanding of its purpose and intent across criminal justice agencies and ultimately the successful interpretation and application of laws by the courts.

A Case Study: Queensland's Move-on Laws and the Impacts on the Courts

Some of the most complex community and parliamentary work I undertook as an elected representative involved consideration of laws relating to police powers. A particular example is the consideration by the Queensland Parliament of amendments to the *Police Powers and Responsibilities Act 2000* (Qld) of laws to expand police move-on powers.

Queensland's move-on powers authorise police, in particular circumstances, to issue a direction to an individual or a group of people to move on or leave a public place. The move-on powers are discretionary in nature, allowing a police officer to consider the circumstances of an incident prior to exercising these powers, and failure to obey a move-on direction may result in a person being charged with the offence of 'contravening the direction or requirement of a police officer'. Police move-on powers had developed incrementally, and prior to 2006 were enforceable in designated areas. In 2006, the Queensland Parliament considered, and passed, legislation to expand the powers to apply state-wide.

Allowing police officers to have a discretionary power to require a person to leave a public space was a very controversial issue within sections of the Queensland community. The strongest opponents of the laws enabling this power were organisations representing disadvantaged communities or people who might be disproportionally subject to a move-on direction. Representatives of youth organisations, Indigenous communities, homelessness and social housing advocates, migrant and refugee leaders and civil rights groups raised concerns.

In consulting my local community, it was also clear that there was significant general support for move-on powers. This was based largely on the rights of people to peaceful enjoyment of public spaces and the right to feel safe around designated spaces such as schools, banks and railway stations. The local community also comprised large migrant and refugee populations with social and cultural expression that involved gathering in public places. Issues raised by the older and newer communities in relation to perceptions of safety and policing powers reflected a lack of shared cultural awareness rather than an identified need for police action.

The views of senior police officers were strongly in favour of greater move-on powers and the expansion of these powers state-wide. Police made the case that state-wide powers would reduce community confusion and policing complexity about where the powers applied, and further that move-on powers could assist police to reduce crime by diffusing potentially violent events, moving people away from opportunity to commit crime and providing an alternative to arrest.

With compelling arguments made by all sides of the debate, the conundrum for the parliamentarian as a criminal justice practitioner was vast. Protecting the disadvantaged, general community safety, peaceful enjoyment of public spaces and providing alternatives to arrest met community expectation of laws being 'fair' and 'just'. Complicating the matter was that in a nine-month period in 2005 there had been approximately 2,000 uses of move-on directions resulting in 700 arrests from the limited locations where the laws currently applied. This suggested large-scale usage of the powers by police to control public spaces but also that their substantial failure as a mechanism to avoid arrest would flow to the courts being increasingly required to interpret the appropriate use of the powers.

The key issue that emerged for me as a member of parliament and a criminal justice practitioner in this matter was that the debate centred on the appropriate usage of move-on powers. A significant challenge in the protection of minority or vulnerable groups is that these groups are less likely to have access to the resources necessary to challenge the usage of a move-on order. Ultimately protections for minority or vulnerable members of the community, along with general safety in public places and the success of the courts, could be improved through clarifying the appropriate use of move-on powers by the police service.

The 2006 legislation to expand the application of move-on powers in Queensland did not contemplate in detail the appropriate usage of the powers and passed through the parliament. Advocacy within the government during the debate however highlighted the need for the then Crime and Misconduct Commission (CMC) (2008) to review the application of the powers. In 2010, the CMC found that young people and disadvantaged groups continued to be disproportionally subject to move-on orders, that arrest rates for disobeying orders remained high and that move-on powers were not substantially diverting young people from the justice system including the courts. The CMC recommended major changes to the application of the powers however substantial change was not supported by government. Recommendations regarding better data collection on the use of the powers and greater agency collaboration to implement diversion programmes for disadvantaged people who frequent public spaces were supported. A recommendation regarding the police officers recording their usage of the powers was noted by government.

Conclusion

The wheels of government move slowly and elected representatives are confronted with a legislative agenda dominated by competing economic and social interests. Whilst the community is invested in the success of the courts to deliver justice and fairness, the challenge for the Australian lawmaker as a practitioner in the criminal justice system is balancing the strengths of representing community expectations with the limitations of being ultimately subject to the views of the majority.

Reference

Crime and Misconduct Commission. (2008, December). *Review of Queensland's police move-on powers: Invitation for public comment*. Crime and Misconduct Commission. https://www.ccc.qld.gov.au/sites/default/files/Docs/Legislative-Review/Police-move-on/Review-of-Queenslands-police-move-on-powers-Invitation-for-public-comment-2008.pdf

Legislation

Police Powers and Responsibilities Act 2000 (Qld).

3

Juries in the Digital Age: Managing Juror Online and Social Media Use During Trial

Jane Goodman-Delahunty and David Tait

Introduction

Questions about the contemporary relevance of juries, their ability to make impartial decisions and their ability to respond to emerging challenges have long been a focus of debate. This chapter considers these questions and explores the extent to which juries continue to ensure that an accused person receives a fair trial. Whilst jury processes remained largely unchanged throughout the twentieth century, jurors have evolved in the twenty-first century—becoming more highly educated and with access to information through technology in the palm of the hand.

J. Goodman-Delahunty (✉)
Newcastle School of Law and Justice, Newcastle, NSW, Australia
e-mail: jane.delahunty@newcastle.edu.au

D. Tait
Western Sydney University, Penrith, NSW, Australia
e-mail: d.tait@westernsydney.edu.au

M. Camilleri and A. Harkness (eds.), *Australian Courts*,
https://doi.org/10.1007/978-3-031-19063-6_3

Access to digital information can both enhance and pollute a criminal trial. This chapter advocates reforms to ensure jurors are kept engaged and active, are well informed through written collaborative jury directions, and deliberate more thoroughly without being tempted to seek their own digital advice. Australian juries today are directed not to undertake internet research. To do so comprises an offence in three states (Queensland, New South Wales and Victoria) and is prohibited by the common law of contempt. Nonetheless, juror internet use has persisted. This chapter reviews the risk of 'online prejudice' that may impact an accused's right to a fair trial before an impartial jury.

Contextualising Jury Trials and Online Information

Since the fourteenth century, trial by jury has been a part of the common law justice system (*Cheatle v The Queen* 1993). Community participation through jury service has several potential benefits for the justice process: it provides greater legitimacy to verdicts; it educates the citizens who take part; and it tends to bring trial outcomes into line with changing social values.

One of the underlying assumptions of contemporary life is that the smartphone is an extension of the self (Park & Kaye, 2019), so that jurors—like most citizens—live their everyday lives through their devices. The average Australian owns multiple internet-enabled devices, and the total number of mobile handsets in service far exceeds the population (ACCC, 2021).

Contemporary daily life has been transformed by smartphone use (Miller et al., 2021). Information is embedded within social networks which facilitate sharing of news, mobilise opinion and shape identity. Nine out of ten Australian social media users access social channels via mobile devices (Mohsin, 2021), with Facebook as their predominant social media platform (Tasmania Law Reform Institute, 2020). A series of international ethnographic studies by researchers at the Centre for Digital Anthropology at University College London uncovered the 'perpetual opportunism' prompted by the omnipresence of smartphones, not the least of which is to look up information (Miller, 2021).

Since around 2010, members of the Australian judiciary, court administrators and academics have expressed significant concern over juror misuse of digital media and social media (Buckley, 2013; Johnston et al., 2013). Law academic Anne Wallace forewarned that the release of pretrial publicity on social media could undermine a jury's ability to keep an open mind, resulting in cases of "trial by Facebook" (Wallace cited in ABC News, 2014). Some trials were aborted after jurors posted information on Facebook or searched the internet for information (Tasmania Law Reform Institute, 2020). The same concerns have registered international alarm (Braun, 2017). Because "a verdict that is not based exclusively on evidence adduced in court contravenes the principle of open justice" (Bowcott, 2013) juror misconduct in the form of 'trial by Google' posed a threat to the integrity of the United Kingdom's justice system.

Another threat to fairness could result from prosecutorial misconduct, faulty forensic procedures or police fabrication of evidence, displayed in a number of United Kingdom state trials such as that of the Birmingham Six in 1974. If jurors in that trial had been able to find out through their own sources (in a time before the internet) that some of the accused had been deprived of food and sleep, beaten up by police and subject to mock execution (or that there was no forensic evidence), they may have been less willing to convict (Edmond, 2002). The celebrated 1734 New York Zenger case involved a jury refusing to convict a newspaper editor for seditious libel (Scott, 1989). Jury common sense, informed by social media or popular knowledge, may on some occasions act as a bulwark of liberty. These cases might be rare, but the case for restricting juror use of external information (including social media) does need to be balanced by the political role of the jury in avoiding government overreach.

Controversies in Juror Internet and Facebook Use

To manage juror internet and Facebook access effectively, it is critical to understand the juror uses of digital and social media, factors that precipitate juror non-compliance with judicial directions and the risks of online prejudice.

Types of Juror Internet and Facebook Searches

The extent to which the use by Australian jurors of digital and social media might impact the right of an accused to a fair trial before an impartial jury requires an examination of types of internet and Facebook searches undertaken following warnings not to resort to the internet. These were analysed by the Tasmania Law Reform Institute (2020), and three categories of information were implicated. First, jurors sought definitions of critical legal terms such as elements of the offence charged, or the meaning of 'beyond reasonable doubt'. Second, jurors looked up technical terms used by expert witnesses. Third, they searched for information about the accused and other parties, primarily on Facebook.

An illustration of a jury seeking to better understand legal terms in the case before them comes from a terrorist trial in the Melbourne Supreme Court. That jury conducted searches on Wikipedia for definitions of 'organisation', 'intention' and 'member' and on Reference.com for definitions of 'membership', 'intentional' and 'organisation'. In addition, they consulted a hard copy dictionary to look up the word 'foster'. The trial judge did not dismiss the jury (*R v Benbrika* 2009). The Victorian Court of Criminal Appeal held that it was not inappropriate or improper for a jury to consult a dictionary about the meaning of an ordinary English word which they were told was a question for them (*Benbrika v The Queen* 2010). The Court noted the paradox facing jurors who are advised to use their common sense and everyday experience but are precluded from accessing the everyday resources that they rely on to acquire context and to check their beliefs and their knowledge.

This case underscores long-standing research demonstrating that most jurors approach their role seriously and conscientiously (Warner et al., 2011) and strive to return the appropriate verdict. Juror non-compliance with a judicial direction to refrain from conducting their own internet research about the accused is not necessarily a failure to take their role and duties seriously.

Other cases illustrate the need to distinguish innocuous juror internet and social media use from exposure to potentially biasing information. For example, at the close of deliberations over 12 charges in a trial in New South Wales, after 10 verdicts had been reached, the jury foreperson informed the judge that one juror had Googled the requirements for a Working with Children Check. This topic had been mentioned in the trial but was unrelated to the offences. The juror motivation was curiosity as to why they themselves had not been required to undergo this check when working as a teacher. The trial judge concluded that the misconduct was minor, did not seek information about the accused or any matters relevant to the trial, and did not give rise to unfair prejudice against the accused, so the verdicts already reached were taken. However, the juror's conduct breached the New South Wales Jury Act, so the juror was discharged. The New South Wales Court of Criminal Appeal clarified that this juror's Googling was not prohibited internet misconduct, could not give rise to the risk of a substantial miscarriage of justice in the trial, and thus the discharge of the juror was erroneous (*Hoang v R* 2018).

In a joint judgement, the High Court disagreed on grounds that Sect. 68C(1) of the *Jury Act*, 1977 (NSW) provides that it is an offence for a juror to make an inquiry for the purpose of obtaining information about any matters relevant to the trial. The High Court noted that what is a "matter relevant to the trial" will vary from trial to trial, and determined that in this case, the juror was seeking information relevant to the trial, notwithstanding her motivation for doing so. Thus, the judge should have immediately discharged the juror before taking the verdicts reached. The guilty verdicts entered before the juror was discharged were set aside, and a new trial was ordered on those counts (*Hoang v The Queen* 2022).

Conversely, when jurors research the parties to a case on Facebook, the consequences are often more egregious because jurors may be exposed to biasing information. On the tenth day of a trial before the Supreme Court of Queensland, one juror reported to a fellow juror the results of a Facebook search about the accused and the murder victim's ex-wife. This misconduct resulted in the discharge of the entire jury (Keim, 2014).

Juror social media misconduct is not limited to seeking information: it can also involve providing information. A 2005 New York robbery trial was declared a mistrial after the foreperson confided to her Facebook followers that she was "trying to remain positive" but was in fact "dying from boredom" (Matyszczyk, 2015).

Factors that Increase Juror Internet and Social Media Use

International studies have identified juror factors and case factors that increase the likelihood of proscribed independent internet research (Thomas, 2010). Jurors, who are conscientious, internet-aware and accustomed to daily use of the internet, and who are younger in age, are more prone to look things up on the internet. Most jurors want to use the internet to assist them in their jury duties because they are accustomed to using social media this way on a daily basis to inform their decision-making on important issues such as health care, finances and education (Hannaford-Agar et al., 2012a).

Two case-related factors pose a high risk of prohibited internet use. In high-profile trials or a trial of a high-profile accused person, more jurors are prone to violate the judicial direction not to conduct internet research (Hannaford-Agar et al., 2012b; Tasmania Law Reform Institute, 2020; Thomas, 2010). Problems identified include the relative permanency of prejudicial online material, the immediate accessibility of this material and the increasing volume of national media coverage of high-profile criminal matters (Buckley, 2013). For instance, an analysis of 33,067 trial-related tweets during a high-profile criminal trial in Brisbane (*R v Baden-Clay* 2014) revealed more prejudicial tweets as the trial approached the end, and that most prejudicial tweets were from non-journalists (Hews & Suzor, 2017). Once information about a trial is posted on the internet, juror compliance with the judicial admonition is reduced (Hannaford-Agar et al., 2012a).

A second case-related factor that can instigate juror internet use is when the evidence against the accused appears incomplete. Incomplete evidence presented during the trial is said to 'liberate' jurors to use their prior views to fill in the gaps (Kalven & Zeisel, 1996). The same argument can be applied to jurors' use of digital media to inform themselves about the background to the trial, the history of the accused or any other topics about which jurors may perceive that the information presented at trial is incomplete.

Prejudicial Effects of Exposure to Online Pretrial Publicity About an Accused Person

When a juror accesses pretrial or in-trial publicity about the accused via the internet, the effects may not be trivial. Media coverage of crimes is demonstrably one-sided, biased towards the prosecution and police (Bakhshay & Haney, 2018), and often contains information that is inadmissible at trial (Daftary-Kapur et al., 2014). Decades of research have established that exposure to pretrial publicity regarding an accused person exerts an unconscious influence (Kramer et al., 1990) on jurors and judges (Wistrich et al., 2005). When asked whether they were influenced, jurors tend to deny this, contrary to what studies show is a robust effect (Studebaker et al., 2000, 2002).

Exposure to pretrial publicity leads to a decision in support of the party favoured in the publicity (Daftary-Kapur et al., 2014). Both positive (favourable) and negative (unfavourable) publicity exert an effect, but negative publicity has approximately twice the impact of positive publicity. A distinction is made between the effects of exposure to general information pertinent to an accused person's case and information specifically about the accused person. The latter has a more significant impact (Vidmar, 2002). Accordingly, exposure to negative publicity on the internet about an accused person poses a risk to justice.

Exposure to negative pretrial publicity about the accused person produces two effects. First, since that information is considered along with other trial evidence, it impacts how other information is perceived and interpreted (Ruva, 2018; Ruva & Guenther, 2017). Second, it impacts the case outcome, the verdict (Hoetger et al., 2022; Simon, 2012). Media reports which depict an accused person in a negative light tend to cause jurors to judge that person more harshly, and to convict the accused significantly more than jurors who have not been exposed to the negative media reports (Steblay et al., 1999).

Certain features of pretrial publicity elicit stronger biasing effects and increased conviction rates, as shown in two separate meta-analyses (Hoetger et al., 2022; Steblay et al., 1999). For example, the presence of limited information about the defendant's background, personality or character, specific details about the charge, descriptions of injuries to alleged victims of the crime charged, the mention of illegal drugs or when the defendant is charged with a nonviolent crime had a stronger influence than other features. Publicity in multiple forms, such as written information plus visual images, exerted a more potent effect than that via a single mode of communication. Exposure to repeated publicity (a more concentrated dose within a single media report, or multiple reports) increased its biasing effect.

The stronger the effect at the outset, the more likely it was to persist throughout the trial and through deliberation (Jones et al., 2021; Ruva et al., 2022). Whilst some studies have shown that deliberation magnified the bias (Ruva & Guenther, 2015) and that the information was spread to jurors who had not been exposed to the negative media reports (Ruva & Coy, 2020), in other studies, the biasing effects disappeared after group discussion and deliberation (Bruschke et al., 2016; Taylor & Tarrant, 2019).

In sum, "the consumption of prejudicial material relevant to the trial is the problem" (Tasmania Law Reform Institute, 2020, p. 43). Concerns about juror non-compliance with legal directions about internet research need to be understood in light of an extensive body of research on the inefficacy of most curative instructional practices. Results of a meta-analysis of 48 studies with 8,474 mock-jurors showed in general that directions to disregard negative media exposure are ineffective (Simon,

2012), and that in some studies they increased conviction rates (Steblay et al., 2006). Put simply, undoing the harm of exposure to prejudicial information is unlikely.

The Challenge of Juror Non-compliance with Judicial Instructions

A challenge to contemporary courts is selecting effective measures to ensure that juror internet use and access does not expose them to biasing information that may compromise the accused's right to receive a fair trial. Insight into the reasons for juror non-compliance with the prohibition is helpful in this regard.

Juror non-compliance with directions not to conduct internet research occurs for a variety of reasons. One explanation is that contemporary citizens learn through active exploration. It is how they are taught to learn at school or university. The judicial admonition is counter-intuitive to contemporary jurors, especially for younger jurors who are most accustomed to reliance on the internet (Bartels & Lee, 2013; Johnston et al., 2013; Waters & Hannaford-Agor, 2014). Yet, the process that jurors are expected to endure in court is passive—jurors are expected to sit back and listen to evidence presented to them—sometimes for lengthy periods, fighting back the lure of sleep—without the opportunity to engage in ongoing dialogue, either with the speakers or each other (Dann, 1992; Yarnell, 2006). The jury is treated as an "empty vessel to be filled" (Yarnell, 2006, p. 24).

Studies of ex-jurors revealed that approximately one-third of jurors misunderstand the judicial admonition regarding internet and social media use (Yarnell, 2006). Thus, they regard independent internet research conducted in the course of exercising their functions as a juror as exempt from the judicial proscription. For example, some jurors hold the view that Googling' does not comprise 'research', rather a more informal activity.

Other jurors perceived that use of the internet to obtain general information was exempt because they understood the prohibited conduct to apply to searches for specific information about the parties and case

(Hannaford-Agar et al., 2012b). Many jurors perceive that checking definitions of terms is exempt, non-prejudicial extrinsic information. In the Melbourne terrorism trial of Benbrika, the presiding judge commented that it was possible that jurors understood from the jury direction to "be wary of any newspaper reports concerning this case, television reports, or reports of similar cases here or anywhere else in the world" that they must not seek any information about the particular case, not that seeking definitions of key terms was proscribed (*Benbrika v The Queen* 2010; Benbrika v R, 2010).

About two-thirds of jurors understand the judicial admonition as intended but may disregard it. Insight into juror motivations to engage in internet and other investigations emerged in an Australian study of 78 New South Wales jurors who served on criminal trials in the period 2005–2006 and 2011. The results disclosed that conscientious jurors felt compelled to conduct prohibited independent research to reach a fair decision (Hunter, 2013; Hunter et al., 2010). These jurors knowingly defied judicial directions to refrain from internet research because they perceived a higher duty to return a robust verdict, and more so when the evidence presented at trial seemed incomplete (Horan, 2012; Hunter et al., 2010). This research illustrates that lay jurors' understanding of fairness and of an accused's right to a fair trial, may rest on flawed assumptions. These jurors justify accessing social media and/or the internet on the grounds that their behaviour is consistent with and in pursuit of a "fair trial" and "fairness to an accused" (Tasmania Law Reform Institute, 2020, p. 59).

Managing a Time of Change: Juror Online Social Media Use During Trial

Judges, practitioners, court administrators and academics acknowledge that the traditional paradigm of judicial directions and a threat of sanctions, premised on passive pre-internet jurors, is not working reliably with contemporary active, information-seeking, internet-aware jurors (Sweeney, 2011). The gap between practice and reality has widened (Blackman & Brickman, 2011).

In some jurisdictions, a judge-alone trial can be requested following "significant pre-trial publicity that may affect jury deliberations" (Buckley, 2013, p. 47). However, the right is rarely invoked and is an unpopular option (Small, 2021). Although judges are susceptible to the effects of prejudicial publicity (Wistrich et al., 2005), demands to replace the jury with judge-only trials resurfaced in relation to juror disregard of instructions to refrain from internet and social media platform use. This option is unsatisfactory as it compromises community participation in the criminal justice process. More effective procedures to safeguard an impartial trial for the accused in the digital age are (i) active juror engagement; (ii) collaborative instructions and education for jurors; and (iii) more diverse jury deliberation.

Active Juror Engagement

Jury reforms in Arizona (United States) introduced features to make jury duty more active, such as encouraging jurors to ask (written) questions, take notes and discuss the case amongst themselves before the formal deliberation. These were already standard practices in some non-US jurisdictions. In Queensland, for example, jurors were sometimes given the opportunity to put questions to expert witnesses directly without having to submit them in writing. Evaluation of the Arizona intervention suggested that the opportunity to ask questions made jurors less likely to seek their own answers to questions about which they were curious. This could be extended to topics that prompt jurors to do their own research.

Insights from Arizona jury reformers can be taken one step further. If carrying out their own research is re-conceptualised as part of the active learning style encouraged in most other areas of life, rather than as misbehaviour, then the challenge for courts is how to accommodate this. Judges could in-principle ask jurors on regular occasions whether they have 'inadvertently' learned something about the case that the court could 'clarify'. Jurors could be reminded that in their discussions, part of their task is to challenge any preconceptions or impressions that other jurors have formed about the case, whether from their neighbourhoods, their experiences of life or indeed from social media. Rather than seeing these 'external' sources of information as forms of contamination, they could be seen as part of the common sense that a diverse group of citizens bring to the jury room, all of which should be subject to testing against the evidence provided in court.

In French juries, a juror might from time to time be given the floor to pursue a line of questioning. One of the authors of this chapter observed a case in Montpellier where an expert witness was trying to explain a complicated scientific idea, apparently without great success. A juror, who happened to be a high school science teacher, asked if he might ask the witness a few questions and managed to get the witness to clarify the issue.

Collaborative Jury Directions and Education

Results of a controlled experiment that included content analyses of 30 mock-jury deliberations showed that exposure to pretrial publicity made jurors either unwilling or unable to adhere to instructions admonishing them not to discuss the media report, and further that they rarely corrected other jury members who mentioned it in the course of deliberations, in contravention of the judicial direction (Ruva & LeVasseur, 2012). On the other hand, a judicial instruction that draws attention to the issues raised in media articles may serve to focus jury debates on these matters. A more 'collaborative' instruction that explains the reason for the rule was recommended to put the issues in context (Diamond & Vidmar, 2001).

Accordingly, courts and jury researchers have advocated providing more explanation to juries about the risks of an unfair trial, starting with the information in the jury orientation video, and giving written information to jurors on the prohibition before they are empanelled and during the trial. Results of a jury simulation study testing whether an educational video designed to reduce implicit biases would also reduce pretrial publicity bias showed it failed to reduce the effects of exposure to pretrial publicity (Jones et al., 2021). The Tasmania Law Reform Institute recommended replacing abstract references to fairness with a discussion of the concept of fairness, plus definitions of terms such as 'impartiality' and 'according to the evidence'.

Directions that address jury behaviours are advised. For example, in conjunction with the discussion of the jury role, the New South Wales model jury direction specifically addresses problems with jury research to fill in gaps in the evidence (Judicial Commission of New South Wales, cited in Tasmanian Law Reform Institute, 2020, p. 84):

> You are not investigating the incident giving rise to the charge(s). You are being asked to make a judgment or decision based upon the evidence that is placed before you. Jurors might in a particular case feel frustrated by what they see as a lack of evidence or information about some particular aspect of the case before them. In some rare cases this has led jurors to make inquiries themselves to try to fill in the gaps that they perceive in the evidence. But that is not your function, nor is it mine ... If you felt that there was some evidence or information missing, then you simply take that fact into account in deciding whether on the evidence that is before you the Crown have proved the guilt of the accused beyond reasonable doubt.

In New South Wales, the model jury direction also describes problems that may arise (Judicial Commission of New South Wales cited in Tasmanian Law Reform Institute, 2020, p. 143):

> ... the result of your inquiries could be to obtain information that was misleading or entirely wrong. For example, you may come across a statement of the law or of some legal principle that is incorrect or not applicable in New South Wales. The criminal law is not the same throughout Australian jurisdictions and even in this State it can change rapidly from time to time. It is part of my function to tell you so much of the law as you need to apply in order to decide the issues before you.

Examples of more detailed explanations from the Judicial College of Victoria (cited in Tasmanian Law Reform Institute, 2020, pp. 152–153) of the rationale for the restriction and of consequences of juror non-compliance are as follows:

You may have a question about what could happen if you acted on outside information or conducted your own research.

The immediate outcome is that the jury may need to be discharged and the trial may have to start again. This would cause stress and expense to the witnesses, the prosecution and the accused. It would also cause stress and inconvenience to the other jurors, who will have wasted their time sitting on a case which must be restarted.

Second, it is a criminal offence for a juror to discuss the case with others or to conduct research on the case. You could therefore be fined and receive a criminal conviction, which may affect your ability to travel to some countries. Jurors have even been sent to jail for discussing a case on Facebook.

More broadly, jurors conducting their own research undermines public confidence in the jury system. The jury system has been a fundamental feature of our criminal justice system for centuries.

More Diverse Juries Promote Compliance

One further potential solution to reduce the risk of inappropriate social media activity is to ensure deliberation by more diverse juries. Conducting research on jury deliberations can be challenging, especially the assessment of opinion changes during the deliberation process (Bruschke et al., 2016). One study showed that members of racially diverse juries are more likely to self-monitor for fear of being seen as bigoted (Stevenson et al., 2017). Extending this argument beyond race, it is argued that individual jurors would be less likely to mention internet searches or use of social media if they thought other jury members would look down on them or report them. Other research has suggested that more gender diverse juries examine the issues more thoroughly than those with a gender skew (Marder, 1986). Even if a range of ideas and information was introduced in deliberation that came from external sources, it would, in more diverse juries, be more carefully scrutinised.

One way to achieve a better gender or racial balance is to mandate it (Forman, 1992). This is not without precedent; juries *de mediatate linguae* (mixed juries) did precisely that in England and Wales until 1870 where the alleged offender was from a different background than the victim (Constable, 1994). A less heavy-handed approach might be to ensure that at least three minorities were represented on a jury, on the grounds that this would produce fuller debate (Fukurai, 1997) and reduce the effects of exposure to pretrial publicity (Taylor & Tarrant, 2019). Which minorities were represented might depend on the nature of the case and the characteristics of the local community.

Conclusion

Controversy over the role and survival of the jury in Australia has been recurrent since the 1960s, and the controversy over internet access by contemporary jurors must be considered in this light (Goodman-Delahunty, 2015). Debates about jury trials are not unique to Australia. In fact, they are so perennial that jury scholars have queried whether any "other institution is simultaneously as sanctified and vilified as the jury" (Bornstein & Greene, 2017, p. 10). The relevance of juries in the criminal justice process in the digital age will remain vital if courts adapt the management of contemporary juries by collaborating with jurors' commitment to assure the accused a fair trial.

References

ABC News. (2014, April 10). *Academic warns of 'trial by Facebook'.* Australian Broadcasting Corporation. https://www.abc.net.au/news/2014-04-10/academic-warns-of-trial-by-facebook/5380946?utm_campaign=abc_news_web&utm_content=link&utm_medium=content_shared&utm_source=abc_news_web

ACCC (Australian Competition and Consumer Commission). (2021). *Internet activity report for the period ending 31 December 2020.* Australian Competition and Consumer Commission.

Bakhshay, S., & Haney, C. (2018). The media's impact on the right to a fair trial. *Psychology, Public Policy, and Law, 24*(3), 326–340.

Bartels, L., & Lee, J. (2013). Jurors using social media in our courts: Challenges and responses. *Journal of Judicial Administration, 23*, 35–57.

Blackman, J., & Brickman, E. (2011). Let's talk: Addressing the challenges of internet-era jurors. *The Jury Expert, 25*(2), 1–11.

Bornstein, B. H., & Greene, E. (2017). *Jury under fire: Myth, controversy and reform.* Oxford University Press.

Bowcott, O. (2013, February 7). "Trial by Google" a risk to jury system, says Attorney General. *The Guardian.* http://www.theguardian.com/law/2013/feb/06/trial-by-google-risk-jury-system

Braun, K. (2017). Yesterday is history, tomorrow is a mystery: The fate of the Australian jury system in the age of social media dependency. *University of New South Wales Law Journal, 40*(4), 1634–1662.

Bruschke, J., Gonis III, A., Hill, S. A., Fiber-Ostrow, P., & Loges, W. (2016). The influence of heterogeneous exposure and pre-deliberation queries on pretrial publicity effects. *Communication Monographs, 83*(4), 521–534.

Buckley, I. F. (2013). Pre-trial publicity, social media and the "fair trial": Protecting impartiality in the Queensland criminal justice system. *Queensland Lawyer, 33*, 38–51.

Constable, M. (1994). *The law of the other.* University of Chicago Press.

Daftary-Kapur, T., Penrod, S. D., O'Connor, M., & Wallace, B. (2014). Examining pretrial publicity in a shadow jury paradigm: Issues of slant, quantity, persistence and generalizability. *Law & Human Behavior, 38*(5), 462–477.

Dann, B. M. (1992). Learning lessons and speaking rights: Creating educated and democratic juries. *Indiana Law Journal, 68*, 1229–1279.

Diamond, S., & Vidmar, N. (2001). Jury room ruminations on forbidden topics. *Virginia Law Review, 87*, 1857–1915.

Edmond, G. (2002). Constructing miscarriages of justice: Misunderstanding scientific evidence in high profile criminal appeals. *Oxford Journal of Legal Studies, 22*(1), 53–89.

Forman, D. L. (1992). What difference does it make: Gender and jury selection. *UCLA Women's Law Journal, 2*, 35–83.

Fukurai, H. (1997). A quota jury: Affirmative action in jury selection. *Journal of Criminal Justice, 25*(6), 477–500.

Goodman-Delahunty, J. (2015). The jury box and the urn: Containing our expectations. *Pandora's Box: Crime, Justice and the People, 22*, 9–16.

Hannaford-Agor, P., Rottman, D., & Waters, N. L. (2012a). *Juror and jury use of new media: A baseline exploration.* National Center for State Courts.

Hannaford-Agor, P., Rottman, D., & Waters, N. L. (2012b). *Preventing and addressing internet related juror misconduct: A judicial curriculum.* National Center for State Courts.

Hews, R., & Suzor, N. (2017). "Scum of the earth": An analysis of prejudicial Twitter conversations during the Baden-Clay Murder Trial. *University of New South Wales Law Journal, 40*(4), 1604–1633.

Hoetger, L. A., Devine, D. J., Brank, E. M., Drew, R. M., & Rees, R. (2022). The impact of pretrial publicity on mock juror and jury verdicts. *Law and Human Behavior*. https://doi.org/10.1037/lhb0000473

Horan, J. (2012). *Juries in the twenty first century.* The Federation Press.

Hunter, J. (2013). *Jurors' notions of justice: An empirical study of motivations to investigate and obedience to judicial directions.* UNSW Jury Study. Law and Justice Foundation.

Hunter, J., Boniface, D., & Thomson, D. (2010). *What jurors search for and what they don't get*. UNSW Pilot Jury Study. Law and Justice Foundation.

Johnston, J., Keyzer, P., Holland, G., Pearson, M., Rodrick, S., & Wallace, A. (2013). *Juries and social media: A report prepared for the Victorian Department of Justice.* Standing Council on Law and Justice. https://www.ncsc.org/__data/assets/pdf_file/0013/17230/juries-and-social-media_australia_a-wallace.pdf

Jones, A. M., Wong, K., Meyers, C. N., & Ruva, C. L. (2021). Trial by tabloid: Can implicit bias education reduce pretrial publicity bias? *Criminal Justice and Behavior, 49*(2), 259–278.

Kalven, H., & Zeisel, H. (1996). *The American jury*. Little Brown & Company.

Keim, T. (2014, August 8). Queensland murder trial aborted as juror researches case on "Facebook". *The Courier Mail.*

Kramer, G. P., Kerr, N. L., & Carroll, J. S. (1990). Pretrial publicity, judicial remedies and jury bias. *Law and Human Behavior, 14*, 409–438.

Marder, N. S. (1986). Gender dynamics and jury deliberations. *Yale Law Journal, 96*, 593–612.

Matyszczyk, C. (2015, November 4). *Juror fined for Facebook posts about criminal court case.* Cnet. https://www.cnet.com/news/juror-fined-for-describing-case-on-facebook/

Miller, D. (2021). A theory of a theory of the smartphone. *International Journal of Cultural Studies, 24*(5), 860–876.

Miller, D., Abed Rabho, L. A., Awondo, P., de Vries, M., Duque, M., Garvey, P., Haapio-Kirk, L., Hawkins, C., Otaugui, A., Walton, S., & Wang, X. (2021). *The global smartphone: Beyond a youth technology.* University of City of London Press.

Mohsin, M. (2021, April 5). 10 social media statistics you need to know in 2021 [infographic]. *Oberlo.* https://au.oberlo.com/blog/social-media-marketing-statistics

Park, C. S., & Kaye, B. K. (2019). Smartphone and self-extension: Functionally, anthropomorphically, and ontologically extending self via the smartphone. *Mobile Media and Communication, 7*(2), 215–231.

Ruva, C. L. (2018). From the headlines to the jury room: An examination of the impact of pretrial publicity on jurors and juries. In B. H. Bornstein & M. K. Miller (Eds.), *Advances in psychology and law* (Vol. 3, pp. 1–39). Springer.

Ruva, C. L., & Coy, A. E. (2020). Your bias is rubbing off on me. *Psychology, Public Policy, and Law, 26*(1), 22–35.

Ruva, C. L., Diaz Ortega, S. E., & O'Grady, K. A. (2022). What drives a jury's deliberations? The influence of pretrial publicity and jury composition on deliberation slant and content. *Psychology, Public Policy, and Law, 28*(1), 32–52.

Ruva, C. L., & Guenther, C. C. (2015). From the shadows into the light: How pretrial publicity and deliberation affect mock jurors' decisions, impressions, and memory. *Law and Human Behavior, 39*(3), 294–310.

Ruva, C. L., & Guenther, C. C. (2017). Keep your bias to yourself: How deliberating with differently biased others affects mock-jurors' guilt decisions, perceptions of the defendant, memories, and evidence interpretation. *Law and Human Behavior, 41*(5), 478–493.

Ruva, C. L., & LeVasseur, M. A. (2012). Behind closed doors: The effect of pretrial publicity on jury deliberations. *Psychology Crime and Law Crime and Law, 18*(5), 431–452.

Scott, P. B. (1989). Jury nullification: An historical perspective on a modern debate. *Western Virginia Law Review, 91*(2), 389–423.

Simon, D. (2012). *In doubt: The psychology of the criminal justice process.* Harvard University Press.

Small, A. (2021). Peer to peer: COVID-19 and transforming jury trials in Australia. *Australian Quarterly, 92*(4), 36–43.

Steblay, N. M., Besirivic, J., Fulero, S., & Jiminez-Lorrento, B. (1999). The effects of pretrial publicity on jury verdicts: A meta-analytic review. *Law and Human Behavior, 23*, 219–235.

Steblay, N., Hosch, H. M., Culhane, S. E., & McWethy, A. (2006). The impact on juror verdicts of judicial instruction to disregard inadmissible evidence: A meta-analysis. *Law and Human Behavior, 30*(4), 469–492.

Stevenson, M. C., Lytle, B. L., Baumholser, B. J., & McCracken, E. W. (2017). Racially diverse juries promote self-monitoring efforts during jury deliberation. *Translational Issues in Psychological Science, 3*(2), 187–201.

Studebaker, C. A., Robbennolt, J. K., Pathak-Sharma, M. K., & Penrod, S. D. (2000). Assessing pretrial publicity effects: Integrating content analytic results. *Law and Human Behavior, 23*(4), 317–336.

Studebaker, C. A., Robbennolt, J. K., Penrod, S. D., Pathak-Sharma, M. K., Groscup, J. L., & Devenport, J. L. (2002). Studying pretrial publicity effects: New methods for improving ecological validity and testing external validity. *Law and Human Behavior, 26*(1), 19–41.

Sweeney, D. M. (2011). Worlds collide: The digital native enters the jury box. *Reynolds Courts and Media Law Journal, 1*(2), 121–146.

Tasmania Law Reform Institute. (2020). *Jurors, social media, and the right of an accused to a fair trial* (Final report no. 30) (p. 16). Tasmania Law Reform Institute.

Taylor, J., & Tarrant, G. (2019). Trial by social media: How do you find the jury, guilty or not guilty? *International Journal of Cyber Research and Education, 1*(2), 50–61.

Thomas, C. (2010). *Are juries fair? Ministry of justice research series.* United Kingdom Ministry of Justice.

Vidmar, N. (2002). Case studies of pre-and mid-trial prejudice in criminal and civil litigation. *Law and Human Behavior, 26*, 73–105.

Warner, K., Davis, J., & Underwood, P. (2011). The jury experience: Insights from the Tasmanian Jury Study. *The Judicial Review, 10*(3), 333–360.

Waters, N. L., & Hannaford-Agor, P. (2014). Juror impartiality in the modern era. In J. S. Albanese (Ed.), *Encyclopedia of criminology and criminal justice* (pp. 2735–2745). Wiley Blackwell.

Wistrich, A. J., Guthrie, C., & Rachlinski, J. J. (2005). Can judges ignore inadmissible information? The difficulty of deliberately disregarding. *University of Pennsylvania Law Review, 153,* 1251–1345.
Yarnell, M. A. (2006). Jury reform—Where is the science the Arizona jury: Past, present and future reform. *Australian Journal of Forensic Sciences, 38*(1), 23–33.

Legislation and Cases

Cheatle v The Queen [1993] 177 CLR 541.
Benbrika v R (2010) 29 VR 593, [192]–[216] (Maxwell P, Nettle and Weinberg JJA).
Benbrika v The Queen [2010] VSCA 281.
Hoang v R [2018] NSWCCA 166.
Hoang v The Queen [2022] HCA 14.
Jury Act 1977 (NSW).
R v Baden-Clay [2014] QSC 154.
R v Benbrika [2009] VSC 142, [53]–[75].

Practitioner Perspective: A View from the Bench—Juries in the Digital Age

Judge W. Graham Turnbull SC

The evolution of the parameters of justice is everywhere in the digital age. Things considered sacrosanct before the computer was invented have been changed, and in some instances, discarded. Before becoming a judge, I was a jury trial privateer for decades. Now, all around, books have disappeared into iPads, trolleys are parked up and turning to rust in clerks' mailrooms, and pens have gone the way of paper. The computer has become an educational, fundamental, core skill—and the internet a freely available resource. Recourse to digital resources is going on right under a jury's nose.

The Temptation of Jurors

Pretrial publicity has a potential bearing on jury attitudes and therefore jury outcomes. Think of images of gutter sittings by the cuffed and detained; parading of arrestees escorted handcuffed into or out of police cars or more disconcertingly, guiltily paraded along supposedly discreet secure police station ramps to their custodial endpoint. Pretrial material can prime people to expect that most people charged are guilty. However, each case is different. Each individual case, and count, is required to be viewed in accordance with the evidence referable to that specific case.

The criminal trial has as its starting point the presumption of innocence. The subtlety of its potential erosion is an aspect of the digital age. There are blogs and talkback outrage, the intemperate criticism of judicial decisions, even at a political level; there is an obscuring of the difference between arrest and conviction; and the ongoing lionising of authority. This has moved many sanctions previously imposed by a court to being imposed on the street. One example is on-the-spot fines or bail

Judge W. G. Turnbull SC
District Court of New South Wales, NSW, Australia

laws which can operate to impose a jail sentence before the case is fully heard. The notion that the accused would face their accuser is now—in many instances, and increasingly so—one where the confrontation occurs over a video-link. The jury sees a two-dimensional distant image, not a three-dimensional person coming and going from the courtroom.

In the digital age, there is an evident drive to make complete the incomplete within the moment—TikTok's 60 seconds; Twitter's 280 characters. There may be a perception in the community, constituted as a trial jury, that the trial is frustratingly long, the directions confusingly detailed, and the standard of proof impossibly high. Frustration that, the studies suggest, does provoke outside the courtroom enquiries. These may be via digital sources but, they may also be by asking others, or they may include discreet visits to the crime scene.

Procedural Fairness

In a magistrate's court, and in a judge-alone trial, where evidence is found to be unfairly prejudicial or where it is found to have been improperly or illegally obtained, judicial officers are presumed to be capable of setting aside the excluded evidence in their fact-finding task. It is accepted that they are capable of resisting irrational thinking, identifying and discarding tainting emotional responses and rendering a just decision. No prohibition on internet searches has been suggested for judicial officers. Indeed, in many contexts it is expected. So, there is always the potential for a look at the legislation or the bench book, a review of some case law, the conduct of further study of sentencing statistics, or to find other points of reference.

Like jurors, judicial officers are not immune to the temptation of internet research; and that internet research may occur during the course of a hearing or trial. I once sat at a bar table where the prosecutor took a magistrate to task for referring to his own research about a recreational drug in an interim judgement—concluded views, absent tested expert evidence, not presented by witnesses exposed to the rigours of cross examination. A rational structured analysis leading to a developed adversarial argument is what was required in a court. The Crown submitted that it was not a proper judgement but merely private musings publicly aired as a "judgement". They argued that justice was not done, nor, absent exposure and testing, seen to be done. It was a stern admonition, courageous even, from counsel. Of course, the magistrate was courageous too; he could have kept it to himself as many likely do.

The Crown had made an important point. In the ongoing contest of a criminal trial, the learned magistrate's now identified musings could only be a preliminary judgement at most. Digital research, aligned with book searches and likely colleague consultation, needs to be openly argued, tested and rationally aligned with the expectations of due process and fairness. Procedural fairness reflects the community's expectations and a community understanding. Not every individual in the jury may have the same level of insight into its operation at the legalese level, but there can be no doubt that a 'fair go' is a community standard.

A True Verdict According to the Evidence

The jury trial system necessarily accepts exposure to the risk of prejudice and ignorance from the outset. Aside from a few limited peremptory challenges, there is no jury selection process in the Commonwealth, beyond the calling out of a number to a group gathered by jury summons. This is distinct from the process in many parts of the United States, where selection proceeds by way of surveys, and even questioning, to flush out inter alia, digital influences.

Biasing information can be case or topic specific. The former is the relevant concern to a trial underway. The reality is that flouting a prohibition is too simple a trigger to despondency about the efficacy of directions. It is not the point that directions in the form of prohibitions on internet use, or independent research are likely to be, or are actually, disregarded by some jurors. The point is what is done with the fruits of those breaches. It is the intrusion of prejudice, the erosion of impartiality, the squandering of rationality; the rogue ignorance of the requirements the law sets out, and ultimately, the rejection of the judge's role in providing the framework within which the found facts are to fit, which is the problem.

No one is suggesting that everything done extra-curially by a judicial officer, including digital searches and the like, should be prohibited where it has a bearing on the trial. They are trusted to expose their thinking, and respond to fairly tested and received evidence. No more should be expected of jurors, who themselves are subject to an oath and are expected to act fairly and rationally and indeed, as if it's needed to be done, are directed to do so.

True it is that the verdict of a jury requires no reasons. What a verdict does require is a trial, evidence, the testing of that evidence and the application of the law as directed. Deliberation, often over days, confirms that people are reasoning towards a conclusion. All of that precedes a verdict.

Managing the Risk

'Verdict' is a combination of the French and Latin saying "to speak the truth, to say the truth". The jurors swear or affirm, to "give a true verdict according to the evidence". That's the evidence in the trial concerning the accused, who the jury have in their charge. In reaching their true verdict, the jury apply the directions of the trial judge.

There had been a usual practice of sequestering the jury during a trial. There can be no suggestion of the digital age provoking a return to that practice. People can listen to others' opinions and views, and not adopt them. People can abide by directions, even if they do not agree with them or are frustrated by them. That is the touchstone. That is why there is not a blanket ban on any pretrial reporting or discussion, and people go home every night. They are told not to discuss the case with their confidants, or anyone, apart from their fellow jurors, when all 12 are gathered together.

The jury trial system is based on community, on trust in each other in a multifaceted process that is experienced by a dozen different people. They do not have to reach the verdict by the same route but must agree nonetheless upon it. In the end they are judges too. There is a solemn promise given, in formal circumstances at the outset of the trial, in a courtroom architecturally calibrated to emphasise the solemnity of the tasks undertaken within.

The acuity of jurors to digital pre-publicity, extending typically far beyond any particulars of the trial they come to hear, has to be accepted. It cannot be that the politics of the day, the preferences of individuals, their education, their life experience, their prejudices, their occupations, their relationships and their life events, can ever be adequately vetted in a system that relies upon that very mix. Daily, the jury trial courts address these issues. The totality of the trial process, its forensic issues, its participants, the political and social context, the accused and what they are accused of, the pretrial publicity and familiarities, are all taken as given.

Prohibiting internet or other digital conduct must reflect an understanding of the need for the rules and thus the prohibitions. This is the actual context. Directions, so often isolated and thereafter impugned as insufficient and impotent, often forget the reality. It is not too bold to suggest that there is, abroad, a focus on discrete issues in exceptional cases, which can typically devolve to the use of a single sentence. It is evident in much academic analysis, and equally so in many appeal court judgements.

What has developed, as a usual trial judge practice in recent years, is an invitation to the jurors in waiting, those about to be empanelled, to identify, in their minds, prejudice. An accused is entitled, as anyone in our community is entitled, to an impartial jury. The three simple rules of a criminal trial—presumption, onus and standard of proof—are set out. The panel are told that those are directions of law that must be applied. If a person cannot be impartial and apply the law, then they can identify that to the judge and seek to be excused.

At the point prior to empanelling, the panel in waiting are given a thumbnail of the case the Crown seeks to prove. The panel has already heard the indictment put, and accordingly knows broadly, the type of case that it is. The names of witnesses, others to be referred to, places, times, surrounding circumstances, usually in consultation with the defence, are read out. The detail of the subject matter, well beyond the mere particulars of the indictment, becomes clearer. Pretrial publicity is specifically mentioned, if it can be identified. Any controversy, and any broad canvassing of events in the community in advance, is typically mentioned so as to alert the panel in waiting.

Then, the members of the jury panel are asked if they can bring an open and unprejudiced mind, after knowing what they now know? If it might even look like they are partial because of a witness relationship, or prior knowledge of the events, they are invited to stand aside, or at the very least discuss the matters confidentially with the judge, albeit in open court, being seen but not necessarily heard.

Many take advantage of the invitation because people are there to do, unquestionably, the right thing by the administration of justice. Judges now commonly go a step further. If the subject matter creates strong emotions, might excite outrage or anger, or might cloud rationality, then potential jurors are asked to be honest with themselves, to look inside themselves, to identify their prejudice and to seek excusal. This is particularly, but not exclusively so, in the case of allegations of sexual assault, and it is usual to hear from more than a handful of people. These may be people who are triggered, angry at events before or now, who have, or who have family or friends who have, suffered at the hands of perpetrators; or they are people who cannot, in all honesty, simply start with a presumption of innocence.

To look at the faces of 70 strangers, waiting for their number to be drawn from a box to serve, is salutary. The diversity, the courtesy, the forbearance, the respect for and compliance with the process of a jury trial from the very start is an everyday occurrence in our courts. Twelve people are then chosen, at random, from the community. By joining a jury, jurors are expected to remain people whose independence, common sense, world experience and capacity for rational discussion allow them to sit in judgement on another member of the community.

The reasons why in-trial juror research is unacceptable are explained by the judge before a direction is given. The proven applied simplicity of a jury's duty, in achieving and being seen to achieve just outcomes, has ensured its inter-subjective acceptance as a legal institution. It reflects the way our democracy does its business.

The simple rules for the jury, even in the digital age remain. Accept directions, and ask if in doubt about directions. As for the facts, the jury is directed that they are what is presented in court, tested in court and accepted as relevant by the parties in the particular trial. The Crown can either prove it, or they cannot. If the jury has a doubt, they are directed the benefit of that doubt goes to the accused, and that it can't be an *unreasonable* doubt.

Conclusion

Trials in front of juries are linear and specific; each accused is an individual, each narrative of events unique. Experience of modern jurors reflects their concern for the task at hand. It is understood that fairness requires an open mind without pre-judgement, and that it is part of the process from the start.

The digital age is not inimical to the survival of the jury system. Indeed, the use of digital devices in a trial is now inherent to the process. It is a facet of community life that should be recognised as a facet of the jury system. Serving on a jury is a facet of community life.

It is not that the traditional paradigm is not working reliably. It is just, as for most things involving people and processes, concepts and compromise, that it may not work perfectly every time. That's why there are appeals, and even then, perfection is elusive. It was said by another judge, that the conscience of the jury gives the judge their power (Devlin 1956). The digital age hasn't changed that.

Reference

Devlin, P. (1956). *Trial by jury*. Stevens & Son.

4

Courts and the Media

Lisa Waller and Katrina Clifford

Introduction

Established media organisations have a special role in our democracy—they are uniquely and inseparably linked to open and accountable government. One aspect of that 'watchdog' role is fulfilling our 'right to know' about matters of public interest (Your Right to Know, 2021). Another aspect lies more specifically in court reporting because not only is news media the public's eyes and ears in the proceedings, its presence also encourages the impartial administration of justice, thus protecting

L. Waller (✉)
RMIT University, Melbourne, VIC, Australia
e-mail: lisa.waller@rmit.edu.au

K. Clifford
Deakin University, Melbourne, VIC, Australia
e-mail: katrina.clifford@deakin.edu.au

M. Camilleri and A. Harkness (eds.), *Australian Courts*,
https://doi.org/10.1007/978-3-031-19063-6_4

the values at the heart of our liberal democracy. Historically, the interaction between courts and news media has been somewhat adversarial, with the judiciary lacking trust in media, and journalists challenging legal departures from the principle of 'open justice' which establishes their role in ensuring fair and public hearings by an independent and impartial judiciary (Smartt, 2020).

Routine media reporting of courts conforms to newsworthiness criteria, so of course it is the colourful criminal cases, matters that involve high-profile citizens and key moments in court proceedings, such as sentencings, that attract the most media attention (see Clifford & White, 2017; Moran, 2013). As the boundaries, forms and purposes of media continue to shift, such cases and proceedings are no longer the province of established news reporters alone, with members of the 'un-established media', including 'citizen journalists', getting in on the act through 'new media' formats and practices such as true crime podcasts and live-tweeting of court proceedings.

In the digital environment, the law can seem antiquated as it has not always kept pace with advances in technologies and the realities of media practice, including the use of social media platforms like Facebook to discuss legal cases. Yet courts are increasingly using media technologies for a range of purposes, including direct communication with stakeholders and the public. In some cases, contemporary media practices related to courts are generating new issues and complexities—and it is also true that the courts' powers to make exceptions to the public's 'right to know' continue to stoke controversy.

This chapter explores some of the key concepts that drive the interplay between courts, media and publics, and discusses several contemporary cases to illustrate the challenges and changes that are shaping their symbiotic yet sometimes fraught relationship. It argues that on the occasions when courts and media do clash, it is often a case of the parties not understanding or taking issue with one another's logics, operations or constraints.

The Context of Open Justice

As Justice John Basten (2005, p. 1) has observed of the courts and media dynamic, "a level of tension is healthy and acceptable as part of a lively relationship between two active institutions in a modern society" so long as both parties remember that "any exercise of public power must be constrained by a sense of responsibility, so as to avoid abuse of power". In the context of the courts-media relationship, that sense of power and responsibility is central to the principles and practices of 'open justice'.

'Open justice' is a core principle in British and Australian common law and a cornerstone of the system of justice. The media plays a vital role in "actively safeguarding it" (Smartt, 2020, p. 113) and is therefore "aggrieved in a way that the remainder of society is not" by any perceived departure from it (Douglas, 2016, p. 70). The term 'open justice' refers to the belief that "accountability and legitimacy within the legal process can be achieved through making accessible information about court procedures, court records, laws and judicial decisions" (Biber, 2013, p. 73). In other words, it embraces the principle that justice must be "seen to be done" (Spigelman, 2000), thereby engendering confidence in the courts (Rodrick, 2014).

In its purest form, open justice, therefore, endorses the idea that all court proceedings and the materials associated with them should be accessible to the public and to media—as a "conduit for justice" (Biber, 2014, p. 75)—*without restriction.* And yet, while it is an essential characteristic of courts, it is not an absolute principle. A court can depart from open justice by closing proceedings to the public, concealing information from those present in court or restricting publication of material arising from proceedings. Douglas (2016, p. 70) argues that when these powers are exercised, it is appropriate for media organisations, which have "the greatest stake in open justice to question whether the circumstances warrant the departure".

The privileges for and constraints on journalists covering the courts vary markedly between jurisdictions and there is often little consistency about "which materials are 'open'… the processes to be followed, and about whether reasons need to be given by a requesting party" (Biber, 2014, p. 74). For example, journalists covering the courts in Australia are subject to different court rules and legislation across nine jurisdictions (six states, two territories and the Commonwealth) as well as the implications of publishing and sharing news stories across borders (Pearson & Polden, 2015).

There are, however, some commonalities in the privileges afforded to journalists, including having access to documents tabled in court and transcripts of court proceedings, subject to certain provisos. This includes recognition that there are sometimes necessary exceptions to the open justice principle, resulting in restrictions on the reporting of certain cases—for example, those related to national security, trade secrets or blackmail, allegations of sexual assault, murder or terrorism, or cases that involve vulnerable individuals (Pearson & Polden, 2015). Open justice may also clash with other principles, such as the right to be tried before an impartial jury, especially when the privileges afforded to journalists in terms of access to court proceedings and materials morph into 'trial by media'.

Arguments about the role of open justice in promoting public confidence in the courts and understandings of the criminal justice system implicitly rely on the media reporting court proceedings in a fair and accurate manner because the court has "limited control over the subsequent use of that information for other purposes" (NSW Attorney General's Department, 2008, p. 35), including its use within criminal justice journalism. Open justice, in practice, is, therefore, about getting the balance right—particularly as it relates to the professional imperatives and ideals of news media. As Pearson and Polden (2015, p. 97) argue:

> … "[s]omewhere in between the extremes of a media free-for-all and judicial clampdown" there must be "a legitimate and vital space for journalism, in which courts can be subjected to vigorous examination and criticism in the public interest, while those accused of a crime can still get a fair trial".

But the fraught nature of the relationship between courts and media—particularly the former's distrust of the latter—has meant that, historically, judges have been both cautious and selective in their determinations about the materials sanctioned for media access and use. At other times, the decision has been made at the discretion of individual court staff, such as public information officers, who we return to later in the chapter. This has led to frustration among journalists, who have reported feeling as though they "have had unnecessary barriers placed in their way in obtaining information that their audiences are entitled to know" (Innes, 2008, p. 3).

This is especially true when it comes to suppression orders and non-publication orders, which prohibit or restrict the disclosure of information about a legal case and are more commonly used in Australia than in some other English-speaking jurisdictions. They can be wide-ranging—restricting nearly all, and at times all, information about a trial—or narrow, obscuring just one person's name.

The Controversies of Suppression Orders: A Right to a Fair Trial Versus the Right to Know

One of the key legal issues that arises for news organisations relates to contempt of court. This is nowhere more apparent than when news outlets challenge or breach suppression orders, which are commonly applied by Australian courts to ensure people who face charges get a fair trial. Suppression orders are a significant limitation on freedom of the media to report what happens in criminal courts and the state of Victoria has come in for some of the harshest criticism. According to Australian media reports, Victoria accounts for more than half of the country's total suppression orders. Critics, such as prominent Australian journalist Louise Milligan, have derided Victoria as "The Suppression State" (@Milliganreports, Twitter post, 12 December 2018):

> The editorials of nation's newspapers on Victoria, The Suppression State, are pertinent & timely. The erosion of open courts principle in Vic has troubled me for years. But never more so, more personally and painfully than now. You either believe in open justice or you do not.

When a person or organisation is accused of breaching a suppression order they can be charged with 'contempt of court', which is a serious offence and can result in jail time or heavy fines. For example, 12 Australian media companies including *The Age* newspaper and News Limited's news.com.au were fined a total of more than AUD$1 million by the Victorian Supreme Court in February 2021 after pleading guilty to contempt of court over their reporting of Australia's most senior Catholic cleric Cardinal George Pell's conviction on sexual abuse charges (McGowan, 2021).

Police charged Pell with historical sex offences in June 2017. He immediately denied any wrongdoing. Some pre-trial hearings were allowed to be reported which revealed that Pell faced separate accusations from the 1970s and the 1990s. Consequently, a judge ordered there would be two trials with separate juries. In a bid to prevent the first trial influencing the second, the judge agreed to an immediate suppression order that made it illegal to report that any trial was taking place. Even saying that the suppression order existed was prohibited. The suppression order legally applied only to Australia, but it effectively extended to international media that publish or broadcast into Australia, or whose content can be accessed there, which is a very difficult thing to avoid in the internet age.

In the first trial, Pell was initially found guilty in December 2018. That conviction was overturned by the High Court of Australia in April 2020. The second trial did not go ahead after charges against Pell were dropped in February 2019. But the possibility of a second trial was real when the first trial guilty verdict was handed down. There is a principle in law that a jury must decide guilt or innocence according to the evidence before them, and not allow other evidence (such as a conviction for a similar crime) to influence their deliberations. It was, therefore, crucial that a jury in the second trial (had it proceeded) not know of the first conviction.

Australian news outlets were generally more cautious than their international counterparts, with journalists sitting in regularly on Pell's case and adhering to the ban, but the blackout did not go totally unnoticed publicly. Social media users, for instance, frequently speculated about it (BBC, 2019). Matters escalated dramatically in December 2018, when numerous non-Australian outlets published reports that Pell had been convicted. The words 'George Pell' were soon trending online, including in Australia (BBC, 2019). This prompted some of Australia's biggest media outlets to run front-page editorials criticising the suppression order. Unlike overseas media, they did not name Pell, instead referring to a trial of great importance and, by implication, a guilty verdict that would have been of significant interest to the public.

The implicit, not explicit, nature of the reporting raises an important point: no Australian media company named Pell, but some directed their audiences to international online reports. For example, on 13 December 2018, Melbourne's *Herald Sun* newspaper published a white headline 'CENSORED' across a black front page, thereby fanning the public's interest in seeking out international reports and internet commentary. On the same day, Melbourne's *The Age* newspaper published a front-page story under the headline, 'Why media can't report on a high-profile case', which referred to the suppression order and the availability of news about the case online. *The Age* also published two other articles and an editorial that scrutinised the use of suppression orders in Victorian courts, which was later taken down from its online site. In a specially convened court hearing the same day, Judge Peter Kidd said he was "angry" about media reports though he did not mention specific outlets. The judge left the matter with prosecutors to investigate. Digital versions of some front pages were later unavailable.

Other Australian journalists such as Kate Jones, however, voiced support for the suppression order, expressing concerns that publicity could influence a court outcome (@Kate_Jones7, Twitter post, 12 December 2018):

> Eight years covering Victorian courts, and I've seen more ridiculous suppression orders than most. But that's not what's going on here. This is a contempt of court issue, and it's right that it shouldn't be reported. It would be a tragedy if publicity now meant justice delayed.

Some commentators said the ban was ineffective but others disagreed, arguing that most people did not know about Pell's conviction before it became public when prosecutors withdrew the charges related to the 1970s allegations, announcing the second trial would not proceed.

In an interview with the BBC, Justin Quill, the lawyer who acted on behalf of the Australian news outlets in the contempt case, argued that judges need to "have more faith" in jurors to form their view from a courtroom even if they had seen something related to the case on social media: "for the public to not be told [about Pell's conviction] until nearly three months later, is in my view, a situation that is not appropriate". He also said courts could not "go around charging 10,000 people for one or two comments they've made on Twitter", adding: "Mainstream media is being held to one standard, and the general public is being held to another—it just doesn't make sense" (Quill in BBC, 2019).

In his judgement, Victorian Supreme Court Justice John Dixon took a stern view of what he said were the motives behind the media outlets' contempt of court. He said reporting by *The Age* and news.com.au in particular "constituted a blatant and willful defiance of the court's authority": "Each took a deliberate risk by intentionally advancing a collateral attack on the role of suppression orders in Victoria's criminal justice system" (Dixon in BBC, 2019). Justice Dixon said the media companies had not only usurped the function of the court but had taken it "upon themselves" to decide "where the balance ought to lie" between Pell's right to a fair trial and the public's right to know about it. While people might debate the politics and public interest in the case, Dixon's judgement is clear—balance is a matter for the courts to determine.

The Challenging Tensions Between Legal Orthodoxy and Changing Media Practice

Another contested aspect of court-media relations hinges on the argument that reforms to Australian media law have been too slow to keep pace with the changed conditions of the digital age. Such were the criticisms of the 2021 High Court of Australia decision in the Dylan Voller defamation case, where commentators like media law barrister Matt Collins QC (2021) lamented the missed opportunity they saw for the court to reconsider the applicability of age-old legal principles (such as who is a 'publisher') in an online era.

Voller, then a teenager, came to public attention in July 2016 following disturbing allegations about the mistreatment of young people in the child protection and juvenile detention systems in the Northern Territory. The allegations, revealed as part of an investigation by the Australian Broadcasting Corporation's current affairs television programme, *Four Corners*, were aired with images showing Voller, then a detainee in an Alice Springs correctional centre, strapped to a chair and wearing a spit-hood (see 'Australia's Shame', 2016).

Following the *Four Corners* coverage, several media outlets posted stories about Voller on their Facebook pages. While these were not defamatory, Voller claimed that some of the public comments made in response to the articles indeed were. Without giving prior notice to the media organisations involved, Voller commenced defamation proceedings against them in the Supreme Court of New South Wales. The case stalled after questions were raised about whether media outlets could be considered 'publishers' of comments posted to their public Facebook pages by third parties.

Under Australian defamation law, it is the communication, not the composition, of the defamatory material that lies at the heart of the issue of publication. As the High Court found in *Dow Jones & Company Inc v Gutnick* [2002] HCA 56, harm to reputation is not done until it is comprehensible to a third party (High Court of Australia, 2002, p. 8, par. 26). One of the difficulties for the media outlets involved in the *Voller* case was that, at the time the news stories were posted between July 2016 and June 2017, Facebook did not allow users to turn off the comments function (Byrne, 2021). This functionality has subsequently changed.

In the High Court, the media outlets argued that they could not be considered publishers of the social media commentary because this required an intention to publish and, at the time they were posted to their Facebook pages, the media outlets were unaware of the comments. The court rejected the claim. It found that by creating a public Facebook page and posting content there, the media outlets had "facilitated, encouraged and thereby assisted the publication of comments from third-party Facebook users" and were, therefore, legally, publishers of the comments (High Court of Australia, 2021). The judgement set the ground rules for the litigation brought by Voller.

In advance of an outcome in this case, reform to Australia's defamation laws commenced, introducing "a number of measures designed to better reflect modern publishing" (Schwarz, 2020, p. 41), including a new 'serious harm' threshold and the need for a person to provide a concerns notice to the publisher before a matter can be litigated. But the difficulties that the diversity of digital technologies and more innovative forms of storytelling raises for issues of publication and the administration of justice continue to be something "with which courts throughout the common law world are grappling" (Rolph, 2021, p. 226).

Beyond the courtroom, the High Court's ruling regarding who is a 'publisher' bore practical implications for traditional media organisations for whom social media is an integral part of their business model. As Douglas (2021) explains: "Sharing drives engagement—likes and comments—which makes content visible to more users. Visibility means clicks, which means money for the organization from advertisers". In the wake of the court's decision, several media outlets closed comments or shut down their Facebook pages. US-based news network CNN was one of the first major news organisations to act, disabling its Facebook page in Australia, citing the High Court's decision (Meade, 2021). Others soon followed with online announcements from organisations like Schwartz Media that they would be turning off comments on their publications' social media accounts to reduce their risk of being sued.

The chilling effect of the *Voller* decision also filtered through to non-commercial social media users, such as community and volunteer-run bodies, who similarly contemplated turning off the comments function out of concern for the defamation risks to administrators (see Purtill, 2021). While prohibitive to civic engagement, for many, shutting down public commentary is an easier and less-resource intensive option than the alternative of closely monitoring comments posted to social media pages and actively removing those that might be potentially damaging. Recognising the risks of legal responsibility for 'ordinary Australians', post-*Voller* the Australian government announced it would introduce additional reforms to defamation law to make clear that "Australians who operate or maintain a social media page are not 'publishers' of comments made by others" (Cash cited in Prime Minister, Attorney General, 2021).

Embracing Change: New Technologies and Opportunities for Connection

The demands of the contemporary news cycle and the impacts of advances in mobile and real-time communications technologies have produced not only challenges but also opportunities for courts to demonstrate that they are open to change. One practice, now less contentious than it once was, is live-tweeting news from the courtroom. While it is still not determined how effective a medium Twitter is in serving the principles of open justice and the fair and accurate communication and contextualisation of complex legal arguments (in 280 characters), live-tweeting by professional journalists can add a real-time "sensory dimension to conventional court reporting of high-profile cases" (Clifford & White, 2017, p. 69). It can also allow journalists to connect with audiences who may not otherwise follow legal proceedings through conventional news sources, such as newspapers and broadcast media. Then, there are the opportunities that the immediacy of Twitter affords court reporters in beating the competition to a news story—or in acting as a news source in its own right for journalists who are not able to attend courtroom proceedings (see for example Isaac, 2017).

Concerns about the potentially adverse impacts of live-tweeting (and liveblogging) on the administration of justice have prompted some courts to impose time delay restrictions on the transmission of tweets from inside the courtroom, so as to avoid inadvertent disclosures of information from trial evidence and submissions, which may later become subject to a suppression order. This is while retaining the opportunity for journalists to live-tweet court outcomes and verdicts (Pearson & Polden, 2015).

As Small and Puddister (2020, p. 6) point out, "once information is shared through a tweet, it is difficult to issue a meaningful retraction as authority over the information is surrendered". The loss of control can be particularly problematic in the context of criminal trials, if the information that a journalist shares is later found to be immaterial or prejudicial against the accused. For these reasons, it is typically only accredited court reporters or those with explicit permission from the court—decided on a case-by-case basis by the presiding judge—who are allowed to bring anything more modern than paper and pen to assist with their reporting (in some jurisdictions, laptops or tablets may be permitted for note-taking or filing stories, as long as their use does not disrupt proceedings).

In Australia, courts themselves have increasingly shuffled off their historical conservatism towards social networking technologies to engage with platforms like Twitter, Facebook and YouTube. Where once courts may have relied on mainstream media outlets as intermediaries to make sense of legal proceedings, now they have the capacity to speak directly to publics through their own social media accounts and the use of digital technologies (Clifford & White, 2017). What they post may be constrained by internal restrictions associated with the administration of justice, but social media nonetheless offers courts a useful tool for debunking the myths and misconceptions that surround their operations and for connecting with jurisprudential networks.

The uptake of social media as standard practice has arguably paralleled the widespread appointment of Public Information Officers (PIOs) within the courts system, who take responsibility for effectively managing the courts-media relationship and promoting public understanding of the court's role and functions. To put this another way, courts have over time become more skilled at doing their own public relations, which has inevitably changed the dynamic with mainstream media and the way stories are told. Just as social media has played an increasingly prominent role in court-media relations, so too the importance of television and webcams in the courtroom has flourished alongside the rise of PIOs, who have been credited with also advancing this field of practice (for a comprehensive history of PIOs in Australian courts, see Johnston, 2019).

Courts' adaptation to new technologies, though, has been gradational. Australian judges have historically tended to take a dim view of cameras in the courtroom. The media circus that erupted in response to the live broadcasting of high-profile international cases such as the O. J.

Simpson murder trial in Los Angeles in 1994 and the criminal trial of South African sprint runner and convicted murderer, Oscar Pistorius, in Pretoria in 2014 have been touchstones for concerns that cameras in the courtroom serve to cheapen and "trivialise the serious business of the courts" (Kirby, 2003, p. 51).

Fears among judges, magistrates and lawyers that audio and video recordings of proceedings would be misused by media have, over time, yielded to a better appreciation of the possibilities afforded by emerging technologies. The change has, in part, been borne from necessity but also the comfort that comes from the increased control courts themselves now exercise over the broadcasting of courtroom content.

Events such as the COVID-19 pandemic accelerated changes to the ways in which the judicial system operates, with courts the world over having to move to virtual hearings in March 2020 for civil and criminal cases. The livestreaming of court proceedings has also become a normalised and accepted part of community outreach and engagement activities—and not just within courts responsible for dealing with civil and criminal matters.

In 2012, the findings of then New South Wales Coroner Mary Jerram into the death of Roberto Laudisio Curti were livestreamed, given the significant public interest in the case. Laudisio Curti, a Brazilian national, had died on a pavement in Sydney's central business district eight months earlier after being pursued and restrained by up to 11 police officers who had used physical force to subdue him (see Clifford, 2021). Excerpts of the livestream were carried on a number of broadcast and online media platforms. Cameras have also helped to broadcast parts of major inquiries in Australia, including the Black Saturday Bushfires Royal Commission in Victoria and the Royal Commission into Institutional Responses to Child Sexual Abuse at the Commonwealth level.

Conclusion

Routinely, courts around the world quietly publish a wide range of case-specific information online for media and public use. The Supreme Court of Victoria as an example offers its own on-demand access to webcasts of a selection of sentences, judgements and hearings, as well as the court's award-winning podcast, *Gertie's Law*. As it is for numerous other organisations though—news media included—courts still need to be alert to the potential pitfalls of having an online presence. For one, maintaining this can be a significant resourcing challenge, given the expectations around information provision and interpretation and the conventions of social media, especially the demands for two-way communication and interactivity between users. This makes it difficult to balance online moderation and the shutting down or deletion of dissent and misinformation with the principles of open justice and transparency.

Livestreaming and other real-time communications are not without challenges too. In February 2021, an amateur online sleuth illegally recorded a sensitive Federal Court proceeding about missing (presumed deceased) Sydney businesswoman and alleged fraudster, Melissa Caddick, which involved discussion of suppression orders. The virtual hearing was reportedly shared with thousands of followers of a Facebook group interested in the case. The video remained available online for almost five hours, before being removed once the court had been alerted to it (Gair, 2021).

Examples, such as this and the others discussed in this chapter, point to the need for a real-world approach to current and future law reform processes to ensure the preservation of the ideals of open justice and a balance between the proper administration of justice and the democratic role of journalism. How reporting restrictions and protected evidence, more broadly, come to co-exist with emerging forms of online open justice and possible wider digital innovation among courts over the longer term remains to be seen (McIntyre et al., 2020).

References

Basten, J. (2005, 30 October–4 November). *Court and media relationships*. National Judicial College, Beijing, Conference. https://www.supremecourt.justice.nsw.gov.au/Documents/Publications/Speeches/Pre-2015%20Speeches/Basten/basten_2005.10.30c.pdf

BBC. (2019, February 26). George Pell: Why was conviction kept secret? *BBC News*. https://www.bbc.com/news/world-australia-47366083

Biber, K. (2013). In crime's archive: The cultural afterlife of criminal evidence. *British Journal of Criminology, 53*(6), 1033–1049.

Biber, K. (2014). Inside Jill Meagher's handbag: Looking at open justice. *Alternative Law Journal, 39*(2), 73–77.

Byrne, E. (2021, September 8). High Court to decide whether news outlets responsible for Facebook comments at centre of Dylan Voller defamation case. *ABC News*. https://www.abc.net.au/news/2021-09-08/high-court-to-make-ruling-in-dylan-voller-defamation-case/100440752

Clifford, K. (2021). *Policing, mental illness and media: The framing of mental health crisis encounters and police use of force*. Palgrave Macmillan.

Clifford, K., & White, R. (2017). *Media and crime: Content, context and consequence*. Oxford University Press.

Collins, M. (2021, September 8). A judgment rooted in 1928, when the world couldn't have dreamed of Facebook. *The Sydney Morning Herald*. https://www.smh.com.au/national/a-judgment-rooted-in-1928-when-the-world-couldn-t-have-dreamed-of-facebook-20210908-p58py0.html

Douglas, M. (2016). The media's standing to challenge departures from open justice. *The Adelaide Law Review, 37*(1), 69–99.

Douglas, M. (2021, September 8). High Court decision will help clean up garbage on social media. *The Sydney Morning Herald*. https://www-smh-com-au.ezproxy-b.deakin.edu.au/national/high-court-decision-will-help-clean-up-garbage-on-social-media-20210908-p58pxi.html

Four Corners. (2016, July 25). Australia's shame. *Four Corners* [Television broadcast]. ABC TV.

Gair, K. (2021, February 23). Amateur sleuth livestreams Melissa Caddick hearing. *The Australian*. https://www.theaustralian.com.au/nation/amateur-sleuth-livestreams-melissa-caddick-hearing/news-story/f2a812f401098cc1e2f46f23c800c9c7

High Court of Australia. (2002, December 10). *Dow Jones & Company Inc v Gutnick* [2002] HCA 56. https://eresources.hcourt.gov.au/downloadPdf/2002/HCA/56

High Court of Australia. (2021, September 8). *Fairfax Media Publications Pty Ltd v Dylan Voller; Nationwide News Pty Limited v Dylan Voller; Australian News Channel Pty Ltd v Dylan Voller [2021] HCA 27* [Judgment Summary]. https://www.hcourt.gov.au/cases/case_s236-2020

Innes, P. (2008). *Report of the review of suppression orders and the media's access to court documents and information*. Australia's Right to Know Coalition.

Isaac, M. (2017, January 24). A trial and a Twitterstorm: On live-tweeting from a federal courthouse. *The New York Times*. https://www.nytimes.com/2017/01/24/insider/a-trial-and-a-twitterstorm-on-live-tweeting-from-a-federal-courthouse.html

Johnston, J. (2019). *A history of public information officers in Australian courts: 25 years of assisting public perceptions and understanding of the administration of justice (1993–2018)*. The Australasian Institute of Judicial Administration Incorporated.

Kirby, M. (2003). Judicial accountability in Australia. *Legal Ethics, 6*(1), 41–54.

McGowan, M. (2021). George Pell: News organisations fined more than $1m over reporting of sexual abuse verdict. *The Guardian*. https://www.theguardian.com/australia-news/2021/jun/04/cardinal-george-pell-news-organisations-contempt-court-fined-more-than-1m-over-reporting-of-sexual-abuse-verdict

McIntyre, J., Olijnyk, A., & Pender, K. (2020, May 5). Courts and COVID-19: Challenges and opportunities in Australia. *Australian Public Law (AUSPUBLAW)*. https://auspublaw.org/2020/05/courts-and-covid-19-challenges-and-opportunities-in-australia

Meade, A. (2021, September 29). CNN disables Facebook page in Australia after High Court defamation decision. *The Guardian Australia*. https://www.theguardian.com/media/2021/sep/29/cnn-disables-australian-facebook-page-after-high-court-defamation-decision

Moran, L. J. (2013). Mass-mediated 'open justice': Court and judicial reports in the press in England and Wales. *Legal Studies, 34*(1), 143–166.

NSW Attorney General's Department. (2008). *Report on access to court information*. NSW Government. http://www.nswbar.asn.au/circulars/july/court_info.pdf

Pearson, M., & Polden, M. (2015). *The journalist's guide to media law: A handbook for communicators in a digital world* (5th ed.). Allen & Unwin.

Prime Minister, Attorney General. (2021, November 28). *Combating online trolls and strengthening defamation laws* [Media Release]. https://www.pm.gov.au/media/combatting-online-trolls-and-strengthening-defamation-laws

Purtill, J. (2021, October 4). Facebook pages fall quiet as administrators fear legal action over defamatory comments. *ABC News*. https://www.abc.net.au/news/science/2021-10-04/facebook-pages-are-falling-quiet-as-defamation-fears-take-hold/100501800

Rodrick, S. (2014). Achieving the aims of open justice? The relationship between the courts, the media and the public. *Deakin Law Review, 19*(3), 123–162.

Rolph, D. (2021). Before the High Court—Liability for the publication of third-party comments: 'Fairfax Media Publications Pty Ltd v Voller.' *Sydney Law Review, 43*(2), 225–240.

Schwarz, K. (2020). Reputation: The careful balance in defamation reform. *LSJ: Law Society of NSW Journal, 64*, 40–43.

Small, T. A., & Puddister, K. (2020). Play-by-play justice: Tweeting criminal trials in the digital age. *Canadian Journal of Law and Society, 35*(1), 1–22.

Smartt, U. (2020). *Media law for journalists*. Routledge.

Spigelman, J. J. (2000). Seen to be done: The principle of open justice—Part I. *The Australian Law Journal, 74*, 290–297.

Your Right to Know. (2021). *Get the facts*. https://yourrighttoknow.com.au/media-freedom/get-the-facts/

Cases

Dow Jones & Company Inc v Gutnick [2002] HCA 56.

Voller v Nationwide News Pty Ltd; Voller v Fairfax Media Publications Pty Ltd. Voller v Australian News Channel Pty Ltd [2019] NSWSC 766.

Practitioner Perspective: Pell, the Press and a Pandemic

Danny Tran

The single largest complaint that lawyers level at the press is that the stories they have written are riddled with errors.

Court reporting is a legally hazardous and detail-oriented job, focused on scrutinising a litigious profession that can be sensitive about how things are portrayed, so it is particularly frustrating when those same lawyers vehemently oppose access to documents that would clarify key facts or add valuable context. It is all the more baffling because court reporters share the same values as those at the bar table and the bench—we also believe justice is a fundamental cornerstone of any functioning democracy; that it should be accessed equally by all and must be seen to be done. But unlike those we scrutinise, the press cannot perform this function without the implicit and explicit support of the justice system and all its players including judges, magistrates, clerks and other staff.

The principle of open justice is as important as justice itself, and full confidence in the judicial system can only be achieved if it can be scrutinised without restriction. Yet as it stands, not everyone who participates in the justice system understands or even accepts the role of the press in raising confidence in the courts. This is made even more complex by new technologies that raise fresh ethical and existential issues around open justice, contempt of court, suppression orders and scrutiny.

COVID-19 and the Courts: More Accessible, Less Open

The COVID-19 pandemic brought the justice system to its knees and nowhere was this more keenly felt than Melbourne, Australia—the world's most locked down city during 2020 and 2021. Before the virus struck, it was not unusual to see queues of people stretching out of the

D. Tran
Australian Broadcasting Commission, Southbank, VIC, Australia

Melbourne Magistrates' Court building. Inside, magistrates, police officers and the accused would spend hours together in crowded courtrooms. But in 2020, all of this came to a grinding halt in the face of rising infection rates and a worsening death toll.

Despite historical conservatism, the courts acted quickly, embracing new technologies by moving hearings online and pressing pause on most in-person hearings.

Interestingly, each jurisdiction in Victoria embraced a different digital platform and developed its own procedures. The Magistrates' Court chose Webex and the County Court used both Webex and Zoom, with cases being set up as meetings and the parties being invited as participants. The Supreme Court and the Court of Appeal also used Webex, but livestreamed the hearings via Vimeo. There was no participation, possibly because reporters rarely address or make application before these higher courts without legal representation.

Only the most urgent matters would involve everyone face-to-face. Solicitors and barristers, so used to appearing from the bar table, instead appeared by video link from the kitchen table. Clients would sometimes appear from the couch.

For the press, the change was a double-edged sword. Suddenly, the time it took to move between courts and courtrooms vanished. Reporters were able to have two virtual hearings open at the same time and dip in and out of courtrooms hundreds of kilometres apart. It was a new and powerful way for the press to scrutinise more of the justice system. But there was a trade-off. Before the pandemic, reporters, like members of the public, were able to walk into almost any courtroom and bear witness to what went on inside without declaring ourselves or being questioned about our presence. However, under these new rules, reporters wanting access to cases in the Magistrates' and County Courts had to request access to cases, identify themselves as members of the media and rely on clerks or associates to physically click the button of a mouse and admit us into a hearing. They also had the power to throw us out.

Through its response to the pandemic, half the courts in Victoria inadvertently created a new layer of gatekeeping to open justice. This became another barrier to navigate. The feeling among reporters was that during the pandemic, more courts became more accessible, but they were ultimately less open.

Like all industries adapting to change, there were some teething issues. But for the most part, the press were given access to hearings unless there was a special reason. Although we did notice that, in order for the system to work as intended, every participant needed to be operating at the absolute best of their ability at every single moment of the day; something which no one can do for a sustained period of time. Even the slightest miscommunication—for example a clerk forgetting to tell a public affairs officer that a hearing had started—could mean that a case is never reported.

If the current status quo with online hearings is to remain, it is crucial that the courts keep pace with and understand the news media's logistics, operations and constraints under these new operating conditions.

Pell and the Press: How Australian Democracy Was Undermined by International Reporting

Cardinal George Pell, who would later have his conviction overturned by the High Court, was found guilty of child sex abuse charges on 11 December 2018, but the nation that hosted his trial was effectively in the dark until 26 February 2019 due to a suppression order on the result. It was a significant moment where the courts tried to balance open justice and the right to know, with the right to a fair trial (see Chapter 15 in this volume for further detail).

But on the day of the conviction, the *Daily Beast*, an American online news media outlet, broke the suppression order and published details of the first trial, marking the report with an exclusive tag. It was an incredibly frustrating moment for the Australian press, which was legally bound not to report on the story.

Some of my colleagues and I disagree about the suppression order that was put in place. My belief was that it was a contempt of court issue and necessary in order to preserve one of the most fundamental rights and in our democratic tradition—that a person, accused before a court, is presumed innocent. By suppressing the result of the first trial, the court accounted for unconscious bias, something which is out of a juror's control. But there has been little discussion about the significance of the decision for a foreign outlet to break an Australian suppression order.

Let's be frank—the *Daily Beast*'s decision and its consequences extended beyond the operational. It was more than just an outlet making a call about the right to know. The move was made with callous disregard for the Australian justice system. It was an intervention in our democracy by a foreign media outlet which considered that its interests were more important than the rights afforded in a sovereign nation's democracy. It appears that little to no consideration was given to the alleged victims or the accused, who also deserved the right to a fair trial of profoundly serious allegations.

Our international colleagues would be well-served to remember that the press are not participants in the judicial process. We are observers. The right to know goes hand-in-hand with the right to a fair trial but does not supersede it, a mistake our American neighbours made that day.

A Responsible Press Does Not Forget Its Role

There is no question that the justice system has changed dramatically over time, and particularly since 2020, and as such, so has court reporting. But what has not changed are the fundamental values of our craft, regardless of new technologies or tensions. The press must never lose sight of its role in the system. Our responsibility is, and always will be, to bear witness. We are observers to the justice system, there to scrutinise. Anything more is simply advocacy.

5

Prosecutions in the Summary Jurisdictions

Sophie Ellis and Marg Camilleri

Introduction

In some common law jurisdictions, such as New Zealand, in all six Australian states and the Northern Territory, and to a lesser extent the United Kingdom, police prosecutors are the primary prosecution agency in the summary jurisdictions. In Victoria, Australia, matters heard in the Magistrates' Court are characterised as less serious than matters heard in the County and Supreme courts. However, the increasing seriousness and complexity of matters heard in this jurisdiction would suggest it has moved from its original intent.

S. Ellis (✉)
VIC, Australia

M. Camilleri
Federation University Australia, Ballarat, VIC, Australia
e-mail: m.camilleri@federation.edu.au

M. Camilleri and A. Harkness (eds.), *Australian Courts*,
https://doi.org/10.1007/978-3-031-19063-6_5

The role of police prosecutions within the Magistrates' jurisdiction has been seldom scrutinised. However, an array of concerns exists with regard to the use of police prosecution:

- a lack of independence from investigative police
- the opaque nature of police prosecutor decision-making
- the potential for bias in favour of police informants and police victims
- the standards of and lack of uniformity in training requirements
- a lack of clear, accountable, public guidelines in relation to police prosecutors
- the high workloads of police prosecutors.

These issues may have real impacts upon court outcomes for the accused and victims alike, and upon the public's confidence in the administration of justice.

At a time when the summary jurisdiction is under pressure to hear an increasing number of complex matters and simultaneously ensure that the defendant receives a fair hearing, can we be confident that police prosecutors are well equipped to perform their role within an increasingly pressured and complex jurisdiction?

This chapter considers the questions raised in Australian and international literature and by legal experts about police led prosecutions. It supports calls in Australia and New Zealand for increased scrutiny of police prosecutors' role and consideration of an independent prosecutorial service for the summary jurisdiction.

Context: Prosecutor Practice Within the Victorian Magistrates' Court, an Increasingly Complex Summary Jurisdiction

Police prosecutors are responsible for the majority of summary prosecutions in Magistrates' Court and Children's Court or their equivalent across all Australian states and territories except in the Australian Capital

Territory (ACT) and at the federal level (where summary offences are prosecuted by the Commonwealth Director of Public Prosecutions) (Corns, 2014). Police prosecutors also prosecute Family Violence Intervention Order and Personal Safety Intervention Order proceedings and indictable matters heard summarily. In Victoria, police prosecutors are sworn Victoria Police members who prosecute charges initiated on behalf of the State and appear on behalf of police and Protective Service Officers (PSOs) pursuant to section 328 of the *Criminal Procedure Act 2009* (Vic).

A specialist prosecutorial department was established in 1981 within Victoria Police (Corns, 2000), which now sits within a broader Victoria Police legal services department (Victoria Police, 2019). Police prosecutors in Australia are not involved in investigating offences and are not engaged in 'operational' aspects of policing (Corns, 2014).

As a matter of practice and policy, Victorian police prosecutors do provide some advice to operational police; however, there is no publicly available information on the scope of police prosecutor involvement in the provision of advice to operational police/informants. For example, in 2017–2018, Victoria Police established a *Prosecutions Frontline Support Unit,* which, according to the Victoria Police Annual Report 2017–2018 (2018, p. 26), exists inter alia to provide "real-time prosecutions advice directly to police commanders operationally at high and extreme risk public order events. The unit has also worked with officers to improve the quality of briefs" and in "supporting police by providing advice and assistance in relation to offences against emergency workers" (which include police).

In contrast, indictable matters in Victoria are prosecuted by the Director of Public Prosecutions (DPP)—an independent office created in 1983 when responsibility for indictable prosecutions moved to an office independent of the executive arm of government. Commenting on the establishment of an independent DPP in Victoria, the first Director of Public Prosecutions (DPP, 2008, p. 10) stated that:

> Decisions to prosecute or not to prosecute in the superior courts must be made independently and be seen to be made independently… free from

> direction of any Minister of the Crown or any police office or… any alleged victim.

Similar offices are now established in all Australian state and territory jurisdictions. In Victoria, Office of Public Prosecutions (OPP) solicitors prosecute all indictable offences heard in the County or Supreme courts and carry out committal hearings at the Magistrates' Court. They can also conduct some summary prosecutions, for example in complex or public interest cases (DPP, 2022, p. 21, see rule 56). OPP "prosecutors represent the DPP, not the government, the police, the victim, or any other person" (DPP, 2022, p. 18).

Australia (with the exception of the ACT) and New Zealand are the only common law jurisdictions that still retain police prosecutors in the summary jurisdiction (Beck, 2006; Corns, 2000; McGonigle, 1996). The United Kingdom, which removed most summary prosecution functions from the police in 1985 (Corns, 2000; Devine, 1986), has in recent years moved back towards increasing involvement of police in the summary prosecution of a range of offences on the presumption that it will improve efficiency of the Courts (Ward, 2015). Matters prosecuted by police include (Ministry of Justice, 2012, p. 6):

> … low-level traffic offences… when there is no plea or the defendant fails to appear, avoiding unnecessary adjournments and the handing of cases over to the Crown Prosecution Service. [In addition to extending] this simpler, police-led, approach to a wider range of low-level offences.

Despite significant changes, including the increasing number and complexity of criminal matters heard before it (Magistrates' Court of Victoria, 2018–2019, p. 17)—some aggregated offences heard in the summary jurisdiction carry a potential maximum penalty of up to five years imprisonment (see *Sentencing Act 1991*(Vic) section 113B)—there is limited examination of the role and function of police prosecutors in the summary jurisdiction in Victoria. This includes within both academic literature and also annual reports of the Victorian Magistrates' Court examined from 2012 to 2022. Corns (2014, p. 224) argues that the retention of police in the summary jurisdictions is "the historical result of expediency rather than the considered policy decision of any legislature".

Changes in the Summary Jurisdiction

The Magistrates' Court of Victoria hears approximately 93% of all criminal matters that come before Victorian courts (Magistrates' Court of Victoria, 2021). The numbers of matters before the Magistrates' Court are also increasing, particularly in certain categories, including family violence matters. For example, between 2004 and 2014 the number of proceedings in the Magistrates' and Children's Courts relating to contraventions of intervention orders more than tripled (RCFV, 2016a, p. 21).

Additionally, the severity of sentences and ranges of offences that fall within the jurisdiction of the Magistrates' Court has increased. For example, in 2018 mandatory custodial sentences for a range of indictable offences that can be heard summarily were introduced, including intentionally or recklessly causing injury to an emergency worker, which include police and protective service officers (SACV, 2019). There is also an increasing number of people appearing in the Magistrates' Court without legal advice or representation (Victorian Government, 2016)—an observation Flynn (2016) also makes as occurring in the context of tightening restrictions to representation by Legal Aid.

Since the turn of the twenty-first century, there has been an evolution of specialist courts and court divisions and programmes within the Magistrates' Court in Victoria, providing alternative prosecution pathways to traditional summary justice models. Examples include the Drug Court (2001), Koori Court (2005), Mental Health Court/Assessment and Referral List (ARC) (2010) and Family Violence Court Divisions at Heidelberg to the north of Melbourne and the regional city of Ballarat to Melbourne's west (2005), and at Shepparton in the north of the State and the south-eastern Melbourne suburbs of Moorabbin and Frankston between 2019 and 2021. There has also been enactment of or reforms to significant pieces of legislation that has led to procedural and practice changes. Examples include the *Charter of Human Rights and Responsibilities Act 2006* (Vic), the *Victims Charter Act 2006* (Vic) and the introduction of uniform evidence law in Victoria in 2008.

Available literature indicates that the role of police prosecutors has evolved in response to these changes. For example, dedicated police prosecutors who have family violence training now work within the Family Violence Court Divisions. Across many Magistrates' courts in Victoria, there has also been the introduction of civil advocates (also known as police lawyers) who are unsworn employees of Victoria Police who have specialised training with respect to family violence (Statement by Cooney to the RCFV 2015). However, in general and particularly outside the family violence context, there is a paucity of literature that critically examines the role of police prosecutors in a changed and changing summary jurisdiction.

Issues and Controversies with Police-Led Prosecutions

Several areas of concern about police led prosecutions exist, which are set out below.

Professional Accountability and Regulation of Police Prosecutors

There is little publicly available information about how police prosecutors are regulated, including applicable professional standards, their conduct and accountability mechanisms. No public guidelines or policies exist that are singularly applicable to the police prosecutors' role. Rather, various internal policies and guidelines contained in the *Victoria Police Manual*, which is issued by the Chief Commissioner, provide some guidance on their role. In Victoria, the DPP can establish guidelines for police officers with respect to the prosecution of offences, under section 26(1)(b) of the *Public Prosecutions Act 1994* (Vic). However, only one guideline has ever been issued. Like all police officers, police prosecutors are ultimately accountable up the chain of police command to the Chief Commissioner; in contrast, OPP solicitors report directly to the DPP.

Police prosecutors are required to have completed at least two years as a probationary officer and a specialised 16-week Prosecutor Training Course. They may then elect to complete a two-year Graduate Certificate in Public Safety (Police Prosecutions) and/or a law degree (Victoria Police, 2019). In contrast, lawyers appearing in any jurisdiction, including OPP lawyers, must have a Bachelor of Laws (3 years) and graduate diploma in legal practice (typically 3–6 months in duration). There is no publicly available information on what percentage of police prosecutors have completed the graduate certificate, a law degree and/or a graduate diploma in legal practice.

OPP lawyers, like all Australian lawyers, become officers of the Court and swear or affirm to conduct themselves honestly in their profession in an admission ceremony which allows them to then practice law. OPP solicitors must also comply with national professional conduct rules applying to lawyers Australia wide (the *Legal Profession Uniform Law Australian Solicitors' Conduct Rules 2015*) ('Uniforms Conduct Rules'). The Uniform Conduct Rules set out ethical rules and legal responsibilities in relation to legal practice. For example, it is stipulated that lawyers have a paramount duty to the court and the administration of justice—a duty that prevails above all others (*Legal Profession Uniform Law Australian Solicitors' Conduct Rules 2015*, rule 3.1).

Compliance with the Uniform Rules is monitored by the Victorian Legal Services Board and Commissioner—an independent statutory agency tasked with regulating the legal profession pursuant to the *Legal Profession Uniform Law Application Act 2014* (Vic) and to which members of the public can make complaints. OPP solicitors also report directly to the DPP and are required to comply with the *Policy of the Director of Public Prosecutions for Victoria*—publicly available guidelines that provide standards for how prosecutorial decisions are made (DPP Guidelines). Totalling 26 pages, the DPP Guidelines cover decisions to prosecute and general obligations in relation to their role. These include, for example, requirements to act independently and impartially; to act fairly to an accused; not to make any submissions of fact or law which are not soundly based; to endeavour to ensure that criminal proceedings are completed expeditiously; and avoid any real or potential conflict of interest (OPP, 2022).

As a result of two different regulatory frameworks, police prosecutors and OPP solicitors face vastly different accountability mechanisms in relation to complaints by members of the public, the judiciary and others about their professional conduct. In Victoria, complaints about police prosecutor conduct are managed internally or by the Independent Broad-Based Anti-Corruption Commission (IBAC). There is no public disclosure or reporting of misconduct that occurs by police prosecutors. However, the Victorian Legal Services Board and Commissioner keeps a searchable, public record of disciplinary action against lawyers (Victorian Legal Services Board & Commissioner, 2020).

The DPP, OPP solicitors and police prosecutors share some accountability mechanisms by virtue of being public authorities under the *Charter of Human Rights and Responsibilities Act 2006* (Vic). They are also both bound by the *Victims Charter Act 2006* (Vic). Although "the general principle in Australia is that discretionary prosecutorial decisions are not susceptible to judicial review" (Corns, 2014, p. 479), there are other ways the judiciary can provide oversight of both OPP and police prosecutors' conduct including utilising powers to stay proceedings, acquit an accused when there is no case to answer, and to make cost orders against the prosecutor when a case has been prosecuted improperly (Corns, 2014).

How such mechanisms are used in practice against both OPP and police prosecutors (and the extent to which any variables exist in the use of these judicial mechanism of review in relation to OPP versus police prosecutors) are out of the scope of this chapter. In practice, however, it is conceivable that variables would exist. For example, cost order applications are made by representatives of the successful party to a proceeding. Given the increasing number of unrepresented parties in the summary jurisdiction in the context of restricted Legal Aid eligibility guidelines, it is probable that utilisation of this accountability mechanisms in the summary prosecution context is more limited.

Police Prosecutor Discretion and Decision-Making

Decisions made by police prosecutors include whether to proceed with prosecution, appeal a sentencing decision, or support bail and which witnesses/evidence to call. These decisions have systemic and individual impacts. Corns (2014, pp. 5–6) refers to three spheres of direct or indirect impact of prosecutorial decisions (generally, including police prosecutors):

i. upon individuals (accused, victims, witnesses, police investigators and so on)—what he calls the "human" or "social dimension of public prosecutions"
ii. upon the "efficient and effective administration of justice"
iii. the political impact, noting that who is ultimately tried for crimes affects the "relationship between the citizen and the State and specifically concerns the legitimate boundaries of public power".

In relation to the third sphere, Corns (2014, p. 5) argues that "because of the enormous seriousness and significance of many prosecution decisions, there needs to be very clear justifications and criteria for the exercise of prosecution powers", particularly to ensure confidence in the administration of justice for both victims and accused.

In making decisions, police prosecutors have broad discretion, but that discretion must be made according to law. Clark (2014) identifies the space of police discretion as being bounded not only by legal constraints, but also by institutional and sociological constraints (Clark, 2014). Examples of institutional constraints on police prosecutors' discretion may include internal policy guidelines and instructions and external complaint bodies (such as IBAC). Examples of sociological constraints may include police culture and practice and the culture of the Magistrates' Court.

Much of the literature on the constraints around police discretion concern operational policing, considering for example discretional choices about whether to investigate a crime, how police choose to deploy resources and whether to make an arrest and lay charges (Clark, 2014; Worden & McLean, 2014). Again, though, there is scant literature focusing on the operation of police discretion in the specific context of police prosecutors' decision-making. There are some evident constraints relevant to prosecutors' decisions (e.g. the operation of the law). Clark also identifies internal guidelines as being another tool for guiding the use of police discretion.

As discussed above, a key issue in Victoria is the lack a singular internal guideline *or* publicly available policy that can provide accountability on the particular and unique role of *police prosecutors* and the principles guiding their decision-making. Furthermore, the *Victoria Police Manual* is only available electronically by subscription, with free public access only obtainable through the State Library of Victoria in hard copy. This serves to limit public accountability of police prosecutors and contrasts with information about OPP solicitors' role, regulation, professional standards and conduct (and that of the DPP), which is accessible to the public, for free via the DPP and Legal Services Board websites.

The culture, context and parameters of the Magistrates' Court's jurisdiction can also play a role in affecting the use of police prosecutor discretion. For example, the Magistrates' Court processes the majority of cases within the court system, and therefore, there is a focus on expedient processing (Corns, 2014). In the summary jurisdictions, Krone (2002, p. 82) describes the 'culture of triviality' which may impact on police prosecutors, defined as a systemic public and institutional perception that matters in the summary jurisdiction are more trivial in nature than those matters heard in the higher courts. Krone (2002, p. 82) suggests this culture means "the functions of the [summary courts] are not sufficiently important to demand many of the 'due process' attributes of the trial courts" and suggests the people in the system are accorded less importance. Another factor that may impact upon the police prosecutor decision-making is the sheer volume of work owing to increased funnelling of people into the summary jurisdiction over time as police officers have increased in number along with the types of offences people are able to be charged with.

There is also minimal judicial review of police prosecutor decision to prosecute (Clark, 2014). This reluctance to judicially review decisions to prosecute comes from case law, which dictates that the judiciary needs to be impartial and separate from the executive arm of the State which carries out prosecutorial functions and that the judiciary does not have the experience or knowledge that the police have to hand when making decisions to prosecute (Corns, 2014). However, putting aside the reasons for this general principle *not* to interfere with decisions to prosecute, the how the general *lack* of review may impact upon police prosecutorial culture and decision-making does not appear to have been examined.

Need for Independence

Police prosecutors and police informants—who decide to lay the charges and investigate an alleged crime—are employees of Victoria Police. The informant collates the brief of evidence and may have been a direct witness to an offence (e.g. they may have witnessed an accused driving in contravention of the road rules). They may also be a witness for the prosecution and provide evidence against an accused in Court. Police prosecutors, who represent the informant, belong to the same chain of command (Krone, 2002). Corns (2014, p. 227) argues that as a result, "they share the same formal organisational values and beliefs, as well as the more informal police 'culture'". A survey of 130 police prosecutors conducted by The Police Association of Victoria (TPAV) (2017, p. 52) emphasised the closeness of this relationship and the benefits, as seen by the TPAV, of coming from the same organisation. A police prosecutor of 20 years standing reflected that:

> We all wear the same uniform, we all empathise with the members and we do try to get the best outcomes, because there's no distinction between us, we're all the same. Police prosecutors are integral to the success of police prosecutions.

Corns (2014) argues that this close relationship raises issues of conflict of interest. One conflict which is most evident is when a police prosecutor is confronted by a brief that alleges offences against an emergency worker, and that worker is the informant or other police officer. Another example is where the prosecutor is junior in rank to the police informant, posing a risk that the prosecutor may not bring an impartial mind in exercising their role due to imbalance of power. Ultimately, Corns (2014, p. 5) is of the view that "an independent prosecution system is a necessary component of a free and democratic society and a part of the rule of law", a view that is based on common law principles of prosecutorial independence and impartiality.

Nicholas Cowdery (2010, p. 17), a former Director of Public Prosecutions in New South Wales, has publicly stated that it is:

> … inappropriate to have the principal investigators, the police, conducting prosecutions. While the proven instances of inappropriate conduct in the present system have been very few, public acceptance of the prosecution process is enhanced by having an independent prosecutor in all cases, one who is an officer of the court and not subject to the same hierarchical regime as the investigators.

In a seminal review of the history of summary police prosecutions in Australia, Corns (2000) summarises issues that have been identified in other common law and Australian jurisdictions with locating police in the prosecutorial arm and uses this to argue that all Australian jurisdictions should transition summary prosecutions into the office of the DPP. Calls for an independent body (in the form of the DPP) to prosecute summary crimes have been made periodically in most Australian states and territories (Corns, 2014; Krone, 2002). Most have arisen in the context of recommendations by commissions of inquiry that did not directly list police prosecutors in their terms of reference or have been direct calls made by DPPs or other public figures.

It is difficult to measure the extent to which lack of organisational independence may impact upon prosecutorial decision-making, because of the lack of reporting/data on complaints made against police prosecutors either formally or within the context of the courts. However, notwithstanding difficulties in substantiating real impacts of prosecutorial conflicts of interest, the perception of bias or a lack of independence can harm public trust in the summary courts and procedures (Corns, 2014). The concern is that police may favour fellow police investigators rather than acting impartially. This is particularly acute when police are the victim of crime, the investigator and then the prosecutor of that crime. It is questionable that concerns regarding bias/conflict of interest could be mitigated if prosecutors were trained to manage bias: training does not resolve the issue of conflict. Another safeguard is provisions that give the DPP discretion to take over summary prosecutions when there is an actual or perceived conflict of interest in the police conducting the prosecution, but there is no public information on how often this occurs and how the decision to engage this discretion works in practice.

Police Prosecutor Decision-Making is Opaque

Corns (2014) identifies the lack of 'checks and balances' governing police prosecutor decision-making as being an issue of concern noting, specifically, that there is greater public accountability when it comes to the application of prosecutorial discretion with respect to the DPP.

One example of the opaque nature of the use of police prosecutor discretion is the summary criminal justice diversion program. Diversion—typically open to first-time offenders—allows an accused to avoid a criminal record by completing certain activities on a diversion plan (e.g. counselling/treatment, an apology to the victim and taking responsibility for the offence). If the diversion plan is followed, the charges will be dismissed. However, police prosecutors act as gatekeepers for diversion (Flynn, 2016) and must consent to diversion under section 59 of the *Criminal Procedure Act 2009* (Vic) before a Magistrate or judicial registrar can grant diversion. Flynn (2016, p. 576) argues that:

> Like plea-negotiations, this means there is the potential for a lack of consistency, oversight and understanding of decisions, and it can disadvantage some defendants, particularly those who cannot afford a lawyer who could initially approach the police to discuss this option.

Another example is prosecutorial decisions made during plea negotiations. Plea negotiations are conducted between prosecutors and an accused (or their defence lawyer) in both summary and indictable jurisdictions. This can result in alterations to agreed statements of fact, withdrawal of charges or variation of charges—all which have impacts on sentencing. The *Victoria Police Manual on Court Processes* provides police prosecutors with authority to conduct negotiations with the defence and specifies that in plea negotiations they are authorised to withdraw substantive and alternative charges.

According to Flynn (2016, p. 1), prosecutorial discretionary decisions made in plea negotiations, which can have significant implications for accused and victims alike "operate essentially free from external scrutiny or transparency". In Australia there are no official data on when plea negotiations occur or their outcomes and, in most jurisdictions, plea negotiations are not legislatively defined (Flynn, 2016). They occur outside the courtroom and therefore do not have the same judicial or public scrutiny when a matter comes before a magistrate for mention or contest.

Flynn (2016) conducted observations of plea negotiations carried out in Victoria in 2007 and interviewed legal professionals between 2007 and 2013. Flynn's research is focused on plea negotiations in indictable matters conducted by DPP prosecutors, rather than plea negotiations conducted by police prosecutors in the Magistrates' Court. Nevertheless, Flynn's research provides useful insights into one aspect of prosecutorial decision-making that can be applied to summary jurisdiction. Ultimately, Flynn (2016, p. 566) argues that greater transparency is needed with respect to plea negotiations, particularly:

> … in light of shifts towards more punitive policies that restrict judicial discretion, whilst simultaneously enhancing prosecutors' discretionary charging powers; a concern intensified by the efficiency pressures prosecutors face to swiftly obtain convictions and reduce court backlog. Increased transparency and public understanding of plea-negotiations are also vital given ongoing restrictions to government-funded legal services, which have resulted in high numbers of defendants being left to navigate complex legal processes alone

The lack of transparency regarding prosecutorial decision-making can have a flow on impact, as unfairness to the accused as a result of inconsistency in how discretion is used. This risk has been mitigated by guidelines; however, these are for the most part, not publicly available and light on detail. An example is the *Summary Case Conference Service Charter*.

High Workloads

The lack of resourcing of police prosecutors has been identified as an issue by the Magistrates' Court (Annual Reports, 2015–2016; 2011–2012). In 2015–2016, the Victoria Police Prosecutions Division prosecuted 255,572 criminal matters at 51 different court locations.

As a strong advocate for uniform police, The Police Association of Victoria have highlighted the high workloads of police prosecutors. In a survey of 130 police prosecutors conducted in 2017, approximately "90 percent of police prosecutors surveyed stated they currently work either paid or unpaid overtime to manage their case load" (TAPV, 2017, p. 53). High workloads of police prosecutors are also a cause for concern in other jurisdictions (Beck, 2006).

Challenges to Change

A former Chief Magistrate of Victoria, Ian Gray, called for a review of the use of police prosecutors in the summary jurisdiction, raising concerns about police prosecutorial standards and independence from operational police. Gray (cited in Farouque, 2012) stated that an:

> … 'obvious problem' was that such prosecutors were not genuinely independent from fellow police who investigated the same cases… with crime becoming more complex and the need for a very, very high level of prosecution capability, sophistication, training and expertise – those police are not resourced or trained adequately in the end to deliver to the court.

Despite the concerns raised by the former Chief Magistrate Gray and former New South Wales DPP (Cowdery, 2010), to date there is yet to be a review of police led prosecutions. This lack of scrutiny appears the greatest challenge to achieving change.

This hesitancy to inquire further is also evident at the level of union representation of police and PSOs (including police prosecutors) in Victoria. The police prosecutors survey by TPAV (2017) supports the retention of police as prosecutors in the summary jurisdiction. The survey of 130 police prosecutors suggests that "[a]lmost 60 percent believe there is scope for expanding the role of police prosecutors, with 34 percent believing there exists potential for police prosecutors to operate in the higher courts" (TPAV, 2017, p. 53). Further, "almost all" of the survey participants indicated an inextricable link between their previous role as operational police officers and their current police prosecutor role, describing the experience as "invaluable when dealing with criminal matters, with some adding that intimate knowledge of police procedures helped to foster increased understanding, trust and bonds with the informant in criminal matters" (TPAV, 2017, p. 54).

At a broader level, the lack of appetite to consider opportunities for reform is also apparent at a political level. For example, the 'Inquiry into Victoria's Criminal Justice System' by the Legislative Council's Legal and Social Issues Committee does not include the role of police led prosecutions in the terms of reference (Parliament of Victoria, 2021); nor does the current government review into Victoria's police oversight system (Engage Victoria, 2022).

Change

Key issues associated with police acting in prosecutorial roles in the summary jurisdiction include transparency; efficacy; training; the increasing complexity of cases heard in the summary jurisdiction; and, critically, the lack of prosecutorial independence from police chain of command. Common law countries have overwhelmingly moved to centralising summary prosecutions within an independent DPP type office, as is the case in the ACT.

Given the sheer volume of matters heard summarily and the seriousness of some of these matters, the impact on the accused can be significant and with lifelong implications. While the work by McGonigle (1996) may be dated from a chronological perspective, his sentiments about the implications of decisions in the summary jurisdiction are no less applicable today. McGonigle (1996, p. 54) states that:

> The decision to prosecute, especially in the summary jurisdiction, is a fundamentally important one, affecting thousands of citizens each year. It should be a decision made by a competent public body, with reasons clearly set out, and subject to review.

Corns (2014, pp. 37–39) evaluates public prosecutions systems/agencies in Australia (more broadly) against certain evaluative criteria that have been recognised by the law as being indicative of and critical to a properly functioning criminal justice system, namely: independence; fairness; equality; consistency; accountability and openness. These serve as useful measures by which to review the critical role of police led prosecutions in summary justice outcomes.

Conclusion

Further research would provide a better empirical understanding of police prosecutors' current role, provide greater transparency to the public and allow for greater consideration of reform options to make summary outcomes more just. There exists scant academic work on the role and function of police prosecutors in Victorian summary justice, despite the implications it has on the lives of individuals (both victims and respondents) engaged in the criminal justice system. Finally, the potential implications of the issues raised in this chapter and previous research highlight the need to consider prosecutions in the summary jurisdictions more closely, through a parliamentary inquiry.

References

Beck, S. (2006). Under investigation: A review of police prosecutions in New Zealand's summary jurisdiction. *Auckland University Law Review, 12*(2006), 150–189.

Children's Court of Victoria. (2015, July 13). *Magistrates' Court of Victoria and Children's Court of Victoria Joint Submission to the Royal Commission into*

Family Violence. https://www.childrenscourt.vic.gov.au/magistrates-court-victoria-and-childrens-court-victoria-joint-submission-royal-commission-family

Clark, D. (2014). Filling in the doughnut? Police operational discretion and the law in Australia. *Oxford University Commonwealth Law Journal, 14*(2), 195–224.

Corns, C. (2000). Police summary prosecutions in Australia and New Zealand: Some comparisons [A draft of this article formed the basis of a paper given at the History of Crime Policing and Punishment Conference (1999, Canberra)]. *University of Tasmania Law Review, 19*(2), 280–310.

Corns, C. (2014). *Public prosecutions in Australia: Law, policy and practice*. NSW, Thomas Reuters (Professional) Australia.

Cowdery, N. (2010, November 6). *The rule of law and director of public prosecutions*. Paper presented at the Rule of Law in Australia Conference. https://www.ruleoflaw.org.au/wp-content/uploads/2012/12/RoLIA-Conference-2010-Paper-Cowdery1.pdf

Devine, F. E. (1986). The end of police prosecutions: Symptoms of changing values in English criminal justice. *Journal of Police and Criminal Psychology, 2*, 44–51.

DPP (Director of Public Prosecutions). (n.d.). *The pursuit of justice: 25 years of the DPP in Victoria*. http://www.opp.vic.gov.au/getattachment/ce33b347-34e9-4711-9ee8-553360566636/dpp25th_book-29oct08.aspx

DPP (Office of the Director of Public Prosecutions). (2022). *Policy of the Director of Public Prosecutions for Victoria*. https://www.opp.vic.gov.au/Resources/Policy-of-the-Director-of-Public-Prosecutions-for-/Policy-of-the-Director-of-Public-Prosecutions-for

Engage Victoria. (2022). *Systematic review of police oversight*. State Government of Victoria. https://engage.vic.gov.au/systemic-review-police-oversight

Farouque, F. (2012, 28 May). Police prosecuting duties queried. *The Age*. https://www.theage.com.au/national/victoria/police-prosecuting-duties-queried-20120527-1zd5w.html

Flynn, A. (2016). Plea-negotiations, prosecutors and discretion: An argument for legal reform. *Australian and New Zealand Journal of Criminology, 49*(4), 564–582.

Judicial College of Victoria. (2018). *Victorian sentencing manual*. https://www.judicialcollege.vic.edu.au/eManuals/VSM/63023.htm

Krone, T. (2002). *Fairness and efficiency in summary prosecutions: The independent prosecutor's dilemma in a 'law and order' environment*. Doctoral Thesis,

University of New South Wales, Sydney. http://www5.austlii.edu.au/au/journals/UNSWLawTD/2002/1.pdf

Magistrates' Court of Victoria. (2019). *Annual report 2018–2019*. Magistrates Court of Victoria. https://www.mcv.vic.gov.au/sites/default/files/2019-11/Annual_Report_18-19.pdf

McGonigle, S. (1996). Public accountability for police prosecutions. *Auckland University Law Review, 8*(1), 163–183.

Ministry of Justice. (2012). *Swift and sure justice: The Government's plans for reform of the criminal justice system.* Ministry of Justice. Retrieved from https://assets.publishing.service.gov.uk/government/uploads/system/uploads/attachment_data/file/217328/swift-and-sure-justice.pdf

Parliament of Victoria. (2021). *Terms of reference for the Legislative Council Legal and Social Issues Committee's Inquiry into Victoria's Criminal Justice System.* https://www.parliament.vic.gov.au/lsic-lc/inquiries/article/4531

Royal Commission into Family Violence. (2016a, March). *Magistrates' Court of Victoria and Children's Court of Victoria Joint Submission to the Royal Commission into Family Violence.* https://www.childrenscourt.vic.gov.au/magistrates-court-victoria-and-childrens-court-victoria-joint-submission-royal-commission-family

Royal Commission into Family Violence. (2016b, March). *Report of the Royal Commission into Family Violence, Report and Recommendations* (Vol. III). Victorian Government.

Royal Commission into Family Violence. (2016c, March). *Victorian Government Statement of Alice Katherine Cooney*. http://www.rcfv.com.au/MediaLibraries/RCFamilyViolence/Statements/WIT-3025-001-0001_R-Cooney-12.pdf

SACV (Sentencing Advisory Council of Victoria). (2019). *Imprisonment.* https://www.sentencingcouncil.vic.gov.au/about-sentencing/imprisonment

TPAV (The Police Association of Victoria. (2017). Dealing with criminal minds—The need to keep police prosecutors. *The Police Association (Victoria) Journal, 84*(4), 52–54. https://www.tpav.org.au/files/02_Communications/04_Media/01_Journals/2017/04_August/TPAV_JOURNAL_AUGUST_2017_FINAL_eVersion_Spreads.pdf

Victoria Police. (2011–2020). *Annual reports 2010–11; 2013–14; 2014–15; 2017–18; 2018–19.* https://www.police.vic.gov.au/annual-report

Victoria Police (2022). *Roles and duties of police officers.* https://www.police.vic.gov.au/police-about-role

Victoria State Government. (August 2016). *Access to Justice Review.* Volume One Report and Recommendations State Government. https://s3.ap-southeast-2.amazonaws.com/hdp.au.prod.app.vic-engage.files/3314/8601/7221/Access_to_Justice_Review_-_Report_and_recommendations_Volume_1.PDF
Victorian Government Gazette. (2011, 15 December). No. G 50. http://www.gazette.vic.gov.au/gazette/Gazettes2011/GG2011G050.pdf#page=10
Victorian Legal Services Board and Commissioner. (2020). *Register of lawyers and disciplinary action.* https://www.lsbc.vic.gov.au/consumers/registers
Ward, J. (2015). Transforming 'summary justice' through police-led prosecution and 'virtual courts.' *British Journal of Criminology, 55*(2), 341–358.
Worden, R. E., & McLean, S. J. (2014). Police discretion in law enforcement. In G Bruinsma & D. Weisburd, D. (Eds.), *Encyclopedia of criminology and criminal justice.* Springer.
Yang, K. (2013). Public accountability of public prosecutions. *Murdoch University Electronic Journal of Law, 20*(1), 28–75.

Legislation and Regulations

Charter of Human Rights and Responsibilities Act 2006 (Vic).
Criminal Procedure Act 2009 (Vic) S. 328.
Legal Profession Uniform Law Australian Solicitors' Conduct Rules 2015, rule 3.1.
Public Prosecutions Act 1994 (Vic). s. 26(1)(b).
Victims Charter Act 2006 (Vic).
Victoria Police Code of Practice for the Investigation of Family Violence (3rd Edition, V4, 2019).
Victoria Police Manual Court Processes (as at 29 October 2019), p. 17.
Victoria Police Manual Procedures and Guideline Brief Preparation and Management (as at 29 October 2019).
Victoria Police Manual Procedures and Guideline Disposition of Offenders (as at 29 October 2019).
Victoria Police Manual Policy Rules Briefs of Evidence (as at 29 October 2019).
Victoria Police Manual Policy Rules Disposition of Offenders (as at 29 October 2019).
Victoria Police Act 2013 (Vic).

Practitioner Perspective: Police-Led Prosecutions in the Magistrates' Court

Sophie Ellis

Police prosecutors wield incredible power in the summary jurisdiction. In busy courtrooms that can see lists of over 50 people a day, such as across the Magistrates' Court in Victoria, prosecutors make time-critical and often complex decisions, which in turn play out in the lives of both accused and victims. These decisions include:

- determining whether or not there is sufficient evidence for charges to proceed
- making submissions to the court on appropriate penalties
- determining whether to oppose or support diversionary outcomes in both Children's and Magistrates' Courts
- determining whether or not to oppose applications for bail, or support an informant's application to revoke bail and making submissions on what conditions ought to be attached to any undertaking of bail
- making submissions on what conditions are needed with respect to family violence intervention order (FVIO) applications
- making applications for victim restitution
- making applications for forensic procedures on an accused
- determining which evidence should be called and what witnesses should be examined.

Police prosecutors' actions also influence how quickly matters are resolved; for example, whether charges are thoroughly case conferenced and if and at what stage charges are withdrawn.

Although they operate in what are often seen as 'less serious' court matters, decisions by police prosecutors will have repercussions for a person's entire life. Exercised with due skill and care, the discretion a police prosecutor applies in summary courts can have a positive impact.

S. Ellis
VIC, Australia

For example, a police prosecutor well versed in the specific jurisdiction of the Children's Court will understand the rehabilitative principles of the jurisdiction and assist the court in achieving efficient and rehabilitative dispositions early that limit unnecessary appearances of children in the courtroom and thus their exposure to the criminal justice system.

This is particularly important: acknowledging the impact of court on a child's daily life, including on schooling; and that many children in the criminal justice system are, themselves, victims of crime and have experienced trauma including removal from their families due to exposure to family violence, abuse and/or neglect.

Conversely, a police prosecutor who is not trained in the jurisdiction of the Children's Court may adjourn matters unnecessarily even where the appropriate disposition is clear—for example, a withdrawal because the child is under the presumed age of criminal responsibility, or a diversion because the offending is minor and the child has no prior criminal history.

There are four key factors which may compromise a police prosecutors' ability to carry out their role with due care and skill which diminishes public trust in the criminal justice system.

First, police prosecutors commonly have enormous workloads and often do not see a brief of evidence until the morning of court. If it is adjourned, then the next time the matter comes to court another prosecutor can be on duty, hampering the resolution of matters efficiently and fairly for accused and victims alike. Police prosecutors are also often faced with insufficient information to resolve or progress matters, for example, about the background of a matter.

Second, police prosecutors are frequently required to appear in many 'hearing/court lists' within the summary court and are expected to prosecute across multiple jurisdictions, which each require expertise across procedure and law (e.g. the Children's Court, Family Violence Specialist Courts, general Magistrate Court criminal division lists and bail lists to name just some).

Third, police prosecutors are not always trained to the level of lawyers, with police able to prosecute without law degrees.

Fourth, they are part of the same chain of command as their police informant colleagues. This can be an issue when they are junior to their 'informant' colleagues and feel the need to seek feedback from their informant, for example on whether diversion should be granted rather than acting independently and authoritatively on the matter. This slows the resolution of matters down in already overloaded courts and clouds their independence.

Resourcing and standardisation of training can overcome these difficulties.

Certainly, the adoption of specialist civilian prosecutions teams in recent years has the potential to address some of these concerns. This has occurred in Victoria, where unsworn employees of Victoria Police that are legally trained (with a law degree and have been admitted to legal practice) prosecute in one jurisdiction only—for example, the Drug Courts, Koori Courts or Specialist Family Violence Courts. This approach allows for better-trained prosecutors that understand their specific jurisdiction.

Employing external lawyers as police prosecutors also means police prosecutors have uniformity of training and are bound by the same conduct rules as defence lawyers. For example, specialist police prosecutors in the Children's Court have a deeper understanding of, and experience in, the distinct legal principals pertaining to that jurisdiction (such as the presumption of *doli incapax*—being that children between 10 and 13 are presumed incapable of forming a criminal mind because they are not sufficiently intellectually and morally developed to appreciate right and wrong (RP v The Queen [2016] HCA 53 [8]) and similarly, prosecutors in the specialist family violence courts are especially trained in family violence and distinct principles applicable to that jurisdiction. It could be argued that the adoption of these specialist prosecutors from *outside* the force is an acknowledgement that things need to change.

However, the fundamental issue remains that police prosecutors are still an apparatus of the police organisation. They are employed by the same institution that polices, investigates, compiles the evidence and ultimately prosecutes. They are part of the same chain of command. They are also part of the same institution that might over-police Indigenous communities, resulting in significant over-representation of Indigenous men, women and children in police cells and prisons. All of this has ramifications for the justice system.

The fundamental conflict of interest that police prosecutors have is one I have observed play out in the courtroom. For example, when summary case conferencing, I have observed police prosecutors' apparent reluctance to make decisions and deferral of decision-making, to consult the informant (e.g. on whether or not to revoke a police order or whether to seek diversion). This is not surprising given they are appearing on the informant's behalf, but it nevertheless remains a conflict that is inimical to justice being served.

Clients are also keenly perceptive to this conflict. For example, I have had clients who have been alleged to have assaulted police, but have denied this and have instead instructed that they were the victim of police misconduct. What confidence does my client have of their allegation being responded to appropriately when I put my instructions to the police prosecutor—a fellow police officer and colleague of the informant—that the prosecutor will be able to bring an impartial mind, knowing they will be returning to the same office at the end of the court day?

Civilian (unsworn) police prosecutors who are legally trained and employed by policing agencies do not resolve this issue. For example, my own direct experience has included a police prosecutor seeking an informant's input on a proposed resolution where misconduct by police is alleged.

Ultimately, we do not have insight into those internal discussions and what, if any, pressures police prosecutors (be they sworn or unsworn) may be under. What is clear is that from the outside looking in, from a client perspective, claims that they are acting 'impartially' are not sufficient to address what is an inherent conflict. Furthermore, because of the lack of independent oversight of police (including prosecutors), there is little way to raise concerns regarding police prosecutor conduct or decision-making, particularly for unrepresented accused person.

Police prosecutors have a very difficult role in an extremely busy and stressful jurisdiction. I have seen many examples of police prosecutors acting with integrity and professionalism. However, the systemic issues outlined above nevertheless influence outcomes in our courts.

Even if resourcing could be addressed, the conflict issue remains unresolved. In one case in which I was involved, a police prosecutor withdrew all charges, promptly, after observing and agreeing that the informant had mis-identified the accused (who was actually the family violence victim) and had not followed police guidelines in responding to the incident. However, this took numerous mentions before the outcome was achieved and the police prosecutor had sufficient time to view the material and respond. There was no transparency about how that decision was made and if there was disagreement about the way forward or concerning the evidence between the police prosecutor and the informant.

Ultimately, the reality of conflict, in and of itself, is enough for the legislature to examine alternative options for police prosecuting in the summary jurisdiction. This is especially so when they wield such great influence and in the context of police discretion being very difficult to challenge (just as operational policing discretion is difficult to challenge).

One approach could be to have an independent process for the laying of charges in the summary jurisdiction as much time is wasted in summary system for briefs that should never have been filed due to want of admissible evidence. This comes at a cost: for individuals; for society (unnecessary criminalisation and stigma being attached to accused persons); for victims; and the financial cost to society and the cost of not prioritising matters that really count. However, independent prosecutors are probably a more holistic approach to ensuring independence and confidence and efficiency in our courts of summary jurisdiction.

Case

RP v The Queen [2016] HCA 53 [8].

6

Bail Decisions: Key Challenges Driving Bail Refusal

Emma Colvin

Introduction

The decision to grant or deny bail—the conditional release from custody of a person arrested and charged with a criminal offence—is one that is not made lightly. Multiple considerations, including community safety, victim needs, the integrity of the forthcoming trial, and the potential of the accused absconding prior to hearing must be considered to the satisfaction of the decision-maker, who can be a police officer, a magistrate or a bail justice. For the most part, such decisions go unnoticed by the public unless in instances where further offences are committed. The change of focus on bail decisions from why bail should be granted, rather than why it should not, has caused concern in regard to the issues surrounding the presumption of bail and how bail is addressed across the state and territory jurisdictions. In particular, who are disadvantaged in

E. Colvin (✉)
Charles Sturt University, Bathurst, NSW, Australia
e-mail: ecolvin@csu.edu.au

M. Camilleri and A. Harkness (eds.), *Australian Courts*,
https://doi.org/10.1007/978-3-031-19063-6_6

these decisions and the subsequent flow on effect of prison overcrowding are vitally important considerations (Bartels et al., 2018; Travers et al., 2020a, 2020b).

This chapter will contextualise these issues, commencing with a brief background on how bail operates in Australian jurisdictions. It will then identify some key challenges and controversies in contemporary bail decision-making, such as rising remand rates, particularly for Indigenous women, and consider how a lack of suitable accommodation options is resulting in bail denial, particularly for young people. The chapter concludes by offering some thoughts on pathways for change.

Bail in Context

What Is Bail?

After a person has been charged with an offence, they may just be issued a summons to appear at court on a certain date, done through a document such as a Court Attendance Notice (CAN). However, police may also release a person on bail, which means the charged person makes a promise to appear at court. Sometimes this promise is secured through the use of a surety, where the charged person agrees to pay a sum of money if they do not meet their court date. Sureties are not commonly used in Australian jurisdictions anymore, but some places—such as in the United States—use them frequently (Steel, 2009).

Sometimes the police may impose certain conditions on a person when they are bailed. These conditions can range from surrendering a passport, agreeing to report regularly to a police station, obeying a curfew or promising not to contact witnesses or co-accused. Increasingly, conditions of a 'therapeutic' nature are imposed, such as attending psychologist appointments or completing a drug treatment programme. Some people may have multiple conditions attached to their bail, some of which can be quite onerous. In some instances, it may be decided that a person cannot be granted bail, instead they wait their court date in prison, this is called remand imprisonment.

Why Do We Have Bail?

Bail was essentially created to ensure that a person charged with an offence will appear at court. Those who were deemed a flight risk—that is, likely to flee and not appear to answer their charges—had bail denied and were held in custody to ensure they went to court. Over time the reasons a person might be denied bail have broadened to include the risk of further (alleged) offending, interfering with witnesses or evidence and protection of the defendant. Bail decisions represent a complex balancing act between upholding key principles to the legal system, such as the presumption of innocence and only using imprisonment as a last resort, while ensuring the integrity of the legal system and safety of the community.

How Is Bail Decided?

Actors in the criminal justice process who make bail decision include police officers, generally more senior experienced officers are able to make this decision; for example, a senior sergeant in Victoria (Coghlan, 2017). However, police do not have the authority to remand a person per se: they can, though, deny bail and detain a person until a magistrate decides to refuse bail. In Victoria, a bail justice can perform an out of hours decisions-making hearing, usually at the police station and they have power to remand people for short periods of time, after which a magistrate must hear an application (Colvin, 2017).

Bail can be decided or applied for at several stages of the criminal justice process. At the time a person is charged, police may decide whether to release a person on summons and a court attendance notice can be issued; or, a decision can be made as to whether the charges or circumstance warrant consideration of bail. If a person is denied bail or wishes to contest the conditions under which their bail has been granted, they can make an application. In the first instance, this may be done at a police station with the charged person's legal representation. If the police deny bail, their decision must be reviewed. This means the charged person remains in custody until the next opportunity for them to be brought before a court.

Once the charged person appears before the court, or in Victoria when a bail justice attends, they can apply for bail. Generally, duty solicitors attend the court cells every morning to see who has been remanded and work out options for applying for bail. If bail is denied, a change of circumstances, for example, more serious charges being dropped or access to accommodation has been found, a new application for bail may be made. Increasingly, legislative reforms have restricted the number of times a person can apply for bail (see, e.g. the *Bail Act*, 1977 (Vic)).

To ensure individual human rights are upheld during the criminal justice process, Australian jurisdictions have a general presumption for bail. This means that the default position of a decision-maker is that the person should be bailed unless an argument is made to the contrary. Bail legislation governs how these decisions are made and what factors should be considered in the decisions. For certain serious offences or circumstances, the presumption of bail can be reversed, placing the onus on the defence to show why bail should be granted. This is known as a reverse onus. Since the turn of the twenty-first century, law reform has resulted in a gradual rolling back of the presumption for bail as more and more offences are exempted from the presumption (Bartels et al., 2018; Steel, 2009; Travers et al., 2020a, 2020b).

Legislation in each jurisdiction provides the parameters for bail decision-makers. In some jurisdictions, legal tests are applied when bail is considered. This can include whether or not a person is in a 'show cause' position. This relates to the reverse onus situation, where the defence must show cause to justify why bail should be considered or demonstrate 'exceptional circumstances' to justify why bail should be granted (Bartels et al., 2018). Generally, there is some sort of threshold test that the decision-maker must consider, the threshold provided in legislation is 'unacceptable risk'. This means the decision-maker must consider whether there is an unacceptable level of risk that the charged person is, for example, a flight risk or a risk of committing further offences if released on bail. In New South Wales, a decision-maker must consider four elements and if the charged person is deemed an unacceptable risk in any of these elements, bail can be denied. These four concerns are:

(i) risk of not attending court; (ii) risk of committing serious offences; (iii) endangering people or the community; and (iv) interfering with witnesses or evidence (*Bail Act 2013 (*NSW), s17).

There are avenues to mitigate levels of risk when a decision-maker is deliberating. This can be done by way of attaching conditions to bail to mitigate identified risks. Both the prosecution and the defence may put forward submissions for certain conditions to be attached to bail. For example, the prosecution might submit that the accused is a flight risk and should be denied bail and the defence then submits that the charged person's passport can be surrendered to mitigate that risk. This may allay concerns about unacceptable risk and result in granting of bail. A rise in the therapeutic jurisprudence movement has seen the expansion of conditions to include drug treatment, counselling and other mechanisms to address the root causes of offending and/or needs posed by people seeking bail (Colvin, 2019; Travers et al., 2020a, 2020b).

Who Is Refused Bail?

More than one in three prisoners are on remand in Australian prisons. This proportion has risen dramatically since 2010. In 2000 approximately, 15% of prisoners were on remand. In the decade between 2006–2016, the remand imprisonment rate across Australia increased by almost 90% (Baldry & Russell, 2017). In the 2022 March quarter, the number of remandees had increased to 14,884 from 14,662 from the pre CovID-19 March quarter in 2019 (ABS. Certain groups of people are increasingly over-represented in remand figures. Australian Bureau of Statistics data indicates that one in three remandees identified as Aboriginal and/or Torres Strait Islander, an increase from under one in four in 2006 (ABS, 2020; see also Productivity Commission, 2021).

According to a report by YFoundations (2021), in 2019–2020 in New South Wales almost 60% of young people in custody were on remand, yet only 14% of those on remand ended up serving a custodial sentence. Forty-five percent of young people in custody identify as Aboriginal and/or Torres Strait Islander where approximately six percent of children and young people in New South Wales are Aboriginal and/or Torres

Strait Islander. The number of women, particularly Indigenous women, on remand has also increased. This is exemplified by data released by Corrections Victoria in 2020 that demonstrate an increase in Indigenous women entering remand of greater than 400% over the previous ten years, noting an overall increase of entering remandees of 200% during this timeframe.

There are serious implications of denial of bail for people from even a very short term of imprisonment. People who are in custody may lose their employment, access to housing and custody of their children (Sullivan et al., 2019). There are long-lasting health and welfare repercussions for people who have served time in prison. Given remand imprisonment is generally of a relatively short duration—the average time spent on remand is less than six months (Productivity Commission, 2021)—denial of bail can result in serious disruptions to a person's life (ALRC, 2017).

Of significant concern is the high rate of deaths in custody within the remand population. Fifty percent of prisoners who committed suicide were on remand at the time of their death (Willis et al., 2016). Despite 30-year-old recommendations from the Royal Commission into Aboriginal Deaths in Custody, which stressed the importance of diverting Aboriginal people away from custody when making bail decisions, there are still Aboriginal people dying in custody while on remand for very minor offending (Russell et al., 2021; Whittaker, 2020).

Bail Decisions: Critical Issues and Controversies

There are a number of critical issues and controversies in the way bail is decided in Australian jurisdictions. This includes the tightening up of bail laws in a 'law and order' approach underpinned by reactions to high profile incidents, the role of family and domestic violence law reform in restricting access to bail, and how a lack of access to services, particularly housing for young people, is limiting decision-makers (Klauzner, 2021; Russell et al., 2021; YFoundations, 2021).

There has been a gradual rolling back of the presumption for bail and a number of changes to bail laws across Australia in recent decades in the context of a 'law and order' political response to crime (see also Harkness in Chapter 14 of this volume). After the terrorist attacks in the United States on 11 September 2001, Australia introduced a range of counter-terror legislation, some of which focused on removal of presumption for bail for terrorism related offences. Since that time, law reform has continued to follow this trend.

From 2010, significant changes to bail legislation have come swiftly after serious, and unusual, events that heightened public fear of crime and led to an increased law and order approach to bail (Auld & Quilter, 2020; Brown & Quilter, 2014). For example, a man on bail perpetrated the Lindt Café siege in Sydney in 2014 which led to the inclusion of bail refusal for terrorism charges unless there are 'exceptional circumstances' (s22A, *Bail Act 2013* (NSW)). In Victoria, a man on bail used his vehicle as a weapon in the busy pedestrian Bourke Street mall, killing six people and triggering a raft of amendments to legislation in that State. The amendments included a 'tightening' of the Bail Act in 2017 and 2018, and the introduction of the 'reverse onus test' requiring the *applicant* to prove why they should *not* remain in custody awaiting trial (Coghlan, 2017; McMahon, 2019).

Russell et al. (2021) identified the impact of law reform on family and domestic violence (FDV), and related policing practices, as drivers of increasing numbers of women, particularly Indigenous women, being denied bail. They identify a "constellation of circumstances" (Russell et al., 2021, p. 5) that explain how this occurs, including homelessness, a background of trauma and experiencing domestic and family violence. Increased use of intervention orders and the introduction of legislation aimed at increasing reporting of FDV has resulted in more women receiving these types of orders, even when they have been victimised.

Additional challenges arise when women's access to suitable housing is affected by legal responses to FDV. For example, an intervention order may restrict a woman from returning to her home: without access to formal and informal support mechanisms, this may result in homelessness. If criminal charges are associated with the intervention order, this may trigger a bail refusal because the charged woman has no suitable accommodation. Indeed, previous research by Russell et al. (2020) indicates that access to accommodation is the key barrier to accessing bail. For Indigenous women, access to suitable accommodation and culturally appropriate services is an added challenge. Increasingly, as the practitioner section which accompanies this chapter expands, this is becoming a concern for children with FDV-related charges.

Accommodation is one of the key challenges in seeking bail, not just for women but also for children and young people (YFoundations, 2021; Richards & Renshaw, 2013). A key principle of the legal system is that children should only be remanded as a last resort, but a lack of suitable accommodation options sees some children remanded for a lack of fixed address. This is a particular issue for children within the child welfare system (Colvin et al., 2020). Section 28 of the *Bail Act 2013* (NSW) was originally designed to allow homeless children to seek bail more readily. In reality, though, this may result in children spending more time on remand. Examining this particular issue provides a case study on a particularly disadvantaged group—children with unstable housing—and allows for reflection more broadly on bail systems in Australia.

Bail refusal is a significant issue for children, particularly those who are Aboriginal and/or Torres Strait Islander and/or in out-of-home care (Colvin et al., 2020; Klauzner, 2021). The significant overlap between these groups of children and over-representation in the criminal justice system is compounded for Aboriginal and/or Torres Strait Islander children, many of whom also have care experience (Colvin et al., 2020; Davis, 2019; Mendes et al., 2019). Further accentuating this issue is access to accommodation. Almost a third of children who tried to access accommodation or homelessness services were Aboriginal and/or Torres Strait Islander (YFoundations, 2021). The key conclusion of the YFoundations report was that children were being remanded because of a lack of accommodation. Klauzner (2021, p. 2) notes that "despite their vulnerability and relatively low chance of being sentenced to detention, young defendants are bail refused at a much greater rate than adults". Klauzner and Yeong (2021) also note that periods of remand for children are very short and that 60% ultimately are granted bail after a term in remand custody.

In New South Wales, Section 28 of the Bail Act (2013) introduced an accommodation requirement that was partly designed to address the remanding of young people for long periods of time because they did not have access to appropriate accommodation. This section of the Act allows a decision-maker to set an accommodation requirement as a bail condition for young people. Essentially, this means that bail can be granted, subject to appropriate accommodation being found. Once that accommodation is sourced, the young person can immediately be released to that place. To ensure accommodation is sourced quickly, the matter must be re-listed every few days so that the magistrate can track how the accommodation search is progressing and ensure that the matter is prioritised for those responsible, for example, Family and Community Services as part of the Department of Communities and Justice.

This legislative provision aims to address the problem of young people remaining in custody for long periods solely because they lack suitable accommodation to be bailed. This is crucial as the consequences for young people spending time in custody are particularly significant, and contrary to key human rights principles stipulated in international law through the Beijing Rules that require deprivation of liberty only to be used as an absolute last resort for children and young people (McGrath, 2016; Richards & Renshaw, 2013).

Challenges in Seeking Solutions

There exists a number of challenges brought about by refusal of bail in Australian jurisdictions. First, there is a need to collect more data regarding people on remand. It can be challenging to track remand rates given that people may be remanded for only very brief periods of time, sometimes overnight but ranging to several months or even years. A person may be remanded briefly then released on bail, then remanded again for breaching bail. The intersectional nature of many people being denied bail is not necessarily captured in statistics. Although race, gender and age are generally included in statistics, more information needs to be collected on factors such as intellectual disability, experience of FDV, or cognitive impairment. Further, collection and analysis of additional data on multiple intersecting factors is imperative.

Compounding these issues is the disparity between jurisdictions. The Australian Bureau of Statistics presents some data, as provided by states and territories, but each jurisdiction has varying levels of data collection and analysis. Notably, the Bureau of Crime Statistics and Research in New South Wales and Crime Statistics Victoria provide useful data. However, there are limitations as to what can be extrapolated: for example, evidence of the specific factors that drive remand rates (Productivity Commission, 2021; Weatherburn, 2020).

It is important to consider the threshold of risk that is considered acceptable by decision-makers. Making decisions about bail is a balancing act between key competing principles of the legal system and the probability of something happening needs to be weighed against the consequences for that person. As Justice Thomas of the Supreme Court of Queensland Court of Appeal (Williamson v DPP (1999) QCA 356) explains:

> No grant of bail is risk free. The grant of bail however is an important process in civilised societies which reject any general right of the executive to imprison a citizen upon mere allegation or without trial. It is a necessary part of such a system that some risks have to be taken in order to protect citizens in those respects.

What is crucial here is that some level of risk needs to be acceptable. Balancing the safety of the community, including the victim, against the rights of the accused to remain within the community until their trial is undoubtedly challenging. This is even more challenging for decision-makers when the accused is a child. Upholding the due process rights of an individual to be presumed innocent until proven guilty is central to justice in Australia, and the denial of bail for an increasing number of individuals arguably impedes on this right.

However, there is also no doubt that there are some individuals who do genuinely pose a risk to the community—and for that reason should be remanded in custody awaiting trial—but how do we determine such 'riskiness'? And how do we determine risk for a child coming before the court. This is particularly problematic as many children appearing before the courts have experienced trauma or have a cognitive impairment and developmental challenges that may affect their behaviour. Concerningly, children are primarily charged with very low-level offences: for example, in New South Wales more than one third of charges related to fare evasion (YFoundations, 2021).

Access to suitable accommodation is a significant reason for denial of bail, particularly for children, young people and women. This is further compounded for Indigenous people. Despite some measures being implemented to address the lack of accommodation, such as bail hostels in South Australia and bail beds in New South Wales, the options are limited (Klauzner, 2021; Travers et al., 2020a, 2020b).

The YFoundations (2021) report noted hundreds of children needing access to bail beds, yet there were only 17 on offer in New South Wales. Even when there is access to accommodation, it may not be suitable for a number of reasons. If a person is bailed to a hostel-type accommodation, other residents may pose a risk. For example, a person with bail conditions imposed that relate to treatment or abstinence from using drugs or alcohol may be placed with others who are using drugs and alcohol, which may impede any attempts to desist from using and put them at risk of breaching their conditions and ultimately revocation of bail. Further, there is a significant lack of Aboriginal-led, culturally appropriate services and supports for Indigenous people in the criminal justice system, and this is especially the case for Indigenous children (Davis, 2019; YFoundations, 2021).

Avenues for Change

There are several avenues to explore when examining the potential for positive change in bail decision-making that may address rising remand rates. Certainly, looking at means to bail people who have no suitable accommodation is critical, and a long-term solution would involve securing more accommodation. However, there can also be innovations in this space where the criminal justice system needs to look beyond existing practices. These range from, for example, changes to the conditions regarding proof of accommodation and the provision of a fixed address, which see many homeless persons remanded, as they are unable to provide such details to the court.

Improving access to services and better resourcing these services is another critical change. The criminal justice system has seen significant innovation in transferring resources from custodial settings to the community through the introduction of Justice Reinvestment mechanisms. It is incredibly expensive to incarcerate people in Australia: the Productivity Commission (2021) estimates it costs more than AUD$330 per person per night in custody; for youth justice the costs can be much more because of the extra level of care and staffing needed. Yet, many support services that reduce the need for this costly imprisonment are receiving minimal funding and are unable to operate at their full potential. For example, the Bail Assistance Line in New South Wales helped to place almost 10% of young people initially denied bail by the police in a six-month period in 2019 (Klauzner, 2021).

A recent evaluation found that young people who are placed by the Bail Assistance Line were less likely to be in custody six months after placement compared with those who has not been able to access these services (Klauzner, 2021). Yet, the Bail Assistance Line only places a small fraction of children needing services and for Indigenous children and those in more regional and remote settings the options are extremely limited.

The COVID-19 pandemic resulted in significant, instantaneous changes in the operation of the criminal justice systems. As the pandemic raged, prisons became hot spots and high-risk areas for contamination due to the high level of vulnerable people living in close proximity. The system focused on how to reduce the risk, part of the solution was to release many people who were close to the end of their sentence, or who were on remand. It became apparent that the number of people on remand, including children, reduced during the pandemic (Gordon et al., 2021; Lachz & Hurley, 2021; Piquero, 2021).

This unprecedented impact gives us an opportunity to reflect on current bail practices, and in particular the need to use remand to the extent that we did prior to the pandemic crisis. It showed that a significant reduction in incarceration rates was possible and could be done quickly. Research, policy development and practice should focus on the aftermath of these changes, and work out how to implement this change before, inexorably, the rates creep up again, as they are already (Russell et al., 2021).

Conclusion

Significant bail law reform, the impact of law and order approaches and the rolling back of presumptions for bail have limited options for decision-makers and made it more challenging for charged people to apply for and be granted bail. Coupled with a lack of resources, support and suitable accommodation options, remand rates are increasing, contributing significantly to imprisonment levels. Some groups are particularly affected, such as children without access to suitable accommodation. A unique opportunity to re-examine the system has been offered through the criminal justice system's response to the COVID-19 pandemic, which showed it is possible to reduce imprisonment rates quickly in response to a health threat. This case should be examined to see if ongoing trends can arise from this response.

References

Auld, L., & Quilter, J. (2020). Changing the rules on bail: An analysis of recent legislative reforms in three Australian jurisdictions. *University of New South Wales Law Journal, 43*(2), 642–673.

ABS (Australian Bureau of Statistics). (2020). *Prisoners in Australia, 2020.* Australian Bureau of Statistics.

ABS (Australian Bureau of Statistics). (2022). Corrective services Australia. Canberra Australian Bureau of Statistics. https://www.abs.gov.au/statistics/people/crime-and-justice/corrective-services-australia/latest-release#persons-in-custody

ALRC (Australian Law Reform Commission). (2017). *Pathways to justice—Inquiry into the incarceration rate of Aboriginal and Torres Strait Islander Peoples*. https://www.alrc.gov.au/publication/pathways-to-justice-inquiry-into-the-incarceration-rate-of-aboriginal-and-torres-strait-islander-peoples-alrc-report-133/

Baldry, E., & Russell, S. (2017). *The booming industry continued: Australian prisons a 2017 update*. https://www.researchgate.net/publication/312453408_The_Booming_Industry_continued_Australian_Prisons_A_2017_update

Bartels, L., Gelb, K., Spiranovic, C., Sarre, R. T., & Dodd, S. (2018). Bail, risk and law reform: A review of bail legislation across Australia. *Criminal Law Journal, 42*(2), 91–107.

Brown, D., & Quilter, J. (2014). Speaking too soon: The sabotage of bail reform in New South Wales. *International Journal for Crime Justice and Social Democracy, 3*(3), 73–97.

Coghlan, P. (2017). *Bail review: Second advice to the Victorian Government*. Government of Victoria.

Colvin, E. (2017). Bail justices in Victoria: Perceptions and experiences. *Current Issues in Criminal Justice, 29*(2), 123–136.

Colvin, E. (2019). Postcode (in)justice: Location and bail support services. *Journal of Criminological Research, Policy and Practice, 5*(4), 307–318.

Colvin, E., Gerard, A., & McGrath, A. (2020). *Children in out-of-home care and the criminal justice system: A mixed-method study*. Australian Institute of Criminology.

Commission, P. (2021). *Australia's prison dilemma*. Australian Government Publishing Service.

Corrections Victoria. (2020). *Annual prisoner statistical profile 2009–10 to 2019–20: Dataset, December 2020*. Department of Justice and Community Safety. https://www.corrections.vic.gov.au/annual-prisoner-statistical-profile-2009-10-to-2019-20

Davis, M. (2019). *Family is culture: Review report 2019*. Family is culture. https://www.familyisculture.nsw.gov.au/__data/assets/pdf_file/0011/726329/Family-Is-Culture-Review-Report.pdf

Gordon, F., Klose, H., & Lyttle Storrod, M. (2021). Youth (in)justice and the COVID-19 pandemic: Rethinking incarceration through a public health lens. *Current Issues in Criminal Justice, 33*(1), 27–46.

Klauzner, I. (2021). *An evaluation of the youth Bail Assistance Line* (Crime and Justice Bulletin No. 237). NSW Bureau of Crime Statistics and Research.

Klauzner, I., & Yeong, S. (2021). *What factors influence police and court bail decisions?* (Vol. 236). NSW Bureau of Crimc Statistics and Research.

Lachsz, A., & Hurley, M. (2021). Why practices that could be torture or cruel, inhuman and degrading treatment should never have formed part of the public health response to the COVID-19 pandemic in prisons. *Current Issues in Criminal Justice, 33*(1), 54–68.

McGrath, A. (2016). Intersections of Indigenous status, sex and age in sentencing decisions in the New South Wales Children's Court. *Australian and New Zealand Journal of Criminology, 49*(1), 90–112.

McMahon, M. (2019). *No bail, more jail? Breaking the nexus between community protection and escalating pre-trail detention.* Parliament of Victoria. https://www.parliament.vic.gov.au/publications/research-papers/download/36-research-papers/13893-no-bail-more-jail-breaking-the-nexus-between-community-protection-and-escalating-pre-trial-detention

Mendes, P., Saunders, B., & Baidawi, S. (2019). The experiences of Indigenous young people transitioning from out of home care in Victoria, Australia. In V. R. Mann-Feder & M. Goyette (Eds.), *Leaving care and the transition to adulthood: International contributions to theory, research, and practice* (pp. 149–171). Oxford University Press.

Piquero, A. R. (2021). *The policy lessons learned from the criminal justice system response to COVID-19.* Criminology Public Policy. https://doi.org/10.1111/1745-9133.12562

Richards, K., & Renshaw, L. (2013). *Bail and remand for young people in Australia: A national research project.* Australian Institute of Criminology.

Royal Commission into Aboriginal Deaths in Custody. (1991). *Royal Commission into aboriginal deaths in custody.* Australian Government Publishing Service.

Russell, E. K., Carlton, B., & Tyson, D. (2021). 'It's a gendered issue, 100 per cent': How tough bail laws entrench gender and racial inequality and social disadvantage. *International Journal for Crime, Justice and Social Democracy.* Onlinefirst. https://doi.org/10.5204/ijcjsd.1882

Russell, E. K., Carlton, B., Tyson, D., Zhou, H., Pearce, M., & Faulkner, J. (2020). *A constellation of circumstances: The drivers of women's increasing rates of remand in Victoria.* Fitzroy Legal Service and La Trobe Centre for Health, Law and Society. https://fls.org.au/product-category/publications/

Steel, A. (2009, December). *Bail in Australia: Legislative introduction and amendment since 1970.* Paper presented at the Australian and New Zealand Critical Criminology Conference (pp. 228–243). http://citeseerx.ist.psu.edu/viewdoc/download?doi=10.1.1.693.1421&rep=rep1&type=pdf

Sullivan, E. A., Kendall, S., Chang, S., Baldry, E., Zeki, R., Gilles, M., Wilson, M., Butler, T., Levy, M., Wayland, S., Cullen, P., Jones, J., & Sherwood, J. (2019). Aboriginal mothers in prison in Australia: A study of social, emotional and physical wellbeing. *Australian and New Zealand Journal of Public Health, 43*, 241–247.

Travers, M., Colvin, E., Bartkowiak-Theron, I., Sarre, R., Day, A., & Bond, C. (2020a). *Rethinking bail: Court reform or business as usual?* Palgrave Macmillan.

Travers, M., Colvin, E., Bartkowiak-Théron, I., Sarre, R., Day, A. & Bond, C. (2020b). *Bail Practices and Policy Alternatives in Australia.* Australian Institute of Criminology.

Weatherburn, D. (2020). Is tougher sentencing and bail policy the cause of rising imprisonment? A NSW case study. *Australian and New Zealand Journal of Criminology, 53*(4), 563–584.

Whittaker, A. (2020, 3 June). Despite 432 Indigenous deaths in custody since 1991, no one has ever been convicted. Racist silence and complicity are to blame. *The Conversation.* https://theconversation.com/despite-432-indigenous-deaths-in-custody-since-1991-no-one-has-ever-been-convicted-racist-silence-and-complicity-are-to-blame-139873

Willis, M., Baker, A., Cussen, T., & Patterson, E. (2016). *Self-inflicted deaths in Australian prisons: Australian prison suicide statistics 1999–2013* (Trends and Issues in Crime and Criminal Justice, 513). Australian Institute of Criminology.

Yfoundations. (2021). *Young, in trouble and with nowhere to go: Homeless adolescent's pathways into and out of detention in NSW*. Yfoundations. https://yfoundations.org.au/our-work/youth-justice-report/

Legislation and Cases

Bail Act 2013 (NSW).
Bail Act 1977 (Vic).
Williamson v DPP (1999) QCA 356.

Practitioner Perspective: Key Challenges Driving Bail Refusal

Lydia Hamilton

The New South Wales *Bail Act* 2013 along with later amendments were enacted after a lengthy process of consultation and collaboration between a number of relevant stakeholders and key decision-makers. The object of such consultation was to better align decision-making processes and improve consistency in the application of the Act.

From a practitioner's perspective, these changes have disproportionately disadvantaged children and young people—especially those with cognitive impairment, where family and domestic violence (FDV) is concerned, those young people under the care of the Minister, as well as Aboriginal young people. These unintended consequences of bail legislation interpretation can have far reaching negative impacts on young people, the community and the service sector—and create a financial cost that could be more beneficially directed to provide support and intervention services, rather than on actions that ultimately criminalise young people.

When a child (in New South Wales, aged 10 to 12) or young person (aged 13 to 17) is arrested and charged with an offence by New South Wales Police, there are a number of decisions police can make. These include release without bail, a grant of bail or bail refusal to be brought before a magistrate. If a young person is arrested after court operating hours or on a weekend, this process is more complicated for police owing to the lack of available services which might ordinarily be relied upon for support, guidance or assistance in the decision-making process.

The situation is further complicated where a child or young person is arrested after Court/business hours on a breach of bail. A breach of bail is not an offence, and section 77 of the Bail Act provides that a police officer who believes on reasonable grounds that a young person has failed or is about to fail to comply with bail may make one of size decisions: (i)

L. Hamilton
Youth Justice, Department of Communities and Justice, NSW, Australia

take no action; (ii) issue a warning; (iii) issue a notice that requires the person to appear before the court; (iv) issue a court attendance notice if police believe failure is an offence; (v) arrest without warrant and take the person before court or authorised justice; or (vi) apply for an arrest warrant.

There is evidence that police are reluctant to reconsider a grant of bail where a breach of bail is believed to have occurred (Klauzner, 2021), even when fresh information is made available that may mitigate risk. Utilising an 'adult lens' with the Bail Act rather than a focus on young people (whose circumstances and control over their environment is limited) is disadvantageous. For example, in family and domestic violence FDV matters, children and young people can be both victims and perpetrators. The Bail Act stipulates the requirement for police to consider vulnerabilities such as Aboriginality, age and cognitive impairment when considering a grant of bail. However, these requirements have been collapsed into s.18(k) of the determination process and is not always fully recognised or applied at the time of consideration of bail. Further, the 'show cause' decision-making matrix does not apply to children and young people, however, police continue to bail refuse under the 'show cause' test.

We know that children and young people in 'out of home care' (OOHC) are more likely to come to the attention of police and courts where they are subject to bail and are living in residential environments. Children and young people with complex trauma histories can have significant behavioural and emotional challenges. Managing these in a residential environment can be extremely difficult for community workers. However, some non-government organisation providers who are unable to manage behavioural incidents, (e.g. disputes between young people in a residential facility) utilise police to manage conflicts in an attempt to leverage control over young people, citing the condition 'to follow reasonable directions' as a reason to breach bail.

This issue is onerous and difficult for police, who can only use a bail refusal to manage what are behavioural issues, and profoundly impacts children and young people. Further, in a situation where a young person in this circumstance who has been refused bail by police but is then granted bail by a magistrate with a s.28 accommodation requirement, the young person can remain in custody on remand for longer periods, owing to a lack of suitable accommodation and supports. There have been incidences where the amount of time a young person spends in custody on remand with bail granted is longer than what they would have received should they have been sentenced by way of control order.

Short-term remand (the process by which young people are bail refused by New South Wales Police, admitted to a Youth Justice Centre overnight and then released by a magistrate the next day after appearing at a court) is of particular concern. This is because there are negative impacts on young people cycling through the criminal justice system, the contaminating effect of custodial environments and the resource intensive nature of the systems and processes involved in this practice. This includes police arrest, charging, administration, transport and admission to a Youth Justice Centre (in rural, regional and remote areas this is often a lengthy trip, sometimes by air travel), involvement of legal professionals, court administrators and other social services and court resources. These issues are compounded where a young person comes from a rural, regional or remote location, is Aboriginal or has cognitive impairments that are not identified at the time of arrest, where other options could be considered by police.

There are several pilot programmes, collaborations and emerging young Aboriginal leaders in communities across New South Wales (such as ID Know Yourself; Deadly Connections; Just Reinvest NSW; Mounty Yarns) with ideas, practice and expertise that can be more responsive to the needs of this cohort of vulnerable young people. The New South Wales Bail and Accommodation Support Service and 'A Place to Go' are programmes in New South Wales that aim to reduce the need to bail refuse young people, provide support and rehabilitative services and work collaboratively across government and the non-government sectors.

The need for more appropriate short-term housing options for young people across the State is a critical part of responding to the needs of young people subject to bail who are homeless. Government and non-government organisation level commissioning and planning of support services for young people who require flexible accommodation and support options is a priority area currently being addressed. Future positive directions worthy of further exploration include raising the age of criminal responsibility, considering separate bail legislation for children and young people, implementing a standalone provision for Aboriginality and amending s.77 of the Bail Act to broaden the options available to New South Wales Police.

Further educating police officers' perception and capacity to use discretion with the Bail Act where it applies to children and young people would be valuable. So, too, would be an exploration of better opportunities to assist police with decision-making in an environment where they have immense pressures and are not always in possession of all the relevant information required to make balanced decisions. As the initial gate-keepers of who gets granted bail, this is crucial in providing better outcomes for some of the most vulnerable people within the criminal justice system. This collaboration must be underpinned by robust data capture of significant indicators such as Aboriginality, cognitive impairment, OOHC status and FDV offences, to better target services and supports to meet the needs of these vulnerable groups at an earlier stage of the process.

Case Study

To illustrate some of these matters, consider the case of Jay (a pseudonym), a 15-year-old Aboriginal young person arrested by police and refused bail on domestic violence related offences after an altercation with his stepfather. When police rang the Bail Assistance Line to admit the young person to custody after bail refusing on domestic violence matters, Bail Assistance Line staff reinforced that show cause for domestic violence does not apply to children, and asked whether police would consider a release on bail if other accommodation could be sought for the young person.

After gaining consent from the young persons' parental guardian, Youth Justice was able to place Jay into a funded bed operated by a non-government agency, who were able to work with Jay before his next court appearance. Jay had undiagnosed and emerging mental health conditions, which were assessed and managed by referral to a youth community mental health service and with subsequent counselling, education and medication.

Jay was also assisted to enrol in a TAFE (Technical and Further Education) course to learn graphic design, and he engaged well in that learning environment. Jay was also offered support in developing living and conflict management skills during his remand period in the community. When his matters were referred back to court for sentence, the magistrate sentenced him by way of s.33 (mental health grounds) and the matters were dismissed. If Jay had been exposed to the contaminating effects of incarceration, his trajectory may have been very different.

Reference

Klauzner, L. (2021). *An evaluation of the Youth Bail Assistance Line* (Crime and Justice Bulletin, 237). NSW Bureau of Crime Statistics and Research.

7

Delaying Justice

Liz Curran

Introduction

Delays in cases coming before the courts can lead to unfairness, uncertainty and impede effective decision-making and responsiveness. This chapter considers the definition of delay, drawing upon the literature examining justice delays in Commonwealth countries and the impacts in Australia's justice system. This itself can delay justice in the broader sense because it leads to uncertainty for people awaiting determinations and can lead to personal costs that can be irreversible.

The chapter identifies some of the core principles from the literature underpinning a good court system and explores the implications of delays to court proceedings and its flow on effects on attaining just outcomes for the parties before the courts. It also identifies some solutions and highlights why there is also a need for caution. This

L. Curran (✉)
Nottingham Trent University, Nottingham, UK
e-mail: liz.curran02@ntu.ac.uk

M. Camilleri and A. Harkness (eds.), *Australian Courts*,
https://doi.org/10.1007/978-3-031-19063-6_7

is because, sometimes, adjustments designed to reduce delays, streamline court processes and create more efficiencies can have unforeseen flow on effects for justice downstream. This chapter identifies some of these complexities and considers why finding ways to reduce delays can be problematic if not done mindfully and without regard to the core principles underlining the court system.

Governments, economists and the media have often lamented court delays and called for it to be addressed (Callinan, 2002). This chapter does not claim that court delay without its implications for justice; rather, it seeks to explore the underlying reasons for delay and avert simplistic solutions. While the focus is on delays in criminal cases, the chapter does make some observations in a civil context.

Delaying justice can impact on defendants, complainants, witnesses, the legal profession and on justice outcomes. Karpin (1990) has noted that delay in court process may not necessarily be a bad thing. For this reason, it is *unnecessary* delay that ought to be identified and addressed. Court processes, whether civil or criminal, are characterised by disputes that can be deeply personal between the parties and involve human and complex issues that need to be navigated and explored in the interests of justice. This means that court determinations by their very nature will not be an exact or predicable scientific exercise in many cases and issues due for consideration will take time to explore, canvas and resolve for a proper consideration and appropriate orders are made (Karpin, 1990). This is often overlooked in media commentary and by governments keen to make efficiencies.

Delaying justice has an array of causes, with different implications and outcomes each of which can be significant and all need to be carefully managed. These include:

- inadequate resourcing of the court and legal assistance services; delays due to the prosecution being not ready to proceed (without substantive cause);
- problems in listing cases such as management of court timetables (including a lack of transparent or tailored case assessment and triage);

- refusals to consider options that may be more appropriate (such as conflict conferencing, alternative dispute resolution or mediation where it might be appropriate);
- time spent on remand in the criminal context (particularly, when an accused is acquitted subsequently); and
- the financial, social and emotional costs of resolving disputes—on the accused, victims, witnesses and others affected.

Historical and Contemporary Context: Definitions of Delay and the Common Law

The Oxford dictionary definition of delay is to postpone; defer; make later; time lost by inaction or the inability to process; a hinderance. Clause 40 of the *Magna Carta* 1215 states "To no one will we sell to no one will we refuse or delay, right or justice" and a right to due legal process (clauses 39 and 40 in the 1215 charter, clause 29 (in the 1297 statute). Hill et al. (2009) note that the State is responsible for delays by its administrative or judicial authorities.

There is case law on delay and implications. Criminal courts have the right to stay proceedings to prevent injustice caused to a defendant by undue delay (*Jago v District Court of NSW*). In the United Kingdom case of *Attorney-General's Reference (No 2)*, the defendants, prisoners, had been involved in a riot in 1998—yet it took until 2001 for the case to come to trial. A range of considerations included the right to a fair trial within a reasonable time, whether delay by the prosecution itself was enough to stay proceedings and whether a fair hearing might still be possible, or the prejudice caused by the delay could be cured. In this case, Article 6(1) of the *European Convention on Human Rights and Fundamental Freedoms* was a consideration. The court concluded that the inherent jurisdiction of the court to stop a prosecution to prevent an abuse of process is to be exercised only in exceptional circumstances. It will turn on the facts of each case. To illustrate this, consider the New Zealand case of *Martin v Tauranga District Court*, a nineteen-month delay from charge to trial due to unwarranted delay by the prosecution was found to require a stay of proceedings, Cooke P citing Sopinka J in *R v Morin* notes:

> The general approach to a determination as to whether the right has been denied is not by the application of a mathematical or administrative formula, but rather by a judicial determination balancing the interests which the section is designed to protect against factors which either inevitably led to delay or are otherwise the cause of delay…

In *R v Smith* it was noted, "it is axiomatic that some delay is inevitable. The question is, at what point does the delay become unreasonable?"

In the Australian Capital Territory case of *Kara Lesley Mills v The Queen,* Higgins CJ examined justice delayed considering the *Human Rights Act* 2004 (ACT) section 22 and the right to a fair trial in criminal proceedings and circumstances constituting 'unreasonable delay'. The accused filed an application for a permanent stay of proceedings on 27 January 2010 based on unreasonable delay based on s 22(1)(c) of the *Human Rights Act 2004* (ACT) which guarantees a person be tried without unreasonable delay. The judge examined implications including prejudice by faded recollection due to delay; the defendant not causing the delay; a lack of communication within the prosecution; and subsequent delays attributed to the lack of resources of the court. The defendant experienced anxiety and the expense of the delayed trial. The delay was for two and a half years from the first trial in a relatively simple case and the prosecution advanced no substantive reason for the delay.

In this instance Higgins CJ (*R v Kara Lesley Mills* 2011) noted that:

> A failure to provide adequate resources will, if unreasonable delay results, be a breach of the human rights entitlements of litigants, civil and criminal, for which the state is then liable… The state cannot on the one hand, confer a right to trial without unreasonable delay and, on the other, provide insufficient resources for its exercise.

In summary, the fundamental tenets that underpin the common law such as the *Magna Carta* connect delay in proceedings to the ability to provide due process. In the case law, especially where human rights instruments exist, as noted above in the cases of *Attorney-General's Reference (No 2)*, *Kara Lesley Mills v The Queen*, and *Martin v Tauranga District Court*, there are also constraints on government requiring them to make efforts to reduce delay so that human rights considerations can be addressed and flow on effects for a case if delay is assessed as causing an abuse of process. This all turns on the facts of each case. Often efforts to address delay overlook the issues of resourcing which Higgins CJ highlights is key.

Underpinning Principles for Courts and Challenges of Reconciling Them with Efforts to Resolve Delay

The problems with court delay, its link to due process and core values that sit behind such due process have been the subject of international scholarship. However, efforts to manage and address court delay can end up being siloed from the principles that underpin this due process. Sometimes the purpose or point of the proceeding is lost in court imperatives or managerialism with its focus on efficiency and streamlining. These, while important, should keep central the core reasons we have the court system which is to determine and deliberate on good and just determinations in line with notions of the Rule of Law. Core values (Allsop, 2016) which are stated to need to underpin good courts include:

- equality before the law;
- respect for the integrity and dignity of the individual; and mercy;
- fairness;
- impartiality;
- flexibility and creativity;
- independence of decision-making;
- competence;
- integrity;
- transparency;
- accessibility;

- timeliness;
- certainty; and
- a balancing of rules, principles, precepts, norms and values.

The World Bank (2012) examined justice reform and noted the need for empirically based problem-solving approaches which focus on end users of the court rather than the needs of the court itself. This aligns with the importance of ensuring that the parties that the proceeding is about, and key values such as equality before the law and fairness, are not forgotten and remain at the heart of solutions.

Global measures for court performance by an International Consortium for Court Excellence (2020) have been developed. This consortium is constituted of the Australian Institute of Judicial Administration, the Federal Judicial Centre, the National Centre for State Courts and the State Courts of Singapore. While first acknowledging the core values should be central to court operations, the 11 performance measures the Consortium identify (such as duration of pre-trial custody; case backlog; employee engagement; compliance with court orders and cost per case) to guide different jurisdictions is lost in translation with the focus on efficiencies and performance indicators using managerial language unlinked to stated core values (International Consortium for Court Excellence, 2020).

In Canada, the courts have set out specific formulas to determine implications where there is delay in criminal trials and gauge how they might be managed including presumptive ceilings, such as providing suggested timings for determining if a delay is unreasonable (R v KGK, 2020), for example, recommending 18 months for provincial court trials and 30 months for superior court trials. R v KGK (2020) provides other elements to be determined including considering complexity, exceptional circumstances beyond the parties' control and local contexts (R v Jordan, 2016). In another case, R v Cody (2017), the Canadian court stresses "every actor in the justice system has the responsibility to combat the culture of complacency and that the judge must assess whether the deliberation time took markedly longer than it reasonably should have in all the circumstances". This approach requires a balancing of justice concerns and their impacts and aims to bring some accountability into the consideration of delay by incorporating an examination of contributing factors by the parties, their lawyers and the State.

The Delicate Interplay of Australian Court Performance Indicators and Due Process

Weatherburn (1996) has examined trial court performance in New South Wales, exploring the possibility of indicators for trial case processing to try and assist in managing delay. He notes that developing performance indicators is difficult in trial court administration and concludes that concerns of the cost of court delays should not be driven by focussing only on efficiency and effectiveness. This, he notes, can overlook the justice and adherence to due process that are integral to seeking timeliness to prevent undue delay. Weatherburn highlights the difficulty in gaining consensus on how to expedite cases and warns that, although there are measures around the efficiency and effectiveness on how a court should be run, these often ignore the compelling case for additional resources or other policies that might be needed to enhance and improve the court process.

Weatherburn (1996) is not arguing that some form of indicators or measurement is not needed, but he warns that the process is complex and there is a need for sophistication and explanation as to the causes around allocations of court time between civil and criminal work; caseload of judges and their availability and cases taking time due to unforeseen circumstances. Factors can include good management practice and triage. He argues for useful and reliable management information, staff training programmes, and sophisticated and reliable computing systems with personnel with requisite statistical knowledge who can analyse the data and input the data and consistency in such data collection. Ongoing open and frank discussions between the executive and the judiciary about the causes of delay, the need for resourcing and the court's core values are all needed to ensure a balance is met between efficiency and justice outcomes (Weatherburn, 1996).

The Australian Productivity Commission (2018) held an Inquiry into Government Services, including Australian courts. Unsurprisingly, given the focus of the Commission on productivity, it looks at the court process through the lens of economic efficiency and cost per finalisation of court matter from lodgement (i.e., the initiation or commencement of a matter before the court). The Commission noted that there are several factors which make things complicated stating “a number of factors are beyond the control of jurisdictions, such as geographic dispersion, economies of scale and socioeconomic factors”. In trying to come to some conclusions about finalisation and backlog, the Commission's report identified problems in the data they collected noting “some finalisations take a short time and require few resources, whereas other finalisations may be resource intensive and involve complicated trials and interlocutory decisions”. In terms of efficiency, it notes “there can be trade-offs between efficiency on the one hand and equity and effectiveness on the other”. This highlights a key theme of this chapter: that there is no ‘silver bullet’ when it comes to trying to fix court delay.

Key Contemporary Controversies

The most helpful analysis focussing on criminal trial delays in Australia is provided by Payne (2006). Payne details results of quantitative and qualitative research conducted across Australia that unravel some of the reasons that criminal trials experience delay. His report is comprehensive in a context of limited available analytical literature on Australian court delay.

In examining trial delays, Payne (2006) examines different jurisdictions including the different states of Australia, New Zealand, Canada and the United Kingdom, exploring pre-trial disclosure, hearings and case management efforts designed to address court delay. He explores the time taken from initiation until finalisation of the case, the complex nature of reasons for adjournments, issues around timely and full disclosure by both prosecution and defence that can help each make decisions. These include the veracity of the case, helping the defendant make early choices about guilty pleas and other causes of delay. Payne also considers the human element, unlike other more managerial approaches. He stresses that this element cannot be predicted or controlled without significant implications for justice. Any effort to make changes to the criminal justice system should be informed by practice and academic rigour, including evaluation.

Underlying problems during criminal (and civil) trials and has implications on delay (Payne, 2006; Weatherburn, 1996). Payne identifies some inefficiencies in the trial system. For every ten trials listed in the Australian criminal jurisdiction, on average three will proceed as scheduled, four will be finalised without trial either by guilty plea or withdrawal by the prosecution, and three matters will be adjourned and relisted for another hearing. In some jurisdictions there has been an increased level of pre-trial supervision by the courts, which can consume additional judicial and court resources resulting with more time spent by defence and prosecution counsel as they manage and oversee these additional processes. This can be counter-productive, effecting cost and consuming significant resources which may cause further delay (Payne, 2006).

Payne's (2006) report highlights that the considerable uncertainty in the criminal trial process renders delays somewhat inevitable. This includes that it is not possible for all the information including forensic analysis to occur at the front-end as sometimes things are unknown at this stage and evidence needs to be gathered. Often there are issues about the adequate resourcing of other elements in the chain of evidence gathering. Examples that are offered include where prosecutorial demands are particularly burdensome (for instance, a new priority in gathering lengthy materials around terrorism) where they wade through mountains of recorded transcripts and where there are increasing demands on forensic institutions with limited staff and resources to provide such evidence.

In addition, there can be an unequal ability to obtain forensic evidence and expert evidence by defence counsel especially if there are limitations on resources and limited Legal Aid criteria. This can be an issue in criminal cases and civil matters where expert evidence is required, and expert reports can cause delay. Also, defendants have limited access to funds to secure such reports in comparison with the prosecution. Sometimes the costs of securing health reports can be prohibitive. There are also delays if expert reports are secured at low or no costs as they end up lower on the expert's priority list and so are not provided in the timeliest manner.

Owing to the COVID-19 pandemic, there have also been flow on effects that cause delay. For example, in Victoria criminal trials were adjourned because the Office of Police Prosecutors found a shortage of prosecutors who fell ill or left because of the strain. This leads to reliance on less experienced prosecutors who lack experience and confidence in making assessments early or who need supervisions thus, causing further delay and case backlogs, a phenomena referred to as 'juniorisation'.

Witness and Victim Alienation from the Court Process

One of the primary problems with court delay is that it further alienates people from the legal system, whether it be a criminal process or a civil process. Reasons for this alienation include witnesses having had a previous negative experience of court proceedings and no longer wishing to be involved; the witness feeling isolated from the process; and being confused by it with inadequate contact with the relevant entities that ought to provide pathways for them to be heard and informed. Additionally, the witness might have been inconvenienced by the trial process on prior occasions and so are sceptical as to what will happen in the current proceedings; impacted psychologically and emotionally by having to give evidence; or impacted by the time which has elapsed between the incident and the court date and thus becoming disconnected and with issues of memory recall (Payne, 2006).

Sometimes witnesses and victims have unrealistic expectations about the process and how long it may take. As practitioners are accustomed to significant delays, they can neglect to account for the personal toll on witnesses and victims. An example is the case of 'Rachel' (a pseudonym outlined in Hickey, 2019), a mother whose daughter was sexually abused. The case took 30 weeks over four years in court with numerous delays and adjournments. This witness reported that the time required away from work to give evidence and be available meant that her employment contract was not renewed, thus causing financial strain and stress on the family.

There are also complications for many First Nations people who live in remote and isolated locations. Many have limited competence in written and spoken English, might have negative experiences of colonial structures, limited capacity for communication either with the court, counsel and/or other services associated with the court, and conflicting community and cultural values. Some of these factors are equally present for people from culturally and linguistically diverse backgrounds. These challenges lead to delays but are caused by structural systems issues including the lack of resourcing, complexity of lives, impacts of colonisation, access to legal help and support, and limited timely access to interpreters and translators. Overlooking these aspects in trying to address delay can lead to implications on equality before the law and due process, all of which underpin the rule of law

COVID-19 Pandemic and Delays

Throughout the COVID-19 pandemic there were significant impacts on court workloads owing to lockdowns and restrictions. The courts and tribunals have had to pivot to online hearings at short notice with implications on court backlogs and the processing of claims. At the same time, it has forced the courts into a position where they have become quicker in embracing the value of technology both in the hearing cases on the paperwork and in conducting more civil and criminal cases online (Legg & Song, 2021). The Federation of Community Legal Centres notes important improvements to court processes and facilities that have been facilitated by changes. A benefit of online hearings for rural and regional areas, where people who would otherwise have felt unsafe attending court, was the ability to use remote witness facilities to give evidence via video link (FCLC, 2020).

There are family violence matters, however, which are still undertaken in person and cannot be facilitated remotely. Although there have been some benefits of online hearings, these changes have had implications on fairness and justice. The Federation of Community Legal Centres notes some of the difficulties that Victoria Legal Aid and community legal centres encountered in the initial stages of the pandemic where different entities were using different online platforms. The Federation called for consistency in relation to safety, accountability and privacy in the use of these platforms and enabling individuals to fully participate in hearings (FCLC Victoria, 2020). Many people do not have access to online systems or do not have the financial wherewithal to have Wi-Fi connection or data sufficient to attend or participate in hearings. In addition, utilising online technology from the home may be unsafe. This applies equally to victims, alleged offenders and witnesses. The Federation stresses the need for a client-centred approach and the ability for participants in the justice system to avail themselves of legal advice and technological support at the earliest opportunity.

Late Guilty Pleas

The entering of guilty pleas late and prosecutorial withdrawal of charges are issues which also contribute to delays (Payne, 2006). Payne explores reasons that sit behind these issues, noting how complicated it is for parties to make decisions earlier. This can occur because evidence may not have been collected at an earlier stage allowing for consideration. From the defence perspective, strategies may be at play in whether a guilty plea is appropriate or raising a defence at the last minute because they are waiting on assessments or to assess total evidence held by the prosecution before making such decisions. Sometimes there are delays in communications or late communications with witnesses leading up to the trial date. This may not be available either through short notice given to witnesses by the prosecution or defence counsel or for normal reasons such as ill-health. Often there is an arrest-driven culture by local police, so charges are poorly considered or they do not adequately prepare the case. This can lead to withdrawal by the prosecution at a late stage (Payne, 2006).

It is critical to the interests of justice that defence counsel and clients have sufficient time to consider and analyse evidence that is presented so they can adequately prepare their cases. This is not only relevant in criminal cases but can be a factor in civil cases as well. Similarly, the prosecution may not be able to proceed because of the withdrawal of witnesses or the production of evidence which is contradictory to sustaining a charge. Another complication is the availability of senior prosecutorial officials at an early stage with the ability to assess the accuracy of charges and to challenge errors or inappropriate charges. Inexperienced prosecutors may lay more charges than are appropriate or without legitimate basis. Not having delegated authority to make decisions can also prolong decisions being made, and if senior staff with authority are unavailable this can lead to delay.

At a human level, defendants may find it difficult to face the reality of their plight and therefore do not engage and are not ready to engage or need time to digest what is for them often an alien decision. For defendants, circumstances can also compound interactions and engagement with defence lawyers over the long time it takes from charge to trial such as being homeless or mentally unwell. It would not be in the interests of justice for a defendant to plead guilty early with such a lack of clarity, an ability to test charges against them and their capacity and that of their defence counsel to weigh up their options. The human elements involved in making a plea are understandable and cannot be overlooked or easily resolved.

Adjournments

Adjournments are a further cause of delay. This applies not only to criminal trials but also impact civil cases before courts and tribunals (Thomas & Tomlinson, 2017). The multiple reasons for adjournments are explored in Payne's (2006) report into criminal trial delay. Two key reasons for adjournments include that the matter is not reached by the court or that a request for an adjournment is made by either of the parties. Matters often do not proceed for a range of reasons including that witnesses, defendants or legal counsel are not available on the day of trial. In the case of legal counsel, sometimes they over-list anticipating that a certain number of cases will not proceed for trial. This practice, particularly at the Bar, occurs where they pass the brief to another legal practitioner because the initial representative has over-booked themselves and subsequently further time is needed for the defendant to be adequately represented.

Other matters may not be ready to proceed because additional information is required, there is a delay in receiving the additional evidence needed, or there is further need for clarification on funding (e.g. by a legal aid commission or where parties are inadequately prepared themselves). Other judicial processes such as a *nolle prosequi* (a decision by the prosecution not to prosecute leading to a dismissal of charges often because some criteria for proof has not been met), *voir dire* (a matter of law needs to be decided by legal parties without the jury present in closed court) or a Basha enquiry (where a prosecution witness appears in a preliminary examination before a judicial member where a court considers it would be unfair to proceed to trial) may be needed to ascertain whether a matter is ready to proceed.

Highlighting complexity and those adjournments do not always cause a delay also complicates the discussion. Court practice of 'over listing' matters is an endeavour to ascertain if cases do not proceed, whether other cases can be heard in their place. It is a genuine attempt by courts to use their finite resources efficiently. In this circumstance, delay is reduced as other proceedings further down the line may be reallocated by judicial case management. This means cases scheduled for later can be reached earlier and thus heard earlier (Weatherburn, 1996).

The reasons for adjournments from the court perspective include limited court facilities for example limited access to information technology services, closed-circuit television services or court support staff or unexpected unavailability of personnel (including judicial officers) and not enough appointments to the bench. The latter means there are not enough judicial officers to deal with the cases before the courts.

All these factors highlight reasons why a court may not reach a case. These factors are not straightforward or in the court's control. Trying to reduce adjournments and streamline to address delay can have downstream implications. Limited resources are often not addressed by the government and yet they a critical element in addressing delay.

Bail in Criminal Cases and Lengthy Remand Periods

In 2018 the bail laws in Victoria were amended, reversing the onus provision and presumptions against bail. These reforms have seen a large number of people, including vulnerable women and First Nations people, being imprisoned on remand when they would otherwise have been eligible for bail. In the context of the COVID-19 pandemic, time on remand has only increased due to the delays in cases being heard (FCLC, 2020). The irony is that often when cases are eventually reached, the nature of the offence would often not have warranted a sentence of imprisonment or the people are found innocent, having already spent prolonged periods in prison. This has significant implications for First Nations people and women (Russell, 2021) and the flow on impact on the future lives of children and young people should not be ignored (FCLC, 2020).

Delays in Decisions by Judicial and Tribunal Members

Another area where there is delay is in the delivery of judgements. It is anecdotally known in legal practice that delays of this nature can arise for a range of reasons including a lack of judicial officers to match the caseload and in areas of civil law, and members being unfamiliar and lacking expertise in areas of law (Refugee Council, 2021). This can all contribute to delay in providing reasons for decision. For instance, in the Administrative Appeals Tribunal members may feel they lack competence in the often increasingly complex areas of law (Law Council of Australia, 2021) or vexed issues are presented. Significant media commentary or government scrutiny puts them under pressure, fear of being wrong (which has implications for people without the wherewithal to appeal), or concerns about an outcome being overturned on appeal are significant considerations. Such delays can lead to non-determinations in areas of family law where relationship dynamics and children's rights can be compounded (e.g. a lack of access to child support payments) or delays occur in the provision of critical social supports (such as the Disability Support Pension).

In employment law in the Federal Court, delays in decision and judgement were ruled to have implications for employees. For example, in a case where the classification of a person as employee or independent contractor where there is a 20-month delay. This led the employee to have significant time away from work to give evidence, and an employment contract not being renewed which subsequently caused financial strain and stress on the family.

Long or excessive delay in a case determination or delay in publication of reasons can in some circumstances render the judgement or decision unsafe (*Expectation Pty Ltd v PRD Realty Pty Ltd*; *Tattsbet Limited v Morrow*). The decisions also explore the pressures that can be bought to bear in decision-making in judicial determination. Alssop CJ considered the issue on appeal to the Federal Court *Tattsbet Limited v Morrow* 2015). He observed that:

> The practical realities of life as a judge may mean, sometimes, a degree of delay in decision-making. Pressure and volume of other judicial work, complexity, and size of the particular decision-making task at hand, a lack, sometimes, of useful assistance from litigants or the profession, and illness or incapacity are but examples of reasons for delay… Whatever the cause of any particular delay (and there was no explanation available here), its consequences must be examined with an eye to the fair administration of justice.

This observation highlights that delaying justice can impede the administration of justice which is so critical in building trust and in and integrity of the legal system.

Challenges and Change: Cause for Caution in Seeking Reform to Address Delay and Some Ways Forward

As many jurisdictions internationally attempt to grapple with court delay—for example, the move in the United Kingdom to digitise justice post COVID-19 in the drive for efficiency—great care is essential. While information technology, performance monitoring, transparency and efficiency are all important, issues around adequate resourcing and human factors (such as advice seeking behaviour and poverty) can compromise due process and equality before the law because they are compounded by inadequate access to legal services, language services and barriers caused by language and trauma. An over-reliance on information technology without awareness of these factors can thwart justice (Denvir, 2018).

Endeavours to make efficiencies in relation to delays should not be undertaken in isolation from a consideration of these factors nor should they overlook the critical importance of people being able to better understand and present fully their case. Alternatively, the cost in human lives of delays or the costs to lives of trying to expedite matters without full and proper determination can cause harm.

Key to addressing delay issues is service coordination and integrated service delivery. The need for an assessment process to be undertaken by the court as to the capacity and capability of individuals whose evidence is required or who are participants in the court process or tribunal process being able to give fulsome evidence cannot be over-accentuated. One cannot underestimate that human interaction has a significant role in building trust, confidence and in identifying pressures and stresses on individuals which when understood properly can then be addressed. These might not be evidenced or visible in the short periods of the online interactions at a hearing or in canvassing factors that may be pertinent to legalistic considerations of the court or tribunal (Curran, 2021a). If these needs are understood, then delays will be limited because more information can enable improved responsiveness and informed decision-making so that delay can be understood and addressed.

There are areas in need of major cultural change to improve communication between parties and to increase dialogue. Clearer communication between all parties would reduce delay: this includes court staff, defence counsel, the prosecution, police informants, witnesses, victims, applicants, respondents and defendants. Earlier discussions between different counsel to ascertain issues in dispute and to negotiate earlier possible outcomes is required. The provision of earlier triage and assessments and the adequate resourcing of the justice system with the requisite number of judicial officers with expertise and resources will help. Acknowledging the increasing cost associated with securing senior professional experience may reduce delay and speed up trials and justice processes. There is also the need for closer adherence to the Australian Solicitors Conduct Rules (Law Council of Australia, 2015) and *Model Litigant Rules* (Australian Government Attorney General's Office) in how matters are conducted by, for example, not unduly delaying matters or dragging them out to drive up legal costs.

In looking to alternate processes which are more expeditious, there may also be a place for restorative justice, alternative dispute resolution and restorative practice as an alternative to the adversarial process where appropriate which may provide for speedier outcomes. Sourdin and Burstyner (2014) noted that in the 1980s there were numerous court-led alternative dispute resolution initiatives that served to clear court backlog. In civil matters, they observed that alternative dispute resolution helped to identify and resolve matters in dispute and thus lead to earlier resolution leaving the court or tribunal time to focus on key issues.

Opportunities exist for restorative practice averting harmful adversarial processes in cases involving institutional abuse, consumer law and family violence. Restorative practice, as well as being less harmful, is also less burdensome and quicker. These options are neglected in discussions around the repertoire of solutions (Curran, 2021b) and may be worthy of consideration in trying to address delay.

Conclusion

Justice needs to be tailored to individual circumstances, enabling participation in navigable systems and processes. Evidence of unnecessary delay and its causes need to be better understood and clearer. Earlier communication between all parties in ways that do not compromise rights will assist. Resourcing enough skilled judicial officers and the central and integrating the central focus on the values that ought to underpin the justice systems operations in all efforts is needed with benchmarks and performance indicators to reduce delay being linked to such values. This will help determine, consider and test downstream implications of efforts to address delay on justice.

At the end of the day, it must be remembered the courts exist to service the community and uphold the rule of law which includes the right to equality before the law, lawful conduct and due process. Delaying justice is problematic but finding solutions is also complex and challenging and must be carefully thought through so that the aims of the justice system are not compromised by illusory easy fixes.

References

Allsop, C. J. (2016). *Values in law: How they influence and shape rules and the application of law.* A paper presented to the Centre for Comparative and Public Law, Faculty of Law, University of Hong Kong. https://www.fedcourt.gov.au/digital-law-library/judges-speeches/chief-justice-allsop/allsop-cj-20161020

Australian Government Attorney General's Office. (2017). *Legal services directions and guidance notes.* Office of Legal Services Coordination. https://www.ag.gov.au/legal-system/office-legal-services-coordination/legal-services-directions-and-guidance-notes

Australian Productivity Commission. (2021). *Report on government services: Part C—Courts.* https://www.pc.gov.au/research/ongoing/report-on-government-services

Callinan, R. (2002). Court delays in NSW: Issues and developments. New South Wales Parliamentary Library Research Service, Briefing Paper No. 1 of 2. https://www.parliament.nsw.gov.au/researchpapers/Documents/court-delays-in-nsw-issues-and-developments/01-02.pdf

Corrections Victoria. (2020). *Annual prisoner statistical profile 2009 to 2010–2019 to 2020.* https://www.corrections.vic.gov.au/annual-prisoner-statistical-profile-2009-10-to-2019-20

Curran, L. (2021a). *From fragmented to holistic: Starting the evidence base the client centred practice through a navigator: A report on the research evaluation of the Hammersmith Fulham Law Centre's 'Women's Crisis Navigator Service Project Pilot'.* Curran Consulting. https://papers.ssrn.com/sol3/papers.cfm?abstract_id=3899573

Curran, L. (2021b). *Better law for a better world: New approaches to law practice and education.* Routledge.

Denvir, C. (2018). *Assisted digital support for civil justice system users: Demand, design, and implementation.* University College London. https://www.judiciary.uk/wp-content/uploads/2018/06/cjc-report-on-assisted-digital-support.pdf

Federation of Community Legal Centres Victoria. (2020). *A just and equitable covid recovery: A community legal sector plan for Victoria.* https://www.fclc.org.au/just_and_equitable_victoria

Hickey, S. (2019, 14 March). *Justice delayed is justice denied: Calls for speedier outcomes to criminal cases.* Sydney Criminal Lawyers Blog. https://www.sydneycriminallawyers.com.au/blog/justice-delayed-is-justice-denied-calls-for-speedier-outcomes-to-criminal-cases/

International Consortium for Court Excellence. (2020). *Global measures of court performance* (3rd ed.). Secretariat for the International Consortium for Court Excellence. http://www.courtexcellence.com

Karpin, A. (1990). Delays in local courts. *Current Issues in Criminal Justice, 2*, 49–58.

Legg, M., & Song, A. (2021). The courts, the remote hearing and the pandemic: From action to reflection. *UNSW Law Journal, 44*(1), 122–166.

Law Council of Australia. (2021). *Submission on the performance and integrity of Australia's administrative review system.* Legal and Constitutional Affairs References Committee. https://www.lawcouncil.asn.au/resources/submissions/performance-and-integrity-of-australias-administrative-review-system

Lord Lester of Herne Hill, QC, Lord Pannick, QC, & Javan, H. (2009). *Human rights law and practice* (3rd ed.). Butterworths.

Payne, J. (2006). *Criminal trial delays in Australia: Trial listing outcomes.* Research and Public Policy Series, No. 74. Australian Institution of Criminology. https://www.aic.gov.au/sites/default/files/2020-05/rpp074.pdf

Refugee Council of Australia. (2021). *Submission 16 on the performance and integrity of Australia's administrative review system.* Legal and Constitutional Affairs References Committee on the Performance and Integrity of Australia's Administrative Review System. https://www.refugeecouncil.org.au/performance-and-integrity-of-the-aat/

Richards, S. (2021). Justice denied as Aboriginal people left without translators in court. *In Daily.* https://indaily.com.au/news/2021/03/11/justice-denied-as-aboriginal-people-left-without-translators-in-court/

Russell, E. (2021). Number of women on remand in Victoria soars due to outdated bail laws. *The Conversation.* https://theconversation.com/number-of-women-on-remand-in-victoria-soars-due-to-outdated-bail-laws-165301

Sourdin, T., & Burstyner, N. (2014). Justice delayed is justice denied. *Victoria University Law and Justice Journal, 4*(1), 46–60.
Thomas, R., & Tomlinson, J. (2017). Mapping current issues in administrative justice: Austerity and the 'more bureaucratic rationality' approach. *Journal of Social Welfare and Family Law, 39*, 380–399.
Victorian Premier's Office. (2021). *Supporting our courts: Drive down Covid 19 Backlogs.* Media statement. https://www.premier.vic.gov.au/supporting-our-courts-drive-down-covid-19-backlogs
Weatherburn, D. (1996). Measuring trial court performance: Indictors for trial case processing. *NSW Bureau of Crime Statistics and Research Crime and Justice Bulletin: Contemporary Issues in Crime and Justice, 30*, 1–11.
World Bank. (2012). *New Directions in Justice Reform: A Companion piece to the updated implementation plan strategy on strengthening governance and tackling corruption.* Retrieved from https://documents1.worldbank.org/curated/en/928641468338516754/pdf/706400REPLACEM0Justice0Reform0Final.pdf

Legislation and Cases

Attorney-General's Reference (No 2 of 2001) [2004] 2 AC 72.
Jago v District Court of NSW (1989) 168 CLR 23 (High Court).
Kara Lesley Mills v The Queen [2011] ACTSC 109–210.
Martin v Tauranga District Court ([1995] 2 NZLR 419.
R v KGK, 2020 SCC 7.
R v Jordan, 2016 SCC 27, [2016] 1 SCR 631.
R v Cody, 2017 SCC 3.
R v Smith (1989) 52 CCC (3d) 97.
R v Morin (1992) 71 CCC (3d) 1, 105.
R v Kara Lesley Mills [2011] ACTSC 109.
Spiers (Procurator Fiscal) v Ruddy [2008] 1 AC 873.
Tattsbet Limited v Morrow [2015] FCAFC 62.
Law Council of Australia (2015). *Legal Profession Uniform Law.*
Law Council of Australia (2015). *Conduct Rules 2015* (Solicitors' Conduct Rules).
Legal Profession Uniform Continuing Professional Development (Barristers) Rules 2015.
Expectation Pty Ltd v PRD Realty Pty Ltd (2004) 140 FCR 17, 32–35 [66]-[83].

Practitioner Perspective: Justice Delayed

Sharon E. Lacy

Only very urgent cases are heard immediately after proceedings are initiated. In my experience as a barrister practising for over 20 years, the resolution of civil or criminal litigation involves some delay. Generally, much preparation is involved by all parties before a matter can be properly tried. But the balance of fairness can tip, and justice will less likely be achieved when the delay between initiation and resolution is unreasonably extended. The common law concept of 'unreasonable delay' is rooted in principles of equity and fairness, referring to delay that causes unfair harm or disadvantage to a party which cannot be rectified.

Consequences of Unreasonable Delay

The most extreme consequences of extended delay are usually found in criminal courts, where an accused person's liberty and livelihood are curtailed between charge and verdict. There are many examples of an accused person who is charged, remanded in custody, refused bail, and ultimately upon trial, is acquitted. The burden of being an accused person waiting for trial cannot be under-estimated. Detention in custody invariably has an enormous impact on their personal life, family connection, mental health, employment prospects, housing and financial security. At some point the delay in resolution of their case has the effect of undermining the presumption of innocence—their detention awaiting trial punishes them as if they were guilty.

Other consequences of extended delay in both criminal and civil litigation that can affect an assessment of its reasonableness include that:

- witnesses' memories can fade and the reliability of their account is diminished;
- physical evidence can be lost;

S. E. Lacy
The Victorian Bar, Melbourne, VIC, Australia

- relationships can be damaged;
- assets can be frozen;
- personal and professional development can be stalled; and
- court outcomes may become less meaningful.

Causes of Extended Delay

For matters to be resolved in a timely fashion requires all stakeholders to be committed to this end. Litigants, their lawyers, court services officers, judicial officers, police and security personnel and witnesses all have capacity to unwittingly, or otherwise, cause significant delay. There is a lot of room for things to go wrong and problems to arise along the journey of a legal dispute.

There needs to be appropriate capacity in resourcing of courts, court services, judicial officers, prosecutorial and legal aid services, technological facilities and support networks to avoid a court caseload backlog that entrenches extended delay in case resolution, quite apart from that which might be caused by the individual players along the way. Where the government introduces legislative or resourcing changes to legal practice, this invariably has a flow on effect to the role or workload of other players essential to the system. For example, where a large number of additional police officers are funded through a government law and order campaign, the police force has a greater capacity for the investigation and charge of offending—more people are charged with offences and more cases initiated in court.

These increased resources at the front-end of the criminal justice process cause a bottleneck at the resolution end, unless there is a corresponding increase in resources to all other entities involved. Similarly, if sentencing laws are amended to create mandatory jail terms for particular offences, people accused of those offences are less likely to plead guilty and will join the list of cases heading for trial.

Since the outbreak of the COVID-19 pandemic in early 2020, justice systems around the world have been grappling with how to keep the wheels of justice turning amid a public health crisis and population lockdowns. Some jurisdictions found creative ways, mostly through the expanded use of technology, to administer justice under extreme conditions. Others simply ground to a halt, leaving an unprecedented backlog of criminal and civil litigation that has entrenched long-term delay for many years to come.

Alleviating Delay and Its Consequences

There are practical things that can be done to reduce litigation backlog, limit delay or relieve some of the detrimental effects of extended delay. Delays are at greatest risk of extending unreasonably where a trial is required for resolution, because processes involving the calling of contested evidence, legal submissions, judicial rulings and jury empanelment, charge and deliberation, all require a great deal of time and resources. Any processes which assist case resolution without the need for extended court time, will reduce caseload backlog and limit entrenched delay.

Following are some practices that have been embraced in various jurisdictions to combat case backlog and resolution delay. Many of them apply particularly to criminal jurisdictions, because overwhelmingly this is where the most significant delay and the greatest consequence of delay occurs.

1. Case conferences can force parties to apply themselves to identifying the issues in dispute before an impartial judicial officer, who weighs in and attempts to settle the case. The process can be 'without prejudice' and provide a forum for flushing out the issues the really matter to each party.
2. Administrative caseload management and triage of cases can allow for prioritisation of the most vulnerable litigants and the cases for which extended delay would impose the greatest prejudice or disadvantage to a party.
3. Building greater agility into court resolution processes can mean that cases are not caught by rigid compliance procedures that slow down resolution. Introducing or better utilising lower-level court officers,

like judicial registrars, at an early stage in proceedings, is one means of efficiently identifying the most direct route to resolution.

4. Less serious offences, like drug possession and petty theft, could be removed from the court system and offenders diverted through a caution process with supports available.
5. Prosecuting authorities could prioritise that offending which matters most to protecting the community and preserving social cohesion. They could adjust policies so as to more readily withdraw from pursuing less serious matters and those matters where prosecution is less likely to be successful.
6. Legislative provision could remove some of the uncertainty of outcome for accused people by allowing judicial officers to indicate the likely sentence to be imposed on an accused if they were to plead guilty. With outcome surety, an accused person is more likely to plead guilty to an offence they have committed.
7. Governments could legislate greater inducements for accused people to plead guilty, like increased sentencing discounts.
8. Alternative dispute resolution mechanisms can provide more purposeful outcomes for litigants and achieve case resolution more quickly and less onerously. Often plaintiffs or complainants do not want to go to court and do not necessarily want the accused prosecuted and punished—they simply want the wrongdoing acknowledged and for an apology.
9. The pre-recording of witness evidence can reduce the burden on witnesses while waiting for a trial to be reached. It also limits problems that arise with depreciation of memories and reduced reliability of evidence, caused by delay.
10. The amendment of bail laws can assist in preventing the unnecessary remand of accused people awaiting trial. The main purpose of bail is to ensure that an accused person attends their trial. There are many alternative means to provide some security to this end, other than detention in custody.

Conclusion

A fair process of justice, by which disputes are resolved and wrongs are accounted for, is an integral component of a civil society. If this cannot be achieved within a reasonable time, then justice cannot be said to be done. Around the world justice systems are in crisis by virtue of crippling delay. In many jurisdictions, much more substantial philosophical and structural changes may be required.

8

Injustices and Inequitable Outcomes: Miscarriages of Justice and Wrongful Convictions

Rachel Dioso-Villa and Caitlin Nash

Introduction

One of the most serious forms of injustice is the wrongful conviction of innocent persons who did not commit the crime. Such failures of justice undermine the integrity of the criminal justice system and result in devastating and long-lasting consequences for wrongfully convicted individuals. Since the first DNA exoneration in the United States in 1989, the problem of wrongful convictions has become more widely acknowledged globally, with the growing number of exonerations demonstrating beyond doubt that criminal justice systems have convicted innocent

R. Dioso-Villa (✉)
Griffith Criminology Institute, Griffith University, Brisbane, QLD, Australia
e-mail: r.diosovilla@griffith.edu.au

C. Nash
Griffith Criminology Institute, Griffith University, Brisbane, QLD, Australia
e-mail: c.nash@griffith.edu.au

M. Camilleri and A. Harkness (eds.), *Australian Courts*,
https://doi.org/10.1007/978-3-031-19063-6_8

persons. This issue has been most extensively documented in the United States, where the Innocence Project has helped exonerate 375 innocent persons since 1989, with this number increasing to nearly 3,000 with the exonerees documented by the National Registry of Exonerations (2022).

The Australian criminal justice system is not immune to this problem and has also convicted innocent persons. Although Australia lacks a national registry such as in the United States, there are over 70 documented cases in Australia where a factually innocent person was convicted of crimes they did not commit (Dioso-Villa, 2015), including well-known cases like Lindy Chamberlain, John Button, Andrew Mallard and Kelvin Condren. As conservatively estimated by Sangha and Moles (2014), there may be somewhere near 300 wrongfully convicted persons across Australian prisons, suggesting that these known cases represent only a fraction of a much more widespread problem.

Access to justice is fundamental to the rule of law in Australia, yet inequitable experiences and unjust outcomes prevail for some individuals. This chapter reflects an intersectional approach to understanding how and why experiences in court may be inequitable for some individuals relative to others. It identifies contemporary controversies and challenges by exploring system-wide pressures and structural mechanisms and barriers that can produce an environment susceptible and conducive to error. The chapter concludes by highlighting strategies to reduce the occurrence of future wrongful convictions and to identify and correct potential cases in the Australian justice system.

Context and Controversies in Convicting the Innocent

Structural Over Causal Factors

For many years, the list of 'causes' or factors contributing to wrongful convictions was limited to faulty eyewitness identification, false confessions, jailhouse informant testimony, false or misleading forensic science, police and prosecutorial misconduct, ineffective defence representation and the like (Garrett, 2011; Gross & Shaffer, 2012).

While there is strong consensus over these factors, they have been criticised for focusing on only the legal or immediate causes of wrongful convictions, neglecting the broader systemic issues that may be contributing to this issue (Leo, 2017). Instead, injustices and inequitable experiences are generally the result of entrenched institutional and systemic factors, beyond the control of any one individual or malicious act. As Siegel (2005, p. 1223) states, "most erroneous or unjust results that emerge from our criminal justice system are the consequence not of extraordinary events, but of the ordinary operation of a flawed system". As such, it is essential to explore the structural features of the Australian criminal justice system that increase the risk of error, particularly, for disadvantaged and marginalised groups.

Imbalance in the Australian Adversarial System

The adversarial criminal justice system itself has been criticised for its tendency to produce wrongful convictions (see Findley, 2011; Huff, 2004). As noted by Roach (2010), this critique is not new, and was hinted at in Edwin Borchard's pioneering book detailing 65 miscarriages of justice, in which Borchard (1932, cited in Roach, 2010, p. 390) stated that convictions were often regarded "as a personal victory calculated to enhance the prestige of the prosecutor" while "the inability to engage competent attorneys makes it often impossible for the accused to establish his innocence".

While the Australian adversarial system *in theory* ascertains truth by having two adversaries present their own competing versions of facts, *in practice* it has been criticised for prioritising values such as autonomy, efficiency and finality over factual accuracy (Hamer & Edmond, 2019). Further, while an implied assumption in the idealised model is that the adversarial parties are roughly equal, the two parties are argued to be "anything but equal", with an imbalance between resources and access to evidence making true adversary testing "virtually impossible" (Findley, 2011, pp. 912–914).

In Australia, while the State-sponsored prosecution will generally have access to all the crime scene evidence and the government's resources to conduct a thorough investigation, the defence will be generally unable to compete with these resources (Findley, 2011; Hamer & Edmond, 2019). Rather, the vast majority of defendants lack the resources required to fund a vigorous defence and are often left with no other option but to be represented by over-burdened and under-prepared defence lawyers. Poor and inadequate defence representation—'bad lawyering'—is a common cause of wrongful convictions, where overwhelming caseloads and a lack of resources hinder a defence lawyer's ability to properly investigate and defend their clients' cases (Yaroshefsky & Schaefer, 2014). They may also put pressure on innocent persons to plead guilty without spending adequate time on their cases or providing sufficient legal advice (Joy & Uphoff, 2014; Sherrin, 2011).

This is pronounced for marginalised and disadvantaged persons who face increasing difficulties in accessing well-prepared and culturally appropriate defence representation (MacFarlane & Stratton, 2016). These defendants are unlikely to receive the benefit of a thorough investigation, careful analysis of the evidence against them, or the funds required to gather expert evidence that can effectively challenge the prosecution's case (Joy & Uphoff, 2014). As a result, while the parties are expected to be equal, the defence can be "frequently outgunned" by the police and prosecution who benefit from much greater power and resources (Bibas, 2013, p. 1292).

The adversarial system has also been criticised in its failure to screen forensic science evidence within the court (Edmond, 2020). False or misleading forensic science is a leading cause of wrongful convictions, contributing to nearly one-third of the wrongful convictions in Australia (Dioso-Villa, 2015). Despite official reports revealing that many forensic science disciplines lack scientific foundation and have not been shown to be valid or reliable, courts have been criticised for being "utterly ineffective in addressing this problem" and continue to permit unreliable evidence that lack solid scientific foundation (National Academy of Science, 2009, p. 53). Defence attorneys can expose the potential bias or invalidity of forensic evidence; however, they often lack the scientific understanding or resources required to effectively cross-examine forensic testimony or retest evidence and provide rebuttal experts (Hamer & Edmond, 2019). Problems may also arise when forensic scientists or lab analysts testify as expert witnesses at trial. As they are often employed by the State, some scientists and experts can identify too closely with the police and prosecution, lacking the necessary independence to give objective evidence.

Cases of misconduct, negligence or incompetence, have highlighted the risks associated with the system's heavy reliance on forensic evidence. For example, in 2008 Farah Jama was wrongfully convicted in the County Court in Melbourne and imprisoned for 15 months for raping a woman he had never met. The case against Jama was completely reliant on DNA evidence, with no other circumstantial evidence presented at trial (that is, no eyewitnesses, the victim had no memory of the assault, and the accused had an alibi). His conviction was quashed on appeal with a subsequent inquiry raising the prospect that a forensic medical officer had cross-contaminated the sample from the rape victim with a prior sample collected from Jama for an unrelated incident (Dioso-Villa, 2015). There are other examples of lax procedures in forensic laboratories, with poor standards in Victoria resulting in the Director of Public Prosecutors in 2009 ordering a review of all cases from the preceding five years that had relied on forensic evidence (Silvester, 2009).

False Guilty Pleas

While the main focus of the adversarial system is a jury trial, with numerous procedural protections and safeguards built into this system over hundreds of years, trials have become rare events in common-law jurisdictions, with the majority of criminal cases being resolved by a guilty plea. In Australia, over 80% of all criminal cases adjudicated in the higher courts are resolved by the defendant pleading guilty (ABS, 2012). Legal scholars have highlighted numerous problems associated with a system built of pleas, including the lack of transparency in plea-negotiations, prosecutorial discretion and unequal sentencing, among others (see Edkins & Redlich, 2019).

While guilty pleas have traditionally been viewed as reliable indications of guilt, criminal defendants can face numerous psychological, social and structural pressures to plead guilty (Redlich et al., 2017). For instance, defendants may feel pressure to plead guilty in order to receive the lesser penalty associated with a plea (Sherrin, 2011). Defendants accused of minor offences may also plead guilty to avoid the financial, psychological and time costs of going to trial, with pressure that is exacerbated when held in pre-trial detention, as defendants may plead guilty simply to get out of jail (Edkins & Dervan, 2018). Criminal defendants can also plead guilty due to legal misunderstanding (Sherrin, 2011). Misunderstandings can arise from a lack of cultural or linguistic understanding of the legal system (Joyner, 2018), or to access alternative justice processes or specialised courts, such as drug courts or Indigenous courts (Bressan & Coady, 2017).

In Western Australia in 2011, Tammy Lysaght pleaded guilty to assaulting her 16-month-old daughter after being threatened by her abusive former partner to take responsibility for the assault. Although she maintained her innocence, Lysaght said she was pressured into pleading guilty by both her lawyer and the Department of Child Services, as she was told that was her best means of being able to see her children (McNeill, 2018). This illustrates gender-specific pressures women may face to plead guilty, including threats from abusive relationships and childcare concerns (Jones, 2011).

The wrongful conviction of Gene Gibson highlights the increased vulnerability to false guilty pleas likely experienced by Indigenous Australians and those with mental disabilities, and how systemic issues can contribute to this issue. Gibson was a young Indigenous Australian from a remote Aboriginal community, he had limited understanding of English and significant cognitive impairments. In 2012, he was arrested and charged with murder after making contradictory and incriminating statements to the Western Australian police. Although this interview evidence was later deemed inadmissible as Gibson had been interviewed for nine hours without a lawyer or native language interpreter (*State of Western Australia v Gibson* 2014), Gibson pleaded guilty to manslaughter on the advice of his defence lawyer and was sentenced to seven and half year's imprisonment.

In 2017, after spending nearly five years in prison, the Court of Appeal unanimously quashed Gibson's conviction on the basis that he did not adequately understand the legal process, the case against him, or the nature and implications of his plea of guilt, and that there was a real risk that his guilty plea was not attributable to a genuine consciousness of guilt (*Gibson v The State of Western Australia* 2017). The Corruption and Crime Commission (2015, p. 50) found "systemic failures" with the Western Australian Police's handling of Aboriginal witnesses and suspects. There were also issues associated with under-funding of legal aid and Indigenous language interpretation services, as they did not have the resources available to provide Gibson with an interpreter accredited in his native language or the finances to administer a cognitive assessment (*Gibson v The States of Western Australia* 2017).

Vulnerable Populations: Equal Before the Law?

Equal access to justice represents a core tenant of human rights and modern legal systems. Yet, for many disadvantaged and vulnerable persons that come before the courts, the justice system can be largely inaccessible. People that come before the Australian courts are vulnerable in numerous ways, with levels of poverty, homelessness, poor education and literacy, unemployment, mental health conditions, intellectual disability, histories of alcohol and drug abuse, language barriers, financial constraints, or a lack of knowledge around rights and where to go for advice or assistance (Law Council of Australia, 2018). However, while it may be expected that vulnerable and disadvantaged persons are furnished within adequate procedural protections from abuses of power and injustices, they can instead be impeded rather than empowered by the law.

One of the major sources of injustices and inequity within Australian society is the persistent over-representation of Indigenous Australians in all aspects of the criminal justice system. Despite representing only 3.3% of the total Australian population, Indigenous Australians make up 29% of all prisoners (ABS, 2020). It is generally accepted that this over-representation is not a result of higher rates of offending within Indigenous communities, but rather reflects pervasive issues of colonialism, racial bias and systemic discrimination (Snowball & Weatherburn, 2007; Stratton & Sigamoney, 2020). Indigenous persons are subjected to laws, policies and practices that disproportionately disadvantage and incarcerate them (Anthony & Blagg, 2020; MacFarlane & Stratton, 2016) and are more than six times as likely to die in police custody and 10 times as likely to die in prison than non-Indigenous people (Allam et al., 2021).

Owing to their over-representation and differential treatment, it is suggested that Indigenous people are at a disproportionally high risk of suffering from miscarriages of justice and wrongful convictions (Dioso-Villa, 2015; MacFarlane & Stratton, 2016; Roach, 2015). Language and translation difficulties and cultural differences can cause inadequate and insensitive defence representation, and racist stereotypes that associate Aboriginal people with crime can make this population particularly vulnerable to miscarriages of justice (MacFarlane & Stratton, 2016; Roach, 2015). These systemic issues can also make Indigenous defendants more vulnerable to pressures to plead guilty, creating a particular barrier for Indigenous defendants to have their wrongful convictions recognised and remedied (Joyner, 2018; Roach, 2015).

The high number of persons with intellectual disabilities or mental illnesses throughout the Australian justice system also represents a significant problem, with the Australian Human Rights Commission (AHRC, 2014) finding numerous barriers that limit or prevent access to justice for persons with disabilities. In Australia, as well as internationally, persons with mental illness and cognitive impairments are over-represented in the criminal justice system compared with prevalence rates in the general population (Ogloff et al., 2007).

Inherent vulnerabilities that typify mental disorders likely increase their risk of wrongful convictions, such as judicial and jury prejudices, falsely appearing to lack remorse, difficulties in assisting in one's defence from deficits in language, an inability to understand abstract legal concepts and limitations in social functioning (Carl, 2020). Research also suggests that persons with mental illness are at an increased risk of falsely confessing or pleading guilty to crimes they did not commit (Redlich et al., 2010). The Australian Human Right Commission (2014a, 2014b, p. 25) found that persons with mental illness or intellectual disability are more likely to be "pleaded out" by duty lawyers who do not have sufficient time available to identify the disability, with the report concluding that systematic approaches to identify disabilities do not exist within the courts.

Contemporary Challenges in Accessing Justice

The High Cost of Justice and Unrepresented Litigants

One of the biggest barriers to justice is the prohibitively high financial legal costs, with the legal system being unaffordable and out of reach for most Australians (Productivity Commission, 2014a, 2014b). Given the high costs associated with going to court, the availability of legal aid represents a fundamentally important factor in determining the extent of access to justice. However, chronic under-funding of legal assistance services by the Australian government has resulted in increasingly restricted access to legal aid, forcing legal aid services to limit eligibility to people on very low incomes (Community Law Australia, 2012; Flynn & Hodgson, 2017). In 2014, the Productivity Commission estimated that only eight percent of Australians are likely to meet the restrictive means test for legal aid, leaving the majority of low to middle income earners with "limited captivity" to afford large legal costs (Productivity Commission, 2014a, 2014b, p. 20). This has been termed the 'missing middle', in which significant numbers of Australians are unable to afford legal representation but nevertheless are ineligible for legal aid.

Without legal representation, there is no alternative but to represent yourself in court; therefore, it is no surprise that increasingly restrictive access to legal services has resulted in rising numbers of self-represented litigants (Hunter et al., 2003; Law Council of Australia, 2014; Productivity Commission, 2014a, 2014b). Owing to the complexity of the law and the legal process, self-represented defendants can face numerous disadvantages in the legal system and may encounter significant difficulties in representing themselves effectively (Law Council of Australia, 2018; Stewart, 2011). Self-represented litigants are also suggested to take up much more time and resources than legally represented litigants, increasing the load on already over-burdened courts (Flynn & Freiberg, 2018; Law Council of Australia, 2018; Stewart, 2011; Walsh, 2017).

Limited access to legal representation can also put pressure on criminal defendants to plead guilty rather than attempt to represent themselves in legal proceedings (Helm, 2019). In their study on plea-negotiations in Victoria, Flynn and Freiberg (2018, p. xii) found that unrepresented defendants were at an increased risk of "succumbing to pressures to make agreements without fully understanding the implications of their guilty plea", raising concerns over the potential for unrepresented defendants to enter "coerced or misunderstood guilty pleas". In a study on Australian appellate court judgements in which a guilty plea conviction was overturned (Nash et al., 2021), it was found that unrepresented defendants were more likely to enter a guilty plea without fully understanding the charges against them, the availability of potential defences, or the implications of a guilty plea. This raises significant concerns over the impact of restrictive access to legal aid, and the real risk of injustice that unrepresented defendants may face within the legal system.

Courts Under Pressure: Court Backlog and Pressured Pleas

Another major challenge facing the court system is the growing backlog of cases, exacerbated during COVID, and the increasing costs associated with proceeding to trial. While litigants have the right for efficient and timely resolution of matters, the Australian court systems are under-resourced and overwhelmed with large caseloads, resulting in long court delays (Powell, 2017). While delays impact the efficiency of the courts, it can also create additional barriers to justice as the inability of the courts to provide timely access to justice imposes additional stress and costs for litigants and witnesses (Economides et al., 2015) and can cause people to give up or settle for outcomes that are not in their interests (Powell, 2017). Long delays can also impact on an accused's decision to plead guilty, especially those held in pre-trial detention (Mack & Roach Anleu, 2000).

To address court inefficiency, there has been an increasing reliance on resolving cases through a guilty plea in order to avoid the cost and time associated with a trial, with the consensus being the court system simply could not function if all cases proceeded to trial. This has resulted in the introduction of numerous inducements and incentives designed to encourage defendants to plead guilty as early as possible, such as sentence discounts, sentence indications, case conferencing and plea-negotiations (see Moynihan, 2008; New South Wales Law Reform Commission, 2014a, 2014b; Tasmanian Sentencing Advisory Council, 2018; Victorian Sentencing Advisory Council, 2007). The system benefits from guilty pleas by saving on the costs and inconvenience of trials, reducing court delays and sparing victims and witnesses from having to give evidence. However, inducements to plead have been argued to diminish the 'safety' of guilty pleas convictions and to prioritise efficiency and cost-effectiveness over just and fair outcomes (Nobles & Schiff, 2020).

Limited Avenues for Correcting Wrongful Convictions

Once convicted, a wrongfully convicted person in Australia can face significant legal obstacles in having their injustices recognised and remedied, with Australia being criticised for "falling behind" its international counterparts when it comes to implementing reforms for better identifying and correcting wrongful convictions (Weathered, 2013, p. 86, see also Hamer, 2014; Sangha & Moles, 2014). For instance, following several high-profile cases of miscarriages of justice, the United Kingdom established the Criminal Cases Review Commission, providing an independent body to investigate claims of miscarriages of justice to send to the Court of Appeal. Since its establishment in 1997, over 760 cases have been referred to the Courts of Appeal, of which 64% of appeals have succeeded (Criminal Cases Review Commission, 2021, p. 13). Canada introduced a similar body in 2002 with its Criminal Conviction Review Group, which expanded upon the mercy provisions previously applied to claims of wrongful conviction (Weathered, 2013). More recently, New

Zealand introduced their own Criminal Cases Review Commission in July 2020, and within a year of its operation had already receive 220 applications of defendants claiming innocence (White, 2021). This is a much greater number of applications received by the previous system of royal prerogative of mercy, which received only 172 applications in 25 years (White, 2021).

In contrast, Australia has not implemented any significant governmental bodies or other legal mechanisms for the identification and correction of wrongful conviction (Weathered, 2013). Instead, there are limited options for errors to be discovered and corrected, with the Australian Human Rights Commission (AHRC, 2011) expressing concern that the current appeal system fails to comply with Australian's international obligations. For instance, current appeal provisions in Australia generally limit a criminal defendant to only one appeal, which must typically be launched within one month of the conviction. Further, the rules of appeal are generally technical and narrow, often focusing entirely on legal or procedural irregularity rather than claims of innocence. While defendants may request for their conviction to be heard in the High Court of Australia, as it operates as an appellate court, it is reluctant to admit any new or fresh evidence even if it demonstrates that the defendant is wrongfully convicted.

As a result of these limitations, many wrongful convictions come to light not through legal processes but because of prolonged media and public campaigns. Well-known wrongful convictions such as Lindy Chamberlain, John Button, Darryl Beamish, Andrew Mallard and Graham Stafford all involved groups of journalists, lawyers and concerned citizens agitating for justice. For many wrongly convicted people, justice is only achieved outside the system because of the efforts of interested bystanders. This is of course a haphazard and unfair remedy, as it largely depends on wrongfully convicted persons attracting the attention of dedicated activists.

Once a wrongfully convicted person has exhausted their rights to appeal, the only recourse available is to petition the Attorney General and the Governor for pardon or to exercise the royal prerogative of mercy. The Attorney General or Governor can also choose to refer the matter back to the appeal court for fresh consideration, or to refer it elsewhere for investigation, such as to a royal commission. However, this process has been heavily criticised for lacking transparency, accountability and independence, and a petition could be rejected for arbitrary reasons or for no reason at all (Sangha et al., 2014). Further, any decision for review is made entirely at the whim of a participant in the political process, who is very likely to be strongly influenced by the public climate rather than questions of justice.

For Change: Strategies to Minimise Unjust and Inequitable Outcomes

Increasing Avenues to Appeal

Since the turn of the twenty-first century, attention and effort has been paid to overturning wrongful convictions globally, including within Australia. In 2013, South Australia enacted legislation that allowed for a second or further appeal where there was fresh or compelling evidence that demonstrated a substantial miscarriage of justice (*Statutes Amendment (Appeals) Act* 2013). Other jurisdictions have since followed suit, with similar legislation being enacted in Tasmania in 2015 (*Criminal Code Amendment (Second or Subsequent Appeal for Fresh and Compelling Evidence) Act*, 2015) and Victoria in 2019 (*Justice Legislation Amendment (Criminal Appeals) Act*, 2019).

While these new laws allow for increased avenues for judicial review, they have been criticised for being insufficient (Sangha et al., 2014), with no assistance provided to convicted persons who believe themselves to be innocent. As a result, wrongful conviction applicants with limited resources can still face significant obstacles in attempting to prove their innocence. For instance, since South Australian enacted their legislation, only two convictions have been overturned, and the Full Court in both cases ordered that a new trial be held (*R v Drummond (No 2)* 2015; *R v Keogh (No 2)* 2014). Instead, to improve post-conviction mechanisms, numerous Australian scholars have called for the creation of a Criminal Cases Review Commission like those established in the United Kingdom and New Zealand (Hamer, 2014; Rego, 2021). Having an independent body to review cases would allow for increased appellate access and ensure claims of wrongful convictions are systematically investigated.

Alleviate System Pressures

In addition to improving post-conviction mechanisms, there also needs to be an enhanced focus on reducing the potential for error, as the "slow, expensive, complicated" legal system drastically needs to be improved (Farrell, 2014). This requires increased funding for the courts and legal aid services to ensure that they are capable of dealing with the overwhelming caseloads and are able to provide representation that can effectively challenge the prosecution's case. Given that Indigenous Australians can be particularly vulnerable to legal problems and require culturally appropriate legal services from specialist experts, there needs to be increased funding and recourse provided to meet legal needs in remote communities.

Since our adversarial system has transformed from one that has historically revolved around trials to a system of pleas, the system's processes and protections thus need to adapt from trial-based protections to plea protections. The justice system must also ensure that especially vulnerable people receive adequate protection throughout any investigative and court process, whether as defendants or as witnesses.

Conclusion

Efforts to put matters right will never be completely satisfactory nor will the job of reforming the criminal justice system, so as to avoid future errors, ever be complete. Rather than interpreting these errors as generally the result of individual malice or incompetence, we should understand them as systemic errors that can occur at all levels and areas of the justice system. Additional safeguards are needed to reduce the risks of future miscarriages such that defence lawyers are not disadvantaged relative to the prosecution, that police investigators are not put under pressure unfairly to solve high-profile cases, that courts and parties have access to objective scientific evidence and that adequate remedies exist to redress wrongful convictions. These will go a considerable way to reducing the risks of future miscarriages, since without them, the criminal justice system will continue to struggle to find an appropriate balance between truth, fairness, finality and efficiency.

References

ABS (Australian Bureau of Statistics). (2012). *Year Book Australia, 2012* (Cat No. 1301.0). http://www.abs.gov.au/ausstats/abs@.nsf/Lookup/by%20Subject/1301.0~2012~Main%20Features~Courts~67

ABS (Australian Bureau of Statistics). (2020). *Prisoners in Australia.* https://www.abs.gov.au/statistics/people/crime-and-justice/prisoners-australia/latest-release

Allam, L., Wahlquist, C., & Evershed, N. (2021). Aboriginal deaths in custody reports to be increased to every six months after years of delays. *The Guardian.* https://www.theguardian.com/australia-news/2021/may/26/aboriginal-deaths-in-custody-reports-to-be-increased-to-every-six-months-after-years-of-delays

Anthony, T., & Blagg, H. (2020). Hyperincarceration and Indigeneity. *Oxford Research Encyclopedia of Criminology.* https://doi.org/10.1093/acrefore/9780190264079.013.656

AHRC (Australian Human Rights Commission). (2011). *Inquiry into the Criminal Cases Review Commission Bill 2010.* https://humanrights.gov.au/our-work/legal/inquiry-criminal-cases-review-commission-bill-2010

AHRC (Australian Human Rights Commission). (2014). *Equal before the law: Towards disability justice strategies.* https://humanrights.gov.au/our-work/disability-rights/publications/equal-law

Bibas, S. (2013). Shrinking Gideon and expanding alternatives to lawyers. *Washington and Lee Law Review, 70*(2), 1287–1308.

Bressan, A., & Coady, K. (2017). *Guilty pleas among Indigenous people in Canada.* Department of Justice Canada. https://www.justice.gc.ca/eng/rp-pr/jr/gp-pc/gp-pc.pdf

Carl, A. E. (2020). Dead wrong: Capital punishment, wrongful convictions, and serious mental illness. *Wrongful Conviction Law Review, 1*(3), 336–363.

Community Law Australia. (2012). *Unaffordable and out of reach: The problem of access to the Australian legal system.* http://www.communitylawaustralia.org.au/wp-content/uploads/2012/07/CLA_Report_Final.pdf

Corruption and Crime Commission. (2015). *Report on Operation Aviemore: Major crime squad investigation into the unlawful killing of Mr Joshua Warneke.* Corruption and Crime Commission. Retrieved from https://www.ccc.wa.gov.au/sites/default/files/Report%20on%20Operation%20AvieMore%20Major%20Crime%20Squad%20Investigation%20into%20the%20Unlawful%20Killing%20of%20Mr%20Joshua%20Warneke.pdf

Criminal Cases Review Commission. (2021). *Annual report and accounts 2020/21.* Criminal Cases Review Commission. https://s3-eu-west-2.amazonaws.com/jotwpublic-prod-storage-1cxo1dnrmkg14/uploads/sites/5/2021/07/CCRC-Annual-Report-and-Accounts-2020-2021.pdf

Denniss, R., Fear, J., & Millane, E. (2012). *Justice for all: Giving Australians greater access to the legal system* (Institute Paper No. 8). The Australia Institute. https://australiainstitute.org.au/wp-content/uploads/2020/12/IP8-Justice-for-all_4.pdf

Dioso-Villa, R. (2015). A repository of wrongful convictions in Australia: First steps toward estimating prevalence and causal contributing factors. *Flinders Law Journal, 17*(2), 163–202.

Economides, K., Haug, A. A., & McIntyre, J. (2015). Toward timeliness in civil justice. *Monash University Law Review, 41*(2), 414–444.

Edkins, V. A., & Redlich, A. D. (Eds.). (2019). *A system of pleas: Social sciences contributions to the real legal system.* Oxford University Press.

Edkins, V. A., & Dervan, L. E. (2018). Freedom now or a future later: Pitting the lasting implications of collateral consequences against pretrial detention in decisions to plead guilty. *Psychology, Public Policy, and Law, 24*(2), 204–215.

Edmond, G. (2020). Forensic science and the myth of adversarial testing. *Current Issues in Criminal Justice, 32*(2), 146–179.

Farrell. (2014, April 10). 'Slow, expensive, complicated' legal system must be improved. *The Conversation.* https://theconversation.com/slow-expensive-complicated-legal-system-must-be-improved-25382

Findley, K. A. (2011). Adversarial inquisitions: Rethinking the search for the truth. *New York Law School Law Review, 56*(3), 911–942.

Flynn, A., & Freiberg, A. (2018). *Plea negotiations: Final report to the Criminology Research Council.* Criminology Research Advisory Council. https://research.monash.edu/en/publications/plea-negotiations-final-report-to-the-criminology-research-counci

Flynn, A., & Hodgson, J. (2017). Access to justice and legal aid cuts: A mismatch of concepts in the contemporary Australian and British legal landscapes. In A. Flynn & J. Hodgson (Eds.), *Access to justice and legal aid: Comparative perspectives on unmet legal needs* (pp. 1–22). Hart Publishing.

Flynn, A., Hodgson, J., McCulloch, J., & Naylor, B. (2016). Legal aid and access to legal representation: Redefining the right to a fair trial. *Melbourne University Law Review, 40*(1), 207–239.

Garrett, B. (2011). *Convicting the innocent: Where criminal prosecutions go wrong*. Harvard University Press.

Gross, S. R., & Shaffer, M. (2012). *Exonerations in the United States, 1989–2012*. Report by the National Registry of Exonerations. https://www.law.umich.edu/special/exoneration/Documents/exonerations_us_1989_2012_full_report.pdf

Hamer, D. (2014). Wrongful convictions, appeals, and the finality principle: The need for a criminal cases review commission. *University of New South Wales Law Journal, 27*(1), 270–311.

Hamer, D., & Edmond, G. (2019). Forensic science evidence, wrongful convictions and adversarial process. *University of Queensland Law Journal, 38*(2), 185–236.

Helm, R. K. (2019). Conviction by consent? Vulnerability, autonomy and conviction by guilty plea. *The Journal of Criminal Law, 83*(2), 161–172.

Huff, C. R. (2004). Wrongful convictions: The American experience. *Canadian Journal of Criminology and Criminal Justice, 46*(2), 107–120.

Hunter, R., Giddings, J., & Chrzanowski, A. (2003). *Legal aid and self-representation in the family court of Australia*. Socio-Legal Research Centre, Griffith University. https://apo.org.au/node/8535

Innocence Project. (2022). *DNA exonerations in the United States*. https://innocenceproject.org/dna-exonerations-in-the-united-states/

Jones, S. (2011). Under pressure: Women who plead guilty to crimes they have not committed. *Criminology & Criminal Justice, 11*(1), 77–90.

Joy, P. A., & Uphoff, R. J. (2014). Systemic barriers to effective assistance of counsel in plea bargaining. *Iowa Law Review, 99*(5), 2103–2130.

Joyner, T. (2018). Aboriginal defendants are pleading guilty due to language and cultural barriers, legal officials warn. *ABC News*. https://www.abc.net.au/news/2018-09-27/aboriginal-defendants-pleading-guilty-by-accident/10129268

Law Council of Australia. (2014). *Erosion of legal representation in the Australian justice system*. http://lca.lawcouncil.asn.au/lawcouncil/images/LCA-PDF/a-z-docs/fmsdownload079a.pdf

Law Council of Australia. (2018). *The Justice project, Final report*. https://www.lawcouncil.asn.au/justice-project/final-report

Leo, R. A. (2017). The criminology of wrongful conviction: A decade later. *Journal of Contemporary Criminal Justice, 33*(1), 82–106.

MacFarlane, J., & Stratton, G. (2016). Marginalisation, managerialism and wrongful conviction in Australia. *Current Issues in Criminal Justice, 27*(3), 303–321.

Mack, K., & Roach Anleu, S. L. (2000). Choice, consent and autonomy in a guilty plea system. *Law in Context, 17*(1), 75–95.

McNeill, H. (2018, January 23). 'I'm innocent': Perth mother's desperate fight to get her kids back. *WA Today.* https://www.watoday.com.au/national/western-australia/im-innocent-perth-mothers-desperate-fight-to-get-her-kids-back-20180123-h0n8ew.html

Moynihan, H. M. (2008). *Review of the civil and criminal justice system in Queensland.* Queensland Government. https://cabinet.qld.gov.au/documents/2009/jul/review%20of%20civil%20and%20criminal%20justice%20system%20in%20qld/Attachments/Review%20by%20Moynihan.pdf

Nash, C., Dioso-Villa, R., & Porter, L. (2021). Factors contributing to guilty plea wrongful convictions: A quantitative analysis of Australian appellate court judgments. *Crime & Delinquency*, online first. https://doi.org/10.1177/00111287211054723

National Academy of Sciences. (2009). *Strengthening forensic science in the United States: A path forward*. The National Academies Press.

National Association of Community Legal Centres. (2017). *Annual Report 2016–2017*. National Association of Community Legal Centres. https://clcs.org.au/sites/default/files/resources/2020-06/2017-10-30-NACLC-Annual-Report-final-web.pdf

National Registery of Exonerations. (2022). National Registery of Exonerations. https://www.law.umich.edu/special/exoneration/Pages/about.aspx

New South Wales Law Reform Commission. (2014a). *Encouraging appropriate early guilty pleas,* Report 141. New South Wales Law Reform Commission. https://www.lawreform.justice.nsw.gov.au/Documents/Publications/Reports/Report-141.pdf

Nobles, R., & Schiff, D. (2020). The supervision of guilty pleas by the court of appeal of England and Wales–workable relationships and tragic choices. *Criminal Law Forum, 31*(4), 513–552.

Ogloff, J. R., Davis, M. R., Rivers, G., & Ross, S. (2007). The identification of mental disorders in the criminal justice system. *Trends & Issues in Crime & Criminal Justice*. https://www.aic.gov.au/publications/tandi/tandi334

Peay, J., & Player, E. (2018). Pleading guilty: Why vulnerability matters. *The Modern Law Review, 81*(6), 929–957.

Powell, R. (2017). Family Court underfunded, letting people down, chief justice says. *ABC News*. https://www.abc.net.au/news/2017-04-30/family-court-letting-families-down-chief-justice-says/8483858

Productivity Commission. (2014b). *Access to justice arrangements: Inquiry report*. Commonwealth of Australia. https://www.pc.gov.au/inquiries/completed/access-justice/report

Redlich, A. D., Bibas, S., Edkins, V. A., & Madon, S. (2017). The psychology of defendant plea decision making. *The American Psychologist, 72*(4), 339–352.

Redlich, A. D., Summers, A., & Hoover, S. (2010). Self-reported false confessions and false guilty pleas among offenders with mental illness. *Law and Human Behavior, 34*(1), 79–90.

Rego, R. (2021). A critical analysis of post-conviction review in New South Wales, Australia. *The Wrongful Conviction Law Review, 2*(3), 305–347.

Roach, K. (2010). Wrongful convictions: Adversarial and inquisitorial themes. *North Carolina Journal of International Law & Commercial Regulation, 35*(2), 387–446.

Roach, K. (2015). The wrongful conviction of Indigenous people in Australia and Canada. *Flinders Law Journal, 17*, 203–262.

Sangha, B., & Moles, R. (2012). Mercy or right: Post-appeal petitions in Australia. *Flinders Law Journal, 14*(2), 293–328.

Sangha, B., & Moles, R. (2014). Maccormick's theory of law, miscarriages of justice and the statutory basis for appeals in Australian criminal cases. *The University of New South Wales Law Journal, 37*(1), 243–270.

Sangha, B., Moles, R., & Economides, K. (2014). The new statutory right of appeal in South Australian criminal law: Problems facing an applicant-unanticipated interpretive difficulties. *Flinders Law Journal, 16*(1), 145–186.

Sherrin, C. (2011). Guilty pleas from the innocent. *Windsor Review of Legal and Social Issues, 30*(1), 1–35.

Siegel, A. M. (2005). Moving down the wedge of injustice: A proposal for a third generation of wrongful convictions scholarship and advocacy. *The American Criminal Law Review, 42*(4), 1219–1237.

Silvester, J. (2009, December 4). Damning report on police lab. *The Age*. https://www.theage.com.au/national/damning-report-on-police-lab-20091203-k8sz.html

Snowball, L., & Weatherburn, D. (2007). Does racial bias in sentencing contribute to Indigenous overrepresentation in prison. *Australian & New Zealand Journal of Criminology, 40*(30), 272–290.

Stewart, R. (2011). The self-represented litigant: A challenge to justice. *Journal of Judicial Administration, 20*(3), 146–166.

Stratton, G., & Sigamoney, A. (2020). Why we don't see race: How Australia has overlooked race as an influence on miscarriages of justice. *Race and Justice*, online first. https://doi.org/10.1177/2153368720922294

Tasmanian Sentencing Advisory Council. (2018). *Statutory sentencing reductions for pleas of guilty: Final report No. 10.* Tasmanian Government. https://www.sentencingcouncil.tas.gov.au/__data/assets/pdf_file/0003/449553/Web-version-Sentencing-Discounts-Final-Report-October-2018.pdf

Victorian Sentencing Advisory Council. (2007). *Sentence indication and specified sentence discounts: Final report.* Sentencing Advisory Council. https://www.sentencingcouncil.vic.gov.au/sites/default/files/2019-08/Sentence_Indication_and_Specified_Sentence_Discounts_Final_Report.pdf

Walsh, K. (2017, January 31). Justice system costs rise but courts miss out. *The Australian Financial Review.* https://www.afr.com/politics/federal/justice-system-costs-rise-but-courts-miss-out-20170131-gu1xhd

Weathered, L. (2005). Pardon me: Current avenues for the correction of wrongful conviction in Australia. *Current Issues in Criminal Justice, 17*(2), 203–216.

Weathered, L. (2013). The growing acknowledgement of wrongful conviction: The Australian response within an international context. *Victoria University Law and Justice Journal, 3*(1), 79–92.

White, M. (2021). Hundreds tell new wrongful conviction body that they're innocent. *Stuff*. https://www.stuff.co.nz/national/crime/125579598/hundreds-tell-new-wrongful-conviction-body-that-theyre-innocent

Yaroshefsky, E., & Schaefer, L. (2014). Defense lawyering and wrongful convictions. In A. D. Redlich, J. R. Acker, R. J. Norris, & C. L. Bonventre (Eds.), *Examining wrongful convictions: Stepping back, moving forward* (pp. 123–140). Carolina Academic Press.

Legislation and Cases

Gibson v Western Australia [2017] WASCA 141.
R v Drummond (No 2) [2015] SASCFC 82.
R v Keogh (No 2) [2014] SASCFC 136.

State of Western Australia v Gibson [2014] WASC 240.
Criminal Code Amendment (Second or Subsequent Appeal for Fresh and Compelling Evidence) Act 2015 (Tas).
Justice Legislation Amendment (Criminal Appeals) Act 2019 (Vic).
Statutes Amendment (Appeals) Act 2013 (SA).

Practitioner Perspective: Wrongful Conviction—*The Case of Terry Irving*

Michael O'Keeffe

In mid-1994, I had taken up a position as Solicitor in Charge of Legal Aid Queensland's Townsville Office. I was on my first visit as duty lawyer at Townsville's Stuart Creek Correction Centre when I first met an Indigenous man, Terry Irving, then aged 38. So vehement and convincing was his claim of innocence, and so angry was he because legal aid had been refused that, in the weeks and months that followed, I was determined that I would assist him pro-bono in an appeal to the High Court.

On obtaining what few investigation and trial documents were available, I became increasingly disturbed that the Queensland criminal justice system had failed this Indigenous man comprehensively, at each stage from investigation to appeal.

Terry Irving wrongly served four and a half years of an eight-year sentence for an armed bank robbery in Cairns in 1993. In 1997, by order of the High Court, he was exonerated and released from prison. In the High Court judgement, Chief Justice Sir Gerard Brennan criticised the prosecution as "very disturbing", adding a long list of evidential failures, going on to say that the High Court " had the gravest misgiving about the circumstances of this case" (Irving vs R (High Court of Australia) 1996).

Requests for an apology, financial compensation and an independent inquiry were refused by successive Queensland Attorneys General. The case (Mr Terry Irving vs Australia 2002) went to the United Nations Human Rights Committee (2002), which stated:

M. O'Keeffe
QLD, Australia

> The facts laid out in the communication, which have not been contested by the State party, show that Mr. Irving was subject to manifest injustice... It would therefore appear that Mr. Irving should be entitled to compensation.

While still not concluded in 2022, Irving's case is Australia's longest running litigation. His quest for justice has travelled for almost 30 years through all Queensland domestic courts—criminal (to gain his freedom) and civil (to obtain reparations)—and to the highest Australian and international tribunals. He has undergone fully contested hearings in the Queensland District Court (in 1993, 1998 and 1999), the Queensland Supreme Court (in 2019 and 2020), the Queensland Court of Appeal (in 1994 and 2021), the United Nations Human Rights Committee (in 2002) and in Australia's High Court (in 1997 and 2022).

In December 2021, the Queensland Court of Appeal found that Terry Irving had been maliciously prosecuted on one count by Detective Helen Pfingst and the State of Queensland, and awarded him damages, and 50% of costs (Irving v Pfingst and the State of Queensland). In July 2022, that judgement was considered by Australia's High Court, which refused special leave to appeal, leaving the Queensland Court of Appeal judgment unchanged. The result is that Terry Irving has been awarded damages (quantum yet to be determined), interest, and 50% of his costs, all of which will fall to be paid the Queensland taxpayers, who will also be obliged to pay the legal costs of Detective Pfingst and the Queensland Government, which could run in the millions in fees.

International Law and Practice

Human rights following exoneration are not merely a matter of public interest, to be balanced against other competing public interests, or left to the discretion of the State. Restitution is one part of the process by which the State, as part of its social contract to the citizen, is able to acknowledge that it sometimes makes mistakes, that no justice system is perfect, and that where such mistakes are made, proper attempts are made to right the wrong.

The human right of compensation after exoneration has been a fundamental international human rights obligation since at least 1983 under Article 14(6) of the United Nations International Convention of Civil and Political Rights (ICCPR). That human right has been adopted by all Western democracies except Australia, either by specific domestic legislation, or by enforceable guidelines. With the exception the ACT, no Australian jurisdiction complies with international law in allowing exonerees their human rights under the ICCPR.

Queensland has expressly refused to incorporate this international obligation into law, most recently in 2019 when the Queensland *Human Rights Act 2019* was passed in State Parliament. For exonerees, that Act disrespected the human rights values mandated by the UN and the community of nations.

Apology

The act of apology does not come easily to Australian politicians. But, at a justice process level, apology forms part of recognised law in Queensland as a key element in certain areas—for instance in restorative justice programmes. For victims, an apology reduces feelings of abandonment and powerlessness, and may provide some closure through a specific recognition that they have been wronged. Terry Irving's claim for an apology has not been responded to by Queensland over three decades.

Inquiry

Since exoneration, all pleas to four successive Attorneys General seeking an independent inquiry for Irving have been refused or not responded to. The outstanding exception as Attorney General was Kerry Shine who agreed to meet with Irving and myself personally, and who ordered former Supreme Court Justice Martin Moynihan to conduct a review into the circumstances of Terry Irving's wrongful conviction. However, Shine's successor as Attorney General, Cameron Dick, sat on the papers for nine months and then simply abolished the Moynihan inquiry (Giles, 2009, 2010).

Official delay by the justice authorities was a notable feature in the Irving case. Delays by Crown Law were protracted during the court proceedings for malicious prosecution. There were few concessions on procedure, the various trials were fully contested, and document discovery was, at times, very delayed. One trial had to be abandoned, and another ordered, for reasons within the purview of Crown Law. There is an old well-known legal maxim, that dates back to *Magna Carta* in 1215: "Justice delayed is justice denied".

The prolonged litigation meant that Irving's case has been subject to a claim of *sub-judice* for much of its legal journey. This has enabled the Queensland Government to refrain from having to make any explanation, if asked.

Requests for Ex-gratia Payment

Shortly after Terry Irving was released from prison by the High Court, I wrote to Attorney General Matt Foley seeking an ex-gratia payment. After many unanswered reminders over the next 14 months, the prospect of the expiry of time under the Queensland *Limitations of Actions Act 1984* to bring a civil suit drew very close. Because of this failure to respond, I decided that Terry Irving's interests were best protected by issuing writs to preserve the single very limited tort remedy he had: the tort of malicious prosecution. After the limitation period had expired, Terry Irving's request for ex-gratia payment was subsequently refused, with the Attorney General noting that he would not further consider such payment as Mr Irving had now issued civil proceedings (Queensland Attorney General Matt Foley, communication to Michael O'Keeffe, 29 October 1999). The next Attorney General, Linda Lavarch, after a further eight months and many reminders, also refused all our pleas.

In Queensland, we are told that restitution after exoneration is not dealt with by law, but by a policy which refuses payments to exonerees unless there are 'exceptional circumstances' (Queensland Attorney General Linda Lavarch, communication to Terry Irving, 8 May 2006). The effect of this policy is that the State retains complete control over post-exoneration decisions, and issues of payment and quantum of restitution (if any) are left to the absolute discretion of the Queensland Attorney General. Any assessments which may have taken place in Irving's case were conducted in secret, without reference to any published guiding principles including guidelines as to what might constitute 'exceptional circumstances'.

As no procedure is set down by Queensland justice authorities, questions of procedural fairness—such as legal representation, calling witnesses, freedom from bias and the right to be heard—need not, and do not, arise. No reasons are given, and such decisions as the Queensland justice authorities choose to make, are not reviewable by the courts.

Malicious Prosecution

Terry Irving's sole available legal remedy was to prove malicious prosecution against the police officer who conducted the police investigation into the robbery. Malicious prosecution is recognised as the most difficult of torts for a plaintiff to establish (Hull, 2015; Sappideen & Vines, 2011; Whealy, n.d.). Many millions of taxpayer dollars were spent by the State of Queensland opposing Terry Irving, who dared to challenge the justice authorities of the State of Queensland after his exoneration. Notwithstanding this almost impossible legal and resource intensive task, in 2021 Irving's pro-bono legal team successfully persuaded the Queensland Court of Appeal to find that he was maliciously prosecuted, ordering damages and costs in his favour in respect of one of two charges, a judgement maintained by the High Court in 2022.

Conclusion

It takes a lot of gall to disregard the findings of Australia's highest court, and the highest international human rights tribunal in the world. But that is what the Queensland justice system has done in Terry Irving's case. More broadly, there is in Queensland an inability to respect accepted international law and values relating to exonerees. There seems to be an entrenched Queensland government philosophy that wrongful convictions for Queenslanders are very much accepted by the justice system as unexceptional, and that any criminal miscarriage of justice is somehow cured simply by release from prison.

In my experience, the real objective of the Queensland justice authorities regarding exonerees has not been about justice at all. The opposite is true: denying justice by refusing to admit that any mistake had been made; and delaying attempts by exonerees to right the grievous wrongs caused by the State's errors. Without the political will to introduce sweeping legislation and without reform of the culture of Queensland justice authorities, the Queensland Government will continue to inflict taxpayer-funded, cruel and unnecessary grief on innocent Queenslanders.

References

Giles, D. (2009, January 11). Words are cheap in a battle for Justice. *Sunday Mail* (Brisbane).

Giles, D. (2010, January 3). No review after innocent man served four years for robbery. *Sunday Mail* (Brisbane).

Hull, C. (2015, September 18). Australia should follow ACT on wrongful prosecution laws. *The Canberra Times.*

Sappideen, C., & Vines, P. (Eds.). (2011). *Fleming's the law of Torts* (10th ed.; Chapter 2). Thomson Reuters Professional.

United Nations. (2002, April 1). Terry Irving v. Australia. Human Rights Committee, 74th session. U.N. Doc. CCPR/C/74/D/880/1999, Communication No. 880/1999. http://www.worldcourts.com/hrc/eng/decisions/2002.04.01_Irving_v_Australia.htm

Whealy QC, Hon Andrew. (n.d.). Malicious prosecution. *Civil trial bench book*, paragraph [5-7120]. https://www.judcom.nsw.gov.au/publications/benchbks/civil/intentional_torts.html

Cases

Irving v R (High Court of Australia, No B96 of 1996), 8 December 1997, Transcript p. 7, per Brennan CJ, Hayne J and McHugh J). Retrieved from http://www.austlii.edu.au/cgi-bin/viewdoc/au/cases/cth/HCATrans/1997/405.html

Irving v Pfingst and the State of Queensland [2021] QCA 280, per Fraser, McMurdo P, Mullens JJA. https://www.queenslandjudgments.com.au/caselaw/qca/2021/280?mview=irving|pfingst|

9

Problem-Solving Courts

Lacey Schaefer and Caitlyn Egan

Introduction

Problem-solving courts developed from the recognition of the limited capacity for traditional court processes to address the causes of offending (and its cyclical nature with punishment), thus advocating for therapeutic rather than legal means of addressing justice-enmeshed individuals (Bartels, 2009; Wexler & Winick, 1996). Since their introduction to Australia in the 1990s, problem-solving courts have been met with mixed reviews.

L. Schaefer (✉)
Griffith University, Brisbane, QLD, Australia
e-mail: l.schaefer@griffith.edu.au

C. Egan
Griffith University, Brisbane, QLD, Australia
e-mail: caitlyn.egan@griffithuni.edu.au

M. Camilleri and A. Harkness (eds.), *Australian Courts*,
https://doi.org/10.1007/978-3-031-19063-6_9

Although problem-solving courts are popular among the public for embodying the rehabilitative ideal and a therapeutic jurisprudence approach (Thielo et al., 2019), they are not without philosophical and practical problems (Schaefer & Beriman, 2019). While the manifestations of these speciality courts vary greatly across Australia, they embrace the same fundamental framework: By targeting the underlying reasons why a person offended through a collaborative case management approach, the individual will be less likely to reoffend. Yet problem-solving courts encounter difficulties in fulfilling this ideal; these are not fatal flaws, however, and can be remedied with thoughtful reforms.

Toward this aim, this chapter reviews the context, controversies, challenges and considerate changes relevant to problem-solving courts in an Australian context. Specifically, it begins by outlining the origins of problem-solving courts in Australia, explaining how the guiding philosophy of individualised responses—both between and within courts—means that the manifestation of these courts varies substantially.

As a loose definition, the chapter focuses on speciality courts that are outcome-focused and advocates for the enacting of system reforms—reforms which rely on a collaborative courtroom workgroup with case co-ordination and which utilise judicial authority for leveraging behaviour change (Bartels, 2009). It highlights some of the ideological controversies associated with Australian problem-solving courts (including issues with boundaries, sentencing and participation) in addition to the practical challenges observed (such as matters of access, assessment and treatment and case co-ordination). The chapter concludes with thoughtful suggestions for reforms, emphasising that key elements of 'justice' should not be lost in the problem-solving movement.

Context: The Origins and Context of Problem-Solving Courts in Australia

The emergence of problem-solving courts in Australia followed a journey comparable to their introduction elsewhere in the world, yet scholars have suggested that there are elements to local versions that are uniquely Australian (Freiberg, 2001; Kornhauser, 2018; Nolan, 2012). Since first appearing in 1997, Australian problem-solving courts can be characterised as the development of native solutions to local crime problems (Payne, 2006). It is perhaps for this reason—thoughtful, tailored responses—that the presence and shape of problem-solving courts varies markedly within and between states and territories as well as across time and governments (Schaefer & Beriman, 2019).

Just as the problems and solutions of problem-solving courts are native to each locality, the discussion in this chapter of the controversies and challenges of Australian speciality courts is likewise contingent on context. As such, before unpacking some of the shortcomings and prospects for reforms to problem-solving courts, 'setting the scene' by describing the development, manifestations and guiding frameworks of these specialty courts is necessary.

The Development of Problem-Solving Courts

Problem-solving courts have rapidly popularised following their introduction in a drug court in 1989 in Dade County in the state of Florida in the United States. The Dade County drug court remains in use, with the primary objective of offering an alternative to prison for offenders with drug-related offending, along with the ability to rehabilitate and recover (Eleventh Judicial Circuit of Florida, n.d.). Since 1989, there has been a proliferation of similar problem-solving courts across the United States, including mental health courts, domestic and family violence courts, driving courts, recidivist courts and community courts.

In the United States alone, there are now over 3,000 problem-solving courts (Haskins, 2019), with rising numbers also seen in Australia, Canada and the United Kingdom (Nolan, 2009). However, not all problem-solving courts and court models are the same. As described by Nolan (2009), the 'transplantation' of problem-solving courts has varied, creating differences in their processes. For instance, the United States is considered to function under an audacious approach, while countries such as Australia and England tend not to stray away from legislative and government order (Nolan, 2011). Scholars have noted that problem-solving courts in the United States rely greatly on the charismatic authority of judges, while Australian courts tend to lack this feature (Nolan, 2009). Yet, while Australian problem-solving courts were initially quite distinct from the models implemented in the United States, they have become more 'Americanised' in their current forms (Nolan, 2012).

Manifestations of Problem-Solving Courts in Australia

The features of Australian problem-solving courts differ considerably across the nation, especially considering the definitional inconsistencies observed between jurisdictions. Given how rapidly these courts emerge and evolve—and particularly provided how quickly political shifts and associated funding structures can occur (Payne, 2006; Stobbs, 2017)—it is not possible to quantify the number or caseloads of problem-solving courts in Australia. As a suitable starting point, however, it is useful to consider the frequent targets of these speciality courts.

A former director of the Australian Institute of Criminology, Toni Makkai, has remarked that there are priority areas that deserve specialised judicial approaches, including "reducing crime related to drug dependency and mental health, reducing the over-representation of Indigenous offenders and reducing the incidence of domestic violence" (cited in Payne, 2006, p. 1). Accordingly, Australian problem-solving courts tend to focus on the matters of alcohol- and drug-induced offending, forensic mental health, domestic and family violence and Indigenous justice (Schaefer & Beriman, 2019).

A notable starting point is that of the New South Wales pilot drug court programme in 1999 (Indermaur & Roberts, 2003). Despite a tumultuous commencement, this drug court remains active, focusing on the well-being of drug-dependent offenders who have pleaded guilty to a non-violent offence. Drug courts have been implemented across several Australian states, including Victoria, Western Australia and Queensland. Across these courts, eligibility requires a plea of guilty to a non-violent or summary offence, sufficient evidence to support a dependency issue, a sentence of possible imprisonment and residency in the court's region (*Drug Court Act 1998* [NSW]; Queensland Courts, 2021).

The first mental health court was trialled in South Australia, also in 1999 (Nolan, 2009). Since then, there have been several mental health courts implemented in Australia, although their manifestations vary greatly. For instance, the Queensland Mental Health Court is charged with assessing the 'state of mind' of an offender and determines fitness for trial (Queensland Courts, 2020). Alternatively, the Start Court in Western Australia is focused on providing support to mentally ill individuals who have found their way into the justice system, presumably as a result of their mental illness. Similar to the drug courts, there is also a guilty plea required (Magistrates Court of Western Australia, 2021a). Western Australia also has a separate court to assist offenders with a cognitive or intellectual disability, as well as those with Autism Spectrum Disorder (Magistrates Court of Western Australia, 2021b).

Domestic and family violence courts were introduced in Australia with two pilot programmes in 1999 in South Australia and Victoria (Nolan, 2009), with several similar courts following in Queensland and Western Australia. A notable exemplar is the specialist domestic and family violence court in Southport, Queensland. Following its trial period in 2015, the court has become the first established domestic and family violence court in Queensland (Department of Social Services, 2020; Queensland Courts, 2019). Evaluations of the Southport court have revealed promising outcomes (Bond et al., 2017), leading to a rollout of similar programmes across the state (Department of Social Services, 2020).

One of the difficulties in classifying problem-solving courts in Australia is that there are unclear concepts and ambiguous definitions used across jurisdictions. These definitions are not a matter of mere semantics but impact the scope of who is drawn into these specialist courts and what happens therein (Schaefer & Beriman, 2019). Such boundaries are of significant consequence, as "if a court's jurisdiction is defined too narrowly, it may not generate enough business to warrant developing an infrastructure; if it is too broad, it may lose its special focus and be unclear about its mission and expertise" (Freiberg, 2001, p. 22).

These definitional inconsistencies are not easily remedied, since individuals processed through the criminal justice system are subject to local legislation and how it is interpreted and applied (Duffy, 2011), and exacerbated by changing governments and associated criminal justice policy (Payne, 2006; Stobbs, 2017). Subsequently, there is considerable debate over the judicial distinctions between problem-solving justice and other justice innovations (Bull, 2010; Schaefer & Beriman, 2019).

Guiding Frameworks in Problem-Solving Courts

Given these difficulties in conceptualisation and classification of problem-solving courts, it is instructive to return to the philosophies that undergird this justice innovation. The guiding framework of problem-solving courts is 'therapeutic jurisprudence', an approach that incorporates the functions of therapy into the practice of law and justice. This framework is non-adversarial and rehabilitation-oriented, focusing on effectiveness and evidence-based outcomes. Therapeutic jurisprudence as the underlying philosophy is evident in an Australian context, drawing heavily upon the United States' problem-solving court models that seek to reduce the harms of traditional justice responses (Bull, 2010; Nolan, 2009).

Within this framework, problem-solving courts aim to hold offenders accountable for their actions, but further provide them the opportunity to heal and receive treatment with the support of the criminal justice system and affiliated social service agencies. In adopting therapeutic jurisprudence, these courts emphasise the welfare of participants (Stobbs, 2017), including defendants, victims and support persons (Bull, 2010). Problem-solving courts periodically and systematically review an offender's progress and recovery, with the overarching aim that at the completion of the programme, the participant will have been effectively treated and will be able to function pro-socially within their community.

The Controversies of Problem-Solving Courts in Australia

Australia's problem-solving courts exhibit many meritorious features. Given the scrutiny justice innovations face, these speciality courts have been the subject of considerable outcome, cost and process evaluations. As a result of these enquiries, we are beginning to understand how, for whom and under what circumstances problem-solving courts are most effective (Schaefer & Beriman, 2019). Yet, conversely, researchers have likewise documented many of the shortcomings of traditional criminal courts that are maintained or worsened in Australian problem-solving courts.

Blurred Boundaries and Muddied Missions

In design, problem-solving courts have a distinct definition and purpose. They are specialised dockets that aim to identify and treat the underlying causes of an individual's offending. Five key features are: (i) an emphasis on case outcomes; (ii) reframing government schemes; (iii) reducing an individual's offending; (iv) inter-agency communication; and (v) unorthodox responsibilities of courtroom staff (Berman & Feinblatt, 2001).

A problem-solving court's *aim* is to find the solution for the *problem* that caused a criminal offence (Freiberg, 2001). Yet this is not always the case. Some problem-solving courts do not address the underlying reasons for offending (Schaefer & Beriman, 2019). For instance, mental health courts are not solving the *problem*. Instead, the purpose is to refer an offender to a treatment programme, or to determine whether the offender was of sound mind during the offence and can subsequently stand trial (consider, e.g. the Queensland Mental Health Court, Queensland Courts, 2020).

There are also several Australian problem-solving courts that do not meet traditional definitions and create confusion over the use of the term. As an illustration, there are arguments that community courts and Indigenous courts do not meet the typical definitional criteria of a 'problem-solving court', as they do not seek to *solve* a cause of offending. Some scholars have argued that these courts may be better considered as 'problem-*oriented* courts', as they focus on an array of elements that may not necessarily have caused offending, but do, in fact, need to be addressed (Schaefer & Beriman, 2019).

Pressured Participation

Problem-solving courts vary in terms of eligibility criteria. Yet, there are two central requirements for entry in most Australian problem-solving courts: a guilty plea and voluntary participation. The idea that an offender can volunteer for such programmes is problematic, as they may not understand the process, may be invited to participate when under less than suitable circumstances, and the invitation may be to either volunteer or face potential imprisonment (Freeman, 2002; Jeffries, 2005). These recruitment procedures and eligibility requirements could be considered coercive and a violation of due process rights (McCoy et al., 2015).

Slippery Sentencing

Participating in a problem-solving court is not easy and can have unforeseen consequences. In the Queensland Drug and Alcohol Court, for example, participants must remain drug and/or alcohol free and are subject to regular court appearances and urine testing (Queensland Courts, 2021). If any breaches are noted, the offender may be subject to re-sentencing (possibly resulting in incarceration), where the original sentence may be imposed. Considering the pressure placed on offenders to partake in problem-solving courts, the possibility of further harm being done if not meeting the requirements poses threats to due process and human rights (Blagg, 2008).

The Challenges of Problem-Solving Courts in Australia

At the heart of ideas for innovations are questions of implementation. In particular, considering the multiple agencies and their protocols that make up the criminal justice system, making changes at the system-level can prove challenging. Since their implementation in 1997 and explosive growth, Australian problem-solving courts have not been immune to these challenges. While these hurdles are not insurmountable, they have been demonstrated to take considerable creativity and effort to be addressed. From a national lens, the challenges cited most frequently include issues of inequitable access, insufficient assessment and treatment options, and a lack of case co-ordination between agents across agencies, each of which is addressed in turn in the proceeding subsections.

Inequitable Access

Australia is geographically vast, with large rural and remote areas covering the nation between densely populated metropolitan areas. Unfortunately, as a side effect of this distribution of people and services, most problem-solving courts have been established within or adjacent to large cities. This is particularly problematic given that these courts intend to address segments of the offending population that have complex and under-serviced criminogenic needs, including those outside of metropolitan areas where access to treatment and other support services is less readily available (Payne, 2006).

Evaluations of problem-solving courts show that participants are generally pleased with the alternative to incarceration and are grateful for the access to treatment and services (ALRC, 2010; Birdsey & Smith, 2012). However, as Australia is one of the most urbanised countries internationally, with two-thirds of the population living in capital cities (ABS, 2018), many services are concentrated in these places. Consequently, problem-solving courts are naturally more readily established in such locations, although this inhibits access to those living in more rural settings.

Assessment and Treatment

Proponents of problem-solving courts often cite the inclusion of treatment as their redeeming trait. Unfortunately, however, this is generally premised on the idea that such treatments are rehabilitative or reformative, which may not always be the case (Schaefer & Beriman, 2019). It is possible for interventions for forensic clients to be benign or even criminogenic (Cullen et al., 2017). Some scholars have suggested that these justice innovations "rely on the capacity of the offender to make 'the right' choices once made aware of the consequences of their behaviour" (Bull, 2010, p. 175), yet rational choice theories are demonstrably faulty theoretical frameworks for offender interventions (Cullen & Jonson, 2012).

Within the Australian context, some scholars have noted that the benefits observed in the outcomes of problem-solving court participants are owing to self-selection biases and pre-existing risk levels rather than the treatment itself (Kornhauser, 2018; Lim & Day, 2016). Indeed, there have been questions over whether these speciality courts rely on validated actuarial risk, need and responsivity assessments (Lim & Day, 2013). While these tools *are* available and we *do know* what effective offender interventions entail, there is a need for more structured assessment processes and improved treatment fidelity (Schaefer & Beriman, 2019). In the case of Australian problem-solving courts, these factors may be a consequence of insufficient or eclectic organisational capability (Paparozzi & Schlager, 2009). These matters are of wide-reaching consequence when government agencies are prescribing treatments for crime problems (Cullen et al., 2017; Freiberg, 2001).

Case Co-ordination

Perhaps the most pervasive challenge confronting problem-solving courts is the (in)ability to coordinate between the agencies contributing to a case before the court. One of the elements that sets problem-solving courts apart from other programmes that emphasise participant accountability and judicial monitoring is the focus on a targeted and collaborative approach to offender intervention (Bowen & Whitehead, 2015). The systems, protocols and philosophical orientations between agencies can differ substantially, and these distinctions may prove difficult to overcome. Moreover, these differences *differ further* from court-to-court with unique processes and life cycles (Schaefer & Beriman, 2019).

As an illustration, imagine a forensic client being case managed by the court, a social worker, a drug counsellor, a probation officer and a family therapist, in addition to other system or service contacts (e.g. housing assistance, unemployment aid and disability services). Although the court itself facilitates a group interaction that contains information-sharing and case planning activities, agents may lack required information between these appearances. However, because each problem-solving court is a native solution individualised to a native problem, it is difficult to make state- or territory-wide system-level reforms that address these challenges.

Considerate Changes for Problem-Solving Courts in Australia

Following roughly 20 years of problem-solving court implementations and evaluations in Australia, we now have a significant amount of information regarding the controversies and challenges of these speciality courts. Stated more positively, we likewise have sufficient ammunition for the modifications required to increase the fairness and problem-solving capabilities of problem-solving courts. Four of the most pressing areas in need of court reform are detailed below.

Just Invitation and Participation Procedures

Treatment being legally leveraged is not unique to problem-solving courts. However, when these specialty courts require defendants to 'volunteer' for case management and a treatment-oriented approach when imprisonment is presented as the alternative, it is questionable whether individuals are truly voluntarily opting-in (Jeffries, 2005). It is also a point of contention to consider how well problem-solving courts switch between punitive and therapeutic functions and how these dual aims influence the actors collaborating on a case (Hall & Lucke, 2010; Thomas & Bull, 2013). Thus, in order for problem-solving courts to improve on this front, invitation and participation procedures should be made to be more just. Critically, defendants must be made aware of their legal rights and available options—in plain language and in accessible formats that is non-emotive and easily understood—at each decision-making point of their engagement with a problem-solving court.

Supportive Sentencing

In their summary of the literature, Schaefer and Beriman (2019) highlight 'the problem of constitutionality' as one of the greatest limitations problem-solving courts must address. They note that the role of magistrates in speciality courts may violate the aim of impartiality. Judges must "avoid stepping into the arena or appearing to take sides" (AIJA, 2017, p. 5), yet this is difficult to achieve when the court is medicating rather than adjudicating. In some problem-solving courts, matters of due process are of concern.

Specifically, where participants 'fail' (e.g. a positive drug test; noncompliance with treatment requirements; a reoffence), the original sentence can be imposed thereby subjecting the individual to greater punishment (Blagg, 2008). Australian problem-solving courts have been criticised for tasking participants with unrealistic obligations that are difficult to meet (Bull, 2010; Indermaur & Roberts, 2003) and for implementing excessively harsh procedures and sanctions that outweigh those used in traditional courts (Jeffries, 2005). There are further complications surrounding the timing of events (such as the requirement of a guilty plea to gain eligibility, uncertainty regarding disposition or sentencing when participants wish to withdraw from the speciality court and cases stagnating for extended periods of time), suggesting that the Australian legal system has wrestled with how offenders' due process rights are to be interpreted when moving from traditional judicial processes to those adopted by problem-solving courts.

Inclusion

When problem-solving courts first entered the Australian legal landscape, it seemed a sensible arrangement that they would appear in large metropolitan areas that had the services available to support treatment mandates. However, the lack of access to speciality courts by residents of outer suburbs and rural and remote locations has become unreasonable.

Criminal justice interventions, including case management and treatment, can be facilitated by technology (when certain conditions are met; Cullen et al., 2017), and the COVID-19 pandemic has demonstrated that agencies are able to deliver services virtually. For these reasons, expanding the geographic boundaries of eligibility for problem-solving courts is a necessary reform, particularly given that individuals placed in these areas may be at greater need of treatment and solutions-oriented justice. Indeed, given that criminal behaviour is often contextualised by community circumstances, it may reasonably be prevented and addressed by investing in the informal social bonds that provide guardianship in families, neighbourhoods and institutions (Austin et al., 2019). As such, community courts and problem-oriented justice initiatives may be well-served for investigating the local-level factors that contribute to individual-level offending.

More broadly, Australian specialty courts must consider mechanisms for encouraging participant inclusivity. Some researchers have speculated that now that justice innovations have shown demonstrable impacts on offending, reformers' goals will shift, such that "many now seek to reduce the use of incarceration, fines, and other punitive practices, and to eliminate racial and ethnic disparities" (Berman et al., 2021, p. 54). Problem-solving courts must develop ways to increase participation and completion rates for Indigenous Australians and other groups that are overrepresented in forensic populations (Schaefer & Beriman, 2019). These courts will also need to consider how to support 'non-traditional' perpetrators and victims, such as female intimate partner abusers, male victims and those from diverse cultural and linguistic backgrounds (Bond et al., 2017). Given that problem-solving courts embrace innovation, creating methods for surmounting these challenges should not be a discouraging prospect but should instead be an energising call to action.

Goal Clarity

Problem-solving courts in Australia are still negotiating their identity. Although the methods and modes used in specialty courts vary by jurisdiction, the overarching philosophy is that collaborative case management can be used to develop an individualised intervention that addresses the underlying causes of a person's offending, thereby reducing reoffending risks.

Payne (2006) categorised Australia's problem-solving courts (of the time) into a three-prong typology, as (i) case managers; (ii) specialist adjudicators; and (iii) diversionary operators and case monitors. Schaefer and Beriman (2019) argue that courts fulfilling the latter two functions, while commendable in their pursuits, fail to meet the definition of a problem-solving court because they are not geared toward uncovering and addressing the reasons why an individual commits crime. Toward this end, the problem-solving movement in Australia must carefully distinguish the aspirations of these courts from the contributions of other justice innovations.

Conclusion

The notion of tailor-made courts and case management is laudable, yet the reverse side of the specialisation coin is inconsistency. Australian problem-solving courts are exemplary in developing native solutions to native problems, yet the variation observed between courts can lead to ineffective practices that are swayed by local politics. Accordingly, the agendas of each court's power players will shape its goal orientation (including the procedures that symbolise the enactment of that goal), particularly without the protections of federal legislation that governs the court's scope—seen in documents such as America's Bill of Rights or Britain's Magna Carta (Duffy, 2011; Schaefer & Beriman, 2019).

Problem-solving courts must reign these local-level forces by more clearly stipulating what the court aims to accomplish while also articulating what the court will *not* do. In this way, Australian problem-solving courts will be most effective when they forego efforts to be a panacea for all the ills of the justice system. However, problem-solving courts may still contribute to broader criminal justice reforms by providing clarity about the shortcomings of our traditional responses to crime. Yet when these courts try to be 'everything to everyone' in addressing these limitations, they risk being 'nothing to no one' if further problems are created rather than solved. As such, Australian problem-solving courts will be most useful when they 'solve the problems' of each defendant's offending rather than widening their scope in trying to 'solve the problems' of traditional legal processes.

References

ABS (Australian Bureau of Statistics). (2018). *Interesting facts about Australia's 25,000,000 population*. Australian Bureau of Statistics. http://www.abs.gov.au/websitedbs/D3310114.nsf

AIJA (Australasian Institute of Judicial Administration). (2017). *Guide to judicial conduct* (3rd ed.). Australasian Institute of Judicial Administration.

ALRC (Australian Law Reform Commission). (2010). *Family violence—A national legal response*. Australian Government.

Austin, J., Schiraldi, V., Western, B., & Dwivedi, A. (2019). *Reconsidering the "violent offender."* Executive Session on the Future of Justice Policy.

Bartels, L. (2009). Challenges in mainstreaming specialty courts. *Trends & Issues in Crime and Criminal Justice, 383*, 1–6.

Berman, G., Adler, J., Barrett, J., & Penrose, K. (2021). What comes next? On the evolution of community courts. In P. K. Lattimore, B. M. Huebner, & F. S. Taxman (Eds.), *Handbook on moving corrections and sentencing forward: Building on the record* (pp. 46–57). Routledge.

Berman, G., & Feinblatt, J. (2001). Problem-solving courts: A brief primer. *Law & Policy, 23*(2), 125–140.

Birdsey, E. M., & Smith, N. (2012). *The domestic violence intervention court model: A follow-up study*. NSW Bureau of Crime Statistics and Research.

Blagg, H. (2008). *Problem-orientated courts*. Law Reform Commission of Western Australia.

Bond, C., Holder, R., Jeffries, S., & Fleming, C. (2017). *Summary report: Evaluation of the specialist domestic and family violence court trial in Southport*. Griffith Criminology Institute.

Bowen, P., & Whitehead, S. (2015). *Problem-solving courts: An evidence review*. Centre for Justice Innovation.

Bull, M. (2010). *Punishment and sentencing: Risk, rehabilitation and restitution*. Oxford University Press.

Cullen, F. T., & Jonson, C. L. (2012). *Correctional theory: Context and consequences*. Sage.

Cullen, F. T., Jonson, C. L., & Mears, D. P. (2017). Reinventing community corrections: Ten recommendations. *Crime and Justice, 46*, 27–93.

Department of Social Services. (2020). *Specialist DFV Court Model*. https://plan4womenssafety.dss.gov.au/initiative/specialist-dfv-court-model/

Duffy, J. (2011). Problem-solving courts, therapeutic jurisprudence and the constitution: If two is company, is three a crowd? *Melbourne University Law Review, 35*(2), 394–425.

Eleventh Judicial Circuit of Florida. (n.d.). *Adult drug court*. https://www.jud11.flcourts.org/Adult-Drug-Court

Freeman, K. (2002). *New South Wales drug court evaluation: Health, well-being and participant satisfaction*. NSW Bureau of Crime Statistics and Research.

Freiberg, A. (2001). Problem-oriented courts: Innovative solutions to intractable problems? *Journal of Judicial Administration, 11*(8), 8–27.

Hall, W., & Lucke, J. (2010). *Legally coerced treatment for drug using offenders: Ethical and policy issues*. NSW Bureau of Crime Statistics and Research.

Haskins, P. A. (2019). Problem-solving courts: Fighting crime by treating the offender. *National Institute of Justice Journal, 281*, 70–79.

Indermaur, D., & Roberts, L. (2003). Drug courts in Australia: The first generation. *Current Issues in Criminal Justice, 15*(2), 136–154.

Jeffries, S. (2005). How justice "gets done": Politics, managerialism, consumerism, and therapeutic jurisprudence. *Current Issues in Criminal Justice, 17*(2), 254–268.

Kornhauser, R. (2018). The effectiveness of Australia's drug courts. *Australian and New Zealand Journal of Criminology, 51*(1), 76–98.

Lim, L., & Day, A. (2013). Mental health diversion courts: Some directions for further development. *Psychiatry, Psychology and Law, 20*(1), 36–45.

Lim, L., & Day, A. (2016). Mental health diversion courts: A prospective study of reoffending and clinical outcomes of an Australian mental health court program. *Journal of Offender Rehabilitation, 55*(4), 254–270.

Magistrates Court of Western Australia. (2021a). *Start Court*. https://www.magistratescourt.wa.gov.au/S/start_court.aspx

Magistrates Court of Western Australia. (2021b). *Intellectual Disability Diversion Program Court*. https://www.magistratescourt.wa.gov.au/I/intellectual_disability_diversion_program_court.aspx

McCoy, C., Heydebrand, W., & Mirchandani, R. (2015). The problem with problem-solving justice: Coercion vs. democratic deliberation. *Restorative Justice, 3*(2), 159–187.

Nolan, J. L., Jr. (2009). *Legal accents, legal borrowing: The international problem-solving court movement*. Princeton University Press.

Nolan, J. L., Jr. (2011). The international problem-solving court movement: A comparative perspective. *Monash University Law Review, 37*(1), 259–279.

Nolan, J. L., Jr. (2012). Problem-solving courts: An international comparison. In J. Petersilia & K. R. Reitz (Eds.), *The Oxford handbook of sentencing and corrections* (pp. 150–172). Oxford University Press.

Paparozzi, M. A., & Schlager, M. D. (2009). Reconciling what works and broken windows: The policy relevance of individual and social correlates to recidivism reduction. *Victims & Offenders, 4*(4), 427–434.

Payne, J. (2006). *Specialty courts: Current issues and future prospects*. Australian Institute of Criminology.

Queensland Courts. (2019). *Specialist Domestic and Family Violence Court*. https://www.courts.qld.gov.au/courts/domestic-and-family-violence-court

Queensland Courts. (2020). *About the Mental Health Court*. https://www.courts.qld.gov.au/courts/mental-health-court/about-the-mental-health-court

Queensland Courts. (2021). *Queensland Drug and Alcohol Court*. https://www.courts.qld.gov.au/courts/drug-court

Schaefer, L., & Beriman, M. (2019). Problem-solving courts in Australia: A review of problems and solutions. *Victims & Offenders, 14*(3), 344–359.

Stobbs, N. (2017). Therapeutic jurisprudence and due process—Consistent in principle and in practice. *Journal of Judicial Administration, 26*(4), 248–264.

Thielo, A. J., Cullen, F. T., Burton, A. L., Moon, M. M., & Burton, V. S., Jr. (2019). Prisons or problem-solving: Does the public support speciality courts? *Victims & Offenders, 14*(3), 267–282.

Thomas, N. K., & Bull, M. (2013). Negotiating the challenges of coerced treatment: An exploratory study of community-based service providers in Queensland, Australia. *Contemporary Drug Problems, 40*(4), 569–594.
Wexler, D. B., & Winick, B. J. (1996). *Law in a therapeutic key: Developments in therapeutic jurisprudence.* Carolina Academic Press.

Legislation

Drug Court Act 1998 (NSW) No 150.

Practitioner Perspective: A Reflection on Problem-Solving Courts in Australia

Elizabeth Daniels

I started my legal career in 2011 as a young general practice lawyer in rural Queensland, spending much of my time representing clients in Magistrates Courts for a variety of criminal proceedings. During that period, I did not devote much thought to the purpose of the justice system, nor did I readily recognise the system's shortcomings when it came to interacting with those experiencing or exposed to domestic and family violence (DFV).

To me, courts were a place for justice, punishment and accountability for someone's actions according to the law. Even with my narrow view of the function of the justice system, I still recall questionable practices, particularly in the domestic and family violence (DFV) jurisdiction, which did not serve the needs of those seeking protection. I regularly observed lawyers representing perpetrators enter courthouse saferooms and demand victims withdraw applications for protection orders or make submissions to the court that a domestic violence offence was 'not overly serious' and punishment 'should be at the lower end of the sentencing regime'.

Throughout the second decade of the twenty-first century, we have seen significant government reform and a spotlight on solving the 'problem' of DFV, including the delivery of the ground-breaking report of the Queensland Special Taskforce on Domestic and Family Violence (2015) *Not now, not ever: Putting an end to domestic and family violence in Queensland* (NNNE Report) in February 2015. I am fortunate to say, through the introduction of specialist DFV courts, I have played an active role in one of the more significant justice system reforms in Queensland's history.

E. Daniels
Queensland Magistrates Court, Brisbane, QLD, Australia

Background and Challenges

In response to the recommendations from the NNNE Report, a trial of the Southport Specialist Domestic and Family Violence Court (SDFVC) commenced in September 2015 and a report evaluating this court was released in 2022 (ARTD, 2022). The NNNE Report implored the Queensland Government to reform the justice system to ensure it better protected victims/survivors (and their children), achieved fair and protective outcomes and made perpetrators of violence accountable for their behaviour. Many reported to the Taskforce that the justice system (courts and police) only further victimised or marginalised victims. From inception, the implementation of a specialist court and the key outcomes it was to achieve had overarching support from government and non-government agencies alike; however, factors such as day-to-day operations, how we would achieve reform, and what would be the 'measures of success' remained key challenges.

From the outset, the SDFVC had a clear mandate: to create a justice system response where the safety of victims/survivors was paramount and perpetrator accountability was a key objective. The specialist court model differed from traditional courts as it became a place of engagement for people attending court and provided not only a legal response but encouraged 'wrap-around' DFV support for those who attended. The model required all stakeholders (government and non-government/legal and social work) to work together in a way and to a magnitude which was unprecedented. The concepts of integration, collaboration and co-ordination would become the cornerstones of the court's operation.

A major challenge was ensuring that the model maintained the separation of powers of the court, preserved the functions of individual stakeholder roles (prosecutors, lawyers, DFV support services) and pursued reform. Despite the collaborative spirit being evidenced from the outset, it did not prevent issues arising which placed significant pressures on all to reflect and understand how their organisations internal operations, purpose and traditional functions may be contributing to the ongoing generation of barriers and marginalising or re-victimising those seeking protection/safety. This reflective practice was particularly challenging for government departments with deeply entrenched organisational cultures, which at the time were reported as not consistent with a 'best practice' response to DFV or the specialist court approach.

Some of the more significant challenges for practitioners involved in the implementation of SDFVCs have included:

- an 'open door policy' and broad eligibility criteria for accessing the specialist court, leading to substantial increases in case numbers, workloads and file complexity (which contributed to staff burnout, placed pressure on resources, and impacted the ongoing sustainability of the model);
- integrated methods of working for government and non-government agencies, including the need to proactively share information about parties attending the court to ensure the most appropriate orders were made (including the granting of protection orders)[1];
- a lack of a common risk screening and assessment tool or any uniform terminology[2];
- complexity and confusion, particularly for victims, in navigating the legal processes (combination/intersection of both civil and criminal proceedings in Queensland) and limited support available to assist; and
- limited availability of specialist DFV support services to assist persons attending court (and for legal practitioners to refer clients to). The services available would eventually increase in functionality/scope and assist victims in drafting and filing protection order applications, conduct risk assessments and generate safety plans (including securing emergency accommodation), receive referrals to men's support services and assist entry into behaviour change programmes. These support activities were identified by stakeholders as key engagement opportunities which if conducted at court and in a timely fashion, could assist in promoting the protection and safety of victims, increase engagement and potentially achieve perpetrator accountability.

Reforms and Solutions

In February 2017, Griffith University released its *Evaluation of the Specialist DFV Court Trial in Southport*, making several interim findings and key recommendations (Bond et al., 2017). The evaluation found the Southport SDFVC had made significant inroads toward achieving its desired objectives. Fundamentally the court had taken steps to increase engagement with parties and to create a safe place for victims to attend and seek protection, all the while providing 'wrap-around' support for both victims and perpetrators. Recommendations were made highlighting some of the areas for continued improvement, perhaps most significantly the need for increased perpetrator accountability and access to men's behaviour change programmes, as well as consideration as to how the model might work in other locations in Queensland.

As a practitioner working across the model, I attribute the positive outcomes and the 'specialist' nature of the court to two key initiatives adopted by Southport (and replicated at subsequent specialist court locations). First, the implementation of the Operational Working Group (OWG)—a weekly stakeholder meeting with representatives from each agency and the dedicated DFV magistrates to openly discuss issues, challenges, failures or successes of how the model was operating and developing.[3] This was one of the key 'problem-solving' elements of the model. Second, the commitment to 'continuous improvement' and 'innovation'—this was despite differences in opinion, ever changing court operations and ongoing pressures on stakeholders' resources including funding, staffing, workloads and fluctuations in government agenda/reform momentum. The commitment and collaborative spirit displayed by those involved in the implementation, development and ongoing sustainability of SDFVCs is what has made it a true privilege to be a practitioner involved.

Sustainability of Problem-Solving Courts

Without the delivery of the second evaluation of the Southport SDFVC at the time of writing this reflection, it is difficult to comment on the sustainability of the model from an evidence-based perspective. As a practitioner involved in inception and ongoing implementation, some of the challenges for sustainability include:

- ensuring models are properly resourced and are not 'person-based' or rely upon goodwill to function;
- the ongoing need for clarity about the model and its core elements—as the SDFVC developed at a rapid pace and in an organic fashion, the model continued to evolve making it challenging to define and sustain over a longer period and across multiple locations;
- the need for the model to reflect diversity, be accessible to people from all cultural backgrounds and diverse groups, and to be able to translate notions of 'best practice DFV' to courts across the state of Queensland (including regional areas/First Nations communities); and
- clarity around the concept of 'success', particularly in relation to the goal of perpetrator accountability.

Reflection

Upon reflection of my involvement in the implementation of specialist DFV courts in Queensland, it has been encouraging to see the justice system proactively and creatively adapt in its response to NNNE. From my perspective, it is important to continue reflecting on the model, both internally and externally through independent evaluations and reviews to improve. Building the OWG as a key function/component of the SDFVC was integral to the success of the model and in my view could be adapted to other problem-solving courts.

In my experience, the questionable practices observed during the start of my career are far less likely to be observed in the SDFVC—if they were, the OWG would certainly have something to say. Despite the significant reform to date, it remains imperative the justice system continues its journey to ensure courts are a place of safety for victims seeking protection and perpetrator accountability remains at the forefront of the response. It is these key objectives which must be achieved before the long-term objective of eliminating domestic and family violence can be realised.

References

ARTD. (2022). *The Southport Specialist Domestic and Family Violence Court: Process Evaluation 2017–2020*. Department of Justice and Attorney-General. https://www.courts.qld.gov.au/__data/assets/pdf_file/0010/722674/southport-specialist-dfv-process-evaluation-2017-2020.pdf

Bond, C., Holder, R., Jeffries, S., & Fleming, C. (2017). *Summary report: Evaluation of the specialist domestic and family violence court trial in Southport*. Griffith Criminology Institute.

Queensland Special Taskforce on Domestic and Family Violence. (2015). *Not now, not ever: Putting an end to domestic and family violence in Queensland*. Report provided to the Premier.

Notes

1. This was in comparison with the traditional 'siloed' approach by agencies only submitting to the court 'what they knew'. At the time of commencement of the SDFVCs, there were no uniform processes or platforms for sharing of information between agencies. The amendments to the *Domestic & Family Violence Protection Act 2012 (Qld)* introducing Part 5A regarding increased information sharing did not come into effect until 30 May 2017.
2. In 2017, the Queensland Government introduced the Common Risk and Safety Framework (CRASF). The framework was developed for use by government and non-government community service agencies. It articulates a shared understanding, language and common approach to recognising, assessing and responding to DFV risk and safety action planning, including common minimum standards and approaches for in an attempt to adopt a more uniformed approach.
3. Note that the OWG continues to date, albeit with less frequent meetings, but still as a key part of the model.

10

Indigenous Sentencing Courts

Elena Marchetti and Linda M. Ryle

Introduction

Involving Elders or community representatives in the sentencing process is something which has been occurring for some time around Australia in more informal ways. However, such practices have never been as far reaching nor have they had the formal recognition and support of governments as is the case with Indigenous sentencing courts. Such courts have been established by way of an agreed practice or protocol in either regional towns or cities (as opposed to remote communities) and that involve the usual participants (such as the judicial officer, defence lawyer and prosecutor) in a conventional sentencing process, as well

E. Marchetti (✉)
Griffith University, Brisbane, QLD, Australia
e-mail: e.marchetti@griffith.edu.au

L. M. Ryle
Griffith University, Brisbane, QLD, Australia

M. Camilleri and A. Harkness (eds.), *Australian Courts*,
https://doi.org/10.1007/978-3-031-19063-6_10

as respected members from the Aboriginal and Torres Strait Islander community.

The establishment of these courts reflects an attempt and desire to correct the harmful and discriminatory nature of the criminal court process, and more recently, implement state and territory justice agreements, which seek to reduce the over-representation of Aboriginal and Torres Strait Islander people in the criminal justice system.

This chapter begins by describing the evolution of the courts and the debates surrounding the drivers of over-incarceration of First Nations peoples in Australia. Reasons for the over-representation of Aboriginal and Torres Strait Islander people in the criminal justice system are complex, but the continuing impacts of colonisation in the form of systemic and institutional discrimination cannot be ignored. The chapter then explains how the recommendations made by the Royal Commission into Aboriginal Deaths in Custody (RCIADIC) were a key contributor to changing criminal laws and policy. However, structural and institutional barriers to changing the way courts sentence, including what factors are considered when assessing risk of reoffending, have restricted the power of Indigenous sentencing courts in transforming the racialised and cultural elements of the sentencing narrative. What further steps are needed to improve individualised justice for Australia's First Nations people is detailed in the concluding section of the chapter.

Context: The Evolution of Indigenous Sentencing Courts

Reducing the negative aspects of criminal court processes for First Nations peoples brought before the criminal justice system in Australia is of critical importance, as was recognised in the recommendations made by the RCIADIC (1991). One of the innovations that emerged almost a decade after this Royal Commission tabled its *National Report* was the involvement and active participation of community representatives in sentencing court hearings through the implementation of Indigenous sentencing courts. A review into Aboriginal and Torres Strait Islander incarceration 25 years after the RCIADIC tabled its report highlighted the self-determining aspects originally envisaged when the Indigenous sentencing courts were established (ALRC, 2017).

The first such court was established in Port Adelaide, South Australia in 1999, with a central aim to improve trust in the criminal justice system, court communication and understanding for First Nations peoples (Daly & Marchetti, 2012). Before establishing what became known as the Nunga Court, Magistrate Chris Vass consulted widely over several years with various stakeholder groups including "Aboriginal community groups, State Government agencies, the Aboriginal Legal Rights Movement, police prosecutors, solicitors and Aboriginal people" (Tomaino, 2004, p. 2). In addition to the Nunga Courts, South Australian criminal courts at all levels can now convene an Aboriginal sentencing conference prior to sentencing, pursuant to s. 9C of the *Criminal Law (Sentencing) Act 1988* (SA).

The Nunga Court model informed the establishment of similar courts in other jurisdictions, including in Queensland (Murri courts) and Victoria (Koori courts). The Murri Court commenced operation in Brisbane in August 2002 (Parker & Pathé, 2006), expanding to other cities and towns from 2007. With the expansion came more government intervention in the way Murri Courts operated reducing the originally envisaged self-determination nature of these justice mechanisms.

In some locations, South Sea Islander community members are also represented on the panel of Elders that sit with the Magistrate in sentencing hearings. Unlike other jurisdictions, Victoria introduced specific legislation—the *Magistrates' Court (Koori Court) Act 2002* (Vic) to establish the first Koori Court in the Shepparton Magistrates Court in October 2002, with others later established in Melbourne and in various regional locations. Both Queensland and Victoria also established specific Indigenous sentencing courts for young people, with Victoria embedding the model in its District Court in the Latrobe Valley in February 2009.

Unlike South Australia, Queensland and Victoria, a peak Aboriginal group led the charge for change in the sentencing court process in New South Wales, as opposed to a judicial officer or government department (Potas et al., 2003). The first New South Wales Circle Court was trialled in Nowra in January 2002, with other circle courts established around the state over the following five years and a Youth Koori Court pilot established in Paramatta in Western Sydney in February 2015.

Although the Australian Capital Territory Galambany (formerly called Ngambra) Circle Sentencing Court mirrored the model adopted in New South Wales, its establishment was initiated by an activist judicial officer (Madden, 2007). The Ngambra Circle Sentencing Court was initially only established for six months in May 2004 but remains operational. An important consideration for the Galambany Court was that in the Australian Capital Territory there is no intermediate court, so the jurisdiction vested in the Magistrates' Court (which is where the Galambany Court was situated) was much broader and included more serious offences than in other jurisdictions.

The Northern Territory (which also does not have an intermediate court) and Western Australia were the last two jurisdictions to establish dedicated Indigenous sentencing courts—referred to as Community Courts. The courts in both jurisdictions are currently not funded as a separate initiative to the mainstream Magistrates Courts. The Northern Territory Community Courts, which had expanded to 18 different locations by 2012, were not limited to Aboriginal defendants. According to an evaluation conducted by the Cultural & Indigenous Research Centre Australia (2013, p. 153), "up until the end of June 2012, 179 of the 182 defendants in the Northern Territory Community Court were recorded as Aboriginal". In Western Australia, a Magistrate initiated discussions to establish a Community Court in Kalgoorlie-Boulder (Aquilina et al., 2009), and in the Northern Territory it was the Yilli Rreung Aboriginal and Torres Strait Islander Commission Regional Council which advocated for the initiative (Anthony, 2015; Cultural & Indigenous Research Centre Australia, 2013).

Controversies: Drivers of Hyper-Incarceration of Aboriginal and Torres Strait Islander People

In 1987, the RCIADIC was established within an environment of political, social and cultural controversy. The circumstances and the sheer number of Aboriginal and Torres Strait Islander deaths in custody had fuelled the anger and suspicion of the families and relatives of the deceased. The Royal Commission began as an investigation into Aboriginal and Torres Strait Islander deaths in custody, but its scope was later broadened to encompass a wide range of matters affecting Australia's First Nations people.

Despite the very lengthy time since the RCIADIC tabled its report in April 1991, very few of its 339 recommendations have been implemented although the report remains the most influential piece of work used to steer government approaches to Aboriginal and Torres Strait Islander criminal justice policy. First Nations legal professionals, academics and community members continue to advocate for culturally intelligent, culturally principled and trauma evidenced, understood and informed approaches. They argue that failing to do so will sustain the status quo (see, e.g. Livermore, 2009).

Since the Royal Commission tabled its report, there have been at least 476 Indigenous deaths in custody (Anthony et al., 2021). In handing down the 339 recommendations, the Royal Commission concluded that the deaths investigated were not the result of any system defect per se. That is, the deaths were not "the product of deliberate violence or brutality by police or prison officers" (RCIADIC, 1991, Vol. 1, p. 3). It also concluded that Aboriginal and Torres Strait Islander people did not die at a greater rate than non-Indigenous people in custody when the rate was calculated *as a proportion of Indigenous people in custody* rather than as a proportion of the Australian population. This finding is the same as what the Australian Institute of Criminology reported 25 years later—that the National Deaths in Custody Programme, which commenced collecting data in 1992, showed Aboriginal and Torres Strait Islander people were less likely than non-Indigenous prisoners to die in prison, while also noting that they were unable to make accurate conclusions about police custody since there was an absence of reliable data (Gannoni & Bricknell, 2019).

The issue of over-representation or hyper-incarceration has not improved since 1991—in fact, it has become much worse. The proportion of Aboriginal and Torres Strait Islander adults in prison then was 14.4% of the Australian prison population (Anthony, 2016). By 2020, that rate had almost doubled to 29% (Australian Bureau of Statistics, 2020).

Aboriginal and Torres Strait Islander deaths in custody are still occurring at alarming rates. Despite the RCIADIC's conclusion that Aboriginal and Torres Strait Islander people did not die at a greater rate than non-Indigenous people in custody, a 2020 Australian Institute of Criminology report found that Aboriginal or Torres Strait Islander people are nearly 10 times more likely to die in prison than a non-Indigenous person when the rate is calculated according to adult population numbers as opposed to the number of Aboriginal and Torres Strait Islander people in custody (Doherty & Bricknell, 2020).

The RCIADIC concluded that imprisonment should be a sanction of last resort for Aboriginal and Torres Strait Islander people considering the highly negative and culturally specific impacts on individuals, families and communities. Mandatory sentencing and laws that criminalise drunkenness and public nuisance in some jurisdictions were identified as being particularly damaging, with recommendations 79 to 85 focused on decriminalising drunkenness and diverting people to places of care; recommendation 86 calling for no arrest or charge in cases involving offensive language; and recommendations 87 and 92 highlighting the need for arrest and imprisonment to be sanctions of last resort (RCIADIC, 1991, Vol. 5).

The Australian Law Reform Commission (2017) has noted that Aboriginal and Torres Strait Islander people are over-represented at all stages of the criminal justice system and not just in prison. This over-representation is highlighted by offending rates and patterns (Weatherburn, 2014) and by the effects of systemic and institutional racism within the criminal justice system (Blagg & Anthony, 2019; Cunneen, 2014; Cunneen & Tauri, 2016).

Scholars such as Cunneen argue for a more nuanced and interconnected explanation that includes recognising "historical and structural conditions of colonisation, social and economic marginalisation and systemic racism" while also "considering the impact of specific (and sometimes quite localised) practices of criminal justice and related agencies" (Cunneen, 2001, p. 25). This nuanced and interconnected explanation acknowledges that offending patterns, policing practices, laws, court practices, geographical and socio-economic circumstances and disadvantage, cultural differences, intergenerational trauma and other enduring impacts of colonisation are all contributing factors to Indigenous over-representation.

Other drives of hyper-incarceration are sentencing court practices themselves. Pre-sentence reports (PSRs) prepared by corrective services staff—including the use of actuarial risk assessment tools to determine someone's risk to the community and propensity to reoffend—are one aspect of this process. PSRs and actuarial risk assessment tools have been found to inadequately represent the experiences and perspectives of First Nations peoples and facilitate erroneous risk evaluations (Anthony et al., 2017; Shepherd & Anthony, 2017).

PSRs tend to follow a standard template (which encourages a 'cut and paste' approach to report preparation occurring as a practical response to capacity and resourcing shortfalls). The reports focus on matters such as offending history, family background, substance abuse issues, medical and psychological issues, an individual's attitudes regarding their offending, and sentencing options in assisting a sentencing court to select the most appropriate sentence. These measures and predictors of risk are formulated from and compared to representative samples of white male prison populations resulting in lower predictive accuracy for non-white prison population groups (of any sex) (Shepherd & Anthony, 2017). They are also unlikely to be prepared by culturally principled First Nations practitioners, and as such risk a lack of culturally intelligent influence and unchecked levels of human bias (Livermore, 2009).

Stakeholders informing the 2017 Australian Law Reform Commission inquiry into the incarceration rates of Aboriginal and Torres Strait Islander people criticised the formulaic and discriminatory nature of PSRs on the basis that using such actuarial assessments and information when sentencing leads to systemic bias and contributed to the increasing rates of incarceration. PSRs were described as devoid of cultural context and lacking in information about the continuing impacts of colonisation, matters which Indigenous sentencing courts are more likely to be privy to, due to the involvement of respected Elders and community members. Ultimately, the sentencing decision rests with the judicial officer.

Challenges in Implementing the RCIADIC Recommendations and Indigenous Sentencing Courts

The RCIADIC *National Report* was divided into two parts. The first part, comprising Volumes 1 and 2, described the circumstances of the deaths investigated, how Indigenous people are over-represented in custody and the underlying issues that explain why there had been so many Aboriginal and Torres Strait Islander people in custody. The second part, comprising Volumes 3 and 4, discussed ways in which the incarceration of Aboriginal and Torres Strait Islander people and the risks of dying in custody could be reduced, as well as how their lives in general could be improved. This part provided strategies for achieving change.

Certain recommendations, such as encouraging the recruitment and training of First Nations staff (recommendation 100) and advocating for appropriate training and development of judicial officers, police, and courts, corrections and other legal staff (recommendation 96) are, to a limited extent, reflected in the operation of Indigenous sentencing courts. The idea of involving Aboriginal and Torres Strait Islander community members in legal processes and courts and ensuring justice processes is culturally safe by educating and exposing stakeholders to the values, knowledges and perspectives of First Nations peoples is not new.

Critical legal scholars (such as post-colonial and First Nations whiteness theorists, and critical race and feminist legal scholars) have been drawing attention to the limitations of the Anglo-centric nature of the justice system when matters involve First Nations peoples (see, e.g. Blagg, 2008; Coker, 2006; Delgado, 1995; Monture-Okanee & Turpel, 1992; Pratt, 1999). It is assumed that community input and participation, and better understanding of the experiences and standpoints of First Nations peoples will make a court or justice process more suitable, meaningful and relevant, which will in turn ultimately assist in changing offending behaviour and result in the implementation of more just and equitable outcomes.

There are a number of theoretical frameworks and political movements that might further explain the emergence of innovative justice practices for First Nations peoples. Two of the main approaches that have emerged over the past 20 years are restorative justice and therapeutic jurisprudence. King (2008, p. 1097) identifies the "central tools and inventions of these approaches" as "communicative techniques incorporating understanding, feelings and empathy, and the application of a broad definition of legal problems and outcomes". The two approaches are, indeed, quite different most notably because of their underlying focus. Restorative justice is more victim-centred than therapeutic jurisprudence, which instead focuses more on the wellbeing of a defendant (King, 2008; Marchetti & Daly, 2007).

Transformative justice is another lens through which innovative sentencing processes that attempt to address the "intersecting oppressive systems that operate in the lives of men and women in subordinated communities" can be viewed (Coker, 2002, p. 129). A 2007 study by Marchetti and Daly, which analysed the practices, protocols and other court-related documents of Australian Indigenous sentencing courts, found that Indigenous sentencing courts exhibited broader theoretical and jurisprudential elements than simply those seen in practices reflecting therapeutic jurisprudence and restorative justice. After a detailed analysis of various official and unofficial documents pertaining to the establishment of the courts across all jurisdictions, the study found that "Indigenous sentencing courts are ultimately concerned with transforming racialised relationships and communities. Thus, they are operating according to a transformative, culturally appropriate and politically charged participatory jurisprudence" (Marchetti & Daly, 2007, p. 443).

The importance of changing the relationship between what is seen to be a 'white' non-Indigenous justice system and First Nations peoples, and as a consequence, empowering and rebuilding Aboriginal and Torres Strait Islander communities, are noted as primary goals and aspirations of the courts, imbuing them with a sense of transformative justice. In making these findings, the study did not unpack the terminology used in the court related documents to determine whether the aims and goals contained therein matched community expectations.

Such practices, however, require more time, recourses and emotional work from judicial officers (Dick & Wallace, 2007; King, 2010), which has affected the expansion and adoption of Indigenous sentencing courts. Aside from a lack of funding to support Magistrates Courts (or at times District Courts) establishing more Indigenous sentencing courts, it is not always easy to find suitable judicial officers to preside over the courts. There has been little analysis of how different magisterial or judicial styles affect the operation of an Indigenous sentencing court despite it being a crucial aspect of the process.

Other RCIADIC recommendations that are reflected in the practices of Australian Indigenous sentencing courts are those that endorse imprisonment as a last resort (recommendations 92 to 121), and consultation with community members in discrete or remote communities regarding the appropriateness of sentences (recommendation 104). The practice directions, legislative provisions or court guidelines informing the operation of the Indigenous sentencing courts typically cite achieving more culturally appropriate sentencing outcomes, reducing recidivism and increasing community participation and confidence in the sentencing process as aims of the courts (Marchetti & Daly, 2007). According to Stobbs and Mackenzie (2009, p. 94), such goals are "fairly broad" and "may appear aspirational and ambitious" often making it difficult to achieve satisfactory evaluation results to support continued funding.

Changes to Court Processes for Indigenous Peoples

Despite not offering First Nations peoples an avenue for exercising self-determination, Indigenous sentencing courts, with the support of authentically and community respected Elders and other community members, do foster limited opportunities for 'power sharing' (as opposed to significant and transformational changes to the power structure) between legal personnel and First Nations communities. This leads to more appropriate sentencing determinations that are more likely to resonate and be accepted by the people appearing in the courts (Dick, 2004; Marchetti, 2015).

There is much variation in the ways these courts operate in Australia, both within and amongst jurisdictions. However, and importantly, in all such courts the defendant must either have been found guilty or have pleaded guilty to the offence and have committed an offence within the jurisdiction of that court. The judicial officer presiding over an Indigenous sentencing court retains the power to sentence the defendant. This, of course, means that the process does not provide Indigenous communities with a forum in which to sanction their own people, but it does mean that Elders or community representatives may be protected from being blamed for whatever sentence is imposed. The involvement of Elders or community representatives varies between courts, but in all courts, they aim to speak frankly with the defendant. In Queensland, the recruitment and appointment of Elders is ultimately determined by the sitting Magistrate.

The power of Elders and community representatives to culturally 'shame' defendants is one of the most important aspects of Indigenous sentencing courts. Potas et al. (2003, p. 52) accentuate this point:

> Fundamentally the strongest aspect of the circle sentencing process, as clearly enunciated by the offenders themselves, is the involvement of the Aboriginal community in the sentencing process. Facing one's own community – respected people who have known the offender his or her entire life – is the most powerful aspect of this process.

In particular, the role of Elders or community representatives generates accountability between defendants, victims and the wider community (Cultural & Indigenous Research Centre Australia, 2008; Harris, 2006; Parker & Pathé, 2006; Potas et al., 2003). One defendant cited in Harris (2006, p. 91) said that "[i]t means a whole lot more to be given directions about your future life path from a person who is an Elder of your community and has a better understanding of the shoes us blackfellas walk in". In some circumstances, defendants may hold a different view if they are 'admonished publicly' by a First Nations individual whose status as an Elder is questioned.

Since the mid-2010s, there have been several evaluations and impact studies conducted of the effect these courts are having on various outcomes such as recidivism, penalties imposed and strengthening informal social controls within Aboriginal and Torres Strait Islander communities by reconnecting defendants to their community and improving respect for Elders (Cultural & Indigenous Research Centre Australia, 2008; Fitzgerald, 2008; Morgan & Louis, 2010). It is not easy to compare the findings of all these studies since they are mostly jurisdiction specific, and because they all identify limitations in the way the data were either collected or analysed. Many have used quantitative studies of reoffending and, until recently, found little or no impact on recidivism because of the introduction of such courts.

A Bureau of Crime Statistics and Research evaluation of the New South Wales Circle Sentencing Courts, however, found that Aboriginal and Torres Strait Islander people who had been sentenced in a Circle Sentencing Court were 51.7% less likely to be incarcerated and that those who had gone through the circle sentencing process and had not been incarcerated were 3.9 percentage points less likely to reoffend (meaning a 9.6 decrease in reoffending rates) within 12 months when compared with First Nations peoples who had been through the mainstream court (Yeong & Moore, 2020). Evidence also exists that Indigenous sentencing courts have had an impact on strengthening informal social controls within First Nations communities, improving perceptions of procedural fairness and confidence in the sentencing process amongst defendants and strengthening perceptions of community empowerment (Marchetti, 2014, 2015; Morgan & Louis, 2010).

A call for PSRs to include information about the unique systemic and background factors affecting Aboriginal and Torres Strait Islander people has been made by the Australian Law Reform Commission (2017). This has led to certain states trialling the use of PSRs that include a more detailed narrative about the particular circumstances of First Nations peoples and more suggestions about community-based options that are relevant and meaningful for addressing offending behaviour.

An attempt to provide more information to the Murri Court in Queensland and to collect more administrative data about the people appearing before the court occurred in 2016 when survey-type forms documenting measures such as cultural connection and level of cultural respect were introduced as Murri Court 'Entry and Sentence Reports'. The Murri Court Entry Report is completed prior to the defendant's first Murri Court mention and is used to assess the suitability of the defendant to be referred to the Murri Court, describe the defendant's cultural and personal circumstances, identify things that contribute to the defendant's offending and identify treatment and support services that may benefit the defendant. The Murri Court Sentence Reports are used to record changes in the defendant's life after participating in the Murri Court process. The aim is for a copy of the Murri Court Sentence Report to be provided to the defendant's legal representative, the prosecutor, the Magistrate and Elders at least 48 hours prior to the defendant's Murri Court sentence (which occurs after they have completed the Murri Court bail programme if available or required).

The Murri Court Entry and Sentence Reports are predominantly in a 'tick and flick' format: for example, one of the questions is 'do you know your mob?' and the form has a 'yes/no' box that can be ticked, with a small space to name the Tribal group. Where descriptive answers can be given, the space is limited. One of the Community Justice Groups who service several courts in and around Brisbane is Five Bridges. Five Bridges, realising the information presented in the Murri Court Entry and Sentence Reports was limited, started their own 'Narrative Reports' which are longer, more descriptive accounts of a defendant's connections to family and community, and include their reasons for offending and how they may be supported to not reoffend. Unfortunately, there is no extra funding provided to produce the expanded reports and they are, therefore, still limited in use and in the detail provided.

Conclusion

Indigenous sentencing courts and PSRs that aim to expand on a person's cultural and individual experience of the justice system can exhibit elements of both restorative justice and therapeutic jurisprudence, in that they have a strong focus on court funded support to assist First Nations defendants to reconnect with Elders, community representatives or victims and obtain the help determined by the courts to be necessary to abstain from criminogenic behaviour. These practices can at times also transform the racialised and cultural elements of a sentencing court by silencing the hegemonic voice of non-Indigenous legal players and, instead, allow a different narrative and perspective to be presented.

The potentially transformative nature of Indigenous sentencing courts—and, where available, PSRs that are more culturally authoritative and informative—can result in empowering Aboriginal and Torres Strait Islander communities through Elders and community representatives who participate in the Anglo-centric justice frameworks and sentencing process. Nevertheless, adapting a sentencing process so that it becomes more culturally safe and sensitive and demonstrably trauma-informed requires more than a rudimentary change in processes and procedures; it involves radical changes in post-colonial power dynamics that continue to exist between First Nations peoples and non-Indigenous actors, and adjustments in the perspectives and worldviews of the non-Indigenous players.

In the interests of true, evidenced and equitable justice, legal actors, governments, public servants and the community more broadly are encouraged to apply a critical mind to their work and be reminded that First Nations are distinct and unique peoples, and it would be unjust and counter-productive to apply a broad-brush approach to the true justice needs of those First Peoples and their Nations. Self-determination is demonstrably trauma experienced and informed.

References

ABS (Australian Bureau of Statistics). (2020). *Prisoners in Australia, 2020.* Australian Bureau of Statistics. https://www.abs.gov.au/ausstats/abs@.nsf/Lookup/by%20Subject/4517.0~2019~Main%20Features~Aboriginal%20and%20Torres%20Strait%20Islander%20prisoner%20characteristics%20~13

ALRC (Australian Law Reform Commission). (2017). *Pathways to justice: An Inquiry into the incarceration rate of Aboriginal and Torres Strait Islander Peoples.* Commonwealth of Australia.

Anthony, T. (2015). Two laws: Indigenous justice mechanisms in context. *Journal of Australian Indigenous Issues, 18*(1), 99–115.

Anthony, T. (2016). Data gaps mean Indigenous incarceration rates may be even worse than we thought. *The Conversation*. https://theconversation.com/data-gaps-mean-indigenous-incarceration-rates-may-be-even-worse-than-we-thought-63044

Anthony, T., Jordan, K., Walsh, T., Makham, F., & Williams, M. (2021). *30 years on: Royal Commission into Aboriginal Deaths in Custody Recommendations Remain Unimplemented*. Australian National University, Centre for Aboriginal Economic Policy Research.

Anthony, T., Marchetti, E., Behrendt, L., & Longman, C. (2017). Individualised justice through Indigenous community reports in sentencing. *Journal of Judicial Administration, 26*(3), 121–140.

Aquilina, H., Sweeting, J., Liedel, H., Hovane, V., Williams, V., & Somerville, C. (2009). *Evaluation of the Aboriginal Sentencing Court of Kalgoorlie*. Shelby Consulting. https://www.shelbyconsulting.com.au/wp-content/uploads/2015/06/Kalgoolie_Sentencing_Court_Report.pdf

Blagg, H. (2008). *Evaluation of red dust role models: Assessing the performance of red dust role models in their work with young people and their communities on remote aboriginal communities in the Northern Territory.* http://www.reddust.org.au/assets/files/review/Evaluation-Document.pdf

Blagg, H., & Anthony, T. (2019). *Decolonising criminology: Imagining justice in a postcolonial world*. Palgrave Macmillan.

Coker, D. (2002). Transformative justice: Anti-subordination processes in cases of domestic violence. In H. Strang & J. Braithwaite (Eds.), *Restorative justice and family violence* (pp. 128–152). Cambridge University Press.

Coker, D. (2006). Restorative justice, Navajo peacemaking and domestic violence. *Theoretical Criminology, 10*(1), 67–85.

Cultural & Indigenous Research Centre Australia. (2008). *NSW Attorney General's Department Evaluation of Circle Sentencing Program: Report*. Cultural & Indigenous Research Centre Australia.

Cultural & Indigenous Research Centre Australia. (2013). *Evaluation of Indigenous Justice Programs—Project A: Aboriginal and Torres Strait Islander Sentencing Courts and Conferences, Final Report.* Cultural & Indigenous Research Centre Australia.

Cunneen, C. (2001). *Conflict, politics and crime: Aboriginal communities and the police.* Allen & Unwin.

Cunneen, C. (2014). Colonial processes, Indigenous peoples, and criminal justice systems. In S. M. Bucerius & M. Tonry (Eds.), *The Oxford handbook of ethnicity, crime and immigration* (pp. 386–407). Oxford University Press.

Cunneen, C., & Tauri, J. (2016). *Indigenous criminology*. Policy Press.
Daly, K., & Marchetti, E. (2012). Innovative justice processes: Restorative justice, Indigenous justice and therapeutic jurisprudence. In M. Marmo, W. De Lint, & D. Palmer (Eds.), *Crime and justice: A guide to criminology* (pp. 455–481). Lawbook Co.
Delgado, R. (1995). *Critical race theory: The cutting edge*. Temple University Press.
Dick, D. (2004). Circle sentencing of Aboriginal offenders: Victims have a say. *The Judicial Review, 7*, 57–72.
Dick, D., & Wallace, G. (2007). *Circle sentencing in New South Wales*. Australian Institute of Judicial Administration Indigenous Courts Conference. Australian Institute of Judicial Administration.
Doherty, L., & Bricknell, S. (2020). Deaths in custody in Australia 2018–19. *Australian Institute of Criminology Statistical Report*, 1–111.
Fitzgerald, J. (2008). Does circle sentencing reduce Aboriginal offending? *Crime and Justice Bulletin, 115*, 1–12.
Gannoni, A., & Bricknell, S. (2019). Indigenous deaths in custody: 25 years since the Royal Commission into Aboriginal Deaths in Custody. *Statistical Bulletin*. Australian Institute of Criminology.
Harris, M. (2006). *A sentencing conversation: Evaluation of the Koori Courts Pilot Program October 2002–October 2004*. Department of Justice.
King, M. S. (2008). Restorative justice, therapeutic jurisprudence and the rise of emotionally intelligent justice. *Melbourne University Law Review, 32*, 1096–1126.
King, M. S. (2010). Judging, judicial values and judicial conduct in problem-solving courts, Indigenous sentencing courts and mainstream courts. *Journal of Judicial Administration, 19*, 133–159.
Livermore, D. A. (2009). *Cultural intelligence: Improving your CQ to engage our multicultural world*. Baker Academic.
Madden, S. (2007). *The Circle Court in the ACT—An overview and its future*. Australian Institute of Judicial Administration Indigenous Courts Conference. Australian Institute of Judicial Administration.
Marchetti, E. (2014). Delivering justice in Indigenous sentencing courts: What this means for judicial officers, Elders, community representatives, and Indigenous court workers. *Law & Policy, 36*(4), 341–369.
Marchetti, E. (2015). An Australian Indigenous-focused justice response to intimate partner violence: Offenders' perceptions of the sentencing process. *British Journal of Criminology, 55*(1), 86–106.

Marchetti, E., & Daly, K. (2007). Indigenous sentencing courts: Towards a theoretical and jurisprudential model. *Sydney Law Review, 29*(3), 416–443.
Monture-Okanee, P. A., & Turpel, M. E. (1992). Aboriginal peoples and Canadian criminal law: Rethinking justice. *University of British Columbia Law Review, 26*, 239–279.
Morgan, A., & Louis, E. (2010). *Evaluation of the Queensland Murri Court: Final report*. Australian Institute of Criminology.
Parker, N., & Pathé, M. (2006). *Report on the Review of the Murri Court*. Queensland Department of Justice.
Potas, I., Smart, J., Brignell, G., Thomas, B., & Lawrie, R. (2003). *Circle sentencing in New South Wales: A review and evaluation*. Judicial Commission of New South Wales.
Pratt, J. (1999). Assimilation, equality, and sovereignty in New Zealand/Aotearoa: Maori and the social welfare and criminal-justice systems. In P. Havemann (Ed.), *Indigenous peoples' rights in Australia, Canada and New Zealand* (pp. 316–328). Oxford University Press.
Royal Commission into Aboriginal Deaths in Custody (RCIADIC). (1991). *Royal Commission into Aboriginal Deaths in Custody: National Report, Vols. 1–5*. Australian Government Publishing Service.
Shepherd, S. M., & Anthony, T. (2017). Popping the cultural bubble of violence risk assessment tools. *The Journal of Forensic Psychiatry and Psychology, 29*(2), 211–220.
Stobbs, N., & Mackenzie, G. (2009). Evaluating the performance of Indigenous sentencing courts. *Australian Indigenous Law Review, 13*(2), 90–105.
Tomaino, J. (2004). *Information Bulletin: Aboriginal (Nunga) Courts* (pp. 1–16). Office of Crime Statistics and Research.
Weatherburn, D. (2014). *Arresting incarceration: Pathways out of Indigenous imprisonment*. Aboriginal Studies Press.
Yeong, S., & Moore, E. (2020). Circle Sentencing, incarceration and recidivism. *NSW Bureau of Crime Statistics and Research Crime and Justice Bulletin, 226*, 1–22.

Legislation

Criminal Law (Sentencing) Act 1988 (SA).
Magistrates' Court (Koori Court) Act 2002 (Vic).

Practitioner Perspective: Murri Court

Jacqueline Payne

I have been a magistrate since the late 1990s, mostly working in Southeast Queensland, but working in the Cairns Murri Court in Far North Queensland since 2020. In Cairns, there are much larger numbers of Aboriginal and Torres Strait Islander people before the court and in custody compared to Southeast Queensland. Each day in Cairns, the court receives a list of all defendants (adults and children/young people) in watch-house custody. Almost all defendants appearing before the court in custody are Aboriginal or Torres Strait Islander.

Murri Court is best understood by visiting it: it is experiential. It is the shared human experience that enables the therapeutic processes to be successful. Everyone benefits from Murri Court, not just the defendants and their families but also the Elders who get to make a difference and create real change. Also, lawyers and prosecutors who believe in the principles of therapeutic jurisprudence can work in a court practicing those principles. Court staff get to work in an uplifting and positive court room; as well as everyone else, including government and non-government agencies that provide support to defendants. These agencies get to fulfil their purpose of providing support and facilitating change.

Murri Court has dual processes. The first is the court process that case-manages a matter. The second process is the supports and services provided or organised by the Elders. In Queensland, the Elders form and become members of a Community Justice Group (CJG) that assists the Murri Court and the defendants.

The Court Process

Some of the court processes are procedural to case-manage the matter but there are also processes that promote and support the therapeutic

J. Payne
Cairns Magistrates' Court, Cairns, QLD, Australia

aims of the court. In Cairns. the court room is a standard courtroom with some Indigenous art on the walls. Police prosecutors do not wear a uniform, however at the request of the Elders, the magistrate wears a robe. Importantly, seated next to the magistrate is a 'Bench Elder': in Cairns, this is always the same person and has been with the CJG (Community Justice Group [CJG] are a group of dedicated local Aboriginal and Torres Strait Islander people who are elders or respected persons in the community) since its inception. She is highly respected by the court and the community.

Murri Court aims to be culturally safe and less alienating than the mainstream court process. At the beginning of court everyone is welcomed to Murri Court and the Bench Elder speaks first, acknowledging the local people and introducing herself. I then introduce myself including sharing I am Aboriginal and where I am from. I am Butchulla from K'Gari (Fraser Island). Each person in the court room then introduces themselves in any way they feel comfortable: the Elders; lawyers; prosecutors; court staff; community corrections staff; support agencies staff; defendant's and their families and supporters; and anyone else in the court.

The Murri Court and Youth Murri Court sits in Cairns on two Fridays of each month. What is extremely powerful is that all the Elders are in court on each of the sitting days and are there to support every adult and child defendant. The Murri Courts aim to support defendants in dealing with the problems that underlie their offending. The Elders provide the court an initial 'entry report' setting out some of the defendant's personal and cultural circumstances and then provide—before the mention of each matter—Murri Court Progress Notes with individualised information about what the person is dealing with and what support services, if any, the defendant is engaged with.

However, Murri Court is a conversation. The contents of the report form the basis of the conversation in court. When I speak to a defendant, I also confer with the 'Bench Elder' to ask if there was anything else she wishes to say about the defendant. Importantly, as all the Elders are at also at court, the individual Elder who primarily works with and supports the defendant and his or her family can also speak to the court about the defendant. The defendant and his or her family can also speak.

Everyone in court involved in the defendant's matter can contribute to the conversation. This includes the defence lawyer, prosecutor, and any of the agencies especially those who work directly with the defendant. Often words of encouragement or acknowledgement or support are said but there might also be words of warning or caution.

Amaroo Community Justice Group

The CJG is made up of local Aboriginal and Torres Strait Islander people who are Elders or Respected Persons. In Cairns, the CJG is Amaroo Aboriginal and Torres Strait Islander CJG (Amaroo CJG). They are a dedicated group of Elders who work together from rented premises where they have offices, meeting rooms and a kitchen and conference room where larger meetings and lunches are held.

When working with children, the elders also work with the child's family. If a child has been removed from their family by the Department of Child Safety, the elders still work with the family. If this is not possible, then they work with the child and the child's case worker.

The defendants (adults and children) must meet with the Elders at the Amaroo offices every Monday.[1] Usually, one elder is assigned to work with the same Defendant each week. This continuity and reliability of support from the same Elder is beneficial and good relationships are formed. Also, to stop the need for defendants and their families having to attend various services, the Elders invite service providers to come to their offices on the Monday when the defendants and young people and their families are there.

The Elders have formed excellent working relationships with various service providers to provide supports including housing, Centrelink, medical, resumes and job applications. Elders work with an education specialist when supporting a child to return to school, working out the best school for the child to attend then working with the child, the child's family and the school when the child returns to school. The Elders also have strong connections with a civil construction training company with whom courses can be undertaken with the opportunity of employment at the end.

Noticing that some defendants had to walk long distances to attend their Monday meeting, including at times in harsh conditions of North Queensland heat or rain, the elders decided to provide transport for defendants and the children and their families. The elder who is providing the transport takes the opportunity travelling in the car to connect with the defendants, children and their families.

The lack of transport led the Amaroo elders to initiate the provision of bikes. Elders are often working with men aged 25 to 40 years. To get a bike they must attend regularly for a period of about six weeks a meeting with the Elders and the Alcohol and Other Drugs Service (AODS), or whichever service they have been referred to. Bikes given to adult defendants enable them to transport themselves to Monday meetings have the freedom of transport more generally and transport to be able to get a job. The Elders tell me that the giving of a bike to a defendant can lift the adult defendant's self-esteem and sense of wellbeing knowing someone cares about them. The bikes are well looked after.

Bikes have also been given to children. With children there may be conditions to getting a bike such as visiting the Elders with their family, not running out of the house and wandering the streets and not offending. Thomas was 15 years old and lived about a 45 minutes walk from the Amaroo offices. The Elders spoke with him, and it was agreed he could get a bike. The following week he rode to his meeting with the elders, but he looked close to tears. He told the elders he had once stolen a bike, used it and thrown it away. He said he felt "really bad" for what he had done, knowing if someone stole his bike he would be upset. The bike was valuable in providing transport and giving him responsibility. It also had the advantage of causing him to experience empathy and some insight into the impact of his behaviour on victims.

Successes

There are a variety of outcomes for adults and children who are supported by the Amaroo Elders. There are good outcomes. Here are two stories.

The first was Dennis, an adult. The Elders who met with him said he was in a "vicious alcohol cycle" and he was "absolutely ready to give up", not caring if he lived or died. The elders were upset to see him so lost. They spoke with him, invited him to the Monday lunch to join everyone at Amaroo. When he left, they gave him a $30 food voucher. They reported that he came back the following Monday and that he was totally transformed. They said someone cared about him which gave him hope. Things moved quickly for Dennis and, with the Elders' support, by his third visit he was ready to go into an Indigenous residential rehabilitation at Shanty Creek. The Elders supported him, including the application process to get a place at Shanty Creek. Dennis successfully completed a nine-month rehabilitation programme. Dennis has stayed in touch with the Elders, has stopped drinking, and no longer appears in Murri Court.

The second story is of a child returning to school. Many of the children in Murri Court have disengaged from school. It is always a goal of the Elders, if possible, to get the child back to school. David was one of six children, and his family were homeless. He had dropped out of school and was hanging out with children who were offending. The Elders supported David's mother helping to secure a house for her and all the children. However, as children are only before the Murri Court for a short time, averaging about six weeks, the Elders continued to support David's mother even after David left the Youth Murri Court. Housing stability for the family supported David and he returned to school. The elders provided him with uniforms and books and worked with him, his new school and his family to keep him in school.

There are many measures of success in Murri Court, but the elders say their biggest successes are getting children back to school and supporting adults and older children find work.

Sentencing

Murri Court gives the court a real opportunity to consider a just sentence. Even though courts can receive submissions for individual offenders about trauma unique to their Aboriginality, such submissions are less common in mainstream courts. I am usually told where they are from and if they have children or if they have a job. I might also receive a general submission: for example, "the offender was exposed to alcohol use and domestic violence as a child".

The sentencing considerations are not changed for the Murri Court. It allows the court to receive proper submissions upon which the court can sentence. In Queensland, sentencing legislation provides that when sentencing the court can consider submissions made by a CJG. Submissions can include the offender's relationship to the community, any cultural considerations or any considerations relating to programmes and services established for offenders in the community in which the CJG participates. The time the adult defendant or child has spent in Murri Court allows the CJG to make detailed submissions unique to that person, resulting in a fairer and just process.

The other benefit is that a sentencing option for the court is a probation or a community service order. People may be unable to complete their orders if they face difficult circumstances such as homelessness, addiction, cognitive impairment or domestic violence. However, with the support given by the Elders, combined with the adult or child's progress through Murri Court, they are far more capable and likely to complete community-based court orders.

They are now 'probation ready'. They also continue to have the support of the Elders even though they have left Murri Court, and this supports them in successfully completing orders such as probation or community service.

Conclusion

The Royal Commission into Aboriginal Deaths in Custody (RCIADIC, 1991b, Vol. 2 part C) found "that a multitude of factors, both historical and contemporary, interact to cause Aboriginal people to be seriously over-represented in custody" and that the fundamental causes are not located within the criminal justice system and instead "the most significant contributing factor is the disadvantaged and unequal position aboriginal people find themselves in society – socially economically and culturally" (RCIADIC, 1991a, Vol 1, 1.7.1.) However, the systems are entangled and criminal justice reform is necessary and urgent.

The Australian Law Reform Commission's Pathways to Justice Report (2017, p. 26) Recommendation 10-2 provides:

> Where needed, state and territory governments should establish specialist Aboriginal and Torres Strait Islander sentencing courts. These courts should incorporate individualised case management, wraparound services, and be culturally competent, culturally safe and culturally appropriate.

The Cairns Murri Court follows this recommendation. The success of this court is because its' therapeutic processes are almost entirely designed and managed by the local Aboriginal and Torres Strait Islander Elders. Of course, the court's effectiveness is greatly enhanced by a judicial officer who believes in the court and its' processes. Murri Court respects Indigenous culture and the authority of the Elders. First-hand, I have seen the transformative nature of the court—not only in reducing recidivism but also in empowering the adults and children who may for the first time in their life felt validated and respected.

Murri Court works because the Elders care about the people. As one of the female elders said to me: "We tell them, 'We're blackfellas too, we know what it's like to struggle, to have nothing'. We let them know that we love them, we support them and we don't judge them".

References

Australian Law Reform Commission. (2017). *Pathways to justice: Inquiry into the incarceration rate of Aboriginal and Torres Strait Islander Peoples* (Final Report No. 133). https://www.alrc.gov.au/publication/pathways-to-justice-inquiry-into-the-incarceration-rate-of-aboriginal-and-torres-strait-islander-peoples-alrc-report-133/

Royal Commission into Aboriginal Deaths in Custody (RCIADIC). (1991a). *Royal Commission into Aboriginal Deaths in Custody: National*

Report, Vols. 1. Australian Government Publishing Service. http://www.austlii.edu.au/au/other/IndigLRes/rciadic/national/vol1/17.html

Royal Commission into Aboriginal Deaths in Custody (RCIADIC). (1991b). *Royal Commission into Aboriginal Deaths in Custody: National Report, Vols. 2, Part C.* Australian Government Publishing Service. http://www.austlii.edu.au/au/other/IndigLRes/rciadic/national/vol2/3.html

Note

1. People who cannot meet on the Monday mornings for example because of a set work commitment will meet with the Elders at other times.

11

Coroners Courts and Death Investigations

Fiona Allison and Chris Cunneen

Introduction

The role of Coroners Courts in Australia in investigating deaths of unknown or unnatural causes and deaths in State custody is unique, complex and challenging. These courts and their practices are under immense scrutiny from those awaiting outcomes, including the family of the deceased and other parties such as police, corrections and health. The potential of the coronial system to improve public health and other social

F. Allison (✉)
Jumbunna Institute for Indigenous Education and Research, University Technology Sydney, Sydney, NSW, Australia
e-mail: Fiona.Allison@uts.edu.au

C. Cunneen
Jumbunna Institute for Indigenous Education and Research, University Technology Sydney, Sydney, NSW, Australia
e-mail: Christopher.Cunneen@uts.edu.au

M. Camilleri and A. Harkness (eds.), *Australian Courts*,
https://doi.org/10.1007/978-3-031-19063-6_11

outcomes and to increase accountability of public institutions makes it both important and at times controversial. Despite this, the coronial jurisdiction is relatively under-considered in the broader literature on law and justice.

Drawing upon original research, this chapter examines a range of procedural and integrity challenges facing Coroners Courts in responses to First Nations deaths in custody. In exploring these challenges, the influence on the court of the broader social and political context in which it operates is considered. In particular, deaths in custody raise important questions about ongoing State violence against First Nation peoples, the wider parameters of colonialism and the role of the legal system in both. These questions are of concern to families directly impacted by a death and other First Nations peoples, generating collective anger and frustration given voice over decades in protests calling for justice for those who have died.

Context: Coroners Courts Investigations of First Nations Deaths in Custody

Research undertaken by Allison et al. (2020) has explored the nature of justice demanded by First Nations peoples following a death in custody and the capacity of the Coroners Court to provide this form of justice. Data was obtained through interviews conducted with those working in and interacting with Coroners Courts in Victoria, Western Australia and New South Wales. Indigenous and non-Indigenous participants included coroners and other staff employed by the courts, as well as legal and other advocates supporting First Nations families. This work forms part of a larger Australian Research Council funded research project the authors are currently conducting on Indigenous access to civil law justice.

Analysis of this interview data, parts of which are presented in this chapter, reveals potential for Coroners Courts to perpetuate the very same colonialism and racism First Nations families often identify as associated with a death in custody, including by rendering both issues invisible and irrelevant. Literature on coronial responses to First Nations deaths confirms this finding. Carpenter et al. (2021, p. 527), for example, refer to the "differential treatment of Indigenous people in coronial practice" as a "contemporary feature of the Australian legal, policy, and social landscape", impacting problematically on the categorisation and prevention of deaths, two key functions of the Coroners Court. A further function of the court is investigation of institutional and other accountability for deaths. Citing Razack (2011, 2015), Hay (2019, p. 2) suggests accountability is avoided through methods that include prioritising "decontextualised narratives of First Nation dysfunction" during coronial proceedings over any "structural analysis" of the part played by "racism and colonialism" in the death in question.

The Royal Commission into Aboriginal Deaths in Custody (RCIADIC) concluded in 1991, making sweeping recommendations intended to reduce Aboriginal and Torres Strait Islander deaths in custody through reform, including of the coronial system, policing and prisons (Commonwealth of Australia, 1991). The rate of both Indigenous and non-Indigenous deaths in prison custody has declined since the turn of the twenty-first century and is considerably lower than it was on average in the 1980s. However, the *number* of First Nations deaths remains high because of substantially increased imprisonment rates during the period. The RCIADIC finding that First Nation peoples were not more likely to die in prison custody than non-Indigenous people but were much more likely to be imprisoned is still relevant today (Doherty, 2021, p. 4).

The recommendations from the RIACDIC still require urgent implementation and continue to provide an essential framework for developing further reform pertaining to First Nations (and indeed all) deaths in custody. An important starting point, though it was outside the scope of the research to interview First Nations families impacted by a death in custody, is for reforms to be directly informed by Indigenous voices. This is in keeping with various RCIADIC recommendations, including those related to self-determination.

Controversies in Coronial Responses to First Nations Deaths in Custody

In an inquest into the 2015 death in the Long Bay Correctional Centre in New South Wales, Australia, of Dhungutti man David Dungay Jr, the coroner made no recommendations for disciplinary action for, or prosecution of the correctional officers involved, finding that their conduct was "limited by systemic deficiencies in training". His mother, Leetona Dungay, announced in 2021 she would be lodging a complaint to the United Nations Human Rights Committee, with her legal representatives stating that breaches of her son's right to life and to a full and proper inquiry into his death would form the basis of this complaint: "All I want is justice. I want real justice where the life of an Aboriginal man is worth something", Ms Dungay stated to media during this announcement (Allam, 2021).

A fundamental controversy arises with respect to First Nations deaths investigations by Coroners Courts, that institutional racism within these courts prevents First Nations peoples from attaining the justice to which they are entitled.

Interviews with research participants identified four justice outcomes that ought to be provided by a coronial inquest into a First Nations death in custody:

i. to fact-find or to conduct a search for the truth through identification of the manner and cause of the death;
ii. to prevent future deaths by identifying systemic problems or deficiencies and public interest lessons, to be addressed through the coroner's findings and recommendations;
iii. to ensure accountability for those responsible for a death, including by way of criminal prosecution; and
iv. to deliver more therapeutic outcomes, providing closure and healing for families impacted by a death.

In many respects, First Nations families seek the same justice outcomes as other families and also face similar difficulties in attaining them. There are important differences, however, in how First Nations peoples define the above outcomes, in terms of both preferred approaches and barriers to achieving them. Whilst acknowledging significant diversity within First Nations communities, these definitions are shaped to a large degree by shared cultural and other perspectives, including those framed by experiences of racism and colonialism. This chapter argues that the Coroners Court is institutionally racist, where the differential treatment it affords to First Nations peoples fails to acknowledge and respond to these perspectives and experiences, ultimately reinforcing and reproducing harmful experiences of racism and colonialism.

First Nations families may expect coronial fact-finding to inquire into the relevance of racism to manner and cause of death. For First Nations peoples, the criminal justice system historically and in the present day is deeply mired in a racism that causes them death and injury. To effectively deliver justice, a First Nations death investigation must consider the implications of this fact for the death in question—part of a broader demand made by First Nations peoples for truth-telling related to the use of State violence and other weapons of colonisation. In most cases, Coroners Courts will fail to do this, just as it struggles to ensure accountability for the death of a loved one or to respond to First Nations cultural perspectives.

In the latter context, for First Nations peoples a death in custody may replicate racist colonial practice, triggering significant levels of anger and trauma. Rather than providing a therapeutic outcome in response, coronial proceedings retraumatise where they fail to ensure cultural safety for families. These failures led Whittaker (2021) to describe First Nations death investigations as a "site of fresh administrative violence" rather than of "justice and change". Coroners Courts become, in effect, indivisible from other State institutions (police, corrections, health) implicated both in First Nations deaths in custody and in other past and more contemporary manifestations of colonial violence.

Challenges in Coronial Processes in Achieving Justice Outcomes

For First Nations peoples, a number of challenges are presented in achieving justice outcomes which give rise to and present as institutional racism. Even where other families interacting with the coronial system experience similar challenges, these often have differential impacts on First Nations families owing to their disproportionately higher levels of contact with the coronial system (for all categories of death) (Butler, 2021, p. 5), but also to First Nations specific experiences and perspectives.

Cultural Safety

Interview participants identified that the failure of Coroners Courts to ensure cultural safety for First Nations families is racist. They particularly focused on court procedures, but there are other relevant matters: for instance, those related to notification of a death and autopsy procedures (Butler, 2021). Participants suggested that some coroners do better than others in this regard, incorporating an Acknowledgement or Welcome to Country and smoking ceremonies within proceedings. As a further example, one interviewee noted that sometimes "Aboriginal people have brought artwork into the court room. If you can't be on country at least bring something". Importantly, there is considerable inconsistency between inquests in this and other regards, attributed by participants to individual discretion on the part of coroners owing to their different levels of skill in running inquests and of prior experience with First Nations peoples.

Some participants identified cultural safety and respect as crucial to delivering therapeutic outcomes. As an example, close physical interaction is required during an inquest between families, police and prison officers and others involved in the death in question. One participant identified families as feeling threatened and outnumbered as a result—but one example of "deeply culturally inappropriate practices" in the court "that border on re-traumatising". This same participant identified as good practice use of a spill-over room during an inquest at the Victorian Coroners Court for family members who did not want to be in the "same room as the people who were giving evidence… or where they could be a bit noisier and react more to what was being said".

Truth Telling

Those employed within the coronial system largely control the narrative through which a death in custody comes to be understood, with important implications for court procedures and outcomes. As an example, a focus throughout the investigation on pathology reports and "body parts" means that cause of death is often attributed to a pre-existing medical condition of the deceased person, who is also likely to be described as "diseased or weak" according to one participant. This same participant saw this practice as "re-colonising" for First Nations peoples, but it is also an instance of the courts positioning First Nations 'dysfunction' at the centre of a death rather than failure or liability on the part of the institution in which it occurred. Of note, Walsh and Counter (2019, pp. 152–155) found that in 44% of coroners' reports on inquests into deaths in custody published between 1991 to 2016, a medical issue was identified as the primary cause of death. For Indigenous deaths in custody, this was the case in 60% of the reports. Notably, in 71% of these reports the Indigenous status of the deceased person was not identified.

Coroners are empowered to consider a wide range of matters in investigating a death. They are "uniquely positioned to [deal] with the totality" of circumstances surrounding a death, as one participant suggested, with capacity to "broaden out that idea of manner and cause of death to encapsulate something like history or the culture of a particular geographic area where something occurred, or the culture of the organisation in which the death occurred". This enables coroners to investigate an issue of particular significance to First Nations families—that is, racism. Another participant identified this as an action "central to the purpose of coronial proceedings". Raising this during an investigation, however, appears to be "beyond the pale", even though "for

Aboriginal people, when you're actually in the criminal justice system it's bland as you like. Of course, there's racism!".

Participants described various ways in which racism, particularly in its institutional form, becomes obfuscated during the coronial process, including where it is seen as outside the scope of an investigation. "Up until the last decade", according to one participant, issues of racism "were roundly considered by coroners as being just too remote from the question of the medical cause of death, so they weren't even raised". Furthermore, where racism *is* explored during the inquest it may not make its way at all or in any meaningful way into coronial findings or recommendations. Rather, the failure by individuals in their duty of care is spotlighted, rather than systemic discrimination—described as involving a 'series of decisions' made at a more 'collective' level. Problems related to 'practice and procedure' are sometimes discussed in findings and recommendations and whilst this may help to prevent deaths, one participant stressed that without discussion of racism "blackfellas can't get justice because the truth-telling is never done". There may also be a finding of an individual's unconscious or implicit bias, meaning that "it wasn't their fault". "The system isn't intentionally racist and no-one's really to blame for it".

As further evidence of inconsistency in coronial practice, attributable to some degree in this instance to variations in levels of understanding of racism and its impacts on First Nations peoples, there has been some progress in this respect in recent inquests. Some participants identified the inquest into the 2017 death in police custody in Victoria of Yorta woman Tanya Day as a 'high watermark' in this regard. Ms Day's family wanted the coroner to investigate the influence of systemic racism on the actions of transit staff who reported her to police as an 'unruly' train passenger and the actions of police who then took her into custody, failed to conduct regular physical checks on her or to provide her with timely access to medical treatment after she hit her head on a cell wall.

Tanya Day died of a brain haemorrhage. The coroner determined that whether "racism played a causal part" in the death was within the inquest's scope and numerous witnesses gave evidence on this issue. Inquest findings and recommendations included, however, that transit staff alone were influenced by unconscious bias and ought to receive further training on removing such bias from their decision-making, that there was a "culture of complacency" within police "regarding intoxicated detainees" rather than systemic racism, and that police required training on mandatory requirements applicable for safe management of people in custody and on medical risks of people affected by alcohol (Victoria Courts, 2020). Of note, the family also sought repeal of Victorian laws criminalising public drunkenness that had led to Ms Day's arrest (notably, also a recommendation of the RCIADIC), citing their disproportionate impact on Aboriginal people. The Victorian Government announced in 2020 the repeal of these laws, following an announcement by the coroner that this would be one of her recommendations and a public campaign by Ms Day's family and others.

Accountability

Carpenter et al. (2021, p. 536) point to the relatively modern shift in Australia of "coronial attention away from crime to public health" and from "criminal concepts (such as culpability) to the social purpose of avoiding preventable death... encapsulated in the statutory power of coroners to make recommendations for reform to government agencies and policy maker". Coroners Courts cannot make a finding of guilt, nor can they commit anyone to a trial, though they can refer individuals for prosecution.

The inquisitorial nature of Coroners Courts is identified as problematic for First Nations families seeking retribution for a death in custody. One participant spoke of inquests providing a lesser "second tier of justice" in this context, something less than a criminal trial in which culpability is properly examined and punished. Given the limited capacity of inquests to provide these outcomes participants also spoke of the need to continually manage family expectations: "[N]o one's going to be held accountable"; "That's my advice to people always – you're not going to get anything out of this court". Discussed, too, was that this incapacity gives rise to a perception of bias, of the court colluding with other players in the legal system to protect those implicated in a death.

Police in all jurisdictions currently compile a brief of evidence for the coroner. Families may identify this as compromising the independence of pre-court investigations where a death has occurred in police custody. Participants identified this practice as discriminatory for First Nations families, and as immediately excluding impartiality from *the entire* coronial process and on the part of all inquest participants, including lawyers for all parties and Counsel Assisting, regardless of where the death in question occurred, given the "strong role" of police "in the historic oppression of Indigenous communities". A more specific example of bias cited during interviews is that police appear to investigate deaths in custody as "procedural" failings rather than as potential homicides. For one participant, police should show the "same level of commitment" to finding "who is responsible" and "bringing them to justice" in these investigations that "you would see if a group of black men killed a police officer".

Coroners' decisions that to release video footage of a death in custody would be culturally insensitive, against the wishes of family, were also highlighted during interviews. This occurred during the Dungay inquest, with one participant stating that family members were "furious as you can imagine… There's a fine line between what's called cultural competency and an excuse for paternalism". Furthermore, families want to see individuals referred for prosecution by the coroner, with some participants suggesting that this does not happen nearly often enough. As evidence of an entire legal system stacked against justice for First Nations families, prosecutions following a referral are rarer still and convictions in a criminal court apparently unattainable. As Whittaker (2018, p. 2) states, "Coroners Courts, prosecutors' decision-making, and criminal procedure each build their own walls and hurdles around a vision vital to conviction and accountability alike: culpability".

A further significant issue related to accountability is that coronial recommendations are not responded to or implemented by government agencies and policy makers to whom they are directed. According to one participant, "[E]ven in great coronial inquests that are well-executed… where you get a great result – the families will feel more heard, and they will feel like they got closer to the truth – what you end up with is a series of recommendations" left unimplemented. This was attributed to significant "push back" against implementation and to a lack of political will: "I've certainly never felt that any political party in Australia has ever been concerned about Aboriginal people dying in custody. Certainly, not concerned enough to use any political capital to try and address it".

Change in Coroner Court Practices

Options to improve current First Nations death investigations were identified during interviews. These include to adapt but largely retain coronial inquests as they are, with adaptations having potential to improve functioning of Coroners Courts for all families. Alternatively, a separate stream within the court or an entirely independent First Nations body with greater input from First Nations peoples might be established, both tasked with investigating First Nations deaths.

The United Nations *Declaration on the Rights of Indigenous Peoples* (UNDRIP) sets out four key principles, which are also rights, that define optimal processes and outcomes through which Indigenous people can access justice (UN General Assembly, 2007). These encompass: (i) self-determination; (ii) respect for and protection of culture; (iii) participation in decision-making; and (iv) equality or non-discrimination. These principles or rights ought to underpin development and implementation of any options for change designed to enhance justice responses to First Nations deaths in custody as follows.

To ensure substantive equality for First Nations peoples in Coroners Courts, they should be provided with differential treatment that responds constructively and positively to their particular cultural and other perspectives. Formal equality means treating all persons the same, regardless of their differences. Conversely, substantive equality recognises and responds to difference in individuals and groups and in so doing provides them with different but equitable outcomes, as opposed to the same (and potentially discriminatory) outcomes. The remaining three principles or rights provide direction as to how the court might be adapted to achieve substantive equality, which may include establishment of a separate stream within the court. Alternatively, any independent First Nations centred body would also align with these principles.

Adapting Coroners Courts

To overcome the various challenges hitherto outlined, it is suggested that a number of adaptations could be made to Coroners Courts. Cultural safety related reforms range from hearing evidence and delivering findings on country to respecting the wishes of family about the release of video footage and ensuring coronial processes are informed by First Nations families. Employment of First Nations staff in Coroners Courts is not common practice but was highlighted by interviewees as essential to effective delivery of these and other outcomes. As one participant stated: "I don't think we can justify having this jurisdiction with no Aboriginal staff when Aboriginal people are over-represented in almost every category of reported deaths. It's like having a domestic violence service and not employing any women".

The Koori Engagement Unit was set up and is run by Aboriginal people within the Victorian Coroners Court. Participants described the Unit as creating a culturally safe space for families by, for example, ensuring court processes are informed by Sorry Business: identified as "a cultural strength" in "how it brings our communities together". The Unit also compiles cultural briefs for the coroner about the person who has passed, "painting out kinship models, who the individual is, their connections, their totems". This both "flips" the deficit narrative and builds trust in court processes, it was suggested. Participants identified the Unit as embedding recognition of culture within the court, with one stating that "even though Victoria has had this capacity within the legislation, it has needed people from within the community [Unit employees] … to make it happen, to give a voice in a way the legislation intends to families".

Some suggestions for reform in how Coroners Courts carry out their accountability and fact-finding functions expanded on management of expectations: providing families, for instance, with detailed pre- and post-inquest briefings to improve understanding of the powers and decision-making of the coroner. Other reforms go further, encompassing increased input from families before and during an inquest on manner and cause of death and on whether prosecution should occur. Independent investigators, perhaps located in a specialised (civil) unit within the Coroners Courts, is a further important reform.

A further suggestion is for a restorative justice stream within the Coroners Courts facilitated by First Nations staff, providing opportunity for First Nations families and those involved in a death in custody to come together to understand the circumstances of the death and to process emotions—though concerns include that this would offer First Nations peoples a version of justice even less likely to provide individual or institutional accountability than the Coroners Courts.

In the absence of an entirely First Nations developed and run justice mechanism, it is also essential that coroners and others involved in the coronial process are sufficiently culturally aware and understand the impacts of colonisation and systemic racism on First Nations peoples. This should go some way to addressing inconsistency within coronial practice. There is utility, however, in more formal structural change in this context by way of legislative reforms directing coroners to explore racism as a causal factor and/or to ensure more timely and effective responses to and implementation of coronial recommendations, for instance, or issuing of practice directions that direct coroners to follow Sorry Business protocol, as has occurred in Victoria.

Beyond Adaptation to the Coroners Courts

In terms of self-determination, to "really drive change and remove some of the systemic barriers" for First Nations peoples seeking justice within the coronial system participants identified that "Aboriginal people do need to have a seat at the table". This was raised in discussion of changes the Koori Engagement Unit has brought about in the Coroners Court of Victoria. Hay (2019, p. 16) states, however, that to combat serious deficiencies in First Nations death investigations "Indigenous systems of law, governance, and community safety appear to be the only sensible option… given the current circumstances of apathy and dysfunction" in settler State coronial systems.

In this context, some participants preferred establishment of an independent First Nations investigative body over adaptation to the existing coronial system. This body would be "explicitly about finding responsibility", "tasked with the investigation and carrying it through to potential criminal prosecution… independent of police" and with "First Nations representation central to it". The details and feasibility of establishing this body requires further thought. Would it operate like a Koori or Murri Court (Indigenous sentencing courts, see Chapter 2 in this volume for more), for instance, where Indigenous people ensure culturally informed decisions but are not responsible for decision-making? One First Nations participant felt that this would be more appropriate than Elders having to carry the significant trauma associated with deaths in custody as decision-makers.

Additionally, RCIADIC recommendations were concerned with systemic change likely to disrupt First Nations contact with the justice system, including strategies likely to address underlying drivers of offending (through economic development or improved educational outcomes, for instance). The RCIADIC identified that this requires the "empowerment of Aboriginal people; that control of their lives, of their communities… be returned to Aboriginal hands" (Commonwealth of Australia, 1991, vol. 1, 15 [1.7.6]). In criticising the coronial system, Hay (2019, p. 16) refers to alternative "radical, non-State oriented, and grassroots Indigenous initiatives" such as Indigenous-led community safety patrols that keep Indigenous people out of custody. This is one example of community-led solutions to First Nations deaths in custody and criminalisation. Others include justice reinvestment initiatives and Aboriginal Justice Agreements, with government's role to resource and partner with communities on this important work.

Given the problematic functioning of Coroners Courts, other justice mechanisms for First Nations peoples impacted by a death in custody were also discussed during interviews. Participants talked about the efficacy of public campaigns that incorporate protest in this context. Generally, these were seen as complementary to rather than as a substitute for the investigative work of the Coroners Courts. As an example, the coroner ultimately provided access to footage of Mr Dungay's death. This video—seen "by millions of people around the world", with "more than 100,000 people on a petition saying the guards should be charged", according to one participant—was used to agitate for a prosecution. The Dungay family was also empowered by the significant public support the footage garnered, increasing their sense of feeling heard, which had not occurred during the inquest.

Activism was also identified as encouraging First Nations families to push for inclusion of the issue of racism during the Day inquest. Protest may also achieve what inquests cannot achieve, or not on their own, as seen in the repeal of drunkenness laws in Victoria prior to the Day inquest, but one participant felt protest might also lead to criminal charges. Discussing the charging of a police officer that shot a young Warlpiri man in Yuendumu in the Northern Territory in 2019, this participant suggested that there is "no way you would have seen charges laid… if it wasn't for the fact that there was 700 Warlpiri on their way to Alice Springs … [and] protests in every small community across the Northern Territory in the week leading up to it, [plus] thousands of people on the streets across the country".

Conclusion

First Nations deaths in custody occur within a long history of racism and colonialism in Australia manifested as physical violence, theft of land, and denial of culture and self-determination. The legal system has been a major player in this history and resumes this role and reprises this history where, in investigating deaths in custody, Coroners Courts disregard the justice needs and rights of First Nations peoples. This occurs where they engage in practices perceived by First Nations peoples as culturally unsafe or as concealing and sanctioning individual and more structural violence and racism underpinning deaths in custody. This practice by the Court, it is contended, is a product of and equates to institutional racism.

Part of the solution involves reforming the coronial system. First Nations peoples are demanding that their perspectives and experiences are acknowledged and appropriately responded to within this system, calling for greater accountability—to RCIADIC recommendations, coronial recommendations and, as McCabe (2020) states, "in a legal, prosecutorial sense". The UNDRIP might inform reform in this space that will contribute to ensuring First Nations peoples can access the justice to which they are entitled following a death in custody. As an important step, there needs to be acknowledgement of the shared patterns of racism and colonialism that exist across State institutions, including within the legal and justice systems.

A further essential part of the solution, however, is of course reducing incarceration of First Nations peoples. As McCabe (2020, n.p.) states, "we need to be keeping mob out of this system to begin with". For McCabe, whilst reforms like the recent introduction of Coroners Courts' practice directions in Victoria are "fantastic", "these things mean next to nothing if the reasons why so many Aboriginal people are dying reportable deaths is not addressed".

References

Allam, L. (2021, June 10). UN asked to look into the death in custody of Indigenous man David Dungay. *The Guardian*. https://www.theguardian.com/australia-news/2021/jun/10/david-dungays-death-in-custody-to-be-taken-to-un-human-rights-committee

Allison, F., Cunneen, C., & Schwartz, M. (2020). *Inquiry into the high level of First Nations people in custody and oversight and review of deaths in custody* (Submission No. 108). https://www.parliament.nsw.gov.au/lcdocs/submissions/69040/0108%20Dr%20Fiona%20Allison,%20Prof%20Chris%20Cunneen%20and%20Melanie%20Schwartz.pdf

Butler, K. (2021). *Aboriginal and Torres Strait Islander families in Australian Coroners Courts: A review of the research literature on improving court experiences*. Law and Justice Foundation of New South Wales. http://www.lawfoundation.net.au/ljf/site/articleIDs/EEAEA41E6208041585258710007D512F/$file/Coroners_Court_Report_2021.pdf

Carpenter, B., Harris, M., Jowett, S., Tait, G., & Bray, R. (2021). Coronial inquests, Indigenous suicide and the colonial narrative. *Critical Criminology, 29*, 527–545.

Commonwealth of Australia. (1991). *Royal Commission into Aboriginal Deaths in Custody* (National Report). Commonwealth of Australia.

Doherty, L. (2021). *Deaths in custody in Australia 2020–21*. Australian Institute of Criminology.

Hay, T. (2019). Foreclosing accountability: The limited scope of the seven youth inquest in Thunder Bay Ontario. *Canadian Review of Social Policy, 78*(Fall), 1–24.

McCabe, L. (2020, October 8). Response to Victorian practice direction on deaths in custody. *IndigenousX*. https://indigenousx.com.au/response-to-victorian-practice-direction-on-deaths-in-custody/

Razack, S. H. (2011). The space of difference in law: Inquests into Aboriginal deaths in custody. *Somatechnics, 1*(1), 87–123.

Razack, S. H. (2015). *Dying from improvement: Inquests and inquiries into Indigenous deaths in custody*. University of Toronto Press.

UN General Assembly. (2007, October 2). *United Nations Declaration on the Rights of Indigenous Peoples*. Resolution/adopted by the General Assembly, A/RES/61/295.

Victoria Courts. (2020). Inquest into the death of Tanya Louise Day. File number COR 2017/6424.

Walsh, T., & Counter, A. (2019). Deaths in custody in Australia: A quantitative analysis of coroners' reports. *Current Issues in Criminal Justice, 31*(2), 143–163.

Whittaker, A. (2018). *Carried 'like a dead kangaroo': Culpability and accountability in Australian justice system responses to Indigenous deaths in custody*. Harvard Law School.

Whittaker, A. (2021, April 15). Indigenous deaths in custody: Inquests can be sites of justice or administrative violence. *The Conversation*. https://theconversation.com/indigenous-deaths-in-custody-inquests-can-be-sites-of-justice-or-administrative-violence-158126

Practitioner Perspective: Chasing Professionalism—The Practitioner Role in Responding to First Nations Deaths in Custody

Craig Longman and Alison Whittaker

Reviewing First Nations deaths in custody troubles the principles and design of Coroners Courts—and surviving families and communities are persistent in stretching the limits of what these courts can deliver. In so doing, they reveal the inadequacies of an apparatus unreflective of its position and role within a colonising legal system (and a jurisdiction built on biomedical principles) when dealing with matters of State and colonial violence.

Coronial investigations and inquests into deaths in custody are mandatory in New South Wales, Australia. Commonly, these investigations and inquests are influenced by the historical role of the coroner as a hybrid inquisitorial and judicial institution, whose primary mandate was investigating a narrow conception of the 'manner and cause' of a death. More rarely are coroner's functions exercised alongside a recognition of the context of historical and contemporary colonisation of First Nations people.

Understanding colonisation (both its historical and contemporary manifestations) is essential for the proper representation of First Nation clients in deaths in custody inquests. Too often, we see families' identification of concerns of systemic issues of discrimination disregarded or 'explained away' by practitioners preferencing their 'professional' expertise as to questions of court practice, epistemology and procedure. Practitioners need to remain self-aware that the experience that First Nation families have in living under a colonial legal system gives them a greater understanding and expertise in how the law actually 'works' upon First Nation communities than their lawyer. Failing to recognise

C. Longman · A. Whittaker
Jumbunna Institute for Indigenous Education and Research (Research Unit), University Technology Sydney, Sydney, NSW, Australia

their expertise devalues the client's experience and escalates the trauma experienced by families in an already-hostile Coroners Court, who are too-often told their concerns fall 'outside the scope' of the coroner's focus on the 'manner and cause of death'.

For example, in the inquest into the 2016 death of Wiradjuri woman Naomi Williams in New South Wales—a death in health care rather than in a custodial setting—a coroner initially determined no inquiry was necessary. It was only as a result of the lawyers for the family, the National Justice Project, speaking with community and taking seriously their perceptions of racial bias in health care that an inquest was secured. That inquest was the first in Australia to consider systemic and implicit racial bias against First Nations people within the healthcare setting.

Shortly after, in 2017, a similar issue of implicit bias was examined in the inquest into the death in custody in Victoria of Aunty Tanya Day. As her family said in a statement to the coroner written in her voice (Day, 2020):

> I need you to see, and to acknowledge, that my death was caused by the same system that killed my uncle, Harrison Day, the same system that dispossessed and killed so many of my ancestors and so many other Aboriginal people; that fractured our communities and culture, and caused deep intergenerational trauma. I need you to see that this is not past history, this is the ongoing story of our country.

To professionally represent a First Nations family, practitioners need to be aware of the complicity of lawyers in colonisation. In our experience, this awareness is rare and at odds with the profession's perception of itself as neutral advocates whose duties to the court and to the client require only technical legal skill and moral indifference, a conception of lawyering that is unconcerned with what broader systems and structures they might be enabling.

Whilst other institutions central to the colonial project such as police and healthcare institutions have been repeatedly brought to reckon with systemic bias, the legal profession continues to perceive its role as disconnected from the morality of the colonial project. That perception may seem natural to those of us trained to believe in that idea of the lawyer, but it is not shared by some First Nations families and communities, who see such approaches as confirming the role of the lawyer as a 'cog' in the machine of colonisation.

One of the most repeated mantras of the coroner is that its function is to determine what happened. It is not empowered to make any findings of criminal guilt or suggest an offence has occurred (*Coroners Act 2009* (NSW) s81(3)). While the law requires that Australia ensures accountability of State actors involved in deaths in custody, there has been an abject and systematic failure of the State to do so.

Despite a history of increasingly publicised State-sanctioned and/or perpetrated massacres of First Nations people on the colonial frontier—and the more contemporary history of substantial domestic and international advocacy in the 1980s and early 1990s culminating in the establishment of the Royal Commission into Aboriginal Deaths in Custody (RCIADIC)—Australia has yet to convict a single person of a serious criminal offence arising from a death in custody.

Inaction in the face of continuing deaths can (reasonably) be perceived as a State's indifference at best or enthusiasm for at worst continuing deaths. Of 99 First Nations people investigated by the RCIADIC only one, the death of John Pat in 1983 in Western Australia, involved a criminal prosecution. Since the RCIADIC reported in 1991, there have been at least 500 First Nations people killed in custody in Australia. Only a handful have been subject to formal sanction or prosecution, and of those no serious criminal convictions have been recorded.

More recently, there has been an increase in the number of criminal prosecutions launched against State actors involved in deaths in custody, though these have been limited to prosecutions against Police and Corrective Services officers involved in fatal shootings—and many are still proceeding through courts, resulting in acquittals.

It has fallen to the families of those killed in State custody to attempt to utilise coronial jurisdictions to obtain answers (and evidence) as to what happened to their loved ones and raise public awareness of the circumstances of such deaths, in an attempt to pressure the State to bring criminal prosecutions against their own. Such approaches by families are difficult, intensive and fraught with potential trauma, predicated as they are upon a faith that principles of 'justice' will compel action by the

State where sufficient evidence exists for a prosecution. This faith is at odds with bitter experience.

In an attempt to use the jurisdiction for accountability, they come into conflict with the oft-repeated mantra of coroners to the effect that the court's role is not to apportion blame but rather to obtain answers. In our experience, those answers, however, are almost always presented in a biomedical and policy-centred narrative.

Perhaps the most acute example of this structural disempowerment of families in the Coroners Court was in the inquest into the death of David Dungay Jr in New South Wales in 2015, when family submissions urging the referral of State actors to the New South Wales Department of Public Prosecutions were rejected by Deputy State Coroner Michael Lee, who found that the right of the family to appear in the proceedings did not extend to addressing the court on whether the guards should be referred.

The preventative function of the coronial jurisdiction is designed to identify recommendations that, once enacted, can contribute to the prevention of similar deaths. This function is clearly ineffective in New South Wales. Tragically, in 2021, four Aboriginal people lost their lives either in prison or as a result of police operations. The RCIADIC produced detailed and comprehensive recommendations for implementation that in our view would have prevented these deaths. Non-governmental organisations have called on many occasions for the implementation of those recommendations. The State's response has been decades-long inaction, with monitoring, shifts in policy language and further review creating only the public impression of change. Meanwhile, First Nations deaths in custody only escalated.

In addition to the largely unreflective practices of the legal profession, the broad discretion of coroners and the role of counsel assisting means the court's capacity to properly identify systemic discrimination and violence, and construct recommendations to address it, is inconsistent. Many of the judges who sit on inquests receive no formal training at all in the jurisdiction, and certainly few coroners would have any formal training in questions of discrimination or the role of institutions such as the police, prisons and health services in colonisation. The successful recommendations and findings we are aware of have occurred only where the coroner seeks to include systemic issues in an inquest at the request of the family, with First Nations people again bearing the burden of pushing the court to rethink its bounds in order to inch closer to serving them justice.

It is clear that changes are required in the jurisdiction if coroners are to earn the trust of First Nation families, an essential element to the court's broader legitimacy. But such change requires a fundamental rethink of the Coroners Courts, not just gestures towards cultural competence. Changes in the jurisdiction must be led by First Nations communities, with proper consultation and the free, prior and informed consent from First Nations families who have experienced these courts and know what must be done.

References

Commonwealth of Australia. (1991). *Royal Commission into Aboriginal Deaths in Custody* (National Report). Commonwealth of Australia.

Day, A. (2020, September 2). Without accountability there is no justice for my mother's death in Australian police custody. *The Guardian*. https://www.theguardian.com/commentisfree/2020/sep/03/without-accountability-there-is-no-justice-for-my-mothers-death-in-australian-police-custody

Legislation

Coroners Act 2009 (NSW).

12

Victims' Participatory Rights

Marg Camilleri

Introduction

The experiences of sexual assault victim/survivors in the criminal justice system have challenged, and continue to challenge, their perceptions of the justice system (McGlynn & Westmarland, 2019). Despite numerous legislative, policy and programmatic reforms, victim/survivors' experiences are compounded and exacerbated by a justice system that is designed to be adversarial (Fairclough & Jones, 2018). As many who have traversed the justice system would attest, each stage—commencing with making a report, followed by police investigation and culminating (at times) in court proceedings—can be a traumatic experience which may also result in secondary victimisation (Wemmers, 2013).

Defining what is meant by "participatory rights" is not straight forward. Various scholars have suggested that participatory rights relate

M. Camilleri (✉)
Federation University Australia, Ballarat, VIC, Australia
e-mail: m.camilleri@federation.edu.au

M. Camilleri and A. Harkness (eds.), *Australian Courts*,
https://doi.org/10.1007/978-3-031-19063-6_12

to processes and procedures, including to have "powers that require, allow, or mandate a form of treatment, benefit, protection, or privilege" (Kirchengast, 2016, p. 8). Similarly, participatory rights "may involve being in control, having a say, being listened to, or being treated with dignity and respect" (Edwards, 2004, p. 973). In addition, participatory rights have been defined as the right of victims of crime to participate in decision-making at each stage from pre-trial to post-sentencing (Kirchengast, 2016, p. 8). Further, a defining feature is that the rights of victims are enshrined in and "can be enforced through legislation" (Kirchengast, 2016, p. 10).

Drawing upon the threads from these scholarly insights, one could conclude that as the person who has been harmed by a criminal act, a victim has a stake in bringing the perpetrator to justice, and that this stake begins from first report through to trial and post-trial. As such, a victim of crime as a stakeholder means being informed about each stage of the process and afforded the opportunity to provide input into decision-making. Moreover, it also includes that all actors in the criminal justice system are aware of victim participatory rights and that victims' input is consistently valued and their rights enforced.

This chapter highlights some of the reforms implemented since 2004 which elevate the voices of and acknowledge the experiences of victim/survivors. Despite a raft of reforms, victim/survivors continue to feel alienated and, in particular, the voices of victim/survivors with cognitive impairment and complex communication needs are sometimes ignored at the point of first report. Considered are the barriers to the effective implementation of reforms and supports proposed reforms for continuous advocacy. This chapter support calls for a continuous advocate and that legal representation should continue through to the conclusion of trial proceedings.

Context

It is generally accepted that victim/survivors of sexual assault, and victims of crime more broadly, have been dissatisfied with their experience of the criminal justice system (Molina & Poppleton, 2020), describing their experiences as alienating and a source of secondary victimisation (Carroll, 2022). Victim/survivors living with cognitive impairment or complex communication needs (CCN) feel this alienation in both different and similar ways. For example, all victim/survivors experience the alienation and disbelief informed by the gendered myths and stereotypes of sexual assault. However, victim/survivors living with cognitive impairment and CCN also have the compounded impact of their voice being invalidated and their credibility questioned (Camilleri, 2010; VEOHRC, 2014). Victim/survivors of sexual assault and advocate groups have long sought greater participation through the investigation and court stage.

The struggle of victim/survivors for acknowledgement of the impact of crime, to have their voices heard and their interests respected in the criminal justice system, is characterised by Christie (1977) as "ownership of the conflict". Arguably, the sense of "ownership" is central to victim/survivors. After all, the offence was perpetrated against them, and they inform police. From their perspective, victim/survivors have an essential stake in the outcome of their initial report to police.

The extent to which the experience of victimisation and interaction with the criminal justice system is met with difficulties and barriers will depend on many factors, including the type of crime, whether the perpetrator is known to the victim/survivor, the response from criminal justice agencies (including police and courts), previous victimisation and criminal justice experiences, and if support is available. Barriers will often be compounded owing to intersectional dimensions. The seriousness of a crime is not always the defining feature of how a victim will be affected.

In Australia and internationally, there has been a growing awareness about the impact of victimisation and the need for support to understand and navigate the criminal justice system and to recover from the effects of crime (Iliadis et al., 2021). The increased focus on victim/survivors of sexual assault has also generated discussion and debate about procedural justice and participatory rights of victims, including what level of participation might be possible and what form it might take into the future. Concepts such as procedural fairness, participation and justice need to be explored to further understand the perspective of victims within these debates.

Reforms Aimed at Enhancing Survivors' Participation

Since the early 1990s in Victoria, Australia, and in other jurisdictions internationally, there have been multiple legislative and policy reforms aimed at providing a framework for how the justice system responds to sexual assault survivors (Braun, 2019; VLRC, 2004, 2016, 2021), resulting in incremental change to the roles of victim/survivors in the criminal justice system (VLRC, 2016). These reforms have brought Victoria into closer alignment with Australia's signatory obligations under the *Declaration of Basic Principles of Justice for Victims of Crime and Abuse of Power* 6 (b), which states:

> Allowing the views and concerns of victims to be presented and considered at appropriate stages of the proceedings where their personal interests are affected, without prejudice to the accused and consistent with the relevant national criminal justice system [emphasis added].

As Braun (2019, p. 7) suggests, however, this statement is qualified, providing flexibility to signatories to determine the "extent to which victims can participate during domestic criminal trials". Suggested here is that the language of Section 6 (b) of the Declaration is too broad, providing only guidance for signatories to implement: that is, if they wish, enabling signatories to disregard or pay lip service to participatory rights, by introducing minor reforms without substantive change.

In Victoria, various reforms have gradually elevated the voice of victim/survivors within prosecutorial and investigatory agencies and in the courts. The following is not an exhaustive list and as such does not reflect all reforms contained with various legislation, but rather the intent to provide a snapshot of reforms since 1994 in Victoria. These are presented below in chronological order.

Victims Impact Statements (VIS)

The rights of victims (*Sentencing Act 1991* (Vic), Division 1C) to provide a Victim Impact Statement (VIS) prior to sentencing of the accused has been legislated. It is up to the presiding judge or magistrate as to the extent to which a sentence is informed by the VIS.

The Victims Charter Act 2006 (Vic)

Since the first iteration in 2006, this Charter has undergone multiple revisions. The initial 12 principles, now expanded to 17, govern investigation, prosecution and victim service agencies responses to victims of crime. Essentially, the expansion of the principles "recognise[s] that a victim of crime has an inherent interest in the response by the criminal justice system to that crime… and to acknowledge the victim's role as a participant, but not a party, in proceedings for criminal offences".

The Charter provides guidance about communication and treatment of victims by investigating and prosecuting agencies and requires the DPP to seek views from the victim prior to decisions which affect the trajectory and modification of the case, including (but not limited to) decisions about plea bargaining and discontinuation. Importantly, the Director of Public Prosecutions (DPP) also is required to provide reasons behind decisions insofar as communicating these reasons does not "jeopardise any investigation of a criminal offence or prejudice any other proceeding" (*Victims Charter Act 2006* (Vic) p. 13). How influential the views of victim/survivors are on prosecutor decision-making is not clear. Considering that the court or trial process is an area identified by victim/survivors as a source of secondary victimisation, it is surprising that the courts or at the very least Court Services have no obligations under the Charter.

Special Measures

A range of "special measures" are available for victims deemed to be vulnerable either due to age, disability or crime type. Designed to reduce trauma and revictimisation, measures can include providing an audio- and video-recorded (VARE) statement, providing evidence remotely, and installation of screens so that the accused and victim do not have line of sight (see *Criminal Procedure Act 2009* (Vic) division 5 and 6A) limiting factor to providing evidence remotely is that the technology is not always reliable.

Victims of Crime Commissioner Act 2015 (Vic)

While this important legislative reform does not directly increase participation, the codification of the Act does enhance recognition and the potential for broader advocacy and monitoring in some instances.

Disability Bench Book

This is a guide for judicial officers and other justice stakeholders whose agencies interact with people with disabilities and the role of agencies, in particular judicial officers, "on their role in making Victorian courts accessible for people with disabilities" (Judicial College, 2016). It is unclear how often and by which cohorts this resource is utilised.

Victims of Crime in the Courtroom

A Guide for Judicial Officers was developed in response to the 2016 Victorian Law Reform Commission's (VLRC) recommendation that judicial officers be provided guidance when "responding to needs and interests of victims in the courtroom" (Judicial College, 2019, p. 1). It is unclear how often this resource is utilised.

Intermediaries

The Intermediaries programme piloted in Victoria from July 2018 to June 2020 was modelled on a programme in England and Wales. At this point, intermediaries "are only available to 'vulnerable' witnesses in homicide matters or 'vulnerable' complainants in sexual offence matters… [v]ulnerable witnesses or complainants are those who are under 18 or have a cognitive impairment" (VLRC, 2021, p. 322).

The programme is aimed at assisting "vulnerable witnesses" to give their best evidence in court. However, as of 2022 the programme was not available across Victoria or at all police stations. No publicly available data exists that would shed light on the success or otherwise of this programme. However, the VLRC (2021, p. 322) have reported that the programme has been "praised for increasing access to justice and for driving positive change in the practice and attitudes of police, lawyers and judges".

Restorative Justice

In response to the alienation felt by victim/survivors during the criminal justice process, in particular at court, victim/survivors had sought other opportunities to "meet more of victims' most commonly articulated needs, including participation, voice, validation, vindication and offender accountability" (VLRC, 2021, p. 192).

These reforms have begun the process of engagement in dialogue to create a space for victim/survivors in an often-contested terrain of victim participation. Nonetheless, these reforms, while positive, have been fragmented and have lacked monitoring.

Controversies

Unlike victims in some European Union countries (VLRC, 2021), crime victims in an adversarial common law justice system as in Australia are not a party to court proceedings (Doak, 2005). Rather, once a crime is reported crime victims are required to inhabit the role of witness. The experience of being relegated to the status of witness, when it is the victim who has experienced the harm, has highlighted multiple examples of victims' feeling as "outsiders" (Antonsdottir, 2018; Braun, 2019; Eraz et al., 2014), alienated from the process which on entry to the justice system becomes offender focused (Hargrave, 2019).

Such feelings of alienation and those of secondary victimisation is not unique to sexual assault victim/survivors residing in Australia. They are also characteristic of experiences in other jurisdictions, depending on the level and extent victim/survivors are supported and their interests represented. For example, a participant in an Icelandic study (Antonsdottir, 2018, p. 319) described her experience of being assigned the status of witness, as a parallel to her "out-of-body" experience of sexual assault:

> … I am not a party to the case so what happened to me is not my concern. And my role is to be a witness, which is unbelievably alienating. You know, talk about an out-of-body experience. You are a witness, which is somehow a concept for an outsider, and then your body is a crime scene.

Central to how victim/survivors may experience the justice system is that "the wishes and needs of victims are often diametrically opposed to the requirements of the legal system" (Herman, 2005, p. 5). According to (Bluett-Bod & Fileborn, 2014, p.ix) victims needs include, although not limited to:

> … having their voices heard; being believed; having their version of events vindicated; being educated as to how the criminal justice system works, the reason for processes such as cross-examination, what acquittals and convictions mean, and so forth; being able to give evidence remotely; confronting their perpetrator in a public setting; having their perpetrator brought to justice/convicted; and having closure and a sense of finality to their experience'

The experience of interacting with the criminal justice system imprints a lasting memory, influencing future impressions of trust and confidence in the system and will inform decisions of future reports (VEOHRC, 2014). For some victim/survivors, their interactions with the justice system have been linked to their recovery from the crime itself (Wemmers, 2013). According to Herman (2005, p. 574), the very nature of the adversarial system, in particular the court process can elicit "symptoms of traumatic stress".

Numerous policy and legislative reforms have sought to improve the experiences of victim/survivors in the criminal justice system. These reforms have been hard-fought by survivors and advocates alike, and over decades. Advocacy has been required at multiple levels: to convince the justice system that the voices of victim/survivors' matter; to highlight how the processes, practices and legislative frameworks have and continue to be a source of secondary victimisation; and to raise awareness and the status of gendered crimes in the sphere of criminality, rather than simply a matter between two people known to each other. For example, law reform to criminalise marital rape in Australia received significant opposition from various groups, as the proposed reforms were seen to be challenging to "the gender [norms and stereotypes] and the public/private divide" (Featherstone, 2017, p. 87).

Various reforms have addressed and continue to respond to issues experienced by victim/survivors through their interactions with the justice system. As Edwards (2004, p. 967) suggests, "the most controversial issues relating to victims have been questions of participation in the decision-making processes of the criminal justice system".

Challenges

Two key challenges present themselves when responding to the needs of crime victims: the need to recognise victim/survivors' inherent interests; attending to perceptions of trust in the criminal justice system.

Recognising Victims' Inherent Interest

There is an intrinsic link between who has been harmed and their role in bringing the offender to justice and accountable for their actions. The VLRC (2016, p. 30) states that:

> The recognition of victims as participants reflects the reality of victims' inherent interest in the criminal trial process and the various capacities in which they may be involved in that process. It gives proper regard to the hardship experienced by victims as a result of crime, their special interest in the criminal trial process, and their contribution to the detection and prosecution of crime in society.

The objectives of the Charter in Victoria, resulting from recommendations in the VLRC (2016, p. xxi) report, state that the *Victims Charter Act 2006* (Vic) (amended in 2018) include a new objective (4(1)(ba)) which "recognise[s] that a victim of crime has an inherent interest in the response by the criminal justice system to that crime".

Within a "traditional dichotomous" adversarial system (Doak, 2005, p. 295), tensions arise when victims, seen as a third party and whose status is that of witness, seek recognition of the stake they have in holding the offender to account. The expected, logical next step is "to feel included (informed, consulted and heard)" (VLRC, 2016, p. 24).

Arguably the most contentious aspect of victim/survivors' participatory rights is the extent to which their voice will be accommodated (Doak, 2005; Englebrecht, 2011), while simultaneously maintaining the need for due process for the accused (Kirchengast et al., 2019). While the adversarial system is a contest between the prosecution on behalf of the State and the defence representing the accused, the voices in the debate do not occupy dichotomous positions. For example, the following quotes from a Victim Support Agency (2009) report provide insights into the varied perspectives about victims' voices in the court room, in this instance the use of the VIS in sentencing. The first comment by a judicial officer refers to the importance of the VIS to the overall trial (VSA, 2009, p. 77):

> … judgment involves a process as well as an outcome. VISs are a significant element of a fair, balanced and humane process even if in most cases they are not ultimately determinative of outcomes.

Another perspective is offered by the defence counsel in a case who was concerned about the implications of introducing emotion into the court room (VSA, 2009, p. 77):

> [Sentencing is an] intellectual process, which requires a dispassionate, objective point of view. Things that sway you from objectivity are dangerous.

For a victim/survivor, the opportunity to provide some understanding of the impact of the crime was important (VSA, 2009, p. 77):

> It's my life, they are my words so it's only appropriate that I read them. I wanted to take people on the journey with me and let people know what I felt, to help them understand what he did to me.

A recent study by Davies and Bartels (2021) affirms that the importance of a VIS to victim/survivors has not diminished over time.

Victim-centred reforms continue to be implemented in various national and international jurisdictions. While the type and timing of reforms vary, driven by the appetite of the jurisdiction, the discourse about greater victim participation and ensuring fairness to the accused return to the dichotomous positions of the debate.

Central to the debate are concerns about the potential for the erosion of fairness to the accused, when greater opportunity for participation is afforded victims (VLRC, 2016, p. 27). In their submission on the "Role of Victims in the Criminal Trial Process", the Victorian Bar Association and Criminal Bar Association (VBACBA, 2015) indicate that they are supportive of victims' views being considered for specific issues being considered by the prosecution. Decisions such as "to continue or discontinue a prosecution, to accept a plea of guilty to lesser charges" (VBACBA, p. 2), noting however that the views of victims' "should not be determinative" (VBACBA, p. 5). Further, the submission states, that on the question of "victims having a participatory or prosecutorial role in trial proceedings. Such a role is fundamentally inconsistent with our adversarial system of criminal justice" (VBACBA, p. 6).

In response to the redesign of court rooms, the following quote from a member of the judiciary in the United Kingdom was documented in research by Erez (2019, p. 182). It suggests that mitigating the fear and apprehension for victims, by providing a separate space for them to sit while attending court, is viewed as acquiescing to victims at the expense of the accused:

> What you're saying is you're favoring the victim. You're giving the victim a special place to sit. You're giving the victim a television, a library of books,

> toys to play with... The defendants should be entitled to all those same protections until he's proven guilty because he comes to the courtroom with a presumption of innocence.

While other commentators argue that far from the enhanced participation of victims reducing fairness to the accused, it is possible for the participation of victims and the rights of the accused to simultaneously co-exist. Fairclough and Jones (2018, p. 212), "[t]he more that criminal justice can develop these 'win win' processes, the better for victims in particular and justice as a whole".

Eroding Victims' Sense of Justice and Confidence in the Justice System

A theme weaving through the debates is that of diminished trust in the justice system, as a consequence of negative victim/survivor experiences. Confidence and trust in this context are associated with reporting crimes to police and providing evidence in court so that perpetrators are held to account (Ministry of Justice, 2021). Justice that victim/survivors seek to is not necessarily associated with the outcome of a case at court. Justice is multifaceted (McGlynn & Westmarland, 2019; Wemmers, 2013) and means different things to different people. Justice can be experienced at various stages of the justice system. It may, for example, include validation by the police or by the judge; the feeling of safety; or being heard and included. Conversely, feeling alienated from the justice process can have negative consequences for the victim/survivor, and the justice system.

Feeling alienated diminishes the confidence of victim/survivors in the criminal justice system and has the potential impact of not reporting matters in the future. A report by the Ministry of Justice (2021) in New Zealand, which analysed survey data collected from eight thousand adult victims of crime that country, found that confidence in the criminal justice system was high, except for victims who had interacted with the criminal justice system within the preceding 12 months of the research. Victims for whom confidence was most noticeably diminished were those that had been victims of interpersonal violence (Ministry of Justice, 2021).

There is no doubt that every legislative or policy reform has been hard fought and informed by years of difficult and challenging experiences of victim/survivors. While incremental reforms have been and continue to be impactful in addressing the concerns of victim/survivors, the existence of legislation is not a determinant of how such legislation is interpreted or used in the court room. This can result in diverse experiences by victim/survivors. For example, victims may feel that their inclusion via the VIS may seem tokenistic, and a sense of the "victims" voice were not genuine and were not heard' (Hargrave, 2019, p. 2).

Change

Reforms have certainly brought into focus—and incrementally enhanced—the role of victims in the criminal justice process. For instance, reforms such as entrenching the rights of victims to be treated with dignity and respect, to provide a VIS, to receive information about the progress of reports and the processes of justice, and to express views regarding specific prosecutorial decisions are important steps on the path to recognition of the role of victims in the process of justice. While the reforms have, at some levels and for some victims, contributed positively to the experience of victims (VLRC, 2021), further reform across the criminal justice process is still required (VLRC, 2021).

There are three areas where reforms to existing legislation and additional reforms would build on existing changes. These suggestions are not new, but rather echo and extend the work of scholars and as outlined in various VLRC reports.

Between Codification and Implementation

The first suggestion relates to the application in practice of existing legislation relating to victims of crime. As the following extract from the

VLRC (2016, p. xiii) suggests, reforms to date have elevated the confidence of victims in the criminal justice system; however, a misalignment exists between what is written in legislation and practice:

> While victims' experience of the criminal justice system, and their confidence in it, appear to have improved, there is a significant disparity between the victim's role as conveyed in legislation and the victim's experience in practice.

Consistent interpretation and implementation of legislation takes time and necessitates cultural change. The divergent perspectives within the criminal justice system, such as with VISs, is an example of where reforms as codified in legislation would benefit from attitudinal change to achieve reforms required in practice. Another example is that of the acceptance and use of intermediaries during trial. The VLRC (2021, p. 322) report, while recognising that the Intermediary programme was largely positive, also identified that "there were isolated reports of some judicial officers being reluctant to engage with the program".

An example of existing legislation that is unclear is that of the acceptance of various modes of communication to provide evidence in court. The *Evidence Act*, 2008 (Vic) allows "[a] witness who cannot speak adequately may give evidence by any appropriate means" (s.31(2)), and in s.31(3), "The Court may give direction concerning… the means by which a witness may give evidence".

This appears to allow for the use of augmentative and alternative communication (AAC) to provide evidence; however, it is unclear if all forms of ACC are accepted. A level of caution exists within the justice system about the use of some forms of AAC. The apparent lack of clarity results in some victim/survivors who use AAC being unable to make a statement to police (Camilleri & Pedersen, 2019). The broader question here is why all forms of communication are not accepted within the justice system. There are parallels with the level of caution regarding the use of AAC and resistance to the use of language interpreters in court in the 1990s in Australia. Carroll (1995, p. 65) suggests that:

> The reasons for the low level of usage in some jurisdictions appears to relate nor only to the law on whether to allow access to interpreters, but also to the beliefs and attitudes of participants in the legal process, particularly the belief that a court will find it more difficult to assess the credibility of witnesses and to ascertain the truth if an interpreter is used

The time required for implementation to be applied consistently in practice may potentially also depend on the proposed reform. For example, gendered constructions of sexual assault, such as victim blaming, continue to be voiced by some in senior criminal justice roles: comments, for example, about sexual assault victim/survivors made by police and the judiciary. The following two extracts provide insight into some of the prevailing attitudes expressed by some police members and the judiciary. The first occurred shortly after the sexual assault and murder of Eurydice Dixon in Melbourne in 2018 (Pearson, 2018):

> Victoria Police Superintendent David Clayton stood up to tell people there would be 24-hour patrols but in doing so told the community to "take responsibility for your own safety".

The second extract pertains to comments made by a judge in 2017, during a sexual assault trial in Victoria of two men accused of raping a 17-year-old girl (Kinsella, 2021). When asked to describe what she was wearing, the judge commented, "[l]ook, when I was a young man, I might've referred to it as teasing."

The step between codification and practice is vitally important for the successful and consistent implementation of reform. Ideally, this step would include training, disseminating information to those with responsibilities to implement reforms, and monitoring compliance (Kirchengast, 2015)—and enabling sufficient resourcing. Clarity of victims' participatory rights and the reforms which enshrine these rights into legislation and policy will ensure that the reforms are comprehensively understood (Coleman, 2020; Englebrecht, 2011) and lead to greater compliance (VLRC, 2016, p. 29). Alongside these strategies is the need for continuous cultural change which challenges gendered myths and misconceptions about sexual assault and other intersectional identities, such as people with cognitive impairments. Braun (2019, p. 22) concludes that:

> … methodical advancement of victim participation rights cannot occur in a legal vacuum but requires a changed understanding of crime and criminal justice and a related attitude change of actors in the criminal justice system.

Reform implementation is an issue considered by Bluett-Boyd and Fileborn (2014, p. x). Analyses of the responses of 81 professionals from across Australian jurisdictions, who worked at the court found that:

> Participants had varying levels of knowledge of recent reforms. Some participants were unable to identify any reforms or changes to their practice that had occurred, while others were able to provide an exhaustive overview of legislative and other reform. Areas of reform identified by participants were those related to their own role.
>
> Conversely, a lack of understanding of the purpose of reforms, legal actors deliberately undermining the intent of reform, change-resistant agencies and individuals, and a lack of reforms specific to vulnerable groups, were identified by participants as barriers to effective reform.

Although reforms have been incremental, the focus to a substantial extent has been on receiving information, support and being consulted to ascertain victims' views on specific prosecutorial decisions. The offering of options such as restorative justice which indicates a need for greater victim/survivor participation has also gathered momentum.

Another factor which affects the ability for justice agencies and victim support services to implement legislative, policy and procedural reforms consistently and uniformly is that of adequate resourcing. A lack of resources, manifested in reduced or the absence of support or services, has a negative effect on the experiences of victim/survivors. Some reforms, such as the Intermediary programme, may struggle to provide equitable services to victims across Victoria. Similarly, audio visual links, utilised for example by witnesses including expert witnesses, do not function as intended owing to a range of technological issues and the absence of technological support (Forell et al., 2011; Smith et al., 2021). The benefits gained using remote witness facilities are undermined when technology is unsupported.

While there is broad support for enhancing victim participation (VLRC, 2021), the extent and type of participation prompts significant debate. Greater participatory rights for victims will, of course, lead to calls to ensure that the rights of the accused remain paramount. Others (such as Iliadis et al., 2021) suggest a more holistic approach which is inclusive of and protects the interest of the accused and the victim/survivor.

Continuous Advocacy and Legal Representation

The second and third suggestions, relating to the notion of a continuous advocate to support victim/survivors through the criminal justice system from first report to finalisation, are not new (Camilleri, 2008). However, calls to strengthen the role of advocates has gained momentum and forms one of the recommendations in the VLRC report (2021, p. xxxvi).

While victim/survivors have access to a range of services that provide various forms of support and information from point of victimisation to court, the extent and type of support available varies depending on the type of crime. This includes whether the matter is being heard in the summary or indictable courts; the cultural or linguistic background of victim/survivors; whether they have a disability; and where they reside geographically. While there have been numerous attempts to coordinate support services, fragmented and inconsistent service provision is still apparent (Centre for Innovative Justice, 2020). What is clear is that the availability of support depends on one or a combination of these factors. Recommendation 45 contained in the VLRC report (2021, p. xxxvi) suggests that the:

> Victorian Government should consult on and co-design a model of victim support that uses single advocates to provide continuous support for people who have experienced sexual violence across services and legal systems.

The role of advocates would include providing referrals, and to advocate for victims to "services and legal systems" (VLRC, 2021, p. xxxvi). Recommendation 46 contained in the report identified that funding should be available for legal advice for victims "and, where necessary, representation until the point of trial and in related hearings, to ensure victim/ survivors can exercise their rights and protect their interests" (VLRC, 2021, p. xxxvii).

Importantly, the advocate role, if developed, would be continuous, and if resourced appropriately would provide support for victim/survivors as they traverse the complex terrain of the criminal justice system. Recommendation 46 stops short of suggesting that victim/survivors be assigned legal counsel during the trial or hearing in the summary jurisdiction. While at one level this position may be understandable, enabling legal counsel to represent the interests of victim/survivors at court would be a considerable departure from existing processes. The introduction of this role within the current adversarial common law framework would not be impossible (Braun, 2019; Iliadis et al., 2021). For victim/survivors for whom the criminal justice system is unfamiliar and difficult to understand, representation during the trial would appear to make a positive difference. For victim/survivors with cognitive impairment and people with CCN, though, legal representation and continuous advocacy would further increase the potential of matters reaching court.

In a country utilising a mixed criminal justice system (inquisitorial during investigation and adversarial in the trial stage), Sweden allows victim/survivors access to independent legal counsel during trial. The Swedish experience suggests that this level of assistance can "empower victims to access their rights and providing emotional support and connectedness in the criminal justice system" and importantly "mitigate the risks for secondary victimization" (Carroll, 2022, p. 270). While there are benefits to introducing legal representatives for victims in Victoria, such reforms remain contested and controversial (Braun, 2019; Iliadis et al., 2021).

Conclusion

Debates between greater participation of victims on the one hand and fairness to the accused on the other continue to spark controversy. Despite the contestation of "who owns the conflict" (Englebrecht, 2011), various legislative, policy and procedural reforms have, over time, been introduced in Victoria. However, while reforms have, to some extent, improved confidence in the criminal justice system and led to a degree of improved experiences for some victim/survivors, the reforms have been fragmented and inconsistently applied. The barriers that appear to hamper the full implementation of reforms include: (i) the lack of resources to ensure that support programmes are offered across the state; (ii) clarity of legislative reforms and how they are interpreted; (iii) attitudinal issues including myths and stereotypes of sexual assault; (iv) accepting the credibility of victims who live with cognitive impairment or CCN; and (v) accepting evidence of victim/survivors who use AAC.

Evidence collected from other jurisdictions indicates that various strategies, such as continuous advocacy and legal representation for victim/survivors at court, would mitigate the negative impact of the adversarial system on victim/survivors. Importantly, despite the limitations and the impact on victim/survivors, the legitimacy of victims' participatory rights continues to gain momentum and to be reflected in reforms.

References

Antonsdottir, H. F. (2018). 'A witness in my own case': Victim-survivors' views on the criminal justice process in Iceland. *Feminist Legal Studies, 26*(3), 307–330.

Bluett-Boyd, N., & Fileborn, B. (2014). *Victim/survivor-focused justice responses and reforms to criminal court practice: Implementation, current practice and future directions* (Research Report No. 27). Australian Institute of

Family Studies. https://aifs.gov.au/sites/default/files/publication-documents/rr27.pdf

Braun, K. (2019). *Victim participation rights variation across criminal justice systems*. Palgrave Macmillan.

Camilleri, M. (2008, September). *Enabling justice*. Paper presented at the National Victims of Crime Conference 'New Ways Forward—Pathways to Change' (pp. 23–24). Adelaide. Retrieved from http://library.aic.gov.au/cgi-bin/koha/opac-search.pl?idx=&q=Camilleri

Camilleri. M. (2010). *[Dis]Abled justice: Why reports of sexual assault made by adults with cognitive impairment fail to proceed through the justice system* (Doctoral thesis). University of Ballarat.

Camilleri, M., & Pedersen, C. (2019). *Hear us: The experiences of persons with complex communication needs in the justice system*. Federation University. http://www.disabilityadvocacyvic.org.au/static/uploads/files/hear-us-the-experiences-of-persons-with-complex-communication-needs-wfcvuuzcyfnf.pdf

Carroll, C. P. (2022). Accessing rights and mitigating revictimization: The role of the victim's legal counsel in the Swedish criminal justice system. *Violence against Women, 28*(1), 255–276.

Carroll, J. (1995). The use of interpreters in court. *The International Journal of Speech, Language and the Law, 2*(1), 65–73.

Christie, N. (1977). Conflicts as property. *British Journal of Criminology, 17*(1), 1–15.

Centre for Innovative Justice. (2020). *Strengthening Victoria's support system: Victims' service review: Final report*. Centre for Innovative Justice at RMIT. https://cij.org.au/research-projects/victims-services-review/

Coleman, M. (2020). The tension between the presumption of innocence and victims' participation rights at the International Criminal Court. *International Criminal Law Review, 20*(2), 371–393.

Davies, R., & Bartels, L. (2021). *The use of victim impact statements in sentencing for sexual offences*. Routledge.

Doak, J. (2005). Victims' rights in criminal trials: Prospects for participation. *Journal of Law and Society, 32*(2), 294–316.

Edwards, I. (2004). An ambiguous participant: The crime victim and criminal justice decision-making. *British Journal of Criminology, 44*(6), 967–982.

Englebrecht, C. (2011). The struggle for "ownership of conflict": An exploration of victim participation and voice in the criminal justice system. *Criminal Justice Review, 36*(2), 129–151.

Erez, E. (2019). Integrating a victim perspective in criminal justice through victim impact statements. In A. Crawford & J. Goodey (Eds.), *Integrating a victim perspective within criminal justice* (pp. 165–184). Routledge.

Erez, Globokar, J. L., & Ibarra, P. R. (2014). Outsiders inside. *International Review of Victimology, 20*(1), 169–188. https://doi.org/10.1177/0269758013510809

Fairclough. S., & Jones, I. (2018). In S. Walklate (Ed.), *Handbook of victims and victimology* (2nd ed., pp. 2011–228). Routledge.

Featherstone, L. (2017). 'That's what being a woman is for': Opposition to marital rape law reform in late twentieth-century Australia. *Gender & History, 29*(1), 87–103.

Forell, S., Laufer, M., & Digiusto, E. (2011). Legal assistance by video conferencing: What is known? *Justice Issues, 15*, 1–23.

Hargrave, P. (2019). *Victims' voices: The justice needs and experiences of New Zealand serious crime victims.* Research report. Victim Support. https://www.researchgate.net/publication/336868107_Victims'_Voices_The_Justice_Needs_and_Experiences_of_New_Zealand_Serious_Crime_Victims

Herman, J. L. (2005). Justice from the victim's perspective. *Violence Against Women, 11*(5), 571–602.

Iliadis, M., Smith, O., & Doak, J. (2021). Independent separate legal representation for rape complainants in adversarial systems: Lessons from Northern Ireland. *Journal of Law and Society, 48*(2), 250–272.

Judicial College of Victoria. (2016). *Disability Access Bench Book.* https://live-jcv-website.pantheonsite.io/eManuals/DABB/index.htm#59523.htm

Judicial College of Victoria. (2019). *Victims of crime in the courtroom: A guide for judicial officers.* https://www.judicialcollege.vic.edu.au/resources/victims-crime-courtroom

Kinsella, E. (2021, July 18). In the witness box. *ABC Online.* https://www.abc.net.au/news/2021-07-18/how-a-court-case-put-the-spotlight-on-sexual-assault-trials/100281894

Kirchengast, T. (2015). *The role of victims of crime in the criminal trial process.* Public Submission to the Victorian Law Reform Commission. https://www.lawreform.vic.gov.au/wp-content/uploads/2021/08/Submission_CP_19_Dr_Tyrone_Kirchengast_01-10-15.pdf

Kirchengast, T. (2016). *Victims and the criminal trial*. Palgrave Macmillan.

Kirchengast, T., Iliadis, M., & O'Connell, M. (2019). Development of the office of Commissioner of Victims' Rights as an appropriate response to improving the experiences of victims in the criminal justice system: Integrity, access and justice for victims of crime. *Monash University Law Review, 45*(1), 1–28.

McGlynn, C., & Westmarland, N. (2019). Kaleidoscopic justice: Sexual violence and victim-survivors' perceptions of justice. *Social and Legal Studies, 28*(2), 179–201.

Ministry of Justice. (2021). *New Zealand Crime and Victims' Survey: Victims' confidence in the criminal justice system.* Ministry of Justice. https://www.justice.govt.nz/justice-sector-policy/research-data/nzcvs/

Molina, J., & Poppleton, S. (2020). *Rape Survivors and the criminal justice system.* Victims of Crime Commissioner. https://victimscommissioner.org.uk/document/rape-survivors-and-the-criminal-justice-system/

Pearson, E. (2018, June 15). 'Women don't need to change, men do': Eurydice death stirs safety debate. *The Age.* https://www.theage.com.au/national/victoria/a-question-of-risk-eurydice-dixon-death-stirs-women-s-safety-debate-20180615-p4zlne.html

Smith, R., Savage, R., & Emami, C. (2021). *Audiovisual link technologies in Australian criminal courts: Practical and legal considerations.* Research Report. Australian Institute of Criminology. https://www.aic.gov.au/publications/rr/rr22

The Victorian Bar and Criminla Bar Association (VBACBA). (2015, October 14). *Submission to the VLRC consultation paper on the role of victims of crime in the crimianl trial process.* https://www.lawreform.vic.gov.au/wpcontent/uploads/2021/08/Submission_CP_29_Victorian-Bar-and-Criminal_Bar_Association_14-10-15.pdf

United Nations. (n.d.). *Declaration of basic principles of justice for victims of crime and abuse of power.* https://www.ohchr.org/en/instruments-mechanisms/instruments/declaration-basic-principles-justice-victims-crime-and-abuse

Victim Support Agency. (2009). *A victims voice: Victim Impact Statement in Victoria.* Victim Support agency, Department of Justice Victoria. https://www.victimsofcrime.vic.gov.au/a-victims-voice-victim-impact-statements-in-victoria

VEOHRC (Victorian Equal Opportunity and Human Rights Commission). (2014). *Beyond doubt: The experiences of people with disabilities reporting crime.* Victorian Equal Opportunity and Human Rights Commission. https://www.humanrights.vic.gov.au/static/de8c56fa6025cc3cc41d58ac57cfbe46/Resource-Beyond_Doubt-Summary_report-2014.pdffile:///C:/Users/Mcamilleri/Downloads/Beyond_Doubt_-_Research_findings(6).pdf

VLRC (Victorian Law Reform Commission). (2004). *Sexual Offences Inquiry: Final report*. Victorian Law Reform Commission. https://www.lawreform.vic.gov.au/publication/sexual-offences-report-2004/

VLRC (Victorian Law Reform Commission). (2016). *Victims in the criminal trial process: Report August 2016*. Victorian Law Reform Commission. https://www.lawreform.vic.gov.au/wp-content/uploads/2021/07/VLRC_Victims-Of-Crime-Report-W.pdf

VLRC (Victorian Law Reform Commission). (2021). *Improving the justice system response to sexual offences*. Victorian Law Reform Commission. https://www.lawreform.vic.gov.au/publication/improving-the-justice-system-response-to-sexual-offences/

Wemmers, J. (2013). Victims' experiences in the criminal justice system and their recovery from crime. *International Review of Victimology, 19*(3), 221–233.

Legislation

Criminal Procedure Act 2009 (Vic) Division 5
Evidence Act 2008 (Vic) s31 (2) and s31 (3)
Sentencing Act 1991 (Vic) Division 1C
Victims Charter Act 2006 (Vic)
Victims of Crime Commissioner Act 2015 (Vic)

Practitioner Perspective: Victims/Survivors and the Courts—From Alienation and Secondary Victimisation to Participatory Rights

Dagmar Jenkins

I have been privileged to bear witness, in my work as a social worker and sexual assault counsellor of almost two decades in Victoria, Australia, to an array of experiences which have informed my work. Observations have been gleaned from experiences shared by the many survivors I have had the honour of knowing and learning from, and do not represent any single individual. Note that my views are formed by personal experiences, and that I am just one of many practitioners in a varied field.

The role of a counsellor/advocate frequently includes supporting victims/survivors through the process of reporting to police and any subsequent investigation. Cumulative practice wisdom suggests that only a small proportion of people seeking support to report a sexual assault have cases progress to court, with an even smaller number resulting in a conviction. This aligns with the broader statistics on criminal justice outcomes for sexual assault in Victoria (Crime Statistics Agency Victoria, 2021).

The journey towards engagement with the criminal justice system for victim/survivors can be a rapid and confusing whirlwind, or a very gradual process, which may take decades. Where matters proceed quickly, opportunities for reflection can be sparse and decisions about participation can feel rushed. This may occur where a disclosure was unintended, where mandatory reporting requirements apply, or when an assault is recent, and a time-sensitive forensic medical examination is recommended. Whilst hearings are underway, complainants may be required to indicate preferences for different courses of action, with little

D. Jenkins
VIC, Australia

opportunity to take time to consider the ramifications of the options provided.

Once a sexual offence has been reported to police, in many instances a victim/survivor will decide not to complete a formal statement, and the matter will not be taken any further. This is usually easy to achieve. Much harder is having matters proceed from investigation to court, particularly when the victim/survivor wants this and a decision has been made that the case is not strong enough to proceed.

The well-documented barriers to reporting sexual offences for people with disabilities, First Nations people, the LGBTIQA+ community and those from culturally and linguistically diverse backgrounds further contribute to attrition on the journey from first point of contact with police. Victims/survivors are often unsure about reporting, and the extra layer of experiences of systemic discrimination and disadvantage—combined with fear of police, fear of not being believed and distrust in the system that are all based on lived experience—reduce participation in criminal justice processes. For survivors with an intellectual disability, who are neuro-diverse or who have a mental illness, assumptions about capacity or credibility frequently create barriers to participation throughout. A responsive police informant who communicates regularly can make all the difference to a victim/survivor's feeling of engagement in the process.

The court process is complex and takes time for those working within that system to fully understand. For victims/survivors, particularly those who have never previously had any contact with the court system, the process can feel overwhelming, daunting and confusing. It can be difficult for people to make sense of the many elements of the adversarial legal system in Victoria, and to find their place within it.

For instance, an experience of sexual assault may have been the most traumatic experience of a person's life, and the counterintuitive idea that victims/survivors are considered a witness to the alleged crime in a state prosecution case can be experienced as invalidating and confusing, and often requires time for people to comprehend and process.

It is common for people to expect that they will have their own lawyer to represent them, and it can be perplexing and frightening for many complainants in sexual offence matters that this will not be the case.

Some victim/survivors hope that the justice system will be a forum for telling their story and are oftentimes crushed to find that what can be said in court is curtailed by what is legally allowed, and can be further limited if some of the evidence is deemed inadmissible. Regular communication from prosecutors, whether the Office of Public Prosecutions or Police Prosecutions, together with clear explanations of court decisions, goes a long way toward ensuring people reporting sexual offences feel informed throughout the process. This is of particular importance when plea negotiations are underway.

It has been observed repeatedly that the court process is experienced by many survivors of sexual violence as retraumatising. The consequences of experiences of trauma, and the intersection with the stressors of the justice system, can further affect the wellbeing of victim/survivors. Many might fear that the impacts on their mental health of the trauma they have experienced and resulting coping strategies such as drug or alcohol use, will be used to discredit them in the court setting. Often these fears are realised during cross examination. Defence counsel may seek access to counselling and medical records as part of their legal strategy, which many people experience as a gross violation further adding to their distress and feeling of vulnerability within an intimidating system.

One area of therapeutic work with survivors of sexual violence involves exploring and mitigating the effect that victim blaming myths have on a person's recovery from their experience. Court processes can undermine those gains, particularly if defence counsel rely on myths about sexual assault to create reasonable doubt or suggest that a victim/survivor might have lied about what happened. Feelings of shame associated with the offending or core beliefs about being unworthy, bad or of having done something wrong can be amplified by the questions asked and the demeanour of counsel, thus stalling or even undoing the healing process.

The communication environment of court can create barriers to participation and leave people feeling as though it is not a system for them. Sophisticated legal language and the formality of proceedings can reduce a person's opportunity to meaningfully participate and to feel that they are a valued participant in a process that is about what happened to them. This can be particularly the case for children and young people, or those with a cognitive impairment.

The very common anxiety leading up to court dates is exacerbated by repeated timetabling changes and a lack of certainty, as often people may well feel as though their lives are on hold as they await hearings. Victims/survivors have very little say in when and how delays occur. Repeated adjournments can be experienced as further victimisation, particularly when related to the needs of the alleged offender, even when legally appropriate within the context of the Victorian criminal justice system and its role in protecting the rights of the accused.

Adjournments which occur close to the time a victim/survivor was scheduled to give evidence can be enormously distressing and disruptive. People have typically put significant amounts of preparation into planning for a particular date, which may involve safety planning in relation their mental health, arranging a support person to also attend, organising care of a child or a pet, coordinating travel arrangements, and taking time off work. When matters are adjourned just prior to a person giving evidence, they are likely to have already reviewed their statement and attended meetings and legal conferences to prepare for court, all of which can be emotionally taxing and involve revisiting memories of a traumatic experience.

Many victim/survivors experience significant fear that they will have unplanned contact with the offender during court proceedings. Although safety planning is an aspect of court preparation, and complainants in sexual offence matters are able to give evidence from remote witness facilities, when the accused person is in the same court precinct and is watching proceedings, this can contribute to participation in criminal justice proceedings feeling deeply unsafe. The infrastructure at different courts and support services available can be a factor in how successfully safety planning strategies are implemented. Victim/survivors reporting summary offences or living in rural areas may experience greater difficulties accessing support services and a less coordinated approach, which can lead to the process feeling rushed and overwhelming as court dates loom.

Victorian criminal justice processes are ever evolving, and true participation of victims/survivors at all stages of the journey is a work in progress. Some signs that this is beginning to be achieved might include when people consistently feel that they have been heard; that they have been treated with respect throughout the process and feel well informed at all stages; that the systems they have had contact with are trauma-informed and culturally safe; that adjustments and accommodations have been made to ensure equal access; that survivors of sexual violence feel that their role and contribution is valued; and that the outcome has met some of their needs.

Reference

Crime Statistics Agency. (2021). *Attrition of sexual offence incidents through the Victorian criminal justice system: 2021 update*. https://www.crimestatistics.vic.gov.au/research-and-evaluation/publications/attrition-of-sexual-offence-incidents-through-the-victorian

13

Children and Young People in Court

Rosemary Sheehan and Susan Baidawi

Introduction

This chapter provides an overview of jurisdictional approaches to juvenile offending and associated victimisation in Australian courts, canvassing issues such as age of criminal responsibility, effective representation and approaches to diversion and sentencing. Each Australian state and territory have established in its legislation a designated Children's Court and principles that guide its operation. The legislation in each jurisdiction gives paramount consideration to the rehabilitation of the child, and this focus guides the Children's Court in its operation and practice in how

R. Sheehan (✉)
Monash University, Melbourne, VIC, Australia
e-mail: rosemary.sheehan@monash.edu

S. Baidawi
Monash University, Melbourne, VIC, Australia
e-mail: susan.baidawi@monash.edu

M. Camilleri and A. Harkness (eds.), *Australian Courts*,
https://doi.org/10.1007/978-3-031-19063-6_13

the Court, and Court stakeholders, support and process cases involving children. It is an approach that significantly differs from that taken, for example, by the *Sentencing* Act, 1991 (Vic) as applied to adults appearing in the Magistrates Courts jurisdiction.

The Context of Criminal Justice Responses to Children

There is a growing national debate in Australia regarding criminal justice responses to children, with pressure from legal, medical, Indigenous, human rights and youth peak bodies for more effective responses to children with offending behaviours. 63% of all children accused in the Children's Court have experienced trauma, abuse or neglect (Youth Parole Board, 2016, p. 14). This adds complexity where an accused child is also a victim of crime, be it from being a victim of crime by adults either at an early age (such as child exploitation/sex trafficking that occurs with young girls living in residential care), or as a victim of crime by other children whilst the subject child is also committing an offence (such as young people engaging in theft against each other, or 'gang fights' and affray).

The intersections of age, disability, geographical location, ethnicity, gender and lower socio-economic factors add to this complexity in legal decision-making about children before the court for youth offending matters (White & Cunneen, 2006). Victoria's Sentencing Advisory Council (2020a, 2020b) recommends that 'trauma' should become a relevant consideration when sentencing children. This allows the court to consider more relevant factors and the full extent of the context of the child prior to sentencing most particularly in giving attention to rehabilitation and consideration to when diversion might be open to the young person, sought first perhaps through the police and then the magistrate. The Sentencing Advisory Council's report emphasises the importance of 'trauma informed practice' with children—understanding how the effects of trauma relate to offending and possible future offending, especially, when necessary, referrals or early support interventions are not provided for the child.

Preventative interventions using a trauma-informed lens and response are likely to offer both a more positive and tailored impact for early offending children and reduce their entrenchment in criminal justice systems and criminal networks. If such interventions are too late, and the child has already experienced a considerable period of remand, court attendances and a conviction, the consequent stigma and damage for the child affects their future identity and development and can have a significant impact on whether they will continue to offend (Sentencing Advisory Council, 2020).

Controversial Responses to Youth Offending

The range of controversies relating to young people in formal legal hearings into criminal matters in Australian youth courts reflect wider debates about what constitutes an appropriate response to youth offending. Broadly, these debates align with what have come to be known as 'justice' and 'welfare' philosophies, or models, of youth justice (Cunneen et al., 2015). The perspectives underpinning these models reflect divergent attitudes characterising justice-involved children as either "victims or villains" (Shaw, 2012, p. 3), as well as reflecting disagreement about the extent to which a child actively chooses to engage in offending behaviour, the efficacy of punitive responses in changing such behaviour, and how much consideration must be given to community protection.

A central concern is the appropriateness of the adversarial approach to justice with youth offenders, with calls for a more 'participatory' or problem-solving approach. Access to effective legal representation is key to addressing the disadvantage and powerlessness children experience in this jurisdiction, often exacerbated by their young age, socio-economic disadvantage or coming from an ethnic minority community. It is key also to ensuring a young person's access to a fair and equitable legal process. The use of plea bargaining within the adversarial approach is a concern, with the risk of an ill-informed young person admitting guilt for an offence they did not commit or agreeing to plead guilty when they could have achieved a diversion disposition if their legal representative was more informed.

In terms of 'justice' and 'welfare' philosophies, the 'justice' approach emphasises the need for clear boundaries, and predictable and immediate consequences for a child's behavioural infractions. It is influenced by a behaviourist worldview, which posits that consistent, predictable consequences are the effective means to modify behaviour and protect the community (Baidawi, 2020b; Cunneen et al., 2015).

The 'welfare' approach focuses more on principles that are broadly understood as welfare-based, trauma-informed or anti-criminogenic. Advocates for this approach give primacy to addressing the welfare-related drivers of children's offending behaviour, to developing supportive relationships with children, and avoiding children's contact with the criminal justice system given its criminogenic impact.

In contrast to the 'justice' approach, those who support a 'welfare' approach highlight the ineffectiveness of punitive approaches (such as incarceration) in achieving intended behaviour change in children (Baidawi, 2020b). The 'welfare' approach is based on evidence that recognises how children's offending is often underpinned by unmet support needs, disadvantage, and vulnerability. The need for such an approach is evidenced in a key subgroup of child offenders who are over-represented in Australian youth criminal courts, the 'crossover' children who have also contact with the child protection system due to abuse, neglect or parental incapacity (Baidawi & Sheehan, 2019b; the Victorian Sentencing Advisory Council has published three significant reports on issues pertaining to crossover kids in the criminal justcie system—see Victorian Sentencing Advisory Council, 2019, 2020a, 2020b).

The Age of Criminal Responsibility

A contemporary example of the 'welfare/'justice' controversy is the ongoing national debate in Australia about the minimum age of criminal responsibility across Australian jurisdictions. The minimum age of 10 years has drawn censure from international human rights bodies, including Amnesty International (2018) and the UN Committee on the Rights of the Child (2019), who recommend the minimum of 14 years of age for criminal responsibility, and 16 years as a minimum age for incarceration. Raising the minimum age in Australia has most recently been discussed at a meeting of the State Attorneys-General (Parliament of Victoria, 2022). In June 2022, the Tasmanian State Government announced Youth Justice reforms which will raise the minimum age of criminal responsibility to 14 years (Jaensch, 2022). Other states and territories are also considering changes to the minimum age of criminal responsibility. However, it is not clear at this point whether such reforms will align with the recommendations from Amnesty International and the United Nations.

Adopting these recommendations would see Australia meet its international commitments under human rights law, specifically its obligations as a signatory to the United Nations Convention on the Rights of the Child (United Nations, 1989). Raising the age would directly address the current approach of criminalising young children and better acknowledge the growing neuro-developmental evidence that demonstrates how under-developed the brain structures relevant to offending behaviour are in younger children (Delmage, 2013). It acknowledges, too, how this development is impacted by a child's environmental surrounds, which includes their exposure to youth justice systems.

Justice-involved children experience greater levels of adversity, trauma and disadvantage relative to their same-age peers (Kenny & Nelson, 2008; Kinner et al., 2014), and an increased level of complexity of needs and vulnerability is observed in the youngest children in the justice system (Baglivio et al., 2015). Younger children charged with offending earlier than 14 years of age are more likely to have more complex cultural, social and developmental circumstances and needs (AIHW, 2020; Baidawi, 2020a; Baidawi & Piquero, 2020; Baidawi & Sheehan, 2019a; Cho et al., 2019). National pressure from legal, medical, Indigenous, youth peak bodies and experts to reform approaches to early offending has led to the contemporary—but as yet unresolved—review of legislative provisions across Australia to raise the age of criminal responsibility (Ralston & Whitbourn, 2020).

The divide between Children's Courts (who are responsible for adjudication and sentencing) and youth justice systems (which supervise some orders sentenced by the Courts) limits courts' statutory ability to influence the various welfare conditions that often underpin, or at least contribute to, children's offending behaviour. Yet, welfare-related factors such as a lack of adult supervision, child maltreatment, lack of access to treatment services and other supports or placement with offending peers in out-of-home care settings are well-known to influence the emergence and continuation of offending behaviour (Baidawi & Sheehan, 2019a; Loeber & Farrington, 2000). At the very least, coordinated responses alongside other sectors, such as child and family welfare, mental health, disability, and other social supports such as drug and alcohol counselling, are necessary for disrupting children's longer-term justice system involvement.

Children and Young People in the Legal Process

Children and young people appearing in formal summary hearings in the Children's Court are challenged by their capacity for cognitive understanding about the offences for which they are charged, their lack of maturity and their capability to engage in what is in many ways an adult justice process. This involvement is more pronounced for child victims of crime where their inclusion in the legal process is difficult to facilitate, attempting to both maintain their best interests and their voice, but also to avoid repeat victimisation and compounding trauma. The challenge is to engage young people more positively in formal and contested court hearings, mindful of both their experience as offenders and as witnesses, the latter who may have been victimised by the events presented at court. Appropriately responding to factors such as ethnicity, gender and socio-economic status is important to managing how court processes are played out.

Aside from the debate over whether children's problematic behaviour ought to incur criminal justice responses, the involvement of children with often numerous vulnerabilities in a complex legal system brings challenges. There is a need to establish a child's understanding of the fact that they have actually legally committed a crime and are not punished instead for simple immaturity, observing common law principles. *Doli incapax* provisions exist across all Australian jurisdictions—a legal presumption that to be held criminally responsible, a child aged between 10 and 13 years must be proven able to distinguish between acts that are 'seriously wrong' and those that are merely 'naughty or mischievous' (Fitz-Gibbon & O'Brien, 2019). It is a provision that translates to being incapable of crime or of evil, aiming to protect younger children who are insufficiently morally or intellectually developed from the full force of the law.

The application of *doli incapax* relies on a retrospective assessment of a child's understanding of their actions, and therefore on access to *doli incapax* assessment (Fitz-Gibbon & O'Brien, 2019). The presumption to rebut *doli incapax* is with the prosecution, and there is no legal requirement for defence or the Court to provide a psychological assessment of the child to assist the prosecutor to decide whether to rebut this presumption. Yet, in practice, it is often the legal defence that takes on the onus of proving the child's lack of capacity (Fitz-Gibbon & O'Brien, 2019).

The application of *doli incapax* provisions also relies very much on the discretion of police, courts and assessors (UN Committee on the Rights of the Child, 2019); and on how it is applied in the context in which the child is placed, allowing for variations in service provision and access (Fitz-Gibbon & O'Brien, 2019). This is made more difficult where there is no clinical report or assessment and it relies on the prosecution to decide the merit of *doli incapax* on the evidence submitted, records of interview, prior criminal record, school records and so on.

Not only does a child before the court need the capacity to understand the wrongful nature of their actions, but also to sufficiently comprehend the complex legal processes of being arrested and charged by police, to giving legal instructions, to appearing before the court and the processes around this and complying with the requirements of court orders. Being able to comprehend this is central to the child's right to participation in judicial and administrative proceedings affecting them, as outlined in Article 12 of the UN Convention on the Rights of the Child (UN, 1989). Yet children, criminal defence lawyers and youth justice practitioners speak about children's lack of understanding of these aspects (Borowski & Sheehan, 2013).

The application of bail can be confusing—the often-mismatched experiences of being bailed despite a pattern of alleged offending, yet later bail being revoked following a comparatively minor infraction such as breaching curfew appears contradictory. Children can be confused by being placed in custody for staying out at night but not for an alleged car theft or robbery. The child's reliance on (often time-poor) legal counsel and (sometimes absent) guardians to support them through their navigation of these complex adult systems subverts their right to participation and the broader requirement to ensure the fair administration of justice (Cashmore, 2013).

Plea bargaining reveals specific legal difficulties in the children's jurisdiction. The majority of legal matters in the children's criminal jurisdiction are resolved by way of a guilty plea (Naffine & Wundersitz, 1991), but how much this is a result of plea bargaining is unclear. Negotiation around children's criminal matters occurs substantiality pre-trial, generally involving a reduction in the number, or seriousness, of charges put to the court in exchange for a guilty plea (Naffine & Wundersitz, 1991). This process typifies the operation of the children's justice system as the capacity of legal defence to advocate effectively on a child's behalf relies on the child's ability to engage with the process. How able the child is to do this will be influenced by a range of individual, socio-economic and cultural factors.

Children can encounter systemic disadvantage in the criminal justice process where more favourable outcomes will rest on the child's capacity to work with and relate to a variety of adults, including Magistrates, lawyers, youth justice workers, police and other professionals. How well a child can do this can be diminished by their exposure to maltreatment and resultant trauma; challenges dealing with authority figures; a lack of caregiver support for them; along with difficulties with emotional regulation, neuro-disability and other language and communication difficulties (Papalia et al., 2020; Snow & Powell, 2012). Challenges emerge also from a lack of attention to the diversity in children's cultural backgrounds, and the impact of this on their experience of involvement in a highly adult-centric court system.

At the heart of these dilemmas is the question as to whether an adversarial system can provide a fair and equitable legal process for children who disproportionately have disabilities, experiences of trauma, adversity and economic disadvantage and lack parental or caregiver support.

Challenges for Early Offending Children

Early offending children are a particularly vulnerable group who have a disproportionately high-risk for future youth justice involvement (see AIHW, 2013; Sentencing Advisory Council, 2016). For instance, the Australian Institute of Health and Welfare (AIHW, 2013) reported that 85% of young people born in 1993–1994 who came under youth justice supervision at ages 10–14 years returned to (or continued under) supervision when they were aged 15–17 years. Younger offending children are particularly more likely to be from Aboriginal and Torres Strait Islander backgrounds, have child protection involvement, and to have a neuro-disability (AIHW,2020, Baidawi & Piquero, 2020). The age of criminal responsibility across Australia is set at 10 years of age, although the Australian Capital Territory's Legislative Assembly voted in August 2020 to give in principle support to raising the minimum age of criminal responsibility to 14 years (*The Guardian* 2020). The low age of criminal responsibility puts Australia at direct odds with the United Nations Child Rights Committee's 2019 declaration which states that 14 years of age should be the minimum age that children could be held legally responsible (UN Committee on the Rights of the Child, 2019).

Legal decision-making for early offending children increasingly involves diversion either before attending court (a 'caution') or as part of sentencing, seeking to avoid drawing children into the criminal justice system by directing them to early intervention at the police station level without instituting formal charges (Cunneen et al., 2015). The aim is to keep matters out of court and in the pre-charge diversion stage to avoid escalating children into the justice system. Such early interventions include referrals for 'wrap around' service responses where, for example, police work together with youth workers—drawing on education, mental health, speech pathology, culturally specific approaches, mentors and disability services—to provide a holistic intervention response.

Such approaches draw on trauma-informed practices, and the use of intermediaries to help young people navigate the justice system. New Zealand has developed a process of communication assistance, based on the role of the intermediary in England and Wales, to work both with youth justice and parties involved in a court matter, to "help young people have a say, understand and fully participate in interventions designed to help them" (Kedge, 2018). Speech pathologists are actively involved in the New Zealand intermediary approach, advising on communication needs of and processes for those who are vulnerable in the judicial system, both as defendants and as witnesses (Bonetti, 2018).

Diversion is central to court outcomes for children including for more serious offending as it can link such children to support services which are proven pathways to rehabilitation and tailored for their specific circumstances. These decisions must be channelled through Magistrates, prosecutors, defence lawyers and diversion coordinators looking at the child and their individual context, and the nature of their offending. In this, they use a trauma-informed practice lens, substantially different from the straightforward sentencing for offending which typically occurs in the Magistrates Court (Sentencing Advisory Council, 2020). This specialist approach provides a more problem-solving and integrated approach to responding to young people charged with offending.

Changes to Formal Court Processes

In Australia, since the 1990s, reforms to formal court hearing processes have aimed to facilitate the inclusion of children and young people; making available, for example, witness testimony via video link and providing trained support staff. These changes sought to provide more fairness and a non-injurious involvement for young people in the adversarial court process.

Perhaps, the most significant change to Children's Court models over this period has been the introduction of problem-solving approaches to adapt Court processes for specific groups of children and young people. These adaptations reflect the increasing attention in justice systems to adopting diverse approaches, such those seen in Scotland (McAra & McVie, 2010), New Zealand (Fitzgerald, 2018) and Nordic countries (Lappi-Seppälä, 2011) that merge welfare and justice models and focus on 'needs' as much as on 'deeds', looking to treatment and rehabilitation rather than solely imposing punishment. Similarly, Australian and New Zealand youth courts have moved to adopting problem-solving approaches based on restorative justice principles, "balancing young offenders' rights against their responsibilities to the community" (Australian Law Reform Commission and Australian Human Rights Commission, 1997, p. 252).

These specialised approaches include specific 'crossover' Children's Court lists to provide a more integrated court response identifying children and young people with concurrent involvement in criminal and child welfare/child protection jurisdictions. Whilst yet to be implemented, such approaches have been proposed for Australian jurisdictions (Baidawi, 2020b; Bowles, 2015). These approaches have been in place in New Zealand's Youth Courts since 2011 (Fitzgerald, 2018) and in California's Sacramento County in the United States (Farn & Umpierre, 2017). Whilst quantitative evaluation of their impact is still emerging, qualitative feedback suggests that they better address the case coordination challenges characteristic of crossover children's matters (Fitzgerald, 2018).

Youth Drug Courts represent another problem-solving model, operating on therapeutic jurisprudence principles for young people before the youth criminal courts. Although successful, New South Wales' Youth Drug Courts were terminated, with costing concerns cited as the reason (Harvey, 2012). Children's Courts around Australia, though, continue to feature many children and young people for whom drug and alcohol and mental health concerns, among other issues, remain unaddressed despite numerous intersections with the law. These concerning circumstances have led key judicial figures to continue to advocate for problem-solving approaches in Australia's Children's Courts to address the underlying challenges that see children and young people becoming entrenched in youth justice systems (Bowles, 2015).

Along with problem-solving courts, specialist Indigenous courts exist within Children's Courts in several Australian States and Territories. They involve the Indigenous community as part of an overarching strategy to reduce the over-representation of Indigenous young people in the criminal justice system. Established in 2005, the Koori Children's Court Division in Victoria is a sentencing model open to Aboriginal and Torres Strait Islander children who plead guilty. Unlike mainstream Children's

Court models, in which the judge or magistrate sits at a bench with legal practitioners at the bar table and the accused either in the dock or in the public seating behind their legal representative, the Koori Court has all the Court participants sitting around one table. Elders or other Respected Persons sit beside the magistrate or judge, and a family member or support person for the young person is also seated at the table (Children's Court of Victoria, 2021). Courtrooms used for the Koori Court are adapted for this distinctive process, displaying Australian, Aboriginal and the Torres Strait Islander flags and artworks. The courts are 'smoked' in accordance with custom and tradition prior to the first sitting of the day (Grant, 2009).

In the Koori Court model, a sentencing conversation provides the opportunity for the young person to speak, alongside family and community members. Elders or Respected Persons give cultural advice to the judge or magistrate in relation to the young person's situation and speak to the young person about the circumstances which have led to their court involvement, as well as about their current circumstances. Whilst such a model cannot address the broader underlying social and economic drivers of Indigenous over-representation in the justice system, they aim to provide a more culturally appropriate and meaningful court experience for Aboriginal and Torres Strait Islander children.

Conclusion

Whilst some changes have been made to respond to juvenile offending, issues remain around the age of criminal responsibility, effective representation and approaches to diversion and sentencing. There remains key challenges in what is effective and beneficial for children and young people caught up in legal and court processes. With multiple Australian jurisdictions, including the Australian Capital Territory and Victoria now moving towards raising the age of criminal responsibility (Legislative Council Legal & Social Issues Committee, 2021; McArthur et al., 2021), as well as a national focus on the unnecessary criminalisation of children,

Australian Children's Courts and broader social services can anticipate moving towards more therapeutic, integrated and developmentally supportive responses towards children.

References

Amnesty International. (2018). *The sky is the limit: Keeping young children out of prison by raising the age of criminal responsibility*. Retrieved from https://www.amnesty.org.au/wp-content/uploads/2018/09/The-Sky-is-the-Limit-FINAL-1.pdf

Australian Institute of Health and Welfare (AIHW). (2013). *Young people aged 10–14 in the youth justice system 2011–12*. Juvenile justice series no.12. JUV 19. Canberra: Australian Institute of Health and Welfare.

AIHW (Australian Institute of Health and Welfare). (2020). *Young people under youth justice supervision and in child protection 2018–19*. Australian Government. Retrieved from https://www.aihw.gov.au/reports/youth-justice/young-people-in-child-protection/summary

ALRC (Australian Law Reform Commission). (1997). *Seen and heard: priority for children in the legal process*. Australian Government. Retrieved from https://www.alrc.gov.au/publication/seen-and-heard-priority-for-children-in-the-legal-process-alrc-report-84/

Baglivio, M. T., Wolff, K. T., Piquero, A. R., & Epps, N. (2015). The relationship between Adverse Childhood Experiences (ACE) and juvenile offending trajectories in a juvenile offender sample. *Journal of Criminal Justice, 43*(3), 229–241.

Baidawi, S. (2020a). Crossover children: Examining initial criminal justice system contact among child protection-involved youth. *Australian Social Work, 73*(3), 280–295.

Baidawi, S. (2020b). Disrupting the pipeline: Supporting and decriminalising child protection-involved youth. In S. Baidawi & R. Sheehan (Eds.), *"Crossover" children in the child protection and youth justice systems*. Routledge.

Baidawi, S., & Piquero, A. R. (2020). Neurodisability among children at the nexus of the child welfare and youth justice system. *Journal of Youth and Adolescence, 50*, 803–819.

Baidawi, S., & Sheehan, R. (2019a). *'Cross-over kids': Effective responses to children and young people in the youth justice and statutory child protection systems*. Report to the Criminology Research Advisory Council. Retrieved from https://www.aic.gov.au/sites/default/files/2020-05/Cross-Over-Kids-Report-Dec2019a-v2.pdf

Baidawi, S., & Sheehan, R. (2019b). 'Crossover kids': Offending by child protection-involved youth. *Trends & Issues in Crime and Criminal Justice, 582*. Canberra: Australian Institute of Criminology. Retrieved from https://www.aic.gov.au/sites/default/files/2020-05/ti582_crossover_kids-v2.pdf

Borowski, A., & Sheehan, R. (2013). The children's court of Victoria. In R. Sheehan & A. Borowski (Eds.), *Australia's children's courts today and tomorrow* (pp. 123–142). Springer Netherlands.

Bonetti, M. (2018). Communication Assistants (Intermediaries)–Structure, training and support–Lessons for New Zealand. New Zealand Law Foundation Researach Reports. Wellington. See: 2018 New Zealand Law Foundation Research Reports (nzlii.org)

Bowles, J. (2015). What can be done?. *Residential therapeutic treatment options for young people suffering substance abuse/mental illness*. Retrieved from https://www.churchilltrust.com.au/media/fellows/Bowles_J_2014_Treatment_for_young_people_suffering_substance_abuse_and_mental_illness.pdf

Cashmore, J. (2013). Juvenile justice: Australian court responses situated in the international context. In R. Sheehan & A. Borowski (Eds.), *Australia's children's courts today and tomorrow*. Springer.

Children's Court of Victoria. (2021). Koori Court. Available online at https://www.childrenscourt.vic.gov.au/criminal-division/koori-court

Cho, M., Haight, W., Choi, W. S., Hong, S., & Piescher, K. (2019). A prospective, longitudinal study of risk factors for early onset of delinquency among maltreated youth. *Children and Youth Services Review, 102*, 222–230.

Cunneen, C., White, R., & Richards, K. (2015). *Juvenile justice: Youth and crime in Australia* (5th ed.). Oxford University Press.

Delmage, E. (2013). The minimum age of criminal responsibility: A medico-legal perspective. *Youth Justice, 13*(2), 102–110.

Farn, A. & Umpierre, M. (2017). Creating an integrated continuum of care for justice-involved youth: How Sacramento County collaborates across systems. Washington, DC: *Center for Juvenile Justice Reform*, Georgetown University McCourt School of Public Policy. Available from http://cjjr.georgetown.edu/wp-content/uploads/2017/10/Creating-an-Integrated-Continuum-of-Care-in-Sacramento.pdf

Fitz-Gibbon, K., & O'Brien, W. (2019). A child's capacity to commit crime: Examining the operation of doli incapax in Victoria (Australia). *International Journal for Crime, Justice and Social Democracy, 8*(1), 18–33.

Fitzgerald, T. (2018). Children in both youth and family courts: New Zealand. *The Chronicle, 1*, 15–20.

Grant, P. (2009). The Children's Koori Court in Victoria. Presentation to the Prato Conference, 2009. Retrieved from: https://www.childrenscourt.vic.gov.au/sites/default/files/2020-11/Prato%20presentation%20-Koori%20Court.doc

Harvey, A. (2012). Anger as NSW axes youth drug court. *ABC News*. Retrieved from: https://www.abc.net.au/news/2012-07-03/experts-baffled-asaxe-falls-on-youth-drug-court/4108366

Jaensch, R, Minister for Education, Children and Youth. (2022, June 8). *Raising the minimum age of detention*. Retrieved from https://www.premier.tas.gov.au/site_resources_2015/additional_releases/raising_the_minimum_age_of_detention

Kedge, S. (2018). Transforming the communication involved in justice processes in New Zealand. In *ANZSOC Conference*, Melbourne 4–7 December, 2018.

Kenny, D. T., & Nelson, P. K. (2008). *Young offenders on community orders: Health, welfare and criminogenic needs*. Sydney University Press. Retrieved from https://www.justicehealth.nsw.gov.au/publications/ch1-3.pdf

Kinner, S. A., Degenhardt, L., Coffey, C., Sawyer, S., Hearps, S., & Patton, G. (2014). Complex health needs in the youth justice system: A survey of community-based and custodial offenders. *Journal of Adolescent Health, 54*(5), 521–526.

Lappi-Seppälä, T. (2011). Nordic youth justice. *Crime and Justice, 40*(1), 199–264.

Legislative Council Legal and Social Issues Committee. (2021). *Inquiry into Victoria's criminal justice system*. Parliament of Victoria. Retrieved from https://www.parliament.vic.gov.au/images/stories/committees/SCLSI/Inquiry_into_Victorias_Justice_System_/Report/LCLSIC_59-10_Vic_criminal_justice_system.pdf

Loeber, R., & Farrington, D. P. (2000). Young children who commit crime: Epidemiology, developmental origins, risk factors, early interventions, and policy implications. *Development and Psychopathology, 12*(4), 737–762.

McAra, L., & McVie, S. (2010). Youth crime and justice: Key messages from the Edinburgh study of youth transitions and crime. *Criminology and Criminal Justice, 10*(2), 211–230.

McArthur, M., Suomi, A., & Kendall, B. (2021). *Review of the service system and implementation requirements for raising the minimum age of criminal responsibility in the Australian Capital Territory—Final Report*. Australian National

University. Retrieved from https://justice.act.gov.au/sites/default/files/2021-10/Raising%20the%20Age%20-%20Final%20Report.PDF

Naffine, N., & Wundersitz, J. (1991). Lawyers in the children's court: An Australian perspective. *Crime and Delinquency, 37*(3), 374–392.

Papalia, N., Baidawi, S., Luebbers, S., Shepherd, S., & Ogloff, J. R. P. (2020). Patterns of maltreatment co-occurrence in incarcerated youth in Australia. *Journal of Interpersonal Violence, 37*(7–8), NP4341–NP4371.

Parliament of Victoria. Legislative Council, Legal and Social issues Committee. (2022). Inquiry into Victoria's criminal justice system. Volume 1. Parliament of Victoria. Retrieved from https://www.parliament.vic.gov.au/lsic-lc/inquiries/article/4534

Ralston, N., & Whitbourn, M. (2020, July 27). Age of criminal responsibility to remain at 10 until at least 2021. *The Age.* Retrieved from https://www.theage.com.au/national/age-of-criminal-responsibility-to-remain-at-10-until-at-least-2021-20200727-p55fy6.html

Sentencing Advisory Council. (2016). Reoffending by children and young people in Victoria. Melbourne: Sentencing Advisory Council.

Shaw, J. (2012). Professionals' perceptions of offending in children's residential care. *Child and Family Social Work, 17*(3), 359–367.

Snow, P., & Powell, M. (2012). Youth (in)justice: Oral language competence in early life and risk for engagement in antisocial behaviour in adolescence. *Trends & Issues in Crime and Criminal Justice, 435*. Australian Institute of Criminology. Retrieved from https://www.aic.gov.au/publications/tandi/tandi435

United Nations. (1989). *Convention on the rights of the child*. United Nations.

United Nations Committee on the Rights of the Child. (2019). *General comment No 24 (2019) on children's rights in the child justice system, UN Doc CRC/C/GC/24 (18 September 2019).* Retrieved from https://undocs.org/en/CRC/C/GC/24: https://undocs.org/en/CRC/C/GC/24

Victorian Sentencing Advisory Council. (2019). *Crossover Kids—Vulnerable Children in the Youth Justice System Report 1: Children Who Are Known to Child Protection among Sentenced and Diverted Children in the Victorian Children's Court*. Retrieved from https://www.sentencingcouncil.vic.gov.au/publications/crossover-kids-vulnerable-children-youth-justice-system-report-1

Victorian Sentencing Advisory Council. (2020a). *Crossover Kids—Vulnerable Children in the Youth Justice System Report 2: Children at the Intersection of Child Protection and Youth Justice across Victoria.* Retrieved from https://www.sentencingcouncil.vic.gov.au/publications/crossover-kids-vulnerable-children-youth-justice-system-report-2

Victorian Sentencing Advisory Council. (2020b). *Crossover Kids—Vulnerable Children in the Youth Justice System Report 3: Sentencing Children Who Have Experienced Trauma*. Retrieved from https://www.sentencingcouncil.vic.gov.au/publications/crossover-kids-vulnerable-children-youth-justice-system-report-3

White, R. & Cunneen, C. (2006). Social Class, Youth Crime and Juvenile Justice. In B. Goldson & J. Muncie (Eds.), *Youth Crime and Justice*, (pp. 17–29). London, Sage.

Youth Parole Board. (2016). *Annual report*. Department of Health and Human Services: Melbourne.

Legislation

Sentencing Act 1991 (Vic)

Practitioner Perspective a Participatory Approach to Young Offenders in the Children's Court

Laura Chipp

I have worked for over a decade as a defence lawyer at Victoria Legal Aid and as a Prosecutor for Victoria Police in the Children's Court, and in 2020 I undertook a Churchill Fellowship studying New Zealand's youth justice system. There are several changes I would advocate in this context, drawing on an international evidence base of alternate models for reducing recidivism and future victimisation of children and young people.

A Participatory Approach

New Zealand's youth justice system is held in high esteem for its reductions in recidivism and increases in community and victim safety. The New Zealand model emerges as one of the best practices, and the basis for possible changes and reforms to the Australian youth justice system, including the Children's Courts. Children's Courts across Australia could be improved by moving towards New Zealand's 'participatory approach' to justice. This would require in-depth training for each person in the legal process who has contact with a child, including a 'child specialisation' which is absent in the Victorian system. All primary and secondary court users would be trained as specialists in the youth jurisdiction and in trauma-informed practice (Gluckman & Lambie, 2018). Importantly, the majority of children would be kept out of court by diversion with only children with the most serious and complex matters would proceed to court. Those who have matters listed in court must experience 'easy to follow' court hearings, with clear aids and language used by all parties. The majority of other children's matters would then be dealt with

L. Chipp
Specialist Children's Court Prosecutions Unit (SCCPU), VIC, Australia

through the implementation of support services by pre-charge/pre-court cautions or diversions programmes.

These systems utilise a 'participatory approach' and problem solving by the court whereby the young person is at the centre of all decisions and actively participates in court processes and decision-making, being genuinely respected and engaged. Having legal representatives available with the time and adequate training to understand the complex issues that characterise these young people's lives is critical to the model. The New Zealand blueprint provides the foundations to create a similar system in other jurisdictions, including throughout Australia.

Effective Lawyers, Communication and Intermediaries

New Zealand emphasises effective communication processes, which assist the child in their understanding of the court process as well as in understanding court outcomes. All legal decision-makers—lawyers acting for the children and all other parties involved in the court process—must be trained in effective communication with children, understanding the dynamics that may affect the child's ability to understand and comprehend the complex legal issues before them. Legal representatives must have specific training to work with children and be trained in trauma-informed practice. This emphasises the importance of using clear language, speaking at a pace children can process, saying less and pausing regularly, and clearly explaining complex legal options to the child (Howard et al., 2020a).

It is accepted that the lens of trauma can make even the most basic proceedings unclear and impossible for the young person to understand (Gluckman & Lambie, 2018). This is especially when compounded by factors such as disability, mental health concerns, socio-cultural context and socio-economic disadvantage, all of which add challenges for the child trying to understand court process (Talking Trouble Aotearoa NZ, 2022).

There are benefits to using an intermediary before proceedings commence, as well as during court proceedings for child defendants as well as child witnesses and victims of crime (Antolak & MacPherson, 2019). Intermediaries assist children in court understand what is occurring by using simple words to explain what is being said, using visual aids, asking for the proceedings to slow down, asking for breaks and other such things to make it easier for the young person to understand what is taking place in the court hearing, which is often complex and complicated (especially the language used).

For witnesses or victims who are children, it is preferable to use an intermediary, especially in cross examination (Antolak & MacPherson, 2019). This is particularly important for a child with a background of trauma and/or disability when they are giving evidence. In my experience, intermediaries can be the difference between an accused being found guilty or not before a trial.

Visual Aids for Communication of Orders

Simple visual aids should always be used by lawyers to assist in explaining legal processes and court orders to children. The lawyer plays a crucial role for the child's future result, especially as to whether they acquire a criminal record. A defence lawyer should always be trained as a specialist youth lawyer, who understands that a child's cognitive functioning is different from an adult's; understands the concept of *doli incapax*; who is trained in trauma-informed practice; and understands that many children (if not, all children) require a lawyer to speak to them very differently.

This would be tailored to their age and cognitive function in order for the child to understand the lawyer and be able to give full and proper instructions (to the best of their ability and functioning). For example, the defence lawyer would have more success in the child understanding their legal advice and thereafter providing full and proper instructions if the lawyer uses visual aids; drawing options the child has as they explain them; using simple open-ended language; saying less and pausing a lot so the child has time to process and respond. Ideally, with the lawyer using the same above techniques, the child can indeed understand the options, and thus the legal outcome and/or conditions of the diversion plan, the court order plan, bail conditions and so on. In New Zealand when defence lawyers and other stakeholders (including the Magistrates) have used this technique, there was a significant increase in compliance of Court Orders. The outcome was that the child was significantly more likely to understand the Court Order and comply with it, when it was explained in a simple and accessible way that was understandable, and reinforced by all parties.

The organisation *Talking Trouble Aotearoa NZ* provides several resources to improve communication with children, such as an easy-read template to assist children to understand bail decisions and conditions. The resource utilises simple language, pictures, flow charts and diagrams to communicate relevant information about bail to children including where they are required to live, activities they are not permitted to engage in and persons who they are not allowed to communicate with.

These visual aids have been so successful that they have been adopted by the New Zealand Courts to precede final court orders, such as Bail and Sentencing Orders. Judges and New Zealand Police believe these aids have increased children's compliance with bail conditions; at each hearing the Judge requests the child read the conditions aloud to the court expressing what they are required to do or not do, and this increases compliance (Howard et al., 2020b).

Problem-Solving Approach

New Zealand Children's Courts see participants sitting in a semi-circle and the young person taking an equal seat at the table. All parties work closely together using a 'problem-solving approach' including the involvement of holistic wrap-around services. The Judge can see the progress that the young person has or has not made between court dates and can therefore make a fully informed decision about the outcome. Judges have sufficient time to hear each case, including support service submissions and their plan for that child before making the next order as to what the child is to do. The Judge asks the child questions and includes them in discussion. The child's family is also included and asked how they can assist the support services to increase the child's compliance.

This is a very 'hands on' approach which differs from what is seen in Australian Children's Courts where long reports are read in silence primarily by lawyers, and only the Magistrate and youth justice representatives speak. Such conditions result in a very formal, adversarial setting. Unlike my own experience as a Legal Aid duty lawyer representing 20 or more clients per day, the child's lawyer in the New Zealand system appears for a maximum of two children at court per day, permitting them sufficient time to hold extensive knowledge about each young person. The social supports attending court are those supporting the children on their orders (not court workers) who are therefore able to answer any questions based on first-hand experience of the child.

Time Saving in Court and Pre-charge Diversion

Observable in the New Zealand Youth Court system is the provision of multiple support services as well as cultural mentors at court hearings, each with distinct roles. In Wellington, the Youth Court sits just once per fortnight with a list of between six and 12 young people in the Criminal Division. Comparatively in Melbourne (although the population size is considerably bigger), the Criminal Division of the Children's Court sits every weekday and can have three courts at a time with overall listings sometimes exceeding 80–100 per day in a single location. An average smaller suburban court in Victoria sitting once per week might have around 60 cases per day. In order to finish the list in a busy Victorian Children's Court, all cases must be heard quickly owing to the high volume and therefore an armed robbery case may be afforded the same time as a shop theft, which is not ideal and does not provide priority to high harm-high impact offenders who require a higher level of intervention.

During my Churchill Fellowship research in New Zealand, all parties I interviewed advised that they believed that around 80–90% of all young people's charges were successfully dealt with by way of 'alternate action' without any further offending. It is more effective to put in place a pre-charge caution/diversion process undertaken with New Zealand Police solving the issue as a social response rather than as a criminal/court response. However, whilst these numbers may vary around New Zealand, the national average of not reoffending after 'alternative action' after a period of 12 months sits at just under 65% (Spier, 2017, p. 1). Thus, the most serious or complex matters are left for the court, and receive a high level of court intervention and attention. Importantly, it offers lower level and more appropriate out-of-court diversion responses for the remaining children, through both an alternate pathway and 'Family Group Conferencing' processes and supports.

My wish is to see Australian Children's Courts adopt the evidence-based New Zealand system and increase their pre-charge early intervention and diversion pathways, which are shown to assist both the accused child to reduce reoffending as well as the victim in their recovery. We do not need to continue to be 'tough' on crime. In fact, that mantra is contrary to the available evidence and has been shown to significantly increase the likelihood of a child reoffending. Instead, we need to be 'smart' on crime—investing in evidence-based, culturally appropriate and trauma-informed pre-charge and court-based diversion programs. This requires suitable trained intermediaries and speech pathologists available to assist all court users, as well as across-the-board training in trauma-informed practice in the youth sector. Justice reinvestment is the answer, and has been shown to work in New Zealand and many jurisdictions across the world.

References

Gluckman, P. and Lambie, I. (2018). It's never too early, never too late: A discussion paper on preventing youth offending in New Zealand. Ministry of Justice and the Integrated Data Initiative, Second Report. Auckland: Office of the Prime Minister's Cheif Science Advisor.

Retrieved from https://dpmc.govt.nz/sites/default/files/2021-10/pmcsa-Its-never-too-early-Discussion-paper-on-preventing-youth-offending-in-NZ.pdf

Howard, K., McCann, C., & Dudley, M. (2020a). What is communication assistance? Describing a new and emerging profession in the New Zealand youth justice system. *Psychology, Psychiatry and the Law, 27*(2), 300–314.

Howard, K., McCann, C., & Dudley, M. (2020b). "It was like more easier": Rangatahi (young people) and their whānau (family) talk about communication assistance in the New Zealand youth justice system. *Youth Justice, 21*(2), pp. 210–229.

Productivity Commission. (2020). *Report on Government Services 2020*. Youth Justice Services, Table 17A.21, pp. 1–135. Canberra: Productivity Commission. Retrieved from https://www.pc.gov.au/research/ongoing/report-on-government-services/2020/community-services/youth-justice

Spier, P. (2017). Reoffending patterns for youth undertaking Police Alternative Action. Ministry of Social Development (NZ). Retrieved from https://www.msd.govt.nz/documents/about-msd-and-our-work/publications-resources/research/alternative-action-report/offending-patterns-for-youth-undertaking-police-alternative-action-feb....docx

Talking Trouble Aotearoa NZ. (2022). *Links and resources*. Retrieved from https://talkingtroublenz.org/links-and-resources/

14

Family Courts and Family Violence

Thea Brown and Renata Alexander

Introduction

The Australian family law courts have long been criticised for their inability to address family violence when attempting to resolve parenting disputes brought by separating and divorcing couples. Despite many reviews and reforms, the criticisms have continued (Sifris et al., 2021). Nelson (2021), Nelson and Lumby (2021) describe the family courts as having failed in tackling family violence and argue the courts will never succeed given the current family law legislation, and the courts' structures, policies and processes.

T. Brown (✉)
Monash University, Melbourne, VIC, Australia
e-mail: thea.brown@monash.edu

R. Alexander
Monash University, Melbourne, VIC, Australia

M. Camilleri and A. Harkness (eds.), *Australian Courts*,
https://doi.org/10.1007/978-3-031-19063-6_14

The Australian Commonwealth government has made substantial changes to the courts. On 1 September 2021, the former Family Court and the former Federal Circuit Court were merged to make the unitary Federal Circuit and Family Court of Australia (FCFCOA). Moreover, the government has supported the court in introducing the Lighthouse Project, a new specialised program designed to address family violence in parenting disputes. Initially a pilot program operating in the three registries of Adelaide, Brisbane and Parramatta, it will be extended to more registries of the FCFCOA if successful.

This chapter reviews past efforts by the Family Court to address family violence and considers the many criticisms of the adequacy of such efforts. It assesses whether the most recent reform attempt is likely to overcome past criticisms, whether further changes need to be made or whether the reform is yet another doomed to fail. Given the FCFCOA and its predecessors' slow, cautious and piecemeal approach to family violence in the past, it is difficult to be optimistic, but the Lighthouse Project program may become a pathway for litigants with problems of family violence affecting their separation and parenting arrangements.

Family Violence, Partnership Breakdown, Separation and Children in Context

Definitions of violence are contentious, and they change over time. For this chapter, family violence is defined as physical, sexual, emotional, financial and religious violence perpetrated by one partner on the other (known also as domestic violence or intimate partner violence) and/or by parents on children (known as child abuse). These two forms of family violence are linked and can co-occur (Brown & Alexander, 2007; Bagshaw et al., 2010). Victims are more commonly women and children (Alexander, 2015).

Partnership breakdown (legal and de facto partnerships) and family violence are related. Wilcox (2012) depicts family violence as intersecting with family law and family law courts. However, the relationship might be better described as an enmeshment, whereby family violence, family law and family courts are entangled in a complexity of relationships over a long period of time in the lives of the separating partners.

Research provides evidence of these linkages. One study concluded that one in six women, aged from 15 years, were victims of violence from cohabiting partners (AIHW, 2018). Another study of litigated cases showed family violence was present in 51% of cases that had proceeded to court and in 70% of cases that had not (Moloney et al., 2007). Another study found 65% of surveyed women ended their marital partnership because of family violence (Bagshaw et al., 2010). Studies by Brown and Alexander (2007) and Laing (2010) have discovered family violence continues after separation—and sometimes even begins there—demonstrating that intimate family violence leads to separation and separation leads to violence.

Similarly, child abuse is linked to partner separation, though somewhat differently. Child abuse can lead to parental separation and, when that happens, the abuse is frequently multi-type abuse, a more severe abuse than that reported in other contexts (Brown & Alexander, 2007; Cawson, 2002). Family Court research found that while only some five to seven per cent of children's matters in the Family Court of Australia involved allegations of child abuse when court proceedings started, by midpoint of proceedings, they had become 50% of children's matters (Brown et al., 1997). A complication in cases of child abuse allegations in parenting disputes is that, in some cases, the separation has been at the advice or even insistence of child protection services that the protective partner removes the substantiated perpetrator from the marital home.

The extremes of family violence, intimate partner homicide and filicide (a parent or guardian's killing of their child) are rarely discussed in the context of separation and divorce context. However, both are related to parental separation. Reviewing intimate partner homicides with a prior history of domestic violence over a four-year period, ANROWS (2019) concluded that in 55% of all such homicides (carried out primarily by men) partnership separation was a factor. The period immediately after separation is seen as the most dangerous for women (ANROWS, 2018). Studies of filicide demonstrate that parental separation is a factor in these deaths, with the proportion of filicide perpetrators being separated from their partner ranging from 50% in a Victorian study (Brown et al., 2019) to 75% in a New South Wales study (Butler & Buxton, 2013).

Controversies, Challenges and Criticisms Emerging from Omission and Complexity

Spanning over 40 years, a raft of programmatic and legislative changes informing how the Family Court responds to family violence has both addressed issues and created further challenges, complexities and controversies.

The 1975 Family Law Legislation

The original *Family Law Act 1975* (Cth) made no mention of any form of family violence; it was not then acknowledged as a community problem and its relationship to separation and divorce was not understood. Understanding of any aspect of separation was limited and one of the consequences of the establishment of the Commonwealth family law legislation was the creation of the Australian Institute for Family Studies (AIFS) to produce research on Australian families, family stability and divorce.

The sentiments underlying the new legislation were contrary to recognising family violence. The legislation aimed to remove fault from separation and divorce, and this over-rode any mention of marital problems, like family violence, to which fault might be attached. The legislation aimed to remove acrimony from separation and family violence was, again, at odds with this approach (Nicholson & Harrison, 2000). Supporting this framework was a high degree of societal gender inequality that dismissed the possible existence of family violence and its potential severity. Intimate partner violence was framed as being the fault of the woman, or as an allegation, which was false, and which she was making to gain some advantage (Haselschwerdt et al., 2010; Meier, 2009).

Child abuse was framed similarly, as exemplified by Gardner's (1992) theory of parental alienation, developed to explain allegations of child sexual abuse allegations in separating parents' conflicts. It is now discounted, but it remains powerfully attractive to fathers, originally the most commonly accused (Brown & Alexander, 2007; Walker & Shapiro, 2010).

A structural problem was the position of a specialist federal Family Court in relation to state courts of summary jurisdiction, such as the magistrates' courts which unlike the Family Court were clearly mandated to address family violence. For example, the state Children's Court addressed child protection including parental violence and abuse against children. The Family Court was not charged with such responsibilities and its growing role as a forum for the resolution of violence when parents brought parenting disputes with allegations of violence to it, was not appreciated.

Addressing Family Violence Through the Family Court

The Family Court has crept slowly towards recognition of its role in family violence. The first step was in 1991 when the family law legislation was amended to include mention of child abuse (Alexander, 2015). Child abuse was defined as physical and sexual assault, omitting the less tangible forms of psychological and emotional abuse and neglect. In 1996, though, the Court acknowledged intimate partner violence—which it defined more broadly than it had child abuse—describing it as behaviour causing the person (victim) to fear or be apprehensive about themselves or their property. This definition lacked any description of the violent behaviour, and unfortunately set up a measurement of fear as 'reasonable fear', which removed the assessment from the victim and left it to others to decide (Alexander, 2015).

The Magellan Program

Under pressure following the production of three reports on children and family violence (Australian Law Reform Commission and Human Rights and Equal Opportunity, 1997; Australian Law Reform Commission, 2000; Brown et al., 1998), the Court introduced its first specialised family violence program, the Magellan Project or List.

Magellan aimed to better manage parenting disputes when accompanied by allegations of child abuse. Coordinated by a judicial registrar, a pilot program was implemented in two Melbourne registries during 1999. It was judge-led, with the court's steps and timelines set out in advance and with a single judge managing all disputes to their conclusion. All children and all parents were provided with a legal representative funded by Legal Aid. The judge ordered reports in the first hearing from other services, such as from child protection and the police and a family report.

Two evaluations found the program was very successful. The first (Brown et al., 2001) showed the program reduced the time to settle the dispute, the number of court events, costs for Legal Aid, the proportion of cases proceeding to a judicial determination, applications after resolution and the children's distress. The program became a permanent feature in all registries in all states, except in Western Australia where an amended version called the Columbus List was introduced. The second, an evaluation of the permanent program, confirmed the original evaluation (Higgins, 2007).

While the program has continued, it has not been sufficiently modified. It has not expanded the numbers of cases taken into the list in relation to increases in population, but rather it has narrowed to include only serious sexual or serious physical abuse. No further changes or evaluations have since occurred. Had any been undertaken, it might have been noted the program ignored intimate partner violence, even though intimate partner violence was found in 44% of cases in the first of the Family Court child abuse studies (Brown & Alexander, 2007). Also, it ignored the parental murder of children who are, or who have been, involved in Court proceedings, a problem that has emerged more clearly since the program began (Brown et al., 2019; Johnson, 2005).

Changing the Journey to Court

The court's failures in managing family violence were not the only source of criticism of its functioning. One issue, which lead to the creation of a Commonwealth committee—the Family Law Pathways Advisory Group—was the confusion and the distress of couples' journeys to the resolution of disputes. This committee's findings (FLAPG, 2001) urged ways of simplifying and clarifying the journey to court and recommended new pathways to court that offered education on post separation parenting and on negotiating conflict.

New Commonwealth legislation followed in 2006: the *Family Law Amendment (Shared Parental Responsibility) Act* established a network of local Family Relationship Centres throughout Australia as the entry point to the Family Court. A special pathway was created for litigants where family violence was involved. If they could produce evidence of family violence, or of an inability to resolve disputes through mediation, they could proceed directly to court. Studies of these centres (Brown & Cavanagh, 2010; Moloney et al., 2013) showed that couples with family violence circumstances did proceed through these centres, either because the parties did not recognise the violence in the family, or they did not wish to disclose it, or they thought the centres were still the best option for them which for many the centres were. Staff were experienced social workers and psychologists, with past work histories in domestic violence and child protection services (Brown & Cavanagh, 2010).

The 2006 reforms also introduced three concerning changes. One was the definition of family violence whereby a person had to 'reasonably fear' or 'reasonably be apprehensive' for their wellbeing or safety. There was no definition of this concept of 'reasonableness' and this introduced subjective and objective elements in parenting cases. In 2012, the word 'reasonably' was removed from the legislation.

A second change was the introduction of the 'friendly parent' provision in the list of factors that a court was mandated to consider in determining the best interests of a child. That effectively meant that women could be penalised for not being 'friendly' in permitting contact by children with their abusive former partners. Thus, mothers did not raise these concerns or else were ordered to continue to facilitate access with abusive fathers until such time as a court finally determined if there was or was not an unacceptable risk to the child. Also in 2012, this provision was replaced by a more neutral consideration of the extent each parent had or had not participated in decision-making about the child.

A third change was about the awarding of costs. This is usually discretionary, but the 2006 amendments introduced a provision that a court *must* consider awarding costs where there were false allegations or statements knowingly made. This specifically targeted allegations of family violence and child abuse after political and media pressure alleging (without any reputable corroboration) that false claims were rife. Again, this was repealed in 2012 but remained a deterrent for many mothers until then.

Family Violence Best Practice Principles

The 2006 reforms produced an increase in the proportion of parenting disputes involving family violence proceeding to court, as many cases without violence were being resolved earlier in the Family Relationship Centres. To meet this change, in 2009 the court published Family Violence Best Practice Principles for the use of court staff, judicial officers, litigants and family law lawyers. The Principles, since amended, grappled with understanding family violence, attempting to incorporate new research-based knowledge. Nevertheless, the Principles were criticised (Alexander, 2015) for being mistaken in their understanding of violence and ineffectual in addressing it, and for using poor social science research.

The Principles-incorporated family violence typologies, developed mostly from studies emanating from the United States which used a supposedly gender-neutral approach to family violence (Erickson & O'Sullivan, 2011; Kelly & Johnson, 2008). The typologies grouped violence into categories to make it easier to identify and to make risk assessments and predictions for court decision-making. Leaving aside the fact that it is difficult to fit actual behaviour into a typology, the typologies tended to discount male violence. Typologies were also used to tackle the vexing problem of how allegations can be determined to be true or false, rather than using professionals' investigations of alleged victims accounts, information from family members, employers, police and other courts, other services and other sources.

The Principles should have been the heart of the Court's policies and practices on family violence, instructing court staff and decision-makers on recognising, understanding and assessing family violence. Their portrayal of violence and their flow on advice to staff needed to be reliable and kept up to date. Some jurisdictions in the United States established collaborative court/social science projects reviewing the relevant research and jointly developing agreed principles of practice (Salem & Dunford-Jackson, 2008; Ver Steegh, 2008), to impart new knowledge continually.

Further Legislative Change

While the courts (then two, the Family Court of Australia and the Federal Circuit Court) seemed to be moving to a better management of family violence, one conflict arising from the contradictory directions of the 2006 reforms, the direction of sharing parenting responsibility and time and the direction of taking account of family violence in determining parenting orders, became more acute. To overcome this problem, the Commonwealth government commissioned five reports (Australian Law Reform Commission and NSW Law Reform Commission, 2010; Bagshaw et al., 2010; Chisholm, 2009; Family Law Council, 2009; National Council to Reduce Violence Against Women and their Children, 2009) to investigate the impact of the 2006 legislation, with each report considering the views of different significant stakeholder groups and each ordered to proceed independently.

All reports agreed the 2006 legislation was a step backwards in managing family violence in partner separation and, consequently, the Commonwealth government introduced further new legislation. The *Family Law Legislation Amendment (Family Violence and Other Measures) Act 2011* (Cth) provided a wider definition of violence and clarified the conflict between the two opposing directions by placing the child's safety as the paramount principle. Violence was defined as violent or other threatening behaviour by a person that coerces or controls a member of the person's family or causes the family member to be fearful. Some ten examples of various forms of intimate partner violence were specified, but some of the more severe forms of violence, such as choking, strangling, stalking and threats or attempts of self-harm or of homicide of the children or the adult were omitted.

The Lighthouse Project—Pathway for Change?

In the years following, research suggested the legislation had contributed little to improving the courts' management of violence (Kaspiew et al., 2015). In 2018, the federal Attorney-General established a review of all aspects of the family law system, to be carried out by the Australian Law Reform Commission. The review did not focus just on family violence, but its draft report (ALRC, 2018) included two recommendations to manage family violence, namely a triage service and a specialised family violence program or list. The government's response was to agree with these recommendations.

Consequently, in 2021—just over twenty years after the introduction of Magellan—the Court introduced its second specialised family violence program comprising the Family Detection of Overall Risk Screen (DOORS) Screening and Triage component and the Lighthouse Project component, referred to jointly as the Lighthouse Project. The program was to cover risks to children of family violence, parental substance abuse, parental mental illness and or parental criminal behaviour.

Pre-program—Family DOORs Triage Screening

The entry to the program is through the Family DOORS Triage screening when as litigants make an application to Court they also complete a short online questionnaire. The answers are assessed to indicate risks of family violence, substance abuse, mental illness and/or criminal behaviour.

The screening divides litigants into those without risk—who then proceed as usual—and those with risk further categorised as high, moderate and low-risk groups. Each group is treated differently, with the greatest and speediest attention being given to the higher risk families. The pathway for the high-risk group is clear—immediate referral to a counsellor for safety, wellbeing and service referrals. The moderate risk group will receive the same, but possibly not as quickly nor with as much investment. The low-risk group will be offered mediation and hopefully avoid the program in its full sense. Whether such divisions will work is debatable. Risk assessment generally has weaknesses (*Health Technology Assessment and Assessment for Social Services* 2019) and determining risk from a short questionnaire filled in by a parent is dubious. At least, the screening has the value of gathering long overdue data on the social problems which the litigants present to the Court.

The Program Proper—The Lighthouse Program

Once past the entry stage, litigants join the Lighthouse Program proper. This comprises five pre-planned steps, each with a set time and set actions. A senior judicial registrar (SJR) or judge oversees each of the steps. The program does not specify if the judicial registrar or judge will be the same throughout all the hearings, as was the case for the Magellan List. The benefit of this is that the Court is more aware of the actions and issues in the case, helps maintain forward momentum and consistency.

The first step includes ordering a formal child expert independent report be undertaken by an employee of the court. This places the welfare of the children as the most important and immediate priority. It is noted that the SJR does not appoint an independent lawyer as an advocate for the children; whether the child expert is to assume this role is unclear, but they are not qualified to do so. The SJR/judge must also seek reports shedding light on the violence in the family from organisations that have had contact with the family. This instruction recognises that many agencies are likely to have been involved. Family violence is noted to require a coordinated approach to both assess and manage it (Hallet, 1995).

At the second step, the SJR/judge must address any urgent issues, such as needs for temporary orders, for special needs of the litigants or for further information. At the third step, a plan for the trial is made and any further specialised reports that are needed (such as mental health reports) are ordered. The possibility of mediation can be considered at this point. Many would criticise mediation, suggesting it may be used as a delaying tactic or a form of coercion by a violent partner (Brown et al., 2016). It may be useful in some cases, but it seems unlikely given the emphasis in the design of the program for high-risk cases which may include severe violence.

A fourth step is led by the List JR, who is not necessarily the registrar who led the previous events. This is a compliance check prior to trial, and it is difficult to see the necessity for that step given the work done in step three. This duplication appears symptomatic of the problems of court processes—many steps and court events leading to many delays and much emotional and financial expense. And the fifth step is the trial, which may take twelve months to reach.

Change Brings Challenges: Addressing Family Violence in Parenting

The Lighthouse Project, as a specialised court program to address intimate partner violence, is a major step forward for the Federal Circuit and Family Court of Australia. The program has strengths, but also has weaknesses which may ultimately be so many they undermine the program.

Inquisitorial Framework

The greatest strength of the program is that, like the Magellan Program, it moves away from the adversarial approach, long argued by some as unsuitable for family law parenting disputes, and towards an inquisitorial framework, argued as superior (Nelson & Lumby, 2021). The framework is child-centred rather than parent-centred. It places the Court in charge instead of the parents and, led by the SJR/judge, it completes the requisite steps and tasks within set timelines while being supported by counselling and other experts.

Immediately, ordering the child expert's report in the first step begins the focus on the child and gives priority to the child's needs and interests. It is a more neutral and standardised report than assessments from external consultants when engaged at times by parents. Such reports have been challenged (Erickson & O'Sullivan, 2011; Haselschwerdt et al., 2010) because of the consultants' lack of understanding of intimate partner violence, their consequent diminishing of the psychological and physical impact of the violence on child and adult victims, their gender bias and their inconsistency. By keeping the report in-house, it is possible to ensure the proper education and work experience of relevant staff to overcome these problems.

Safety

The framework supports the Court ordering a safety assessment (FCFCOA, 2021) but it does not appear to do so routinely for all in the program. The safety of the children, their parents, other family members and court staff should be a priority in the project. Litigants, their children and court staff have been killed during or after court proceedings (Brown et al., 2019; Johnson, 2005; Marshall, 2014; Nelson & Lumby, 2021). Safety plans should include safety at home, in the community and in court. In this program, the Court should routinely order them to be made rather than ordering them sometimes and otherwise leaving the initiative with the litigant to contact the Court. Litigants do not always recognise their danger and some, who recognise it, are so threatened that they conceal it. Others conceal it because they have had experience of authorities taking little action when violence is reported and so do not mention it again.

One safety protection the Court does offer is remote electronic appearances, through a video link. This does reduce vulnerability to the perpetrator but does not give complete protection. Another protection is arranging for the alleged victim to avoid face-to-face cross examination by the alleged perpetrator, which has been identified as extremely distressing for a victim (Sifris et al., 2021). That risk has been alleviated by the introduction of rules against allowing perpetrators to cross-examine. It must be done through lawyers, but this may be even more distressing.

Length of the Program

The program may take up to a year, which for victims of violence is too lengthy a wait for resolution; a wait which will be accompanied by much distress. The study by Brown et al. (1997) preceding the Magellan Program found every court event provoked anxiety in the children who, doubtless, reflected the anxiety of the parent. Reducing the events and the timelines was very helpful in reducing stress. The program can be shortened by removing Step 3 and integrating it with Step 2 and Step 4. Thus, Step 2 could include additionally the ordering of further specialised reports and a consideration of mediation. Step 4 could include additionally the plans for trial. This should bring the number of steps to four and shorten the time by three months.

Expertise and Education of Key Staff

The success of the program hinges on the roles and performances of three key court staff: the initial counsellor; the SJR/judge; and the child expert. All need expertise in intimate partner violence and child abuse. However, the level of expertise and how it is gained and maintained is not highlighted in the description of the program. Studies show the general community's lack of understanding of family violence (Tucci & Mitchell, 2021). Other studies show the myths and misinformation Australian and overseas courts have displayed about intimate partner violence, child abuse and parenting in this context (Alexander, 2015; Erickson & O'Sullivan, 2011; Haselschwerdt et al., 2010). All the staff working in the project need specialised initial and ongoing education.

Ongoing Issues

Further issues may emerge once the program is well underway. Program capacity may be insufficient. Considering the large number of cases presenting to court where family violence exists, it can be questioned whether the pilot in each registry can handle the number of eligible cases in the time period in that registry. Clearly the risk assessment and review at Steps 1 and 2 will give disputes a priority rating that will mean some cases are dealt with more urgently than others. Less urgent cases may drop so low they will not be dealt with if there is a capacity problem.

The cases will present many problems other than family violence. The first report on the program shows some 54% of parties allege child abuse, 64% intimate partner violence, 39% substance abuse and 40% mental illness (FCFCOA 2021). This places a heavy load on the program; staff will need to make referrals for many services at or around the entry point and staff will also need to be coordinating and monitoring these referrals.

Another significant issue is program suitability for every community group. Violence varies in its expression from one group to another and there are no differences in policies and procedures for groups like Indigenous litigants, litigants from culturally and linguistically diverse backgrounds and LGBTIQA+ groups.

Conclusion

Since the commencement of the Family Court of Australia in 1976, changes have been made to address allegations of family violence in parenting disputes, including new legislation, new policies and procedures, new supporting family law services and greater resourcing. The most recent development has been the creation of the court's second specialist family violence program, the Lighthouse Project, an innovation that has taken so many years to instigate.

The Lighthouse Project echoes the Magellan Program with its semi-inquisitorial framework. However, it lacks avenues for the direct participation of children to communicate what the violence means for them and how they want to manage it. The Lighthouse Project does not incorporate reviews of the impact on children of the court's decisions on violence. There is no feedback or accountability for the Court. The process is still seen as a one decision only process. The Court does not take a longer-term view of the children's best interests, arguably vital when issues of family violence and children are involved.

References

Alexander, R. (2015). Family violence in parenting cases in Australia under the *Family Law Act 1975* (Cth): The Journey So Far—Where are we now and are we there yet? *International Journal of Law Policy and the Family, 29*(3), 313–340.

ALRC (Australian Law Reform Commission). (2000). *Managing justice* (Report No 89). Canberra: Commonwealth of Australia.

ALRC (Australian Law Reform Commission). (2018). *Review of the family law system* (Discussion Paper, No 86). Canberra: Commonwealth of Australia.

ALRC (Australian Law Reform Commission) and NSW Law Reform Commission. (2010). *Family violence—A national legal response* (Final Report). Sydney, ALRC.

ANROWS. (2019). *The facts about intimate partner homicide*, sourced from Australian Domestic and Family Violence Death Review Network Data Report, 2018. https://www.coroners.nsw.gov.au/

Australian Insitute of Health and Welfare. (2018). *Family, domestic and sexual viuoewlecne in Australia* (Cat. no. FDV 2). Canberra, AIHW.

Australian Law Reform Commission and Human Rights and Equal Opportunity. (1997). *Seen and heard: Priority for children in the legal process* (Report No 4). Canberra: Commonwealth of Australia.

Australian National Research Organisation for Women's Safety. (2018). *The facts about intimate partner homicide*. Retrieved from https://www.anrows.org.au/resources/domestic-and-family-violence-lethality-the-facts-about-intimate-partner-homicide/

Bagshaw, D., Brown, T., Wendt, S., Campbell, A., McInnes, E., Tinning, B., Batagol, B., Sifris, A., Tyson, D., Baker, J., & Fernandez Arias, P. (2010). *Family violence and family law in Australia: The experiences and views of children and adults from families who separated post 1995 and post 2006, Vol 1 and Vol 2*. Canberra: Commonwealth Attorney General's Department.

Brown, T., & Alexander, R. (2007). *Child abuse and family law*. Allen & Unwin.

Brown, T., & Cavanagh, J. (2010). *What about the children*? Diversity: Everyone Benefits, FRSA National Conference Proceedings, 3–5 November, Melbourne.

Brown, T., Flynn, C., Fernandez Arias, P., & Clavijo Lopez, C. (2016). *A study of the impact on men and their partners in the short and long term of attending men's behaviour change programs*. Violence Free Families. Retrieved from https://violencefreefamilies.org.au/longitudinal-study-effectiveness-mens-behaviour-change-programs/

Brown, T., Frederico, M., Hewitt, L., Sheehan, R. (1997). *Violence in families: Report No 1*. The Management of Child Abuse Allegations in Custody and Access Disputes Before the Family Court of Australia, Monash University Clayton Vic.

Brown, T., Frederico, M., Hewitt, L., & Sheehan, R. (1998). *The management of child abuse allegations in custody an access disputes before the Family Court of Australia*. Monash University.

Brown, T., Sheehan, R., Frederico, M., & Hewitt, L. (2001). *Resolving family violence to children*. Monash University.

Brown, T., Tyson, D., & Fernandez Arias, P. (Eds.). (2018). *When parents kill children: Understanding filicide*. Palgrave Macmillan.

Brown, T., Tyson, D., Fernandez Arias, P. (2019). Filicide in Australia. In T. Brown, D. Tyson & P. Fernandez Arias (Eds.), *When parents kill children*. Palgrave Macmillan.

Butler, A., & Buxton, E. (2013). Trends and issues in filicide deaths: A review of all NSW Filicide Deaths in the context of domestic violence. *Paper presented to Addressing Filicide: The First International Conference, Prato, Italy.*

Cawson, P. (2002). *Child maltreatment in the family*. NSPCC.

Chisholm, R. (2009). *Family courts violence review*. Attorney-General's Department.

Department of Families, Housing, Community Services and Indigenous Affairs (FaHCSIA), *Time for action: The national council's plan for Australia to reduce violence against women and their children, 2009–2021*. Canberra.

Erickson, N., and O'Sullivan, C. (2011). Doing our best for New York's children: Custody Evaluations when domestic violence is alleged. *NYS Psychologist, XXIII* (2), 9–12.

Family Court of Australia. (2020). *Annual report 2019–2020*. Commonwealth of Australia. Retrieved from https://www.fcfcoa.gov.au/2019-20-family-court-australia-annual-report

Family Law Council. (2009). *Improving responses to family violence in the family law system: An advice on the intersection of family violence and family law issues*. Family Law Council

Federal Circuit and Family Court of Australia. (2021). *Lighthouse Project: Guiding those experiencing family violence and other safety risks through the family law system*. Retrieved from www.federalcircuitcourt.gov.au/lighthouse

Family Law Pathways Advisory Group Report. (2001). *Out of the maze: Pathways to the future for families experiencing separation*. Commonwealth of Australia.

Federal Court of Australia. (2020). *Annual report 2019–20*. Commonwealth of Australia. Retrieved from https://www.fedcourt.gov.au/__data/assets/pdf_file/0017/80117/AR2019-20.pdf

FCFCOA (Federal Circuit and Family Court of Australia). (2021, November 10). *New court initiatives help uncover higher prevalence of family violence and other risks (media release)*. Retrieved from https://www.fcfcoa.gov.au/news-and-media-centre/media-releases/mr101121

Gardner, R. A. (1992). *True and false allegations of child sex abuse*. Creative Therapeutics.

Hallet, C. (1995). *Interagency coordination in child protection: A case study (studies in child protection)*. HMSO.

Haselschwerdt, M., Hardesty, J., & Hans, J. (2010). Custody evaluators beliefs about domestic violence allegations during divorce: Feminist and family perspectives. *Journal of Interpersonal Violence, 26*(8), 1694–1719.

Higgins, D. (2007). *Cooperation and coordination: An evaluation of the Family Court of Australia's Magellan case management model*. Family Court of Australia.

Jeffries, S., Field, R., Menih, H., & Rathus, Z. (2016). Good evidence, safe outcomes in parenting, matters involving domestic violence? Understanding family report writing practice from the perspective of professionals working in the family law system. *UNSW Law Journal, 39*(4), 1355–1388.

Johnson, C. H. (2005). *Come with daddy: Child murder—Suicide after family breakdown*. University of Western Australia Press.

Kaspiew, R., Carson, R., Dunstan, J., Qu, L., Horsfall, B., De Maio, J., Moore, S., Moloney, L., Coulson, M., & Tayton, S. (2015). *Evaluation of the 2012 family violence amendments: Synthesis report*. Australian Government and Australian Institute of Family Studies.

Kelly, J. B., & Johnson, M. P. (2008). Differentiation among different types of intimate partner violence: Updates and implications for interventions. *Family Court Review, 46*(3), 476–499.

Laing, L. (2010). *No way to live: Women's experiences of negotiating the family law system in the context of domestic violence.* University of Sydney and Benevolent Society. Retrieved from https://ses.library.usyd.edu.au/handle/2123/6255

Marshall, D. (2014). *The family court murders.* Ebury Press.

Meier, J. (2009). A historical perspective on parental alienation syndrome and parental alienation. *Journal of Child Custody, 6*(3), 232–257.

Moloney, L., Qu, L., Weston, R., & Hand, K. (2013). Evaluating the work of Australia's family relationships centres: The first five years. *Family Court Review, 51*(2), 234–249.

Moloney, L., Smyth, B., Weston, R., & Qu, L. (2007). Allegations of family vIolence and child abuse in family law children's proceedings, Australian Institue of Family Studies, Research Report No. 15, *Family Matters*, pp (8–15).

Nelson, C. (2021). *Can the Family Courts be fixed?: Recognising children's rights as a means of securing children's safety in Australia's family law system.* Policy paper for the Whitlam Institute.

Nelson, C., & Lumby, C. (2021). *Broken: Children, parents and Family Courts.* La Trobe University Press.

Nicholson, A., & Harrison, M. (2000). Family law and the family court of Australia: Experiences of the first twenty-five years. *Melbourne University Law Review, 24*(3), 756–783.

Royal Commission on Human Relationships. (1977). *Final report, volume 4.* Australian Government Publishing Service.

Salem, P., & Dunford-Jackson, B. (2008). Beyond politics and positions: A call for collaboration between Family Court and domestic violence professionals. *Family Court Review, 46*(3), 437–453.

Sifris, A., Young, L., Carroll, R., Parker, A., Fernando, M., & Alexander, R. (2021). *Family law in Australia* (10th ed.). Lexis Nexis Butterworths.

Swedish Agency for Health technology Assessment and Assessment of Social Services. (2019). *Psychiatric risk assessment methods: Are violent act preventable?* Retrieved from https://www.sbu.se/en/publications/sbu-assess/psychiatric-risk-assessment-methods-are-violent -acts-preventable

Tucci, J., & Mitchell, J. (2021). *Still unseen and ignored*. Australia Childhood Foundation.

Ver Steegh, D. (2008). Report from the Wingspread Conference on domestic violence and family courts. *Family Court Review, 46*(3), 454–475.

Walker, L. E., & Shapiro, D. (2010). Parental alienation disorder: Why label children with a mental diagnosis? *Journal of Child Custody, 7*(4), 266–286.

Wilcox, K. (2012). *Family law and family violence: Research to practice. Briefing paper.* Australian Domestic and Family Violence Clearing House. Retrieved from www.apo.org.au/node/28672

Legislation

Family Law Act 1975 (Cth) (Austl.)

Practitioner Perspective: Family Law Professionals and the Court

Renata Alexander

The family law system in Australia depends upon many legal and socio-legal professionals. In the Federal Circuit and Family Court of Australia (FCFCOA) itself, the key players are judges, registrars, family consultants and child experts (social workers and psychologists) and other registry staff. The system also relies on external players being lawyers (solicitors and barristers), social workers, psychologists and medical professionals. Many in this workforce, together with litigants and other advocacy groups, have been critical of the Court's failures in addressing family violence.

The first issue has been the constant changes in legislation, court policy and processes that have brought few noticeable improvements for children (or adults) when violence is involved in parenting disputes. Since the *Family Law Act 1975* (Cth) was enacted, the system and its key players have endured many changes. These changes have meant new courts, new forms, new procedures, new practice directions, new terminology and new specialist lists. No other system, jurisdiction or piece of legislation has undergone so many legislative amendments (over 119), constitutional challenges in the High Court of Australia, parliamentary inquiries (over 50) and academic reviews.

These changes have taken place alongside recurring assaults on various philosophical binaries, namely that of a 'helping court' versus a 'therapeutic court', mandatory versus optional counselling, adversarial practice and procedure versus inquisitorial practices, voluntary versus mandatory alternative dispute resolution, public ordering (litigation) versus private ordering (parenting plans and financial agreements) and specialist courts versus generalist courts. Thus, the professionals and litigants have had to navigate through a challenging and ever-changing landscape.

R. Alexander
Monash University, Melbourne, VIC, Australia

The second issue has been the limitations of a federal structure that has to address problems involving family violence. The FCFCOA continues to operate and co-exist with eight different state and territory hierarchies of courts, family violence protection order regimes and child protection statutory schemes. Apart from the system in Western Australia, Australia does not have one family law system and one hierarchy of courts dealing exclusively with family law. Cases involving family violence and child abuse dominate in all these courts. This creates numerous jurisdictional gaps and conflicts. The system is so fractured and so fragmented that best strategies are almost impossible to develop. There is no obvious solution to this looking ahead.

The third issue is that many professionals are now afraid that with the creation of the new unitary court, the consequent loss of the specialist court will mean that family law cases involving family violence will be lost in a mire of other civil federal law matters, like migration, social security, bankruptcy and industrial/employment law. Will the court ever appreciate the priority that needs to be given to family violence?

Combined statistics from the former Family Court of Australia and Federal Circuit Court of Australia (2019–2020) show approximately 80% of family law cases allege at least one major risk factor, most commonly family violence and/or child abuse, and that family violence and child abuse are 'core business' of the almost 90,000 family law applications filed in 2019 to 2020 (FCFCOA 2020a; 2020b).

Professionals are looking to the Lighthouse Project (refer to Chapter 5 of this volume) to show improvements for the children involved in parenting disputes where violence has been alleged but they are not optimistic given the size of the problem and the problems identified at just the pilot stage without it even being trialled in the two highest-volume registries of Melbourne and Sydney.

However, the majority of cases will not be heard through the Lighthouse Project. The existence of family violence allegations present additional complexities for clients and legal practitioners alike; heighten stress for the families involved; increase emotional and financial cost and sometimes lead to further instances of violence or abusive or controlling behaviour.

The role of the barrister is to assist a party to navigate and make sense of the various processes and court events and to try and help clients grasp the ramifications of the different potential decisions and resultant scenarios. For example, if the court does make an order for a child to spend supervised time with a father whom the mother alleges is abusive but of which the court has not been satisfied on the evidence, who can that supervisor be? How will the parenting capacity of the mother as primary caregiver be affected? What if the time granted is unsupervised? What measures can be put in place? What supports are available, if needed, for the mother or for the child?

It is difficult attempting to justify the cost and delay of court proceedings to clients as well as explaining the unpredictability of any outcome. Family law cases are not decided according to a set formula. Clearly, one size does not fit all. Of course, flexibility and judicial discretion should occur, but there is no doubt that different judges take different views of what does or does not constitute coercive and controlling behaviour. Three of the four typologies and classifications of different types of family violence promoted in the *Best Practice Principles* (see Chapter 5) do not meet the definition of family violence in s 4AB of the *Family Law Act 1975*. In addition, family violence is but one of the two primary considerations (albeit the more important) and 13 additional considerations which a court must look at to determine the best interests of the child under the two-tiered framework prescribed in s 60CC of the same Act.

Again this is value-laden. As recognised by the High Court in *CDJ v VAJ* [1988] HCA 77 at [151], the evidence in parenting cases 'is often such that the same body of evidence may produce opposite but nevertheless reasonable conclusions from different judges. It is a mistake to think that there is always only one right answer to the question of what the best interests of a child require. Each judge is duty bound to make the order which he or she thinks is in the best interests of the child. But the fact that other judges think that the best interests of that child require a different order does not necessarily prove that the first order was not in the best interests of the child. Best interests are values, not facts'. This observation equally applies to the weight attributed, if any, to the existence of high-risk factors such as family violence.

As a practitioner, it is easy to point out the problems with the existing system. The challenge is to propose viable solutions. The loss of a specialist court is irreversible. The integration of state and federal legislation remains glued to the bottom of the too-hard basket. Improving the Magellan List and refining and extending the Lighthouse Project as flagged in Chapter 5 are clearly achievable. We have various screening tools and networks to assist in detecting and supporting family violence victims/survivors (mostly women and children). We have the National Action Plans to Reduce Violence against Women and their Children and the various state and federal funding commitments, particularly at election times. We have burgeoning social science research on the effects of family violence and high conflict on families and in particular, on children.

The real question is whether all the changes and resources, inquiries, summits, plans and legislative reforms are fundamentally attacking the problem of family violence at its core or is our family law system just adding more complications, retraumatising families and creating more hurdles and expense. Our family law system is certainly facing the problem—but is it facing the wrong way?

References

Federal Circuit and Family Court of Australia(FCFCOA). (2020a). *Annual Report 2019–2020*. Canberra: Federal Circuit and Family Court of Australia. Retrieved from https://www.fcfcoa.gov.au/2019-20-family-court-australia-annual-report

Federal Circuit and Family Court of Australia (FCFCOA).(2020b) *Annual Report 2019-2020. Canberra:* Federal Circuit and Family Court of Australia. Retrieved from https://www.fcfcoa.gov.au/fcc-annual-reports

Legislation and Cases

Family Law Act 1975 (Cth) (Austl.)

CDJ v VAJ [1988] HCA 77 at [151] (Austl.)

15

The Ur-controversy of Civil Justice

Joe McIntyre

Introduction

Nothing captures public attention quite like crime. Criminal proceedings tend, consequently, to dominate public discourse of judicial processes. High-profile criminal cases are headline news, attracting interest from the broader population. For example, as his appeal reached the High Court in 2020, George Pell become the fourth most searched for Australian on Google Trends for that year, up from eighth place in 2019 (Google Trends, 2020). In contrast, civil justice rarely enters public consciousness. This is despite that—for most citizens—they are far more likely to personally engage with civil processes, whether through a fencing

The original version of this chapter was revised: Author's affiliation has been corrected. The correction to this chapter is available at https://doi.org/10.1007/978-3-031-19063-6_17

J. McIntyre (✉)
University of South Australia, Adelaide, SA, Australia
e-mail: joe.mcintyre@unisa.edu.au

M. Camilleri and A. Harkness (eds.), *Australian Courts*,
https://doi.org/10.1007/978-3-031-19063-6_15

dispute, planning application, consumer complaint or small claim. It is telling that the only form of civil proceeding that tends to attract media attention are defamation cases—scandalous, often salacious, with famous players and deep pockets.

Unfortunately, with this lack of attention has grown a complacency that "everything is okay". In most cases when citizens turn to the civil justice system, the reality will not meet their expectations. For this is a system facing an existential crisis.

This chapter considers the changing nature, role and function of the civil jurisdiction in Australia, where decades of under-investment have combined with years of well-intentioned reforms—if under-theorised and under-evaluated—which have slowly changed the efficacy and form of the civil jurisdiction. It outlines the place of civil courts in Australia, including the evolution of tribunals which—in the State context in particular—have expanded their jurisdiction to include both administrative and civil dispute resolution roles. The chapter will focus on the classic "civil" disputes between individuals, excluding public and constitutional law.

It is argued that the biggest controversy faced by civil courts is the controversy-by-omission that there is not broader public concern over the perilous state of civil justice in Australia—labelled here as the *ur-controversy*, as it represents a state preceding a controversy. The contemporary great challenge for civil courts and tribunals, then, is twofold: first, to engage the public and politicians in the need for a healthy and accessible civil justice system; second, to create the systems, procedures and practices to deliver such a system.

The Context of Civil Justice in Australia

Bringing a civil action in Australia is often complex and expensive. Sometime even finding the correct institution to bring an action (let alone the potential for forum shopping) can be a real problem in a country with nine principal legal jurisdictions, each with multiple courts and tribunals of civil jurisdiction and distinct substantive and procedural laws. The Commonwealth Attorney General's Department (2009, p. 52) has observed that:

> Looking at the justice system currently, a prospective user is confronted with a collection of disparate institutions and services largely operating independently. This includes the courts, tribunals, legal assistance service providers, [alternative dispute resolution] providers, and ombudsmen.

The situation has since become more acute, with new tribunals, technologies and procedural reforms emerging in attempts to reform or refresh civil justice systems.

The increased use of digital technology in the justice sector has had many positive benefits for the accessibility of law. A generation ago, access to the primary materials of the law—legislation, regulations and case law—was the privilege of the professional few whose fees paid for the prohibitively expensive subscriptions. The digitalisation of law—led by Australian pioneers such as the Australian Legal Information Institute (AustLII), and through increasingly comprehensive parliamentary websites—has now made this primary source of legal information available. Unfortunately, much of this information remains conceptually inaccessible without legal training, and the increased digital coverage has created a mass of data that can easily swamp the unprepared.

However, it is once a party actually engages directly with the civil legal system that the true scale of the stress under which this long neglected system operates becomes truly apparent. The evils of delay, costs and undue proceduralism are well recognised by all those with an interest in the civil justice system (see, for example, Cannon, 2014; Doyle, 2012; Productivity Commission, 2014; VLRC, 2008). The concerns are not new. The withering critique of civil justice in Charles Dickens' *Bleak House* (first published 1853, cited in McIntyre, 2020, p. 5) who contemptuously writes of legal practitioners gouging expansive and improper fees from clients, concluding that the "one great principle of the English law is, to make business for itself" continue to resonate. While that particular form of the current dominant evil may have changed, the underlying sense of crisis has not abated.

Reforms over the last two hundred years have attempted to fundamentally reshape some aspects of the judicial system: the theoretical simplicity of adversarialism (Millar, 1923) has been abandoned for active judicial case management; the rise of Alternative Dispute Resolution

(ADR) and enforced settlement regimes has made the pursuit of less litigation a driving institutional objective; and rising "small claims" limits mean more disputes are removed entirely from the rigours of litigation. Underlying many of these reforms has been a lionisation of ideas of "efficiency".

This highlights an inconsistency at the heart of most of these reforms: in response to litigation that is too expensive and inaccessible, a model is put forth that encourages *less* litigation. The decrease in litigation rates is clear. The South Australian Supreme Court Judges (2019) report that only 14 of the 729 civil matters lodged in the South Australian Supreme Court in 2018 reached final judgement. The reduction in matters lodged in this jurisdiction is indicative of a broader trend, sometimes referred to as the issue of the "Vanishing Trial" (Galanter, 2004. As Galanter (2006, p. 7) notes, there is "an abundance of data that shows that [civil] civil… are declining precipitously". Only around one per cent of actions commenced in court now make it to judgement (Galanter, 2004).

Litigation and judicial resolution have become, in the civil sphere, endangered a creature. Far too often, access to the courts is effectively "rationed by delay and congestion, which increases the attractiveness of settlement or abandonment of claims" (Dingwall & Cloatre, 2006, p. 51). Compounding this is the inherent complexity of the law and the overwhelming cost of professional legal services, which together creates a civil justice system that effectively operates in isolation from the lived experience of the broader population.

The unspoken, unexamined controversy facing the civil justice system is that the alienation of the population from that system is so complete that for most people they have no idea of how incapable that system currently is at serving their needs. This is the ur-controversy of civil justice—the system is in a state of existential crisis, fundamentally incapable of performing its functional objective, but most people are blissfully unaware of this crisis. It is a controversy of omission.

Controversy of Omission: The Problem of Access to Justice and Legal Need

The very attempt to understand how acute the issue of access to justice is in the civil sphere can, of itself, reveal this unacknowledged crisis of the ur-controversy. This is, in part, because there is no civil law equivalent to the academic discipline of Criminology. The systematic and interdisciplinary study of crime and its effect on society has occurred within a distinct academic disciplinary space since the late nineteenth century. In contrast, the systemic study of civil justice systems and the impact of civil disputes on society remain at best protean, and more realistically anaemic. In the civil sphere, issues of delay, expense and inaccessibility are often disguised by a paucity of quality empirical evidence (see Victorian Department of Justice and Regulation, 2016).

The lack of high-quality empirical studies (and the funding necessary to achieve this) has led to the situation where it is not possible for *anyone* to accurately understand how problematic access to justice is in the civil sphere. There is little agreement on basic terms, on the scale of the problem, and even on how the basic issues should be studied (Economides et al., 2015).

The basic proposition that civil justice is now the domain of the very wealthy is one that is well recognised. The Productivity Commission (2014, p. 114) observed that there are "widely held views that accessing justice through the civil legal system is beyond the financial reach of 'ordinary' Australians". For example, a survey by the Australia Institute found that 83% of respondents believed that only the very wealthy can afford to protect their legal rights (Denniss et al., 2012).

The difficulty of unpacking those perceptions is compounded by the challenge of defining the relevant scope of the civil justice domain. This is not so much in the division between criminal and civil, but inherent in the idea of what is a relevant legal "dispute". As McIntyre (2019, p. 35) has noted:

> Disputes, and their resolution, are an inevitable aspect of the human social condition. Disputes range from the domestic "row" amicably settled to the confrontation between nation states resolved through warfare; they may be settled in an afternoon or linger for a generation.

The subset of disputes and conflict that are rightly the concern of the civil justice system is a tiny portion of that broader domain of "disputes". Defining the portion, and how it is measured, is sometimes referred to the problem of "legal need". The Productivity Commission (2014, p. 83), usefully defined "legal need" as occurring when "an individual cannot resolve a problem by his or her own means and a legal remedy to the problem exists". The focus is on those disputes that *may* be resolved by the justice system, rather than those that actually *are* (Genn, 1999, p. 12). This is an important distinction. As Currie (2007, p. 2) notes:

> Even though problems may not be brought to the justice system for resolution, they are, nonetheless, legal problems. Logically, they should not be ignored, assumed not to be serious, or not deserving of assistance because they are not brought to the formal justice system … justiciable problems are very frequently aspects of, and one in the same with, the problems of everyday life.

The most comprehensive contemporary source of information about legal needs in Australia is the *Legal Australia-Wide Survey* (*LAW Survey*), published by the Law and Justice Foundation of New South Wales in 2012 (Coumarelos et al., 2012). The *LAW Survey* was conducted through telephone interviews in 2008 from a statistically representative sample of the Australian population ($n = 20716$ including $n = 4113$ NSW). The findings are stark in their illustration of how prevalent legal need is in Australia, and how poor the civil justice system is at addressing that need.

The study found that "50 per cent of respondents [from across Australia] experienced one or more legal problems in the 12 months prior to interview" (Coumarelos et al., 2012, p. 58). Shockingly, a quarter of the respondents (28%) experienced a "substantial" legal problem in the previous year (p. 61), defined as a legal problem having a "moderate" or "severe" impact on everyday life. These impacts are wide ranging: the most common adverse consequences were income loss or financial strain (29%), stress-related illness (21%) and physical ill health (20%). Relationship breakdown (10%) and moving home (6%) were also evident (pp. 82–83).

In response to these legal problems, Coumarelos et al. (2012, p. 95) found that approximately 20% of respondents "took no action"; 30% were "handled without advice"; and in 50% of cases, the respondent "sought advice" from formal or professional advisers. For those seeking advice, only 32% sought advice from legal advisers (Coumarelos et al., 2012, p. 109).

The vast majority of these legal problems occur within the broad domain of the civil justice system. The Productivity Commission (2014, p. 90) indicates that criminal law is only the fourth most common legal problem, with the rest such as consumer, housing, government, employment and others legal issues fall broadly within the sphere of civil justice:

Coumarelos et al. (2012) revealed that of the disputes surveyed, roughly two-thirds of legal problems were reported to be "now over" or finalised at the time of interview. Most commonly these legal problems were finalised via agreement with the other side (31%), the respondent not pursuing the matter further (29%) or the decisions or actions of other agencies (15%). Only three per cent of issues were resolved through legal proceedings in courts or tribunals, and only a further 3.4% were finalised through formal dispute resolution. While "substantial legal problems"— those with a moderate to severe impact on daily life—were more likely than minor problems to be finalised by court or tribunal proceedings (4.4% versus 2.1%) (Coumarelos et al., 2012), the absolute numbers remain very low. The figures do not reveal how many of these cases were resolved through final judicial determination, and how many were settled after proceedings were initiated.

Again, it is difficult to precisely quantify the scale of the problem, but the case study of South Australia is illustrative. That suggests that the figures used in the *LAW Survey* represent *all* finalisations, not just *final* judicial determination. South Australia has a population of approximately 1.8 million people Australian Bureau of Statistics. On the Law

Survey data, this would suggest around 500,000 "substantial legal problems" every year. Yet only around 26,000 civil matters are "finalised" through the court system every year (Courts Administration Authority of South Australia, 2021, p. 13).

Yet even this paints an inaccurate picture, as the only available data is on "finalisations", which includes settlements, default judgements, abandoned claims, summary and final judgements. Accurately measuring how many matters are resolved through a full trial and judicial determination is functionally impossible given current data. The South Australian Supreme Court Judges (2021) report provide more detailed insight into the Civil jurisdiction of that court there were 1098 finalisation in 2020–2021, yet only in 39 cases was a date set for trial and only 10 cases proceeded to trial and final judgement (Supreme Court Judges, 2021). That is, only 3.5% of cases have a date set for trial, and less than one per cent proceed to judgement. Yet it is that larger figure of 1098 finalisations that appears to support the *LAW Survey* findings.

The data, therefore, paints a very clear picture: a large number of Australians are impacted by serious (civil) legal problems every year (25%+), yet only a tiny proportion (3–4%) are resolved through the civil justice system. Of those that reach the courts, only around one per cent end in a trial and final judgements. The formal civil justice system is effectively only playing an extraordinarily marginal role in resolving *serious legal problems*.

Understanding why this the case, and how it can be addressed is part of the challenge of what is sometimes described as "access to justice", a phrase "capable of meaning different things to different people" (Sackville, 2002, p. 19). A useful definition is provided by Rice (2011, pp. 17–18), who has described access to justice in the following terms:

> the idea is broadly understood as access to law – justice being, in effect, 'justice according to the law'. The idea of 'access to justice' is, therefore, the capacity to understand the law, to get legal advice, to get legal assistance and representation, and to use public legal institutions such as the courts. It requires an ability to, for example, understand, communicate, travel and pay, and also requires the means to overcome the inability to do any of those things.

As this definition makes clear, the capacity of the formal legal system to effectively allow citizens to enforce legal rights and resolve legal problems is a multifaceted issue. It is beyond this paper to examine how these many factors interact, or the proper degree to which the formal legal system is involved in resolving disputes. For these purposes, it is sufficient to observe that for a number of reasons—including financial cost, duration, complexity and emotional/psychological cost—the justice system remains functionally inaccessible and marginalised in the resolution of civil disputes.

This is strikingly illustrated by the 2021 edition of the World Justice Project's *Rule of Law Index*. Australia ranked 63rd out of 139 countries for the extent to which people can access and afford to utilise its civil justice system. This places Australia between such developing countries as Ghana and El Salvador, and 40th out of 46 countries in its relative income bracket. While the overall rating of the civil justice system is far better (17th of 139), this lift is largely owing to the integrity and reputation of the system. The perception of a civil justice system out of reach of the ordinary Australian is reflected in this data, and moreover shows that Australia is out of step with its equivalent nations.

The Productivity Commission (2014, p. 123) recognised the scale of this problem when they observed that the "high costs of taking action do not just impact on tribunal and court users" but actively "discourage many Australians from seeking a remedy to their legal problems". The Commission estimates that "in around one third of substantial civil legal problems that were not acted on, a belief that action would be too costly was a reason for inaction". For example, in 2013, the transaction/legal cost of bringing a claim in the South Australia Magistrates Court was equivalent to 73% of the amount in dispute. That is, it would cost approximately AUD$7,300 to recover an AUD$10,000 claim—and this is in the lowest cost and most streamlined jurisdiction in the state.

This issue of unmet legal need is not merely an issue for marginalised and disenfranchised groups. It is a profound problem for the majority of Australians, the 'missing middle' of the community comprising "the many Australians who would not qualify for legal assistance but who would be unable to afford a lawyer if they had a serious legal issue" (Victorian Department of Justice, p. 119). Even where legal information and support is provided freely and publicly, it tends to overwhelmingly focus on criminal, and to a lesser extent, family law matters.

Despite the high prevalence of serious legal problems experienced, the majority of Australians are effectively alienated from the civil justice system. Where those citizens have a substantial legal problem—one that by definition is having a significant impact upon their life—the civil justice system is profoundly unable, in almost all cases, to practically assist them in resolving it. This should be a scandal of national significance. Yet the ur-controversy persists, with most Australians entirely ignorant as to the scale and impact of the problem.

Challenges: The Future of Civil Justice

The greatest contemporary challenge for civil courts and tribunals is twofold: first, to engage the public and politicians in the *need* for a healthy and accessible civil justice system; second, to create the systems and practices to deliver such a system. Arguably, the first of these challenges is the most significant and pressing.

These challenges are as much directed to *purpose* and *idea* of civil justice as a social good, as they are directed particular civil court or procedure. Issues of procedural fairness, access to justice (both affordability and complexity), the rise of self-representation and the refinement of rules of procedure and evidence are ultimately built on the foundation of this often-unspoken functional role. The challenges facing civil justice are existential—they have reached a point where we must reconsider the very nature and purpose of this institution, and to reflect upon what a commitment to civil justice looks like in contemporary society.

In addressing these challenges, it is necessary to reframe the crisis of civil justice and see that it is not simply a threat to individual rights (a mere private concern) but to the broader social values and interest. A functional and accessible civil justice system is a critical public good. This a point recognised by the Productivity Commission (2014, p. 6):

> A well-functioning civil justice system protects individuals and businesses from infringement of their legal rights by others. The ability of individuals to enforce their rights can have profound impacts on a person's wellbeing and quality of life... But a well-functioning civil justice system serves more than just private interests – it promotes social order, and communicates and reinforces civic values and norms. A well-functioning system also gives people the confidence to enter into business relationships, to enter into contracts, and to invest. This, in turn, contributes to Australia's economic performance.

What then are the basic purposes of a court, and particularly a court of civil jurisdiction? The starting point must be the basic proposition that civil courts are involved in resolving civil disputes (Barak, 2011; Doyle, 2001; McIntyre, 2020). That this function involves a particular form of dispute resolution is evident in those familiar statements of judicial dispute resolution: the judge decides disputes "by finding out the facts of the case and applying the law to those facts" (French, 2009, p. 20) in a process that involves law identification, fact determination and the reasoned application of one to the other (see also French, 2008). As Barak (2002, p. 48) has observed:

> [t]he role of the judiciary is to adjudicate disputes according to law. Adjudication involves three functions: fact determination (done mostly by the trial court), law application and law determination.

As outlined elsewhere, judicial form of dispute resolution ultimately represents a "highly specialised mode of conflict resolution" (Wroblewski, 1992, p. 54), distinguished by the criteria of merit, the nature of the third party, the degree of formality and the decision-making method (McIntyre, 2019).

Dispute resolution is, though, an insufficient (if necessary) description of the judicial role. A court is not "simply a publicly funded dispute resolution centre" (Spigelman, 2002, p. 26), but a core "institution of governance" (Bhagwati, 1988, p. 38) that affects the governance and regulation of society as a whole (Brennan, 1979). Courts are performing a key public role of social governance: maintaining social order and a system of legality, together with clarifying, interpreting and developing legal norms (Legg & Mirzabegian, 2013; McIntyre, 2019). Courts are *the principal* dispute-resolution system of the modern democratic society, providing a key plank in maintaining social order (Devlin, 1979). As Couture (1950, p. 7) forcefully argued:

> [t]he first impulse of a rudimentary soul is to do justice by his own hand. Only at the cost of mighty historical efforts has it been possible to supplant in the human soul the idea of self-obtained justice by the idea of justice entrusted to authorities… A civil action, in final analysis, then, is civilization's substitute for vengeance.

The performance of this role is powerfully aided by the intimate connection between the judiciary and other institutions of government. Compliance with judicial decisions is not left to diffuse social pressure or the goodwill and integrity of the disputants but is ensured through the enforcement abilities of the state (McIntyre, 2019).

In Australia, we do not (yet) have a clear articulation of the value and significance of meaningful access to civil courts. While there are many extrajudicial comments that accept this value (see, for example, Brennan, 1996), the driving doctrinal animus remains that civil justice should be carefully rationed and controlled, and that substantive judicial determination is to be avoided.

Australia has so far lacked the type of "public incident" or "controversy" so often necessary to drive discussion of institutional reform. Obscurity rarely coincides with controversy, and so it is with the civil justice system which seldom generates public attention. The sensationalist nature of defamation law is the exception that proves the rule: high profile fights between politicians, media and celebrities have brought significant attention, and resultant discussion of the need for reform.

Change: The Promise of Technology and Other Seismic Changes

Ultimately, positive change in the civil sphere must be driven by a clear-headed understanding of why civil justice matter, both as a private and as a public good. Reforms are likely to involve the embrace of digital justice technologies and expanded recognition of the role of self-representation. However, the inherent complexity of law, and its role in social governance, requires continued input of the profession and the judiciary in the administration of civil justice. Balancing this value with concerns of the accessibility of justice will require fundamental change in our practice of civil justice. The challenge is in delivering this in a way that honours the underlying conception of civil justice, and the ideals of justice more generally.

Stasis, or incremental change, is inadequate to address a challenge of this degree. Arguably, the reforms of the last generation—the emphasis on alternative dispute resolution and a view of final judicial resolution as a system failure—have compounded rather than improved the problem. To properly address the existential challenge of the scale faced by the civil justice system, radical change will be necessary. However, there are early indications that such change—and the political will to carry it out—may eventually be possible.

Digital justice technology promises to play a major role in democratising civil justice, and the many pieces necessary to affect seismic change through this route appear to be falling into place. Despite being an early leader in digital justice technology, Australian courts have fallen significantly behind other jurisdictions in embracing it. For example, prior to the COVID-19 pandemic, many jurisdictions across the world had begun to examine the opportunities presented by 'online dispute resolution' systems (see, for example, Rabinovich-Einy & Katsh, 2017). These systems seek to integrate different forms of dispute resolution and information provisions tools into single online platform (Waye et al., 2021). Perhaps the most successful of these has been the Civil Resolution Tribunal established in 2016 in British Columbia, Canada (Salter, 2017). More recently, the United Kingdom has introduced an Online Solutions Court to handle civil disputes up to £25,000 (Hodges, 2016). In contrast, no Australian jurisdiction has moved beyond the investigatory stage (VCAT, 2018).

However, the technological responses necessitated by COVID-19 appear to have fundamentally altered the cultural attitude of the judiciary and legal profession to digital justice technology (McIntyre et al.,

2020). There has been a rapid uptake in the use of technology to increase the capacity of courts (Bell et al., 2021). The moves so far are more incremental than revolutionary, and there remains significant untapped potential.

Conclusion

If the civil justice system is to be truly democratised, technological change will not be sufficient. There will need to be major regulatory and cultural shifts in the legal profession. Issues to be addressed are legion and include issues such as the role and extent of professional liability; relaxation of restrictions on the provision of "advice" (as opposed to general "information"); appropriate public funding of civil courts; and costs of litigation relative to amount in dispute. These issues all require careful reflection in the light of underlying principles and objectives (McIntyre, 2013a, 2013b).

Central to this needs to be the clear recognition of the public good civil courtsand of civil litigation itself. Meaningful access to civil courts is critical to the rule of law. Faced with the apathy of the ur-controversy, the political will necessary to affect systemic change is unlikely to crystalise. But the serious legal problems will continue to occur and their costs to citizens and society will continue to mount.

Changing this narrative, engaging the population and politicians with the value and significance of civil justice appear to be a monumental challenge. It is, though, a challenge that we cannot shy away from if we have a commitment to legality and a faith in the social goods delivered by our courts.

References

Ackermann, R. M. (2006). Vanishing trial, vanishing community? The potential effect of the—Vanishing trial on America's social capital. *Journal of Dispute Resolution* (1), 165–180, Article 13.

Attorney-General's Department (Commonwealth). (2009). *A strategic framework for access to justice in the Federal civil justice system.* Commonwealth of Australia. Retrieved from https://www.ag.gov.au/sites/default/files/2020-03/A%20Strategic%20Framework%20for%20Access%20to%20Justice%20in%20the%20Federal%20Civil%20Justice%20System.pdf

Barak, A. (2002). The role of a supreme court in a democracy. *Hastings Law Journal, 53*(5), 1205–1216.

Barak, A. (2011). On society, law and judging. *Tulsa Law Review, 47*(2), 297–318.

Bell, F., Legg, M., McIntyre, J., & Olijnyk, A. (2021). The use of technology (and other measures) to increase court capacity: A view from Australia. *International Journal on Online Dispute Resolution, 8*(2), 102–130.

Bhagwati, P. N. (1988). Role of the judiciary in developing societies: New challenges. In T. M. S. Abas & D. V. Sinnadurai (Eds.), *Law, justice and the judiciary: Transnational trends.* Professional Law Books Publishers.

Brennan, G. (1979). Judging the judges. *Australian Law Journal, 53*(11), 767–770.

Brennan, G. (1996). Key issues in judicial administration. *Journal of Judicial Administration, 6*(3), 138–146.

Cannon, A. (2014). Affordable costs in civil litigation. *Journal of Judicial Administration, 23*(3), 171–181.

Coumarelos, C., Macourt, D., People, J., McDonald, H. M., Wei, Z., Iriana, R., & Ramsey, S. (2012). *Legal Australia-wide survey legal need in New South Wales.* Access to Justice and Legal Needs: Volume 7. Sydney: Law and Justice Foundation of NSW. Retrieved from http://www.lawfoundation.net.au/ljf/site/templates/LAW_AUS/$file/LAW_Survey_Australia.pdf

Courts Administration Authority of South Australia. (2021). *Annual report 2020–2021.* Retrieved from https://www.courts.sa.gov.au/publications/annual-reports/

Couture, E. J. (1950). The nature of the judicial process. *Tulane Law Review, 25*(1), 1–28.

Currie, A. B. (2007). *The legal problems of everyday life: The nature, extent and consequences of justiciable problems experienced by Canadians.* Department of Justice, Canada. Retrieved from https://www.justice.gc.ca/eng/rp-pr/csj-sjc/jsp-sjp/rr07_la1-rr07_aj1/rr07_la1.pdf

Denniss, R., Fear, J., & Millane, E. (2012). *Justice for all: Giving Australians greater access to the legal system.* Paper 8. Canberra: Australia Institute. Retrieved from https://australiainstitute.org.au/wp-content/uploads/2020/12/IP8-Justice-for-all_4.pdf

Devlin, P. (1979). *The judge*. Oxford University Press.
Dingwall, R., & Cloatre, E. (2006). Vanishing trials? An English perspective. *Journal of Dispute Resolution* (1), 51–70.
Doyle, J. (2001). The judicial role in a new millennium. *Journal of Judicial Administration, 10*(3), 133–148.
Doyle, J. (2012). Imagining the past, remembering the future: The demise of civil litigation. *Australian Law Journal, 86* (4), 240–248.
Economides, K., Haug, A., & McIntyre, J. (2015). Toward timeliness in civil justice. *Monash University Law Review, 41*(2), 414–444.
French, R. (2008). Judicial activist—Mythical monsters? *Southern Cross University Law Review, 12*(59), 60–74
French, R. (2009). In praise of unelected judges. *Brief, 36* (9), 19–24.
Galanter, M. (2004). The vanishing trial: An examination of trials and related matters in federal and state courts. *Journal of Empirical Legal Studies, 1*(3), 459–570.
Galanter, M. (2006). A world without trials. *Journal of Dispute Resolution,* (1), 7–33.
Genn, H. (1999) *Paths to justice: What people do and think about going to law.* Hart Publishing.
Google Trends. (2020). *Year in search.* Retrieved from https://trends.google.com/trends/yis/2020/AU/
Hodges, C. J. S. (2016). Proposed modernization of courts in England and Wales: IT and the Online Court. *International Journal of Procedural Law, 6* (1), 149–163.
Judges of the Supreme Court of South Australia. (2019). *Report of the Judges of the Supreme Court to the Attorney-General: Year Ended 31 December 2018.*
Judges of the Supreme Court of South Australia. (2021). *Report of the Judges of the Supreme Court of South Australia to the Attorney-General Pursuant to Section 16 of The Supreme Court Act 1935 (SA) For The Year Ended 30 June 2021.* Retrieved from https://www.courts.sa.gov.au/download/judges-annualreports/?ind=1637210851799&filename=2020_Judges_Annual_Report_SC.pdf&wpdmdl=8308&refresh=61f1e67c05c1c1643243132
Kritzer, H. M. (2004). Disappearing trials? A comparative perspective. *Journal of Empirical Legal Studies, 1*(3), 735–754.
Legg, M., & Mirzabegian, S. (2013). Appropriate dispute resolution and the role of litigation. *Australian Bar Review, 38*(55), 57–63.
McIntyre, J. (2013a). A framework for civil justice reform Pt I: Theory. *The Law Society Bulletin, 35*(8), 26–27.

McIntyre, J. (2013b). A framework for civil justice reform Pt II: Politics and practice. *The Law Society Bulletin, 35*(9), 18–19.

McIntyre, J. (2019). *The judicial function: Fundamental principles of contemporary judging*. Springer.

McIntyre, J. (2020). *Re-examining the judicial function*. SSRN. Retrieved from https://papers.ssrn.com/sol3/papers.cfm?abstract_id=3663530

McIntyre, J., Olijnyk, A., & Pender, K. (2020). Civil courts and COVID-19: Challenges and opportunities in Australia. *Alternative Law Journal, 45*(3), 195–201.

Millar, R. W. (1923). *The formative principles of civil procedure*. North-western University Press.

Productivity Commission. (2014). *Access to justice arrangements* (Productivity Commission Inquiry report, Vol. 1). Canberra: Australian Government. Retrieved from https://www.pc.gov.au/inquiries/completed/access-justice/report

Rabinovich-Einy, O., & Katsh, E. (2017). The new new courts. *American University Law Review, 67*(1), 165–215.

Rice, S. (2011). Access to a lawyer in rural Australia: Thoughts on the evidence we need. *Deakin Law Review, 16*(1), 13–46.

Sackville, R. (2002, July 10). Access to justice: Assumptions and reality checks. Keynote address to the Law and Justice Foundation of NSW, Access to Justice Workshop, Parliament of NSW. Retrieved from http://www.lawfoundation.net.au/report/roundtable/49571BB84EBCB469CA2572730018E0CC.html

Salter, S. (2017). Online dispute resolution and justice system integration: British Columbia's Civil Resolution Tribunal. *Windsor Yearbook of Access to Justice, 34*(1), 112–129.

Spigelman, J. (2002). Judicial accountability and performance indicators. *Civil Justice Quarterly, 21*, 18–45.

VCAT (Victorian Civil and Administrative Tribunal). (2018, November 21). *VCAT's online dispute resolution experience*. Retrieved from https://www.vcat.vic.gov.au/news/sharing-vcats-online-dispute-resolution-experience

Victorian Department of Justice and Regulation. (2016). *Access to justice review: Volume 1 report and recommendations*. Government of Victoria.

VLRC (Victorian Law Reform Commission). (2008). *Civil justice review* (Report No 14). Melbourne: Victorian Government Printer. Retrieved from https://www.lawreform.vic.gov.au/wp-content/uploads/2021/07/VLRCCivilJusticeReview-Report.pdf

Waye, V., McIntyre, J., Knowler, J., Olinjyk, A., Snowden, C., Martini, B., Deegan, G., & Palmer, J. (2021). Maximising the pivot to online courts: Digital transformation, not mere digitisation. *Journal of Judicial Administration, 30*(3), 126–152.

World Justice Project. (2021). *WJP rule of Law Index*. Retrieved from https://worldjusticeproject.org/rule-of-law-index/country/2021/Australia/Civil%20Justice/

Wroblewski, J. (1992). *The judicial application of law*. Kluwer.

Practitioner Perspective: A Reflection on Civil Litigation

Ben Doyle KC and Stephen McDonald SC

Our observations, as practitioners who practice in civil litigation, is that the problem of an accessible civil justice system remains an acute one even for those clients who have accessed legal assistance (either as a claimant or respondent) and have become party to some proceeding. A common problem is that even where initial estimates are made on what is thought to be a conservative basis, a dispute proves to take more time and be more expensive than was anticipated.

In a system where the default rule is 'loser pays', the all too common conclusion that is reached, before a trial is heard and the court is called upon to determine the 'just result', is that neither party can afford to take the risk of that occurring.

The costs to be incurred, or the potential adverse costs exposure, often loom as large as the risks of success or failure on liability for all but the most well-heeled of clients. And even for the well-heeled, if their adversary is not so well-heeled, their likely inability to recover costs if they succeed acts as a significant disincentive to proceeding with the case. This often leads to a negotiated outcome which might come to be viewed as better than running the gauntlet of trial, but which, for a claimant, often leaves them thinking they would have been better off never having engaged with the system.

One of the difficulties in trying to gauge the extent of the problems of access to civil justice—or to measure any potential success in responding to it—is that it seems virtually impossible by empirical means to define and measure a 'successful' attempt at 'accessing' justice. After all, some people who consider they had a genuine legal issue but who did not pursue it for fear of cost may have been mistaken. Of course, reaching

B. Doyle KC
Hanson Chambers, Adelaide, SA, Australia

S. McDonald SC
Hanson Chambers, Adelaide, SA, Australia

the stage of judgment is not to be universally regarded as equating to successful access to justice, at least not without qualification. The matter may only have reached that stage because one party has been unprepared to let a totally unmeritorious matter go. One person's access to justice may be the source of another person's dismay at how the system may permit an impecunious claimant to have their day in court at the great expense of the respondent who may have no realistic prospect of recovering their costs.

To define and quantify the problem is inherently difficult in the sphere of civil justice for a variety of reasons, including because civil disputes are far less homogenous than criminal prosecutions. In the criminal law, the number of charges may be a rough proxy for the expected complexity and time required for the case.

In a civil dispute, by contrast, there may be any number of parties. Some may be claimants, some respondents, or both. A single cause of action may occupy months of trial, or a single issue may involve multiple alternative causes of action and just as many defences.

There are some areas of the civil law (for example, workers compensation or personal injury) where costs rules, or a greater preparedness of lawyers to act on a no-win no-fee basis, seem to facilitate greater access to justice for claimants. This may in part be due to the slightly more homogenous and formulaic nature of the kind of litigation involved. It makes cases slightly more efficient to 'get up' (because they involve activities and preparations with which practitioners are very familiar), and also slightly easier to predict, both of which incentivise practitioners to provide their services on a contingent or concessionary basis.

The lack of homogeneity that attends civil disputes not only makes the quantification of the problem of access to justice difficult; it may contain part of the explanation for the underlying problem.

In a civil justice system in which time-based charging has become entrenched, the more complex a dispute, the more costly it is. To that must be added the risk of paying the other party's costs, which means that any additional complexity comes at twice the cost for the loser. It seems that the inevitable response to this problem is an attempt to simplify *procedure*. An allied but more radical solution that is sometimes proposed is to assist in removing lawyers (and the consequent cost) from the process.

A difficulty with these responses is that they focus unduly on one party's experience of a dispute, and often in the preliminary phases, without considering the implications for the efficient conduct of a dispute if it ever reaches a trial. A system which, to save one party the cost of representation, permits that party to advance their claim or complaint without a proper pleading or articulation of the material facts to be relied upon in support of an identified cause of action, may give a false appearance of access to justice. It may simply result in later interlocutory steps or arguments of relevance and admissibility at trial being rendered more diffuse and ultimately more costly. And undoubtedly it will cast a greater cost on the other party to the dispute, who will lack clarity about the case they need to meet. This cost in turn may rebound on the claimant. The risk of adverse costs orders therefore means that a reform is only worthwhile if it reduces the combined costs of the litigants.

Unless lawyers are excluded entirely from certain types of disputes, if the aim is to reduce the total cost incurred in a civil dispute, the answer may lie not in 'dumbing down' or abandoning basic procedural rules (which generally but not always exist for sound reasons which become apparent when the trial is reached), but in finding ways either to reduce the complexity of disputes themselves, or to bring about improvements in lawyers' abilities to conduct complex disputes efficiently. Apart from legal education and training, another way of improving the quality of lawyering may be to prune back the substantive law itself.

A certain degree of fact-sensitivity, and therefore complexity, is inevitable in the substantive law if it is to accord with demands of fairness. But there comes a point where the sheer volume of substantive law adds to its complexity without aiding its sophistication. Indeed, to our observation, it becomes self-defeating. All too often a problem, in response to which the common law has evolved reasonably satisfactorily, is added to by legislative intervention. This typically spawns its own difficulties as the chosen language gives rise to new and unforeseen interpretational questions. Where the statute law supplements and does not codify or replace the common law, the lawyer advising on and conducting a case must deal with and attempt to master and adduce evidence relevant to a greater volume of law. Even where the real issues in dispute are relatively clear and confined, cases may become unwieldy.

Self-evidently, the more law that must be dealt with in a dispute, the greater the cost of transacting the litigation. But at a higher level, it is hard to resist the conclusion that a familiarity with a vast bulk of substantive law comes at the cost of a mastery of any aspect of it. And whenever the lawyer for one party missteps in relation to any aspect of a dispute, it throws a potential cost burden on all parties the litigation.

The access to justice implications of complexity in the civil law should be a consideration for every Parliament that is contemplating adding to, or tinkering with, the substantive law. Whatever perceived improvement there may be in the new law, or in adjusting the existing law, it will never be realised if the law is rarely if ever applied.

Lawyers are necessary participants in the application of the law, and rightly or wrongly they charge for the time they spend providing services. It is in society's interests that there be simple and relatively stable substantive laws so that the accumulated expertise of lawyers can be quickly deployed in response to a particular dispute. It is against everyone's interests for there to be mistakes, or unnecessary issues raised, because the volume of law applying to a civil litigious controversy is greater than is needed for a reasonably just result.

The scandalous cost of access to justice generally (as opposed to the especially scandalous cost of particular disputes) does not attract the public discussion or political attention that it should. The answer does not lie exclusively in the public- or crowd-funding of access a complex system, nor in seeking to simplify the procedural rules that govern access. To aid access to justice, there may be more value in reducing the volume and complexity of the substantive law which is to be accessed than there is in trying to simplify the procedural rules governing its access, or by encouraging litigants in person to access it directly.

16

Challenging Court Landscapes and Opportunities for Change

Marg Camilleri and Alistair Harkness

Introduction

Courts are complex institutions which must constantly adjust to change, ensuring that they are fulfilling their responsibilities to the accused and society and all those who enter court space, whether virtually or physically. Courts must manage their relationships with other agencies (both justice and community) on whom they rely. Fulfilling these important roles and functions is not without challenges. In an Australian context, these challenges are manifested by the sheer geographical expanse of the

M. Camilleri (✉)
Federation University Australia, Ballarat, VIC, Australia
e-mail: m.camilleri@federation.edu.au

A. Harkness
University of New England, Armidale, NSW, Australia
e-mail: alistair.harkness@une.edu.au

M. Camilleri and A. Harkness (eds.), *Australian Courts*,
https://doi.org/10.1007/978-3-031-19063-6_16

country—and challenges are faced by the various participants in the court processes whether as defendants, victims, witnesses or others.

This chapter considers an array of challenges and assesses a suite of reform proposals, recognising that reform is critical for the continuing evolution of Australian courts and the justice system more broadly.

Challenging Landscapes and Dimensions

Challenges persist in the criminal justice system and attempts at reform are seldom straight forward. The complexities assume added dimensions when considering Australia's geographic expanses and differences between its nine criminal justice systems. Change, therefore, requires multiple agencies working together, balancing the roles of various disparate actors with oftentimes competing demands and requirements.

Geography

Australia is a vast landscape and, whilst some 85% of the population live within 50 kms of the coast, a significant number of people live in rural, regional and remote parts of the country require—and deserve—access to court services as much as any other citizens. Geographic challenges in ensuring "access to justice" (see Camilleri and Harkness, Chapter 1) are magnified in very remote parts of the country. For instance, Schaefer and Egan (Chapter 9) articulate the complexities of providing equity of access to problem-solving courts across wider geographic, as do Marchetti and Ryle (Chapter 10) in their discussion of Indigenous sentencing courts.

Circumstances in the Northern Territory are particularly instructive. Whilst the Northern Territory Supreme Court will sit regularly in the more populated places of Darwin, Alice Springs and to a less regular extent Katherine, finding a sufficient number of impartial jurors in other locations is a very real challenge, and oftentimes a trial will occur some considerable distance from the location of the crime (Blokland, 2016). This, too, presents transportation and other resourcing issues, such as the need to provide interpreters, and finding suitable physical space for lawyers to meet their clients. The number of matters to be dealt with when the court travels to a remote location for a short number of days can also be quite exceptional (Hunyor, 2016).

Challenges in Times of Crisis

When disasters such as pandemics, floods, fires and cyclones strike, access to courts and other justice services is impacted, with both physical (such as closed roads) and social (such as dislocation from social and community supports) barriers created. These can be felt disproportionality by some people and communities more than others, such as those in regional, rural remote communities (Hale et al., 2021).

A significant contemporary disruption was caused by the COVID-19 pandemic, producing numerous challenges for the smooth operation of courts internationally (Sourdin et al., 2020). Australian courts needed to pivot from inherently complex systems which are primarily public facing to virtual spaces whilst continuing to maintain the rule of law, and to be open, transparent and subject to scrutiny.

The spread of the virus necessitated the closure of the Australia's international borders as well as internal borders between states and regions within states. Health regulations mandated mask wearing, travel limitations, hotel quarantine requirements and so on. New enforcement measures, and the swift introduction of regulations led to an increased workload for courts (Parliament of Victoria, 2021); the pandemic created delays in court hearings with consequential implications on defendants awaiting trial and for victims (Curran, Chapter 7).

The impact of COVID-19 and the subsequent early release of incarcerated people highlighted how quickly the system can move—and in the context of providing bail during this time of crisis, extended "an opportunity to reflect on current bail practices, and in particular the need to use remand to the extent that we did prior to the pandemic crisis" (Colvin, Chapter 6).

Various physical impacts were also felt by the criminal and civil courts (McIntyre et al., 2020). Courts were not immune from social distancing and stay-at-home orders, creating a need for innovative flexing to maintain a steady throughput of cases whilst protecting the health and safety of court participants. Key amongst the responses was the pivoting to remote courts and the use of audio-visual links. Reflecting on the increasing role of technology in the court room, Turnbull (practitioner perspective, Chapter 3) notes that confrontations between the accused and their accusers often occur over video link, with events observed by juries in two rather than three dimensions.

An accelerated use of technologies, for a quick transition from face-to-face to online, ensured that hearings could continue—but this was not without impacts on access. Indeed, whilst the use of audio-visual links has been increasingly in use for vulnerable court participants such as children, intimidated witnesses and prisoners, the rapid deployment for all hearings, in conjunction with the use of remote courts, created some distinct challenges. Amongst these are the availability and quality of technology (particularly for rural, regional and remote communities), issues around procedural fairness which may be negatively impacted by an inability to sufficiently cross-examine witnesses; impacts on "open justice" (Legg & Song, 2021); and an array of other practical and legal considerations (Smith et al., 2021).

The courts and key stakeholders who regularly enter the civil court space have identified, through urgent need during the pandemic, the benefits of technology in conducting the daily business of the courts. Whilst the use of technology has been necessarily swift during and in the wake of the pandemic, changes over time have been "more incremental than revolutionary, and there remains significant untapped potential" (McIntyre, Chapter 15).

The increased use of technology in response to the pandemic has shown that technology can play a significant role in the administration of justice. Curran (Chapter 7) warns, however, of the over reliance on technology through online hearings, as a pathway to reducing delays and improving efficiencies "has implications for justice and is complex". Such changes without adequate resourcing of the technologies—and in concert with services and support—can potentially compromise fairness and due process.

Justice for All?

What constitutes "justice" is fraught, much debated and, oftentimes, subject to one's own perspectives and inherent biases. In twenty-first century Australia, though, Beccarian principles of justice for all ought not be considered controversial. Whether this is achievable in practical reality is certainly debatable: after all, the criminal justice system is constituted of an inherently complex and conservative group of institutions. Whilst reforms have been implemented over time, the traditional conservative nature of such systems at times lacks the flexibility for change.

Camilleri and Harkness (Chapter 1) chart the historical emergence of courts in Australia, noting that supplanting a Western colonial system upon the world's oldest continuing culture has produced an enduring legacy of justice-related challenges for First Nations peoples. Procedural and integrity complexities for First Nations peoples include matters of "cultural safety" and, for instance, practices in coroners' courts. Truth telling and accountability are two other areas which exhibit a disconnect of expectations of First Nations families and the inquisitorial nature and processes courts (Allison and Cunneen, Chapter 11).

Decisions about whether to grant or deny bail are similarly complex with various factors to consider, not least of which include the level of risk to community safety and the "potential of the accused absconding prior to hearing" (Colvin, Chapter 6). Another important systemic factor is the limited availability of housing options which disproportionally affects young people, women and First Nations peoples (Russell et al., 2020).

For young people, legislation tightening access to bail has had a disproportionate impact upon disadvantaged children and young people, notably those with cognitive impairment and those in the care of the State (Hamilton, practitioner perspective, Chapter 6). The experiences of children and young people in the criminal justice system can be variable. Sheehan and Baidwadi (Chapter 13) contend that "more favourable outcomes will rest on the child's capacity" to relate to a variety of adults. A child or young person's capacity may be impacted by their past and current experience of trauma, their age and development in addition to any cognitive or psycho-social disabilities.

The Challenge of Changing Societal Attitudes and Legislative Parameters

Changing public sentiment will often lead to the challenge of changing requirements for the courts. A useful example of this revolves around matters of family violence. Public attitude surveys regarding violence against women have been undertaken in Victoria in 1995, 2009, 2013, and 2017 (VicHealth, 2019). The 2017 survey indicates greater awareness of such offending and less supportive attitudes to violence (Webster et al., 2018). In response to the challenge of tackling family violence, changes have been made by law enforcement bodies in the way in which these matters are viewed and dealt with (for example, Victoria Police, 2014), and in legislation such as in Victoria with the *Family Violence Protection Act 2008 (Vic)*. A significant contribution to this space was the Victorian Royal Commission into Family Violence (State of Victoria, 2016).

Heightened attention to family violence matters by police, and changes to community expectations and to legislation, inevitably bring more such matters before the courts. Brown and Alexander (Chapter 14) plot four decades of changes to systems and processes in the Family Court response to family violence. The changes themselves have, at times, created further complexities and challenges for those with the task of implementation, and of course the uncertainty and safety concerns for women and their children living the realities of family violence.

Searching for Balance in Challenging Landscapes

Various chapters in *Australian Courts* (Harkness, Chapter 2; Waller and Clifford, Chapter 4; Colvin, Chapter 6; McIntyre, Chapter 15) address the theme of 'finding balance in challenging landscapes', albeit for different reasons. However, the subject of these chapters reflects the powers of the court, such as in restricting access by jurors to social media and the internet; limiting freedom of the media; balancing the risk of granting bail; balancing the various, often competing demands of advocacy groups, the community and politics; and balancing the need for cost-effective prosecutions with the need for transparency and independence.

Whilst suppression orders are imposed by the court to ensure the accused a fair trial, Waller and Clifford (Chapter 4) highlight that there is a need "to ensure the preservation of the ideals of open justice and a balance between the proper administration of justice and the democratic role of journalism".

Another significant challenge of balance is a lack of reform drive in some parts of the legal system, and this is acutely felt within the civil justice system which McIntyre (Chapter 15) argues has been largely ignored in terms of reform compared to the criminal justice system. This results in civil justice languishing within systems that have become inaccessible because of costs, complexities and consequent negative perceptions. Balance in decision-making of law makers is required, with members of parliament needing to balance sentencing policy with public opinion (Harkness, Chapter 2; Finn, practitioner perspective, Chapter 2), and "the threshold of risk that is considered acceptable by decision makers" is both an important yet complex consideration (Colvin, Chapter 6).

Other Key Challenges

Delays in matters being attended to by the courts is a challenge which "can lead to unfairness, uncertainty and impede effective decision-making and responsiveness", with the potential to alienate people from the legal system whether as defendants or as victims (Curran, Chapter 7). Extended delays whilst a person is held on remand will have potentially detrimental impacts on a prisoner in terms of their personal life, family connection, mental health, employment prospects, housing and financial security—and can have the effect of undermining the presumption of innocence (Lacy, practitioner perspective, Chapter 7).

Goodman-Delahunty and Tait (Chapter 3) warn of the challenge of "juror non-compliance" with directions not to access the internet and social media during a trial. The challenge here is managing a changing cohort of jurors who have a high reliance on mobile devices as they conduct their daily lives, accessing information in a way which "does not expose them to biasing information that may compromise the accused's right to receive a fair trial".

The summary jurisdiction is one of increasing complexity regarding the matters heard within that jurisdiction, yet police-led prosecutions are seldom scrutinised either by scholars or by government. The challenge here is that of potential conflict of interest for prosecutors who are employed by the same organisations that also employs the informant and the victim, in instances where the victim is a police officer (Ellis and Camilleri, Chapter 5). In the problem-solving courts, case coordination is perhaps one of the most complex matters to address (Schaefer and Egan, Chapter 9).

The Case for Both a Micro and Macro Reform Agenda

Courts are inherently conservative institutions with a reputation for being slow to change (McIntyre et al., 2020). That said, numerous historical and contemporary legislative, process and programmatic reforms over decades have occurred in response to calls from various cohorts. Personal perspective, though, dictates whether the pace, scope, depth, and breadth of reforms are considered to have been piecemeal and simply tinkered with, or if reforms have been systemic and transformational.

Notwithstanding the consternation of some about the contemporary pace and scope of reforms, much evidence-based work is undertaken with the aim of positive change. In Victoria, for instance, the Sentencing Advisory Council produces reports on an array of issues such as the effects of media coverage on sentencing (McGorrery, 2022) and produces data on, for example, judging statistics (Simu & McGorrery, 2021). So, too, does the Victorian Law Reform Commission with reports proposing changes to matters such as justice improvements in responding to sexual offences (VLRC, 2021). Various parliamentary committees have similarly conducted inquiries into law reform matters.

Symbolic reform in Victoria has occurred, such as the removal of anachronistic wigs and gowns for judges in the Supreme Court (since 2016) and their voluntary wearing in the County Court (Mills, 2021). Amongst more substantive court reforms has been the introduction of the Koori Court and other specialist courts, and the Neighbourhood Justice Centre (part of the Magistrates Court) which offers place-based, problem-solving justice outcomes (NJC, 2022).

As chapters throughout *Australian* Corts identify, substantive legislative change also occurs regularly. Caution should be exercised, though, in thinking that legislative reform is a panacea: "Whatever perceived improvement there may be in the new law, or in adjusting the existing law, it will never be realised if the law is rarely if ever applied" (Doyle and McDonald, practitioner perspective, Chapter 15).

Whether micro-level "quick fixes" or macro-systemic change over the longer term, ongoing reform is both desirable and essential in responding to the ever-challenging and constantly evolving legal landscape. A key question, though, is whether change ought to be gradualist in the Fabian tradition or a complete rebuild of the system akin to that proposed by "defund police" and prison abolitionist advocates. It is also worth bearing in mind that smaller, gradual changes can, over time, be enormously transformational for the lives of individuals. Let us consider first some major, necessary systemic reforms, and then countenance several other short- to medium-term reform proposals.

Addressing Income Inequality and Social Disadvantage

Strain and other criminological theories developed from an understanding that crime causation relates to social and environmental conditions, rather than necessarily biological or psychological determinants (although largely focus on so-called "street crimes'" overlooking other offending such as white-collar, State and environmental crime). Social disjuncture and processes, as well as blocked opportunities to achieve desired or expected goals, will fuel offending behaviours (see White et al., 2017).

A macro-level reform, therefore, is to address the societal conditions such as lack of housing; blockages to education and skill attainment; employment opportunities; affordable health care; provision of a living wage and a welfare safety net though income redistribution via the taxation system; neighbourhood revitalisation and provision of support (including justice services) where needed; and so on. A 2021 parliamentary committee report from the United Kingdom identified that poor education attainment by working-class white children (especially for boys) in England was contributed to be a set of factors including limited job opportunities, the absence of community infrastructure, social organisations, poor local services and transport options; and multi-generational poverty and disengaged parents. White working-class boys were less likely to pursue tertiary education (Coughlin, 2021; House of Commons Education Committee, 2021).

In Australia, pockets of "concentrated and severe" disadvantage exist (Tanton et al., 2021). Considering the Gini coefficient of income equality, Australia is ranked eleventh of 33 OECD countries (for this and other international comparisons of welfare data, see AIHW, 2021). Income inequality and other forms of social disadvantage will lead to potential for interactions with the criminal justice system, appearances before the courts and thus, depending on the offence, possible incarceration which spurs recidivist offending—and so the cycle continues unless interventions are made, resources provided and political will exhibited.

There can be no doubt that further social justice reform is both desirable and essential. A relatively new reconceptualisation as to how tax dollars are spent in the justice space is "justice reinvestment", an approach originating in the United States and United Kingdom that provokes the redirection of funding from prisons to provide enhanced human and physical resources in areas dominated by high levels of incarceration (see, for example, ALRC, 2018; Brown et al., 2016).

In essence, funds are reallocated from the prison system to the provision of programmes and infrastructure to prevent offending from occurring before matters proceed through the criminal justice system. A number of justice reinvestment inquiries have been undertaken—and some pilots or programmes are underway—in various Australian States and Territories (Willis & Kapira, 2018). Further commitment to the rollout of justice reinvestment programmes would go a long way to addressing the root cause of offending, thus reducing the number of individuals occupying the time of the courts.

Addressing the Needs of First Nations Peoples

One could be forgiven for thinking that addressing issues of cultural inclusion and safety in the justice system may at times seem impossible, particularly given the decades of delays in implementing many of the recommendations from the Royal Commission into Aboriginal Deaths in Custody (RCIADC, 1991). It is not surprising, then, that the consequence of inaction to implement the recommendations have contributed to, perpetuated and compounded the entrenchment of First Nations peoples into the criminal justice system as defendants and as victims (see Marchetti and Ryle, Chapter 10).

Whilst specialist Indigenous sentencing courts have been shown to reduce the likelihood of recidivism (Marchetti and Ryle, Chapter 10) and are less alienating that mainstream courts (Payne, practitioner perspective, Chapter 10), many of the chapters in *Australian Courts* identify that many First Nations peoples are negatively impacted by an array of contemporary criminal justice processes and issues, such as by the coroners court (Allison and Cunneen, Chapter 11; Longman and Whittaker, practitioner perspective, Chapter 11). The key to more equitable, transparent and culturally informed justice responses to First Nations peoples is to understand that using a one-size-fits-all response is insufficient in addressing the needs of First Nations peoples in the twenty-first century.

To address inherent inequalities within the courts system for First Nations peoples, ongoing reforms—both micro and macro—are necessary. Marchetti and Ryle (Chapter 10) suggest several measures to improve outcomes for Indigenous defendants in Indigenous sentencing courts. Whilst these might appear at face value to be simple to implement, such change is contingent on government funding and a willingness on the part of courts to understand why change is important to improving outcomes. They point to the efficacy of "narrative reports" which provide the opportunity for more information that is culturally relevant to the defendant and allowing space to include information about the unique factors affecting First Nations peoples. Ongoing and increased support for Indigenous participation in specialist sentencing courts is vital: as Payne (practitioner perspective, Chapter 10) notes, the "success of [the Murri Court] is because its' therapeutic processes are almost entirely designed and managed by the local Aboriginal and Torres Strait Islander elders".

Allison and Cunneen (Chapter 11) suggest two changes that would increase cultural safety and reduce the potential for retraumatisation experienced by First Nations families through their interaction with the coroner's court. The first is adapting coroners' courts to better suit the cultural and safety needs of First Nations People, such as hearing evidence on country and the employment of First Nations staff. The second is to establish an independent First Nations investigative body—separate from police and placing First Nations peoples as central—although Allison and Cunneen do note that the "feasibility of this option requires further investigation".

Greater Focus on Victims and Participatory Rights

A case can be made for greater participatory rights in recognition of a victim's inherent interest in matters brought to court. Despite a raft of reforms focused on improving the experiences of victim/survivors of sexual assault, including at court, such reforms have been implemented inconsistently, at times owing to insufficient resourcing. Indeed, some victim/survivors with cognitive impairment or complex communication needs may even struggle for their reports to be taken by police. To address this issue, Camilleri (Chapter 12) joins calls for greater monitoring of reforms at implementation; a focus on cultural change amongst key criminal justice stakeholders; consistent advocacy from first report to finalisation; and separate representation for victim/survivors during trials.

Victim participatory rights vary across different criminal justice systems (Braun, 2019) and precisely defining "participation" is somewhat fraught (VLRC, 2016). Jenkins (practitioner perspective, Chapter 12) suggests that the sign that greater participatory rights for victim/survivors is starting to be achieved will be when people feel that their voice has been heard; they have been respectfully treated; systems are trauma-informed and culturally safe; accommodations have been made for equal access to justice outcomes; and outcomes have met needs.

Improving Processes for Children and Young People

Raising the age of criminal responsibility is a reform which would have significant implications for children, the community and the justice system broadly (including the courts, youth justice, police and juvenile justice centres). Research consistently highlights how the age at which a child becomes justice involved will influence their likelihood of continuing justice involvement into adulthood (DeLisi & Piquero, 2011; Sutherland & Millsteed, 2016). Further, justice involvement is precipitated by early and continued experiences of trauma (Duron et al., 2021). As such, raising the age of criminal responsibility would facilitate a focus on welfare rather than punitive responses to child offending, which could potentially have significant cost-saving implications for the justice system well into the future, as well as in the immediate- and medium term.

Momentum for such a change is growing internationally (Goldson, 2013) and in Australian jurisdictions. For instance, a Victorian Legislative Council committee inquiry into the State's criminal justice system made 100 recommendations, amongst them the need to raise the minimum age of criminal responsibility from 10 years of age to 14 (Parliament of Victoria, 2022), although the Premier indicated that a national rather than state-based is the preferred approach (Woods, 2022).

Other suggestions for reforms aimed at better supporting children and young people who are before the courts—and to reduce the potential for increased justice involvement into the future—include introducing a specific "crossover" Children's Court list; diversion programmes; the use of intermediaries for all young people before the court; the reintroduction of youth drug courts; and an expansion of Indigenous youth courts (Sheehan and Baiwadi, Chapter 13). Implementation of a participatory best practice approach, as utilised in New Zealand which places the young person central in decision-making processes, is also advocated (Chipp, practitioner perspective, Chapter 13). In some Australian jurisdictions, community-orientated "night patrols" are used to reduce the involvement of young Indigenous people in criminal justice processes (see, for example, Scott et al., 2021).

Reform of Bail Laws

Not all changes necessarily have a positive effect, but rather might serve to satisfy other wants or occur based on individual headline grabbing cases. The rollback of bail laws in Victora, for instance, have disproportionally affected several groups already experiencing levels of disadvantage. Further implications have been to increase the prison population, thus adding to court hearing delays. For young people for whom the state has responsibility, changes in bail laws have arguably contributed further to their criminalisation. Reforming bail laws back to the previous requirement of showing-cause why the accused should remain in custody would require much in the way of resourcing; however, the positive implications to people's lives would be impactful (see Colvin, Chapter 6; Curran, Chapter 7), although not without controversy (Harkness, Chapter 2).

Appointment of Magistrates and Judges

Whereas once they were overwhelmingly male, white, older and upper/middle class (Gelsthorpe, 2001) and, it could be argued, out of touch with the community at large, strides have been made since the turn of the twenty-first century to make the magistracy and judiciary more representative of the community. Nevertheless, much more work is required in Australia to ensure gender balance (only 39% of judges are women) and cultural representation: there are very few Indigenous judges and only one per cent of judges are Asian-Australia despite the Australian labour force comprising 10% Asian Australians (Leigh, 2021).

Jury Reforms

An ongoing debate centres on the suitability of juries in the modern age and whether reforms to the jury system should be contemplated. Should the jury system be reformed, and, if so, how? Should the task of determining guilt remain with the amateur (jury) or be decided by "rational" experts or a panel of judges?

These are questions oftentimes asked as to whether a jury is capable of understanding all the evidence in certain technical and protracted trials, such as serious fraud trials. In a case at the Old Bailey in London in 2005, after hearing evidence for 140 days across 21 months, one juror refused to take any further part in the trial because of the financial impact it was having on him. This led to the Attorney General introducing legislation to allow for complex fraud trials to be heard without a jury, although the House of Lords defeated this legislation after two years declaring "that trial by jury is a bedrock if the criminal justice system" (BBC News, 2017).

In Australia, there has been some work undertaken on determining ways in which juries can improve their comprehension and use of expert DNA evidence (Goodman-Delahunty & Hewson, 2010). An alternative mechanism for consideration is the use of an expert bench of judges in place of 12 lay people for certain trials.

Other matters around jury reform relate to the inclusiveness of juries, such as allowing people who are hearing or sight impaired the ability to participate in the criminal justice process as a juror. Legislative and practice change in the Australian Capital Territory require courts to make arrangements for prospective jurors who might have limited English proficiency or a disability (VLRC, 2020).

Public Involvement in Court Proceedings

McIntyre (Chapter 15) argues that the challenge facing civil justice is to create systems and practices that are "healthy and accessible". This is achieved, he suggests, through engagement of the public and politicians in the need to "reconsider the very nature and purpose of this institution, and to reflect upon what a commitment to civil justice looks like in contemporary society".

Whether court hearings should be televised, thus opening up court processes to a mass audience, has been a matter of long-running discourse (see, for example, Barber, 1985 in a United States context; Stepniak, 1994 in an Australia context). A key concern of televised trials is the potential for cases to be sensationalised, with courtroom participants dramatising for the camera. New South Wales made legislative changes in 2014 to allow media filming, with permission, of verdicts and sentencing in the Supreme and District courts. The Attorney General declared that it would allow the public to develop a better understanding of sentencing decisions and "demystify" the process (Hall, 2014).

A Need for Greater Clarity

Whilst the judiciary in Australia is generally respected for integrity and impartiality, further reform as to actual and apprehended bias and provision and greater clarity of processes and procedures might maintain public confidence. The Australian Law Reform Commission (ALRC, 2022) made a suite of recommendations in this regard, including the need to strengthen institution structure, changes of appointment processes and judicial education.

Reforms to better clarify and define the role of problem-solving courts are also desirable, so that they can better fulfil their aim of addressing the underlying reasons why a person offends. These include clarifying the invitation and participation procedures; implementing "supportive sentencing" as the dual role occupied by problem-solving courts may "violate the aim of impartiality"; distinguish between the aspirations of such courts and other justice innovations; expand the geographic reach of these courts to facilitate greater access (Schaefer and Egan, Chapter 9); and with regard to in reference to specialist domestic and family violence courts ensuring they remain a place of safety for victims and for perpetrator accountability (Daniels, practitioner perspective, Chapter 9).

Also requiring greater clarity are decisions about journalists' freedom to report what is happening in the courts and the accused's right to a fair trial. Waller and Clifford (Chapter 4) argue that "[h]ow to reconcile public attitudes (and thus parliamentary action) with magisterial, judicial, parole board and bail justice decision-making is a significant challenge". Preserving the tradition of open justice is crucial in the post-pandemic era. The media occupy a unique place and "watchdog" role as, fulfilling the community's "right to know" about matters of public interest and acting, impartially, as its eyes and ears (Waller and Clifford, Chapter 4). A substantive challenge here, though, is that the courts and media have not always agreed on how or what should be reported in the public domain, or indeed the timing of reporting specific content. At times, such disagreements have resulted in tensions and led to a lack of trust by the judiciary. Tran (practitioner perspective, Chapter 4) observes that if online hearings are to remain, it is crucial that the courts keep pace with and understand the news media's logistics, operations and constraints under these new operating conditions.

Accountability and Transparency to Prevent Unjust Outcomes

Transparency and accountability in the justice system are key measures as to whether a justice system is operating as intended and expected, and without which opportunities for injustices or miscarriages of justice arise.

Macro-reforms addressing systemic factors such as racism and negative characterisations of people with disabilities will limit equitable access to the justice system. Reforms which could be achieved with immediacy include improving post-conviction mechanisms to ease pressure on a system that is slow to move, complex and beyond the financial reach of many people, particularly those who experience system disadvantage

(Dioso-Villa and Nash, Chapter 8). A lack of political will to implement cultural change within the courts system—and the absence of acceptance of responsibility—can be detrimentally impactful on innocent people (O'Keeffe, practitioner perspective, Chapter 8).

Police-led prosecutions in the summary jurisdiction is another area lacking sufficient clarity and transparency, and worthy of reform to ensure a greater degree of independence of prosecutions. This could emanate from a wholescale and evidence-based review of police-led prosecutions which considers the impacts on case outcomes, and what other reforms may be necessary (Ellis and Camilleri, Chapter 12) including the degree of legal training prosecutors should have and whether they should be independent of police organisations (Ellis, practitioner perspective, Chapter 12).

Conclusion

Justice system reform occurs on a regular basis and, whilst debate occurs as to the adequacy, pace and depth of reforms, change nonetheless provides evidence of a dynamic system. Although further and ongoing inquiry into an array of issues with the Australian courts might often be both desirable and necessary, reform for reform's sake is not necessarily desirable. For example, in considering the courts and their handling of family violence matters, Alexander (practitioner perspective, Chapter 14) queries whether a skew of changes, inquiries, summits, plans and legislative reforms aimed at addressing the problem of family violence might actually be adding further complications, retraumatising families and creating additional hurdles and costs.

Many agencies, organisations, parliaments, advocates, legal practitioners, the media and the public scrutinise the justice system on a regular basis. In the twenty-first century Australian Federation, there is strong and ongoing need for evidence-based responses to key challenges. In many instances, a national, coordinated approach to responses would avoid cross-border issues and anomalies, perhaps coordinated through the Meeting of Attorneys General (Attorney General's Department, 2022).

Reform of courts, and their processes and practices, takes time. Much work is occurring in this space on a micro level, although much more could be achieved. Beyond the courts specifically, much could also be undertaken on a macro level to address structural and systemic issues which continue to impact specific groups in the community such as children and young people, First Nations people, women, defendants and victims with disabilities. Without further ongoing reform, these groups and others will continue to be at risk of compounded systemic disadvantage in the justice system.

References

AIHW (Australian Institute of Health and Welfare). (2021). *International comparisons of welfare data*. Australian Institute of Health and Welfare. Retrieved from https://www.aihw.gov.au/reports/australias-welfare/international-comparisons-of-welfare-data

ALRC (Australian Law Reform Commission). (2017). *Pathways to Justice: Inquiry into the Incarceration Rate of Aboriginal and Torres Strait Islander Peoples* (Report 133). Canberra: Australian Law Reform Commission. Retrieved from https://www.alrc.gov.au/publication/pathways-to-justice-inquiry-into-the-incarceration-rate-of-aboriginal-and-torres-strait-islander-peoples-alrc-report-133/

ALRC (Australian Law Reform Commission). (2018). What is justice reinvestment? *Pathways to justice—Inquiry into the incarceration rate of Aboriginal and Torres Straight Islander Peoples* (ALRC Report 133). Canberra: Australian Government. Retrieved from https://www.alrc.gov.au/publication/pathways-to-justice-inquiry-into-theincarceration-rate-of-aboriginal-and-torres-strait-islander-peoples-alrc-report-133/4-justice-reinvestment/what-isjustice-reinvestment/

ALRC (Australian Law Reform Commission). (2022). *Without fear of favour: Judicial impartiality and the law on bias* (ALRC Report 138). Australian Law Reform Commission. Retrieved from https://www.alrc.gov.au/publication/ji-report-138/

Attorney-General's Department. (2022). *About the meeting of Attorneys-General*. Retrieved from https://www.ag.gov.au/about-us/who-we-are/committees-and-councils/meeting-attorneys-general

Barber, S. R. (1985). Televised trials: Weighing advantages and against disadvantages. *The Justice System Journal, 10*(3), 279–291.

BBC News. (2017, May 16). Should there be juries in fraud cases? *BBC News*. Retrieved from https://www.bbc.com/news/uk-scotland-39877171

Blokland, J. (2016). Bush courts and beyond. In A. Harkness, B. Harris, & D. Baker (Eds.), *Locating crime in context and place: Perspectives on regional, rural and remote Australia* (pp. 162–167). The Federation Press.

Braun, K. (2019). *Victim participation rights: Variation across criminal justice systems*. Palgrave Macmillan.

Brown, D., Cunneen, C., Schwartz, M., Stubbs, J., & Young, C. (2016). *Justice reinvestment: Winding back imprisonment*. Palgrave.

Coughlin, S. (2021, June 22). Poorer white pupils let down and neglected—MPs. *BBC News*. Retrieved from https://www.bbc.com/news/education-57558746

DeLisi, M., & Piquero, A. R. (2011). New frontiers in criminal careers research, 2000–2011: A state-of-the-art review. *Journal of Criminal Justice, 39*(4), 289–301.

Duron, J. F., Williams-Butler, A., Liu, F.-Y. Y., Nesi, D., Fay, K. P., & Kim, B.-K. E. (2021). The Influence of Adverse Childhood Experiences (ACEs) on the functional impairment of justice-involved adolescents: A comparison of baseline to follow-up reports of adversity. *Youth Violence and Juvenile Justice, 19*(4), 384–401.

Gelsthorpe, L. (2001). Critical decisions and processes in the criminal courts. In E. McLaughlin & J. Muncie (Eds.), *Controlling crime* (Chapter 3). Sage.

Goldson, B. (2013). 'Unsafe, unjust and harmful to wid (Southerland and Millsteed 2016; Delisi and er society)': Grounds for raising the minimum age of criminal responsibility in England and Wales. *Youth Justice, 13*(2), 111–130.

Goodman-Delahunty, J., & Hewson, L. (2010). *Improving jury understanding and use of expert DNA evidence* (Technical and background paper series No. 37). Canberra: Australian Institute of Criminology. Retrieved from https://www.aic.gov.au/publications/tbp/tbp37

Hale, R., Stewart-North, M., & Harkness, A. (2021). Post-disaster access to justice. In A. Harkness and R. White (Eds.), *Crossroads of rural crime: Representations and realities of transgressions in the Australian countryside* (pp. 167–179). Emerald.

Hall, L. (2014, March 25). TV cameras to be allowed in NSW Supreme Court verdicts. *Sydney Morning Herald*. Retrieved from https://www.smh.com.au/national/nsw/tv-cameras-to-be-allowed-in-nsw-supreme-court-verdicts-20140325-35flz.html

House of Commons Education Committee. (2021, June 22). *The forgotten: How White working-class pupils have been let down, and how to change it* (First report of Session 2021–22, HC 85). Retrieved from https://committees.parliament.uk/publications/6364/documents/70802/default/

Hunyor, J. (2016). Law and true justice: A perspective from the Top End. A. Harkness, B. Harris & D. Baker (Eds.). *Locating crime in context and place: Perspectives on regional, rural and remote Australia* (pp. 158–161). The Federation Press.

Legg, M., & Song, A. (2021). The courts, the remote hearing and the pandemic: From action to reflection. *UNSW Law Journal, 44*(1), 126–166.

Leigh, A. (2021, December 21). Why has no person of colour ever served on the High Court? *Financial Review*. Retrieved from https://www.afr.com/politics/federal/why-has-no-person-of-colour-ever-served-on-the-high-court-20211221-p59j8x

McGorrery, P. (2022, July). *Should media coverage affect sentencing? Melbourne: Sentencing Advisory Council*. Retrieved from https://www.sentencingcouncil.vic.gov.au/sites/default/files/2022-07/should_media_coverage_affect_sentencing.pdf

McIntyre, J., Olijnyk, A., & Pender, K. (2020). Civil courts and COVID-19: Challenges and opportunities in Australia. *Alternative Law Journal, 45*(3), 195–201.

Mills, T. (2021, August 2). Wigs stained, tattered and dwindling in Victorian courts. *The Age*. Retrieved from https://www.theage.com.au/national/victoria/wigs-stained-tattered-and-dwindling-in-victorian-courts-20210729-p58e3e.html

NJC (Neighbourhood Justice Centre). (2022). *What we do*. Retrieved from https://www.neighbourhoodjustice.vic.gov.au/about-us/our-story/what-we-do

Parliament of Victoria. (2022, March). *Inquiry into Victoria's criminal justice system, Volume 1*. Parliament of Victoria, Legislative Council Legal and Special Issues Committee. PP No 326, Session 2018–2022 (Volume 1 of 2). Retrieved from https://new.parliament.vic.gov.au/4a2c47/contentassets/053cb654453b446580cce854fb5885af/lclsic-59-10-vic-criminal-justice-system.pdf

Parliament of Victoria. (2021). *Public Accounts and Estimates Committee: Inquiry into the Victorian government's response to the OCVID-19 pandemic.* Parliament of Victoria. Retrieved from https://www.parliament.vic.gov.au/paec/inquiries/inquiry/1000

RCIADIC (Royal Commission into Aboriginal Deaths in Custody). (1991). *Royal Commission into Aboriginal Deaths in Custody: National Report, Vols 1–5.* Australian Government Publishing Service.

Russell, E.K., Carlton, B., Tyson, D., Zhou, H., Pearce, M., & Faulkner, J. (2020). *A constellation of circumstances: The drivers of women's increasing rates of remand in Victoria.* Fitzroy Legal Service and La Trobe Centre for Health, Law and Society. Retrieved from https://fls.org.au/product-category/publications/

Scott, J., Sims, M., Cooper, T., & Barclay, E. (2021). Night patrols: Mobilising collective efficacy in Indigenous communities. In A. Harkness & R. White (Eds.), *Crossroads of rural crime: Representations and realities of transgressions in the Australian countryside* (pp. 45–60). Emerald.

Simu, O., & McGorrery, P. (2021, August). *Judging statistics.* Sentencing Advisory Council. Retrieved from https://www.sentencingcouncil.vic.gov.au/sites/default/files/2021-08/Judging_Statistics.pdf

Smith, R.G., Savage, R., & Emami, C. (2021). *Audiovisual link technologies in Australian courts: Practical and legal considerations* (AIC Research Report 22). Australian Institute of Criminology. Retrieved from https://www.aic.gov.au/publications/rr/rr22

Sourdin, T., Li, B., & McNamara, D. M. (2020). Court innovations and access to justice in times of crisis. *Health Policy and Technology, 9*, 447–453.

State of Victoria. (2016). *Royal Commission into Family Violence: Summary and recommendations* (Paper No 132 [2014–16]). Retrieved from https://www.rcfv.com.au/MediaLibraries/RCFamilyViolence/Reports/RCFV_Full_Report_Interactive.pdf

Stepniak, D. (1994). Why shouldn't Australian court proceedings be televised? *UNSW Law Journal, 17*(2), 345–382.

Sutherland, P., & Millsteed, M. (2016). *Patterns of recorded offending behaviour amongst young Victorian offenders* (In Brief No. 6). Melbourne, VIC: Crime Statistics Agency. Retrieved from https://www.crimestatistics.vic.gov.au/research-and-evaluation/publications/patterns-of-recorded-offending-behaviour-amongst-young

Tanton, R., Dare, L., Miranti, R., Vidyattama, Y., Yule, A., & McCabe, M. (2021). *Dropping Off the Edge 2021: Persistent and multilayered disadvantage in Australia.* Jesuit Social Services. Retrieved from https://www.dote.org.au/full-report

VicHealth. (2019, May 21). Findings from the 2017 NCAS (National Community Attitudes towards Violence against Women Survey) are now available [press release]. Retrieved from https://www.vichealth.vic.gov.au/media-and-resources/publications/2013-national-community-attitudes-towards-violence-against-women-survey

Victoria Police. (2014, May). *Victoria Police Blue Paper: A vision for Victoria Police in 2025.* Retrieved from https://www.police.vic.gov.au/sites/default/files/2019-01/Victoria-Police-Blue-Paper_web.pdf

VLRC (Victorian Law Reform Commission). (2021, June). *Improving the justice system response to sexual offences.* Victorian Law Reform Commission. Retrieved from https://www.lawreform.vic.gov.au/wp-content/uploads/2022/04/VLRC_Improving_Justice_System_Response_to_Sex_Offences_Report_web.pdf

VLRC (Victorian Law Reform Commission). (2016, August). *The role of victims of crime in the criminal trial process.* Victorian Law Reform Commission. Retrieved from https://www.lawreform.vic.gov.au/wp-content/uploads/2021/07/VLRC_Victims-Of-Crime-Report-W.pdf

VLRC (Victorian Law Reform Commission). (2020). *Inclusive juries—Access for people who are deaf, hard of hearing, blind or have low vision* (Consultation Paper). Melbourne: Victorian Law Reform Commission Retrieved from https://www.lawreform.vic.gov.au/wp-content/uploads/2021/07/VLRC_Inclusive-Juries-Consultation-Paper-forweb.pdf

Webster, K., Diemer, K., Honey, N., Mannix, S., Mickle, J., Morgan, J., Parkes, A., Politoff, V., Powell, A., Stubbs, J., & Ward, A. (2018). *Australians' attitudes to violence against women and gender equality.* Findings from the 2017 National Community Attitudes towards Violence against Women Survey (NCAS) (Research report, 03/2018). Sydney: ANROWS. Retrieved from https://www.anrows.org.au/NCAS/2017/home/

White, R., Haines, F., & Asquith, N. (2017). *Crime & criminology* (6th ed.). Oxford University Press.

Willis, M., & Kapira, M. (2018). *Justice reinvestment in Australia: A review of the literature* (AIC Research Report 09). Canberra: Australian Institute of Criminology. Retrieved from https://www.aic.gov.au/sites/default/files/2020-05/rr09_justice_reinvestment_in_australia_160518_0.pdf

Wood, E. (2022, March 24). Raise Victorian criminality age: Report. *The Canberra Times.* Retrieved from https://www.canberratimes.com.au/story/7671888/raise-victorian-criminality-age-report/

Legislation

Family Violence Protection Act 2008 (Vic)

Correction to: Australian Courts

Marg Camilleri and Alistair Harkness

Correction to:
M. Camilleri and A. Harkness (eds.), *Australian Courts*,
https://doi.org/10.1007/978-3-031-19063-6

The original version of Chapters 2 and 15 was inadvertently published with incorrect authors' affiliation information, which has now been corrected to Simon Finn, Former member of the Queensland Parliament, VIC, Australia in Chapter 2 and Joe McIntyre, University of South Australia, SA, Australia in Chapter 15. The corrections to the chapters have been updated with the changes.

The updated original version of these chapters can be found at
https://doi.org/10.1007/978-3-031-19063-6_2
https://doi.org/10.1007/978-3-031-19063-6_15

M. Camilleri and A. Harkness (eds.), *Australian Courts*,
https://doi.org/10.1007/978-3-031-19063-6_17

Index

A

access to justice 8–10, 15, 170, 175–178, 349, 352, 354, 368, 379
attitudes to sentencing 31
Australian courts 2, 6, 13, 15, 77, 84, 150, 175, 178, 200, 297, 357, 368, 369, 384
Australian media law 80
awaiting trial 127, 130, 164, 167, 369

B

bail 11, 12, 19, 22, 23, 30, 65, 103, 115, 116, 121–133, 137–140, 157, 164, 167, 233, 303, 304, 317, 369, 371, 373, 380, 383

C

challenges 38, 45, 67, 74, 83, 86, 122, 127–129, 131, 138, 153, 170, 198, 199, 205, 207, 210, 216–219, 248, 252, 258, 277, 283, 302, 304, 307, 308, 315, 324, 341, 354, 367–372, 384
child abuse 92, 322, 323, 325, 326, 328, 334, 342
children 12, 14, 116–118, 125, 126, 128, 129, 131–133, 137, 138, 140, 157, 174, 216, 238, 240–244, 294, 298–309, 314–319, 322, 323, 325–327, 330, 331, 333–336, 341, 342, 344, 370–372, 376, 379, 385
Children's Court 4, 96, 99, 116, 117, 297, 298, 301, 302, 306, 307, 309, 314, 318, 319, 325, 379

M. Camilleri and A. Harkness (eds.), *Australian Courts*,
https://doi.org/10.1007/978-3-031-19063-6

child victim 116, 138, 302
child witness 316
civil courts 9, 346, 354–356, 358, 369
civil procedure 152
cognitive impairment 8, 130, 131, 137–140, 174, 176, 243, 270, 271, 284, 286, 287, 294, 371, 378
complex communication needs (CCN) 270, 271, 286, 287, 378
conditional release 121
contempt of court 77, 78, 80, 90, 92
coroners courts 247–252, 255, 257–261, 264, 265, 267, 268, 371, 377, 378
coronial system 247, 249, 252, 253, 259–261
court efficiency 98, 149, 150, 178
court participants 206, 308, 370
court reporting 73, 90, 93
court values 147, 149, 228
COVID-19 11, 12, 23, 85, 90, 125, 132, 133, 152, 153, 157, 158, 165, 209, 357, 369
criminal justice system 14, 21, 39, 40, 43, 58, 76, 111, 116, 128, 131–133, 139, 140, 151, 169–171, 175, 176, 182, 183, 190, 202, 205, 222, 223, 226, 243, 251, 269–272, 276, 277, 280, 282, 285–287, 292, 295, 299, 300, 305, 307, 368, 371, 373, 376, 377, 379, 381

D

death investigations 251, 257, 259
deaths in custody 126, 224–226, 248, 249, 251, 253, 256, 257, 260, 261, 264, 266, 267
defamation 9, 80–82, 346, 356

F

Family DOORS Triage screening 330
family violence 8, 10, 11, 14, 99, 100, 115–117, 119, 127, 153, 160, 199–201, 219, 321–331, 334–336, 341–344, 372, 383, 384
Federal Circuit and Family Court of Australia (FCFCOA) 322, 333, 335, 341, 342
First Nations peoples 1, 3, 8, 9, 13, 222, 223, 227–230, 232, 234, 248, 250–254, 257, 259–262, 371, 377, 378, 385

G

geography 15, 368

H

homeless 11, 41, 127, 128, 132, 139, 155, 175, 242, 243

I

Indigenous sentencing courts 11, 221–224, 227–234, 260, 368, 377
inequity 175
injustices 145, 169, 171, 175, 178, 179, 383

J

judicial theory 6
Juries and jurors 45
jury trials 2, 59
justice delayed 146
justice innovation 202, 203, 206, 209, 210, 382
justice outcomes 111, 144, 149, 250, 252, 292, 375
justice system 1–3, 8, 11–14, 20, 43, 46, 47, 90, 91, 93, 118, 143, 154, 159–161, 165, 168, 170, 175, 176, 182, 191, 194, 201, 211, 215, 216, 219, 228, 229, 233, 260, 262, 269, 272, 275–277, 280, 282, 294, 301, 304–308, 314, 346–358, 368, 377, 379, 383–385
juvenile offending 297, 308

L

law and justice 202, 248
legislative decision making 19
Lighthouse Project 322, 330, 332, 335, 342, 344

M

magistrates court 215, 224, 230, 298, 306, 353, 375
miscarriages of justice 14, 171, 176, 179, 383

O

open justice 13, 74–76, 83, 86, 90–92, 373
over-representation 9, 117, 128, 175, 176, 222, 225–227, 307, 308

P

parliament 14, 20, 21, 24, 27, 32, 33, 38, 40, 42, 43, 301, 369, 373, 379, 384
participatory rights 12, 269–272, 278, 283, 285, 287, 378, 379
police 4, 14, 31, 33, 38, 39, 41–43, 47, 51, 65, 78, 85, 91, 95–111, 115–119, 121–123, 132, 137–140, 154, 159, 165, 170, 172–174, 176, 182, 194, 216, 225, 228, 239, 247, 251, 252, 254–256, 261, 265, 267, 269, 271, 280, 282, 283, 292, 293, 298, 303–305, 314, 317, 319, 326, 329, 372, 374, 375, 378, 379
police-led prosecutions 14, 374, 384
politics 30, 47, 65, 69, 80, 210, 373
problem-solving courts 11, 14, 197–211, 219, 307, 368, 374, 382
procedural fairness 67, 194, 232, 271, 354, 370
prosecutors 4, 14, 28, 66, 79, 80, 95–98, 100–111, 115–119, 152, 155, 216, 221, 223, 233, 238–240, 273, 294, 303, 306, 314, 374, 384

R

reform 2–4, 8, 12, 14, 15, 20, 22, 46, 55, 80, 82, 86, 99, 110,

111, 124, 126, 127, 133, 148, 157, 179, 195, 198, 199, 207, 209, 211, 215, 216, 218, 219, 244, 249, 258, 259, 262, 269, 270, 272, 274–277, 279, 281–284, 286, 287, 301, 306, 314, 321, 322, 327–329, 344, 346–348, 356, 357, 368, 371, 373–379, 381–385
remand 12, 23, 122–126, 128–133, 139, 141, 145, 157, 164, 167, 299, 369, 373
rule of law 153, 161, 170, 358, 369

S
self-representation 9, 354, 357
sentencing 7, 11, 19–22, 24–26, 28–32, 66, 74, 103, 107, 165, 167, 173, 198, 208, 221–223, 226, 227, 229, 230, 232–234, 243, 278, 297, 298, 301, 305–308, 373, 374, 378, 382
sentencing reform 19, 22
separation of powers 21, 25, 216
sexual assault 12, 70, 76, 269–272, 275, 276, 283, 284, 287, 292–294, 325, 378
social media 46–50, 53–55, 58, 74, 78, 80–82, 84, 86, 373, 374
specialty courts 199, 207, 209, 210
summary jurisdiction 95, 96, 98, 100, 102, 104, 108–111, 115, 119, 286, 325, 374, 384
suppression orders 77–79, 83, 86, 90, 92, 93, 373
systemic and institutional racism 226

T
technology 45, 153, 154, 156, 159, 166, 209, 274, 285, 347, 357, 358, 370
therapeutic jurisprudence 11, 125, 198, 202, 229, 233, 238, 307
tribunals 4, 153, 155, 159, 160, 191, 194, 346, 347, 351, 353, 354, 357

V
victims/survivors 216, 292, 293, 295, 344

W
wrongful convictions 9, 14, 169–172, 174, 176, 179–183, 192, 194

Y
youth offender 299

The manufacturer's authorised representative in the EU is Springer Nature Customer Service Centre GmbH, Europaplatz 3, 69115 Heidelberg, Germany. If you have any concerns regarding our products, please contact ProductSafety@springernature.com

Printed and bound by CPI Group (UK) Ltd, Croydon, CR0 4YY
30/09/2026
02225243-0016